XML COMPLETE

Robert Zarrow

XML
Complete

Steve Holzner

McGraw-Hill
New York • San Francisco • Washington, D.C. • Auckland
Bogotá • Caracas • Lisbon • London • Madrid • Mexico City
Milan • Montreal • New Delhi • San Juan • Singapore
Sydney • Tokyo • Toronto

Library of Congress Cataloging-in-Publication Data

Holzner, Steven.
    XML complete / Steven Holzner.
        p.   cm.
    Includes index.
    ISBN 0-07-913702-4
    1. XML (Document markup language)   I. Title.
QA76.76.H94H652   1998
005.7'2—dc21   97-44404
                                    CIP

McGraw-Hill

A Division of The McGraw-Hill Companies

   2 3 4 5 6 7 8 9 0 DOC/DOC 9 0 2 1 0 9 8

P/N 471271-4
PART OF
ISBN 0-07-913702-4

The sponsoring editor for this book was Michael Sprague and the production supervisor was Tina Cameron. It was set in Century Schoolbook by Douglas & Gayle, Limited.

Printed and bound by R. R. Donnelley & Sons Company.

McGraw-Hill books are available at special quantity discounts to use as premiums and sales promotions, or for use in corporate training programs. For more information, please write to Director of Special Sales, McGraw-Hill, 11 West 19th Street, New York, NY 10011. Or contact your local bookstore.

 This book is printed on recycled, acid-free paper containing a minimum of 50% recycled de-inked fiber.

DEDICATION

To Nancy, for all the reasons she already knows—plus a few more that won't fit into words.

CONTENTS

Contents

INTRODUCTION

It's hardly necessary to say that the World Wide Web has become a programming phenomenon. The Web has taken off and gets more popular every day. However, as the Web gets used more—and people try to use it for more than the current Web protocols were designed for—life gets more complex. The *Extended Markup Language* (XML) was created to make Web life simpler.

Currently, the most popular Web markup language is HTML. This language has been a powerful asset to Web development, but it lacks the capability for specialization, which restricts its growth tremendously. All of HTML is already defined for you, and if you have a specialized task, such as storing and transmitting the records for a hospital over the Web in an easily readable way, HTML is not a good choice. HTML formats *how* you present a Web page's data, and it is not designed to work with *what* that data represents.

XML is more flexible, because you can define your own markup elements in XML. This enables you to tailor a document to your own needs, storing and structuring the data in that document as you like, far beyond what the HTML <p> and <DIV> tags can do for you. In the case of storing hospital records, for example, you can create a <patient> element that holds other elements, such as <medications>, <room_number>, <admission_date>, and so forth. By letting you define your own elements, XML enables you to structure a document as you want it, without having to restructure your data to fit a predefined markup language.

In this book, we'll cover the three parts of the XML specification: XML-Lang (the XML language specification), XML-Link (the specification for XML links), and XML-Style (the proposal for XML stylesheets). Together, these three parts make up XML, and we'll explore them in this book.

Using XML, we'll see how to *customize* the documents we use on the Web and how to build robust applications that use and interpret those documents. In this way, we'll take the next step after HTML, storing our documents in a "smart" way that can actually explain our data-storage techniques to the applications we'll create. We'll be able to specialize our documents far more than HTML ever could, creating a significant advance in making the Web a serious medium for data transmission.

What's in This Book

This book covers all three parts of the XML specification: the XML language specification, the XML link specification, and the XML stylesheet specification.

To examine the XML specification, we'll pepper this book with dozens of short and powerful examples, because seeing a project at work—from beginning to end—is the best way to learn when it comes to XML. We'll also make our examples bite-sized and to-the-point, without a lot of extraneous details that you have to wade through. We'll create XML applications like browsers, database handlers, document decoders, and more, filling our examples with real-life uses.

Here's an overview of what's in this book by topic:

- Using Java
- Creating windowed Java applications
- Using Java controls
- Using the Microsoft XML parser
- Reading in an XML document
- Displaying an XML document's text
- Retrieving an XML document's title
- Using recursion to unpack an XML document
- Creating your own XML tags
- Declaring XML tags
- Declaring empty XML tags
- Interpreting XML tags
- Creating "valid" and "well-formed" XML documents
- Using external DTDs
- Using a text-indenting XML browser
- Getting an XML document's name
- Extended Backus-Naur notation
- Accessing XML child elements
- Constructing new elements in an XML document from code
- Creating and using XML tag attributes
- Handling XML attribute lists

- Creating XML browsers
- Decoding nested XML tags in XML browsers
- Creating XML databases
- Searching XML databases
- Adding records to XML databases
- Writing XML databases to disk
- Handling variable-length records in XML databases
- Working with XML links
- Using XML locators
- Using XML extended links
- Creating XML extended link groups
- Working with text in XML browsers
- Using graphics in XML
- Creating a circle-drawing XML browser
- Cross referencing in XML documents
- Using entirely graphical XML browsers
- Handling images with XML
- Creating an XML image browser
- Specifying font size and weight in XML browsers
- Creating an XML image map
- Working with XML stylesheets
- Using DSSSL, the Document Style Semantics, and Specification Language
- Defining DSSSL terms
- Creating SGML documents
- Discovering how SGML differs from XML
- Using James Clark's Jade DSSSL processor
- Formatting rich text documents from XML
- Using menus in XML browsers
- Using Java radio buttons and check boxes in XML browsers
- And more

We'll see these topics illustrated in examples as we work through what XML has to offer us. We intend to put XML to work for us.

What You'll Need

Most of the current XML software is designed to be used with the Java language, and to use this book profitably, you should have Java installed on your computer; this book uses the most widespread version of Java: Java 1.0.2. You can get a copy of the *Java Development Kit* (JDK) from Sun Microsystem's site: `http://www.javasoft.com`. You should also have a word processor or editor with which to write Java code files, as we'll see in Chapter 1.

After Chapter 1, we'll use the Microsoft XML parser in all the other chapters except Chapter 9. You can get a copy of the Microsoft XML parser at this Microsoft site: `http://www.microsoft.com/standards/xml/xmlparse.htm`. You can install the Microsoft XML parser, which is made up of Java classes that you import into Java programs, relatively easily using the instructions at the Microsoft site.

Finally, in Chapter 9, we'll take a look at the third part of the XML specification, XML-Style (XS). XML supports the use of a subset of *Document Style Semantics and Specification Language* (DSSSL), and we'll use DSSSL to format the appearance of our XML documents for display. We'll use James Clark's Jade DSSSL processor to create formatted rich text (RTF format) files in Chapter 9 by using XS. You can get a copy of the Jade processor on the CD that accompanies this book or at James Clark's Jade site, `http://www.jclark.com/jade`.

In addition, you can find the three parts of the XML specification at these URLs—part I: `http://www.w3.org/TR/WD-xml`; part II: `http://www.w3.org/TR/WD-xml-link`; part III: `http://sunsite.unc.edu/pub/sun-info/standards/dsssl/xs/xs970522.rtf.zip` (note that the xs970522 document is only a temporary version of what will become part III of the XML specification; check the site `http://www.w3.org/XML/Activity` for the latest version of part III of the XML specification). These three documents make up the formal XML specification, and you should refer to them for all answers not provided in this book.

That's it—that's all we'll need. We're ready to start. We'll use the Java language throughout this book, because most XML software (such as the Microsoft XML parser we'll use) is written to be used with Java. In Chapter 1, we'll spend some time getting up to speed in Java before tackling XML. (If you're already familiar with Java, you might consider just scanning through Chapter 1 and then moving on to Chapter 2.)

ACKNOWLEDGMENTS

A book like the one you hold is the product of the hard work of many people; I'd particularly like to thank Michael Sprague for discussions on both editorial and technical issues, Kelly Dobbs for her excellent and thoughtful work in production, and all the people at McGraw-Hill and Douglas & Gayle who worked hard to make this book a reality. Among those who made significant contributions are Sherry Souffrance, Fred Bernardi, Denny Hager, and Kathy Ewing.

XML COMPLETE

Getting Started

Welcome to XML programming! In this book we're going to take a guided tour of what XML has to offer—we'll see it all, from the basics of XML to the advanced topics, from creating our own XML documents to using XML stylesheets, from creating XML links to creating XML browsers.

What Is XML?

So what, exactly, is XML? Its proper name is the Extensible Markup Language, abbreviated XML, and you use it to format and transfer data in an easy and consistent way (usually on the World Wide Web). XML is actually a specially designed subset of *Standard Generalized Markup Language* (SGML) simplified and targeted at the Web. HTML is another subset of SGML—in fact, if you're familiar with *Hypertext Markup Language* (HTML), you already have a leg up on XML. For example, take a look at this HTML Web page:

```
<HTML>

<HEAD>
<TITLE>The Best Web Page Ever!</TITLE>
</HEAD>

<BODY>
<CENTER>
<H1>
<B>This is the Best Web Page Ever!</B>
</H1>
</CENTER>

Welcome to the best Web page ever!

</BODY>

</HTML>
```

Here, we use HTML *tags* to specify just how we want the text in the Web page displayed:

Markup Tags

Tags in both HTML and XML are text strings enclosed in angle brackets: < and >, and they are directives to the application reading in the HTML or XML document. For example, the first tag in the preceding Web page is <HTML>:

```
<HTML>
   .
   .
   .
```

This informs the Web browser that the document is written in HTML and so is a proper Web page. Next, we set up the Web page header with the <HEAD> and the <TITLE> tag:

```
<HTML>

<HEAD>
<TITLE>The Best Web Page Ever!</TITLE>
</HEAD>
        .
        .
        .
```

This sets the title of the Web page, as displayed in the browser (usually in the browser's title bar at the top); in this case, the Web page title is the (somewhat grandiose) title, "The Best Web Page Ever!"

For each *start tag*, like <HEAD> or <TITLE>, in this example, there is also an *end tag*, like </HEAD> or </TITLE>. End tags enclose the same name as start tags with an added forward slash, "/"; for example, for the start tag <HEAD>, the end tag is </HEAD>. In this way, pairs of start and end tags can enclose regions of the Web page text, specifying how we want that text displayed.

NOTE *Not all start tags require end tags, but most do.*

For example, in the body of the Web page (as specified with the <BODY> tag), we center text with the <CENTER> tag:

```
<HTML>

<HEAD>
<TITLE>The Best Web Page Ever!</TITLE>
</HEAD>

<BODY>
<CENTER>
<H1>
<B>This is the Best Web Page Ever!</B>
</H1>
</CENTER>
        .
        .
        .
```

In addition, we display the page's title as a header with the large font using the <H1> tag (HTML headers go from <H1>, the largest, to <H6>, the smallest), and make it bold with the <B> tag:

```
<HTML>

<HEAD>
<TITLE>The Best Web Page Ever!</TITLE>
</HEAD>
```

```
<BODY>
<CENTER>
<H1>
<B>This is the Best Web Page Ever!</B>
</H1>
</CENTER>
        .
        .
        .
```

In this way, we use HTML to specify how to display the text and graphics in our Web page.

XML is different, although not completely different. Although HTML describes how to display the data in a Web page, we use XML to describe the data itself.

In other words, XML is most often used as a data-description language, allowing us to organize data into data structures—even complex data structures, if we so choose. You can tailor the data as you want it; the most attractive feature of XML is that you can create your own tags. This lets you structure the data in an XML document as you like. Let's take a look at an XML example to make this clearer.

An XML Example

In this example, `grocery.xml`, we'll record which grocery customers purchased what groceries and when, setting up an XML document to record that data. Let's see how this works now.

We start `grocery.xml` with a *processing instruction* indicating that this document is an XML document and uses XML version 1.0:

```
<?XML version = "1.0" ?>
        .
        .
        .
```

Processing instructions start with `<?` and end with `?>`, and they are directives to the *XML processor*—the application that reads in and interprets our XML. In this case, we're indicating the XML version to the XML processor.

Next, we can start inventing `grocery.xml`'s XML tags. We start with a <DOCUMENT> tag ("DOCUMENT" is our own choice for a tag—there is no predefined XML DOCUMENT tag) to show we're starting our XML document:

```
<?XML version = "1.0" ?>
<DOCUMENT>
        .
        .
        .
```

This tag starts our new XML document. We can structure the XML document **grocery.txt** customer by customer, listing the groceries each customer has purchased between <CUSTOMER> and </CUSTOMER> tags:

```
<?XML version = "1.0" ?>
<DOCUMENT>
<CUSTOMER>
        .
        .
        .
</CUSTOMER>
```

Next, let's store this customer's name. We can nest tags in XML to arbitrary depth; in this example, that means that we can set up a name section for each customer by creating and using a <NAME> tag this way:

```
<?XML version = "1.0" ?>
<DOCUMENT>
<CUSTOMER>
    <NAME>
        .
        .
        .
    </NAME>
</CUSTOMER>
```

We can further store the customer's first and last names with tags we can call <FIRSTNAME> and <LASTNAME>:

```
<?XML version = "1.0" ?>
<DOCUMENT>
<CUSTOMER>
    <NAME>
        <LASTNAME>Edwards</LASTNAME>
        <FIRSTNAME>Britta</FIRSTNAME>
    </NAME>
        .
        .
        .
</CUSTOMER>
```

Now we can store the date on which the customer purchased the groceries by setting up a <DATE> tag:

```
<?XML version = "1.0" ?>
<DOCUMENT>
<CUSTOMER>
    <NAME>
        <LASTNAME>Edwards</LASTNAME>
        <FIRSTNAME>Britta</FIRSTNAME>
    </NAME>
    <DATE>April 17, 1998</DATE>
        .
        .
        .
</CUSTOMER>
```

At this point, then, we're ready to store the grocery orders the customer made. We can do that with a new tag we create, the <ORDERS> tag:

```
<?XML version = "1.0" ?>
<DOCUMENT>
<CUSTOMER>
    <NAME>
        <LASTNAME>Edwards</LASTNAME>
        <FIRSTNAME>Britta</FIRSTNAME>
    </NAME>
    <DATE>April 17, 1998</DATE>
    <ORDERS>
        .
        .
        .
    </ORDERS>
</CUSTOMER>
```

We can store each item the customer ordered with an <ITEM> tag:

```
<?XML version = "1.0" ?>
<DOCUMENT>
<CUSTOMER>
    <NAME>
        <LASTNAME>Edwards</LASTNAME>
        <FIRSTNAME>Britta</FIRSTNAME>
    </NAME>
    <DATE>April 17, 1998</DATE>
    <ORDERS>
        <ITEM>
            .
            .
            .
        </ITEM>
    </ORDERS>
</CUSTOMER>
```

Let's say this customer ordered five cucumbers; we can store that data and the price paid with three new tags: <PRODUCT>, <NUMBER>, and <PRICE>:

```
<?XML version = "1.0" ?>
<DOCUMENT>
<CUSTOMER>
    <NAME>
        <LASTNAME>Edwards</LASTNAME>
        <FIRSTNAME>Britta</FIRSTNAME>
    </NAME>
    <DATE>April 17, 1998</DATE>
    <ORDERS>
        <ITEM>
            <PRODUCT>Cucumber</PRODUCT>
            <NUMBER>5</NUMBER>
            <PRICE>$1.25</PRICE>
        </ITEM>
    </ORDERS>
</CUSTOMER>
```

Let's also say that besides cucumbers, this customer also ordered lettuce. We can store that data as a new item this way:

```
<?XML version = "1.0" ?>
<DOCUMENT>
<CUSTOMER>
    <NAME>
        <LASTNAME>Edwards</LASTNAME>
        <FIRSTNAME>Britta</FIRSTNAME>
    </NAME>
    <DATE>April 17, 1998</DATE>
    <ORDERS>
        <ITEM>
            <PRODUCT>Cucumber</PRODUCT>
            <NUMBER>5</NUMBER>
            <PRICE>$1.25</PRICE>
        </ITEM>
        <ITEM>
            <PRODUCT>Lettuce</PRODUCT>
            <NUMBER>2</NUMBER>
            <PRICE>$.98</PRICE>
        </ITEM>
    </ORDERS>
</CUSTOMER>
```

We can even store data for additional customers in the same XML document this way:

```
<?XML version = "1.0" ?>
<DOCUMENT>
<CUSTOMER>
    <NAME>
        <LASTNAME>Edwards</LASTNAME>
        <FIRSTNAME>Britta</FIRSTNAME>
    </NAME>
    <DATE>April 17, 1998</DATE>
```

```
<ORDERS>
    <ITEM>
        <PRODUCT>Cucumber</PRODUCT>
        <NUMBER>5</NUMBER>
        <PRICE>$1.25</PRICE>
    </ITEM>
    <ITEM>
        <PRODUCT>Lettuce</PRODUCT>
        <NUMBER>2</NUMBER>
        <PRICE>$.98</PRICE>
    </ITEM>
</ORDERS>
</CUSTOMER>
<CUSTOMER>
    <NAME>
        <LASTNAME>Thompson</LASTNAME>
        <FIRSTNAME>Phoebe</FIRSTNAME>
    </NAME>
    <DATE>May 27, 1998</DATE>
    <ORDERS>
        <ITEM>
            <PRODUCT>Banana</PRODUCT>
            <NUMBER>12</NUMBER>
            <PRICE>$2.95</PRICE>
        </ITEM>
        <ITEM>
            <PRODUCT>Apple</PRODUCT>
            <NUMBER>6</NUMBER>
            <PRICE>$1.50</PRICE>
        </ITEM>
    </ORDERS>
</CUSTOMER>
</DOCUMENT>
```

In this way, we've stored—and structured—the data we need to keep track of the customers by creating and using our own XML tags. We are free of the HTML restrictions that make us use a set of predefined tags.

However, as you can tell, XML is a free-form language. It will be up to us to make sense of the tags we're using, not some prewritten browser application. We'll see how to interpret XML throughout this book.

In XML, we make up our own tags to describe and structure the data we want to store and use. In larger documents, this can lead to a lot of confusion: how can we be sure we've set up our XML document correctly? That is, what if we omitted the end tag </CUSTOMER> in the preceding listing? Our XML processor might mistake that to mean that we want to store only data from one customer, not two. What if we omit the person's last name and the corresponding tags: <LASTNAME> and </LASTNAME> by mistake? What if we place tags in the wrong place? How will we know?

Document Type Declarations

It turns out that you can define what tags you will use in the XML document, what order they should go in, and what tags other tags can contain; you also can set up other rules in the document's *Document Type Declaration*, or DTD. The DTD is not strictly necessary in many XML documents, but to make sure your document is *valid* (that's the XML terminology), you should include a DTD so that the XML processor can check to make sure the XML document obeys the rules you've set up. We'll see a lot more about DTDs in the next chapters, but here is a DTD for the document we've created, specifying which tags can contain what other tags and in what order, as well as what type of data tags can contain (PCDATA stands for parsed character data, or text, and the * symbol means the item it refers to may be repeated):

```
<?XML version = "1.0" ?>
<!DOCTYPE DOCUMENT [
<!ELEMENT DOCUMENT (CUSTOMER)*>
<!ELEMENT CUSTOMER (NAME,DATE,ORDERS)>
<!ELEMENT NAME (LASTNAME,FIRSTNAME)>
<!ELEMENT LASTNAME (#PCDATA)>
<!ELEMENT FIRSTNAME (#PCDATA)>
<!ELEMENT DATE (#PCDATA)>
<!ELEMENT ORDERS (ITEM)*>
<!ELEMENT ITEM (PRODUCT,NUMBER,PRICE)>
<!ELEMENT PRODUCT (#PCDATA)>
<!ELEMENT NUMBER (#PCDATA)>
<!ELEMENT PRICE (#PCDATA)>
]>
<DOCUMENT>
<CUSTOMER>
    <NAME>
        <LASTNAME>Edwards</LASTNAME>
        <FIRSTNAME>Britta</FIRSTNAME>
    </NAME>
    <DATE>April 17, 1998</DATE>
    <ORDERS>
        <ITEM>
            <PRODUCT>Cucumber</PRODUCT>
            <NUMBER>5</NUMBER>
            <PRICE>$1.25</PRICE>
        </ITEM>
        <ITEM>
            <PRODUCT>Lettuce</PRODUCT>
            <NUMBER>2</NUMBER>
            <PRICE>$.98</PRICE>
        </ITEM>
    </ORDERS>
```

```
        </CUSTOMER>
        <CUSTOMER>
            <NAME>
                <LASTNAME>Thompson</LASTNAME>
                <FIRSTNAME>Phoebe</FIRSTNAME>
            </NAME>
            <DATE>May 27, 1998</DATE>
            <ORDERS>
                <ITEM>
                    <PRODUCT>Banana</PRODUCT>
                    <NUMBER>12</NUMBER>
                    <PRICE>$2.95</PRICE>
                </ITEM>
                <ITEM>
                    <PRODUCT>Apple</PRODUCT>
                    <NUMBER>6</NUMBER>
                    <PRICE>$1.50</PRICE>
                </ITEM>
            </ORDERS>
        </CUSTOMER>
    </DOCUMENT>
```

Now we've seen an XML document. Note that XML is so free-form that it's up to us to interpret it. Can you imagine having one of the major Internet browsers like the Internet Explorer try to read in the preceding document? That browser would have no idea what to make of tags like <CUSTOMER> or <ITEM>. What should it do with them? Should it display that data in a particular format? Should it store the data in a file? It's up to us to interpret the document ourselves (although there are parts of XML that are predefined, as we'll see, and which the major browsers do plan to support).

Parsing and Browsing XML

To interpret XML documents, we'll *parse* them (that is, dissect them into their logical structure). There are a number of XML parsers available that we can work with. Parsing an XML document breaks it up into its component elements. Then, however, it will be up to us to make sense of the result, because only we know what we want to do with the data in the <CUSTOMER> or <ORDERS> tags.

Almost all XML parsers are written in Java these days, which means we'll use a lot of Java in this book. XML parsers come as prewritten Java code that we can place right into our applications. We'll make use of that code in our programs to read in XML documents and determine their structure. In the rest of this chapter, then, we'll come up to speed in Java, getting familiar with—or, if you already know Java, reviewing—the code we'll need to make XML parsers work. Then we'll be able to write programs in Java that load, parse, and process (i.e., display, interpret, analyze as indicated by the document's content) XML documents.

NOTE *If you're familiar with Java and the topics in this chapter, feel free to skip on to Chapter 2, "Working with XML."*

Let's start now with Java, working through the Java we'll need for the rest of the book in this chapter. In the next chapter, we'll start parsing and making use of actual XML documents. Here, we'll use Java 1.02, the version that is the most widely used today (in practice, you can use any Java version, of course, but here we'll use Version 1.02). To make use of the code in this book (and virtually every XML parser), then, make sure you have Java installed on your computer. You can download the Java Development Kit (JDK) from the Java Web site, `http://www.javasoft.com`; to install Java, follow the instructions that come with the JDK.

Our First Java Application: `helloapp`

Our first Java application will be a very simple one, only printing the greeting: "Hello." This will get us started in Java, creating the type of Java applications we'll use throughout the book, so let's take a look at how this works now. In the next chapter, we'll see how to connect XML parsers to our Java applications.

Learning Java is fundamental to working with XML today, because almost all XML software uses Java, and you need to use Java to use that software. XML is designed for the Web, and Java is the most popular programming language used on the Web. We'll be using Java in all the chapters in this book (except Chapter 9 on XML stylesheets).

This first Java application will print only the greeting "Hello.", so we'll call it helloapp. Using a text editor or word processor (if you use a word processor, make sure you store Java programs in plain text format, without any special formatting characters), create the file `helloapp.java`. Note that a Java file's extension must be `.java`; if your editor can't create documents with that extension, save the file with the extension `.jav` and rename it later, giving it the extension `.java`.

To start, place this text in helloapp.java:

```
public class helloapp {
    .
    .
    .

}
```

Here we declare the new Java *class* **helloapp**. And that brings us to the first question: what's a class? To answer that question, we will quickly overview object-oriented programming.

Object-Oriented Programming: Classes and Objects

Object-Oriented Programming (OOP) was originally invented to deal with larger programs, and it provided the programmer with a way of *encapsulating* code and data into easily conceptualized bundles called *objects*. This cleared the program's general workspace of many unrelated data items and functions.

What Are Objects?

To understand how objects work, consider a refrigerator as an example. A refrigerator has many internal parts—regulators, a compressor, thermostats, and so on. Imagine how difficult it would be to use a refrigerator if you had to deal with all the parts of a refrigerator yourself—turning the compressor on and off, regulating the temperature, and so forth. What makes a refrigerator useful is that it performs all these operations itself, internally. What's left is an object with one easy-to-remember purpose: to refrigerate foods. You don't have to concern yourself with the internal operation of the refrigerator at all.

OOP works in much the same way; if you have functions, subroutines, and data that manage screen displays, you can put everything—functions, subroutines, and data—together into one object named, say, *display*. Then everything having to do with the display is in this object. Many functions will remain internal to this object, called by other internal functions, and because they're internal, they no longer clutter up the rest of the program. Internal data and functions are called *private* data and functions. Data and functions accessible from outside the object are called *public* data and functions. For example, if the display object had a public function named `drawCircle()` to draw circles, we could call that function, referring to it this way: `display.drawCircle()`. Here, the dot operator—"."—indicates that the `drawCircle()` function is a public function of the display object.

That gives us an overview of objects.

What Are Classes?

Classes are to objects as cookie cutters are to cookies. That is, a class is an object's *type*, much as an integer named `myInteger` is a variable of the Java `int` type. If we had a class named `dataClass`, then we would could create objects of that class named, say, `dataObject`. The `dataObject` object is what we would actually use and refer to in our program—the `dataClass` class is only that object's type. For example, if `dataClass` has a public function named `getData()`, then we would first declare an object of class `dataClass` named `dataObject` this way in Java:

```
dataClass dataObject;
          .
          .
          .
```

NOTE   *Like C or C++, you end lines of code in Java with a semicolon, ;.*

To actually create that new object, dataObject, we use the Java **new** operator this way (we'll see more about this process later in this chapter):

```
dataClass dataObject;

dataObject = new dataClass();
          .
          .
          .
```

Now that the `dataObject` object has been created, we are free to use the `getData()` function in that object like this:

```
dataClass dataObject;

dataObject = new dataClass();

dataObject.getData();
```

.
.
.

An object's built-in functions are called its member *methods*, just as its built-in data (stored in variables, data structures, or other, internal, objects) is referred to as member data. You reach member data just as you reach member methods: if `dataObject` has a public data member named, say, `dataInteger`, we can reach that in Java this way:

```
dataClass dataObject;

dataObject = new dataClass();

dataObject.getData();

dataObject.dataInteger = 0;
```

That completes our overview of classes and objects. The best way to learn about these programming concepts is to see them at work, so now that we have some of the terminology down, let's return to our Java example, `helloapp.java`.

Java Class Files

This is what our file `helloapp.java` looks like so far:

```
public class helloapp {
    .
    .
    .
}
```

Here we're declaring a class named `helloapp` and making it public. When we make this class public, Java will create a *class file* named `helloapp.class`, and it is this class file that we'll actually run to see our program work. When we run it, Java will create an object of this class and give it control, as we'll see.

Now we've declared the new class we need, but how do we make it do anything? It turns out that there is a special method in Java applications named the `main()` method, and when you run a Java application, Java runs this method first. The next step, then, is to add that method to our program.

The `main()` Method

You declare the `main()` method as you would any other method in Java, giving its name and the arguments passed to it. In this case, Java passes any command-line arguments to the program in an array of text strings that we can name `args[]`. In addition, the `main()` method does not return a value, so we set its return type to *void*:

```
public class helloapp {

    public static void main(String args[]) {
        .
        .
        .
    }
}
```

Note that we enclose the body of the class definition and the `main()` method in curly braces, `{` and `}`. Like C and C++, this is the way you set aside class definitions, method bodies, and other code blocks in Java; we'll soon become very familiar with this notation. The *static* keyword in the preceding example makes sure that no matter how many objects of the `helloapp` class we create in a program, all the code in those objects' `main()` methods share the same data; you need to declare the `main()` method as static in Java applications.

Now we're ready to complete the program and write the actual code to display the text "Hello.". We do that with these lines:

```
public class helloapp {
    public static void main(String args[]) {
        System.out.println("Hello.");
    }
}
```

The `System` class is built into Java, and it gives us access to many features, including simple *Input and Output* (I/O). The `System` class is an entirely static class, which means we can't create objects of that class; to use its methods, we refer to the class itself: `System`. In the preceding code, we use the `println()` method (`println()` stands for print line) to print the line "Hello." This line goes to the Java *output console*. In Windows 95, that means a DOS window. (We'll see all about windowed output in the next example.)

Our program is ready to run, and we'll see how to run it now.

Creating `helloapp.class`

The first step in running our helloapp program is to create the *bytecode* file, `helloapp.class`. Java bytecodes are special codes that the Java interpreter, called the *Java Virtual Machine* (JVM), reads and runs.

To create the `helloapp.class` bytecode file, we use the Java compiler, `javac.exe`, which comes with the JDK. You run this utility in a DOS session. To compile `helloapp.java`, then, we pass it to javac like this:

```
C:\>javac helloapp.java
```

This compiles `helloapp.java` and creates `helloapp.class`. Now we're ready to run the example; we can run this file and (finally) see our greeting.

Running helloapp.class

To run `helloapp.class`, we use `java.exe`, which comes with the JDK. All we need to do is to type this line in the DOS session:

```
C:\>java helloapp
```

When the program runs, it creates the greeting "Hello." and displays it:

```
C:\>java helloapp
Hello.
```

And that's it—our first Java program is a success. However, it's a pretty modest program, and if that was the extent of our Java expertise, this would be a very short book. Let's start expanding our Java skills now by seeing how to work with and display a window.

Programming Java Applets

In our next example, let's display the string `Welcome to XML!` in a Web browser:

```
┌─────────────────────────────────────────────┐
│                                             │
│  Web Browser                                │
├─────────────────────────────────────────────┤
│  Welcome to XML!                            │
│                                             │
│                                             │
│                                             │
│                                             │
│                                             │
│                                             │
│                                             │
│                                             │
│                                             │
│                                             │
│                                             │
│                                             │
└─────────────────────────────────────────────┘
```

This will show us how to set up Java *applets* (our previous program was a Java application). Java applets are targeted at the Web and usually displayed in Web browsers. Applets will be useful for us in this book because they have a great deal of graphics capability built-in, which will let us create and run XML browsers.

However, there is one consideration: because of security restrictions, Java applets displayed in Web browsers don't support file handling, which means they can't work with XML documents. To fix this problem, we'll set up our programs in this book as applications that display a window, and in that window, we'll display an applet to produce our graphics output. This is the standard way of working with graphical output in stand-alone (i.e., no browser involved) Java applications, so we will spend a little time seeing how applets work before proceeding. After we learn how to create applets, we'll see how to display them in their own window—that is, without using a Web browser—so we can use file handling and therefore read in and write out XML documents.

Let's name this new example applet, say, **app1**. We start this new applet's code file, **app1.java**, by declaring the new class, **app1**:

```
public class appl extends java.applet.Applet
{

}
```

When we compile this applet, the javac compiler will produce the file **appl.class**.

Note the keywords extends **java.applet.Applet** in the preceding code. Here we indicate to Java that our **appl** builds on the predefined **java.applet.Applet** class. This Java class, **java.applet.Applet**, has a tremendous amount of graphics and other resources already built-in, which saves us the time we'd need to write them. Here, the name **java.applet.Applet** refers to the Applet class of the Java *package* named *applet* (a Java package is a library of prewritten classes, ready for us to use).

By extending the Applet class, we are *inheriting* all the functionality of that class. Inheritance is one of the most important and essential characteristics of OOP, and it allows us to build classes on top of class. Using inheritance, we can use the prewritten Java classes to provide our own classes with a foundation full of resources that we can use. We'll see more about inheritance in this chapter when we create our own stand-alone window from the **Java Frame** class. (*Frame* refers to a window with a border you can use for resizing.)

Now we're ready to display our text string **Welcome to XML!** as graphics in the applet.

Note: *You might be surprised to see text like* **Welcome to XML!** *referred to as graphics. However, even text is just another graphical element in a windowing environment that uses a GUI.*

Displaying Graphics in an Applet

We usually display graphics in the **paint()** method in applets. This method is called when the applet's window needs to be drawn or redrawn (the window is redrawn when its content changes, or the window is re-opened after being minimized, or another window is moved, uncovering the applet's window, and for other, similar, events). We add the **paint()** method to our applet like this:

```
public class appl extends java.applet.Applet
{
    public void paint( Graphics g )
    {
                .
                .
                .
    }
}
```

The **Applet** class has a built-in **paint()** method, but that method is simply a default and does nothing. By writing our own **paint()** method, we are *overriding* the default **paint()** method. Overriding methods like this is another important part of OOP.

Note that we are passing an object of the **Java Graphics** class in the **paint()** method, and we name that object **g**. We will use this object to create our graphics display in the applet.

The **Graphics** class is part of the Java AWT (Abstract Windowing Toolkit) package, the package that supports graphics displays in Java. To make sure the Java compiler knows about the **Graphics** class, we import that class into our program like this:

```
import java.awt.Graphics;

public class appl extends java.applet.Applet
{
    public void paint( Graphics g )
    {
                .
                .
                .
    }
}
```

We're ready to display our greeting as soon as we determine where in the applet's window we want to display it. The applet's coordinate system starts at the upper left; x increases to the right, and y increases downwards as shown on the following page.

Measurements in Java are in pixels, so we can display our string starting at, say, (60, 30) using the **Graphics** class' **drawString()** method:

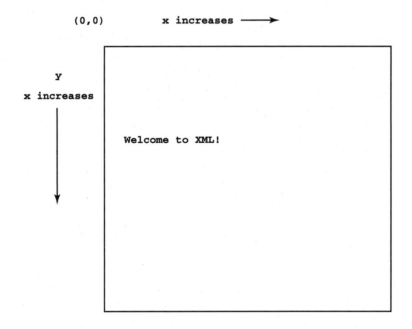

```
import java.awt.Graphics;

public class appl extends java.applet.Applet
{
    public void paint( Graphics g )
    {
        g.drawString( "Welcome to XML!", 60, 30 );
    }
}
```

NOTE   *The origin of displayed text strings, like (60, 30) in our example, refers to the lower-left corner of the text string as it appears in the applet's window.*

And that's it for our Java code. Use **javac.exe** to create **appl.class** now. We're almost ready—the final step is to display our applet in a Web browser, and we'll need a Web page for that.

Creating a Web Page for Our Applet

We'll write the applet's Web page in HTML, starting with a heading and title like this:

```
<HTML>

<HEAD>
<TITLE>HELLO</TITLE>
</HEAD>
        .
        .
        .
```

Now we embed our applet, **appl.class**, in the Web page with the HTML <APPLET> tag, displaying the applet in a region of 200 x 200 pixels:

```
<HTML>

<HEAD>
<TITLE>HELLO</TITLE>
</HEAD>

<BODY>
<HR>

<APPLET CODE=APPL.CLASS WIDTH=200 HEIGHT=200>
</APPLET>

<HR>

</BODY>
</HTML>
```

When we open this Web page in a browser such as the Microsoft Internet Explorer, we see our applet at work, displaying the greeting **Welcome to XML!**, as shown in Figure 1-1.

That's it—now we've gotten a Java applet running. The next step is to get an applet running in a stand-alone Java window (because we want to avoid Web browsers, which won't let us undertake file handling), and we'll look into that now.

Running an Applet in a Stand-Alone Window

Because of security issues generated by file handling (i.e., reading in and writing out XML documents), we won't be able to run our applets in Web browsers (although this may change as Web browsers add XML support). This means that we will run our applets in their own stand-alone window instead. We can start by placing the applet we just developed—which dis-

Figure 1-1.
Our first applet at
work.

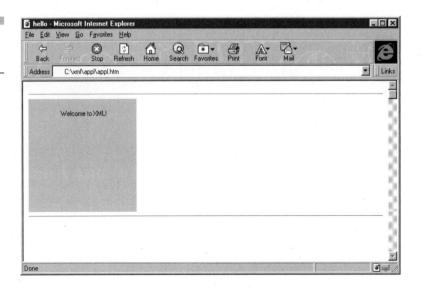

plays the string `Welcome to XML!`—in a stand-alone window as shown on
the following page.

We can call our new windowing application `winapp.java`. Create that
file now and add the code for the applet we just developed:

```java
import java.awt.*;

public class winapp extends java.applet.Applet{

    public void paint( Graphics g )
    {
        g.drawString( "Welcome to XML!", 60, 30 );
    }
}
```

The only difference here is that instead of importing only the `Graphics`
class, here we import all the classes in the Java AWT with this statement
(the * character functions as a wildcard, and indicates that we want to import all `AWT` classes):

```java
import java.awt.*;

public class winapp extends java.applet.Applet{

    public void paint( Graphics g )
    {
        g.drawString( "Welcome to XML!", 60, 30 );
    }
}
```

```
Welcome to XML!
```

We want to import all **AWT** classes because the window we're about to set up makes use of many methods in those classes.

Tip: *Importing extra classes does not make your bytecode file bigger if you do not use those extra classes in your program.*

Now our applet is ready to be inserted into a new stand-alone window, but first we have to create that window.

Creating a New Window

To create a new window, we'll use the **Java Frame** class (as mentioned previously, *Frame* refers to the frame that surrounds the window which you can use to resize the window). In fact, we'll customize the **Frame** class by *deriving* a new class, **winappFrame**, from it. When you derive a new class from a foundation class, you inherit all the functionality of the foundation or *base* class while being able to add new functionality in the derived class. For example, we'll add code to our window class to allow the user to close the window smoothly.

We'll write the actual code for the **winappFrame** class in a minute. First let's write the code that uses that new window class, installing our applet in the window and displaying it. This should be the first operation of our new application, because we can't do anything with the applet until it's visible. As you might recall from our earlier discussion at the beginning of this chapter, Java first runs a program's **main()** method, so we'll place the window-creation code in that method. We add that method now to our program:

```java
import java.awt.*;

public class winapp extends java.applet.Applet{

    public static void main(String args[])
    {
        .
        .
        .
    }

    public void paint( Graphics g )
    {
        g.drawString( "Welcome to XML!", 60, 30 );
    }
}
```

Now we'll create a new object of the window class, **winappFrame**, named **frame**. To show the new window, we will simply use the frame object's **show()** method. This means we have to declare and create the new object named **frame**; as you might recall from our discussion of OOP, making a new object is a two-step process: first you declare the new object and then you create it with the new operator, like this:

```java
dataClass dataObject;

dataObject = new dataClass();

dataObject.getData();
    .
    .
    .
```

Java allows us to perform both operations on one line, as follows, where we declare and create the new object named **frame** of the **winappFrame** class:

```
import java.awt.*;

public class winapp extends java.applet.Applet{

    public static void main(String args[])
    {
        winappFrame frame = new winappFrame("The winapp
application");

              .
              .
              .

    }

    public void paint( Graphics g )
    {
        g.drawString( "Welcome to XML!", 60, 30 );
    }
}
```

Here we're declaring a new object, frame, of the `winappFrame` class, using the new operator. Note also the text we enclose in parentheses—`"The winapp application"`:

```
winappFrame frame = new winappFrame("The winapp
        application");
```

This is the title we want to display in the title bar of our new window: **The winapp application**, and we're passing that title to the `winappFrame` class' *constructor*.

Java Class Constructors

In our object-creation example at the beginning of the chapter, we created a new object this way:

```
dataClass dataObject;

dataObject = new dataClass();

dataObject.getData();
              .
              .
              .
```

In this case, we didn't enclose anything in the parentheses that follow the class name, but if we had wanted to initialize the new object in some way, we could have put some data there if the class named **dataClass** was set up to make use of that data. For example, if we had wanted to initialize the new object with a value of 5, we could have passed it that value this way:

```
dataClass dataObject;

dataObject = new dataClass(5);

dataObject.getData();
        .
        .
        .
```

What we're really doing is passing a value of 5 to the **dataClass'** constructor.

A constructor is a special method that you write to initialize an object in some way, most often to store data. In fact, we'll write the constructor for our window class, **winappFrame**, in a minute, and we'll see how constructors work in detail. In the **winappFrame** constructor, for example, we'll take the string passed to us and make that into the window's title.

After declaring, creating, and passing the window's title to the new frame object, we give our new window a size with the **Java Frame** class' **resize()** method. In this case, we will give our window the dimensions 400 x 300 pixels:

```
import java.awt.*;

public class winapp extends java.applet.Applet{

    public static void main(String args[])
    {
        winappFrame frame = new winappFrame("The winapp
            application");

        frame.resize(400, 300);
            .
            .
            .
```

NOTE   *if you don't give a window a size before displaying it, only the title bar will appear on the screen.*

Now that our window has been given a size, we are ready to place our applet in that window in preparation for displaying the window on the screen.

Installing an Applet in a Window

To install our applet in our new window, we have to create a new applet object; then we can install that applet object in the window. In this case, we'll create a new object of our applet's class—the **winapp** class—and name that new object applet:

```
import java.awt.*;

public class winapp extends java.applet.Applet{

    public static void main(String args[])
    {
        winappFrame frame = new winappFrame("The winapp
            application");

        frame.resize(400, 300);

        winapp applet = new winapp();
            .
            .
            .
```

Next, we add the new applet object to the window using the window object's **add()** method and centering the applet in the window:

```
import java.awt.*;

public class winapp extends java.applet.Applet{

    public static void main(String args[])
    {
        winappFrame frame = new winappFrame("The winapp
            application");

        frame.resize(400, 300);

        winapp applet = new winapp();

        frame.add("Center", applet);
            .
            .
            .

    }
```

Now that we've installed the applet in the window, we can initialize the applet in preparation for displaying it.

Calling the Applet's `init()` and `start()` Methods

If we run the applet in a Web browser, the applet's environment calls the applet's `init()` and `start()` methods to get the applet started. The `init()` method, as we'll see in the next example, is where we place code to initialize the applet, and the `start()` method actually starts the applet.

Tip: *The `start()` method is where we can start additional threads if we want to make our program multitasking; a thread is a stream of execution, and if we have multiple threads we can execute code in multiple locations in a program.*

In this example, we won't override either the applet's default `init()` method or its default `start()` method, but we call those methods now to show how you start an applet after installing it in a window:

```
import java.awt.*;

public class winapp extends java.applet.Applet{

    public static void main(String args[])
    {
        winappFrame frame = new winappFrame("The winapp
            application");

        frame.resize(400, 300);

        winapp applet = new winapp();

        frame.add("Center", applet);
        applet.init();
        applet.start();
            .
            .
            .
```

Finally, we show the window itself, using the `show()` method:

```
import java.awt.*;

public class winapp extends java.applet.Applet{
```

```
public static void main(String args[])
{
    winappFrame frame = new winappFrame("The winapp
        application");

    frame.resize(400, 300);

    winapp applet = new winapp();

    frame.add("Center", applet);
    applet.init();
    applet.start();
    frame.show();
}
```

That's it—now our applet is created and running. When it comes time to display it, the code in the **paint()** method will display the **Welcome to XML!** string:

```
import java.awt.*;

public class winapp extends java.applet.Applet{

    public static void main(String args[])
    {
        winappFrame frame = new winappFrame("The winapp
            application");

        frame.resize(400, 300);

        winapp applet = new winapp();

        frame.add("Center", applet);
        applet.init();
        applet.start();
        frame.show();
    }

    public void paint( Graphics g )
    {
        g.drawString( "Welcome to XML!", 60, 30 );
    }
}
```

We're all done, except for one crucial task. We still have to write the code for the window class, **winappFrame** (the class that takes the place of a Web browser for us).

Creating the `winappFrame` Window Class

The `winappFrame` class is the class for the window we display our applet in, and we'll write the code for that class now.

We can place the code for the new `winappFrame` class at the end of our file, `winapp.java`; note that this class extends (that is, is derived from) the `Java Frame` class, which is the built-in Java window class:

```java
import java.awt.*;

public class winapp extends java.applet.Applet{

    public static void main(String args[])
    {
        winappFrame frame = new winappFrame("The winapp
            application");

        frame.resize(400, 300);

        winapp applet = new winapp();

        frame.add("Center", applet);
        applet.init();
        applet.start();
        frame.show();
    }

    public void paint( Graphics g )
    {
        g.drawString( "Welcome to XML!", 60, 30 );
    }
}

class winappFrame extends Frame
{
        .
        .
        .
}
```

We'll write the code for this new window class now. As you might recall, we passed the string we wanted to use as the window's title to the window's constructor when we created the window object in the `main()` method:

```java
import java.awt.*;

public class winapp extends java.applet.Applet{

    public static void main(String args[])
    {
```

```
winappFrame frame = new winappFrame("The winapp
    application");

frame.resize(400, 300);
                        .
                        .
                        .
```

To write the `winappFrame` class' constructor, we simply create a new method with the same name as the class itself—`winappFrame`—and pass this new method a Java String object:

```
class winappFrame extends Frame
{
    public winappFrame(String str)
    {
            .
            .
            .
    }
}
```

That's how you write constructors—as class methods with the same name as the class itself (and with no return value). In this case, we want to get the title for the window and install that in the window itself. To install the title in the window, we simply pass that title to the `Frame` class' constructor (the `Frame` class is `winappFrame`'s base class).

How do we reach the `Frame` class' constructor? Java has a special way of doing this; the base class is also called the *super* class, and you can reach that class' constructor by calling the special Java `super()` method. In our case, we pass the title to the `Frame` class' constructor this way:

```
class winappFrame extends Frame
{
    public winappFrame(String str)
    {
        super (str);
    }
```

Now our window's constructor is all set.

We also want to let the user close the window smoothly, so we'll add code for that process next (if we didn't add code to let the user close the window, they'd have to end the program by pressing ^C or by terminating the program at the system level).

When the user closes our window (using the close button in the title bar), Java passes a special value, WINDOW_DESTROY, to the `handleEvent()`

method. We can intercept that message and close the window from code at that point. Let's see how that works now.

First, we add the `handleEvent()` method to the window class:

```
class winappFrame extends Frame
{
    public winappFrame(String str)
    {
        super (str);
    }

    public boolean handleEvent(Event evt)
    {
        .
        .
        .

    }
}
```

We are passed an object of the Java Event class, which we name `evt`, in this method; if the id data member of this object is equal to the constant `WINDOW_DESTROY`, we should close our window.

This constant, `WINDOW_DESTROY`, is defined in the `Java Event` class, so we refer to it as `Event.WINDOW_DESTROY`. Because there might be other window events we want to handle in the future, we'll set up a Java `switch` statement here, allowing us to handle various window events depending on the value we're examining, `evt.id`:

```
class winappFrame extends Frame
{
    public winappFrame(String str)
    {
        super (str);
    }

    public boolean handleEvent(Event evt)
    {
        switch (evt.id)
        {
            .
            .
            .

        }
    }
}
```

A `switch` statement contains one or more *cases*, and if the value we're examining (`evt.id` here) is equal to the value specified in a particular case, the code in that case is executed. Here, we check whether `evt.id` id equal to `Event.WINDOW_DESTROY` this way:

```
class winappFrame extends Frame
{
    public winappFrame(String str)
    {
        super (str);
    }

    public boolean handleEvent(Event evt)
    {
        switch (evt.id)
        {
            case Event.WINDOW_DESTROY:
                .
                .
                .
        }
    }
}
```

If **evt.id** is indeed equal to **Event.WINDOW_DESTROY**, we get rid of our window with the **dispose()** method this way:

```
class winappFrame extends Frame
{
    public winappFrame(String str)
    {
        super (str);
    }

    public boolean handleEvent(Event evt)
    {
        switch (evt.id)
        {
            case Event.WINDOW_DESTROY:
                dispose();
                .
                .
                .
        }
    }
}
```

Then we indicate that we want to shut down the program by calling the **Java System** class' **exit()** method:

```
class winappFrame extends Frame
{
    public winappFrame(String str)
    {
        super (str);
    }
```

```
public boolean handleEvent(Event evt)
{
    switch (evt.id)
    {
        case Event.WINDOW_DESTROY:
            dispose();
            System.exit(0);
               .
               .
               .

    }
}
}
```

Finally, we can return a value of **true** to the Java framework to indicate that we've handled the message:

```
class winappFrame extends Frame
{
    public winappFrame(String str)
    {
        super (str);
    }

    public boolean handleEvent(Event evt)
    {
        switch (evt.id)
        {
            case Event.WINDOW_DESTROY:
                dispose();
                System.exit(0);
                return true;
                  .
                  .
                  .

        }
    }
}
```

And that's it—now we've handled the case in which our window is closed. We can pass all other window messages back to the base class' **handleEvent()** method, letting it take care of them. We can catch all other window messages by adding a *default* case to our switch statement:

```
class winappFrame extends Frame
{
    public winappFrame(String str)
    {
        super (str);
    }
```

```
public boolean handleEvent(Event evt)
{
    switch (evt.id)
    {
        case Event.WINDOW_DESTROY:
            dispose();
            System.exit(0);
            return true;

        default:
            .
            .
            .

    }
}
}
```

If no other case statement matches the value of **evt.id**, the program executes the code in the default statement, and we'll just pass the event back to the super class by calling the super object's **handleEvent()** method:

```
class winappFrame extends Frame
{
    public winappFrame(String str)
    {
        super (str);
    }

    public boolean handleEvent(Event evt)
    {
        switch (evt.id)
        {
            case Event.WINDOW_DESTROY:
                dispose();
                System.exit(0);
                return true;

            default:
                return super.handleEvent(evt);
        }
    }
}
```

That's all we need, now our program is ready to run. When we use **java.exe** to run it (i.e., type **java winapp** at the DOS prompt), a window appears with our applet in it, as shown in Figure 1-2—no Web browser needed.

Our applet-in-window example is a success; the code for this example, **winapp.java**, appears in Listing 1-1.

We've made considerable progress in Java, but there is still more work

Figure 1-2.
The winapp Java
application at work.

Listing 1-1.
winapp.java.

```java
import java.awt.*;

public class winapp extends java.applet.Applet{

    public static void main(String args[])
    {
        winappFrame frame = new winappFrame("The winapp
            application");

        frame.resize(400, 300);

        winapp applet = new winapp();

        frame.add("Center", applet);
        applet.init();
        applet.start();
        frame.show();
    }

    public void paint( Graphics g )
    {
        g.drawString( "Welcome to XML!", 60, 30 );
    }
}

class winappFrame extends Frame
{
    public winappFrame(String str)
    {
        super (str);
    }

    public boolean handleEvent(Event evt)
```

Listing 1-1.
winapp.java.

```
{
    switch (evt.id)
    {
        case Event.WINDOW_DESTROY:
            dispose();
            System.exit(0);
            return true;

        default:
            return super.handleEvent(evt);
    }
}
}
```

before we're up to speed. Many of our XML examples will use two Java
controls: text fields and buttons (a control is a visual object used for user
input or output, like list boxes, scroll bars, buttons, and so on). We'll take
a look at how to use those controls in the rest of this chapter.

Using Text Fields

In our next example, we'll use a Java text field (you may be more familiar with this type of control under its standard Windows name—the text
box). We can display a text field in an applet in a stand-alone window and
our standard greeting, **Welcome to XML!**, in the text field.

This new example will be named **textfields.java**, so create that file
now and add this starting code—note that the class name is **textfields**,
matching the name of the file:

```
import java.awt.*;
import java.applet.Applet;

public class textfields extends Applet{
    .
    .
    .
```

Next, we add the **main()** method to install the applet in a stand-alone
window; this time, we'll call the window class **textfieldsFrame**:

```
import java.awt.*;
import java.applet.Applet;
```

```
┌─────────────────────────────────────┐
│                                     │
├─────────────────────────────────────┤
│                                     │
│                                     │
│         ┌─────────────────┐         │
│         │                 │         │
│         │ Welcome to XML! │         │
│         │                 │         │
│         └─────────────────┘         │
│                                     │
│                                     │
│                                     │
│                                     │
│                                     │
└─────────────────────────────────────┘
```

```java
public class textfields extends Applet{

    public static void main(String args[])
    {
        textfieldsFrame frame = new textfieldsFrame("The
            textfields application");

        frame.resize(400, 300);

        textfields applet = new textfields();

        frame.add("Center", applet);
        applet.init();
        applet.start();
        frame.show();
    }
```

In addition, we create and add the new **textfieldsFrame** class, our window class, to textfields.java:

```java
import java.awt.*;
import java.applet.Applet;

public class textfields extends Applet{

    public static void main(String args[])
    {
        textfieldsFrame frame = new textfieldsFrame("The
```

```
                    textfields application");

              frame.resize(400, 300);

              textfields applet = new textfields();

              frame.add("Center", applet);
              applet.init();
              applet.start();
              frame.show();
         }
     }

     class textfieldsFrame extends Frame
     {
         public textfieldsFrame(String str)
         {
             super (str);
         }

         public boolean handleEvent(Event evt)
         {
             switch (evt.id)
             {
                 case Event.WINDOW_DESTROY:
                     dispose();
                     System.exit(0);
                     return true;

                 default:
                     return super.handleEvent(evt);
             }
         }
     }
```

Now our applet will appear in the window. We only have to add the text field and place our message in it.

Declaring and Creating a Text Field

To add a text field to our applet, we first declare it as an object of the Java **TextField** class:

```
import java.awt.*;
import java.applet.Applet;

public class textfields extends Applet{

    TextField text1;
```

```
    public static void main(String args[])
    {
            .
            .
            .

    }
}

class textfieldsFrame extends Frame
{
            .
            .
            .

}
```

Declaring this new object, **textfield**, outside of any method gives it global *scope* (a variable or object's scope is the part or parts of the program in which it may be referenced), which means we can use it in any method of our applet class.

Now that we've declared our new **TextField** object, we have to create it with the Java new operator. We do that in the **init()** method, which is where you initialize an applet and add new controls to it. Here, we create our new text field and give it a width of 20 characters by passing 20 to the **TextField** class' constructor:

```
import java.awt.*;
import java.applet.Applet;

public class textfields extends Applet{

    TextField text1;

    public static void main(String args[])
    {
            .
            .
            .

    }

    public void init(){
        text1 = new TextField(20);
            .
            .
            .

    }
}
```

```
class textfieldsFrame extends Frame
{
        .
        .
        .

}
```

Next, we set the text in the text field to `Welcome to XML!` with the `TextField` class' `setText()` method:

```
import java.awt.*;
import java.applet.Applet;

public class textfields extends Applet{

    TextField text1;

    public static void main(String args[])
    {
        .
        .
        .

    }

    public void init(){
        text1 = new TextField(20);
        text1.setText("Welcome to XML!");
        .
        .
        .

    }
}

class textfieldsFrame extends Frame
{
        .
        .
        .

}
```

Finally, we add the text field to the applet's display with the applet's `add()` method:

```
import java.awt.*;
import java.applet.Applet;

public class textfields extends Applet{

    TextField text1;
```

```
public static void main(String args[])
{
    .
    .
    .
}

public void init(){
    text1 = new TextField(20);
    text1.setText("Welcome to XML!");
    add(text1);
}
}

class textfieldsFrame extends Frame
{
    .
    .
    .
}
```

Java Layout Managers

You have to add each new control you want in an applet using the **add()** method. You can specify how to place your controls in an applet by using one of the Java *layout managers*; in this book, we'll only use the

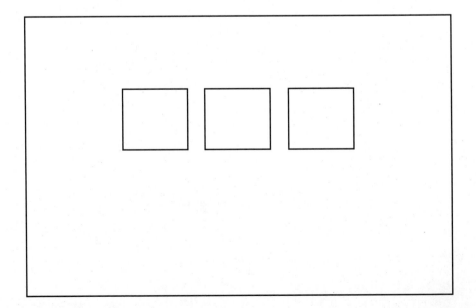

default layout manager, the Flow Layout manager. Using this layout manager means that when you add controls to an applet, they are simply added one after the next, like words on a page, except that they appear centered as shown at the bottom of the preceding page.

When you come to the edge of the applet, the next controls are simply placed on the next line, again just like words in a page:

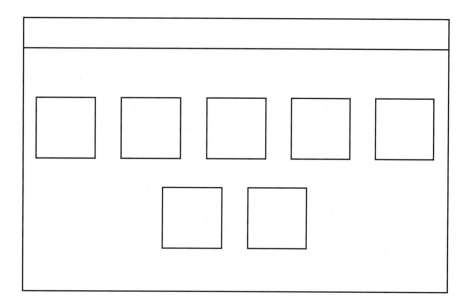

Compile the new program, **textfields.java**, using **javac.exe** now and run it with **java.exe**. When you do, you see the result in Figure 1-3—a window with a text field displaying our message in it.

Our program is a success; now we've been able to add a Java control—a text field—to our applet and display that applet in a window. You can even edit the text in the text field by selecting the text field with the mouse and editing the text there as you would in any standard Windows text box. The code for this example, **textfields.java**, appears in Listing 1-2.

Now we've seen how to use text fields in Java. The next step is to add one more common control to our programs—buttons. We'll use buttons in our example XML programs throughout this book, so let's look into how to use buttons in Java now.

Figure 1-3.
The textfields
program at work.

Using Buttons

In this next example, we'll display both a text field and a button, giving the button the caption `Click Me`:

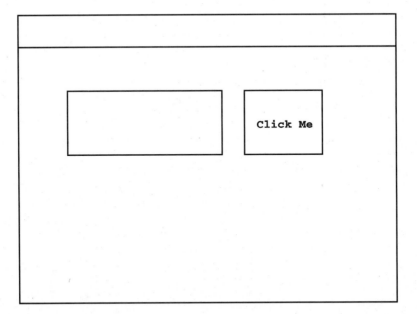

When the user clicks the button, the program displays the string `Welcome to XML!` in the text field:

Listing 1-2.
textfields.java

```java
import java.awt.*;
import java.applet.Applet;

public class textfields extends Applet{

    TextField text1;

    public static void main(String args[])
    {
        textfieldsFrame frame = new textfieldsFrame("The
            textfields application");

        frame.resize(400, 300);

        textfields applet = new textfields();

        frame.add("Center", applet);
        applet.init();
        applet.start();
        frame.show();
    }

    public void init(){
        text1 = new TextField(20);
        text1.setText("Welcome to XML!");
        add(text1);
    }
}

class textfieldsFrame extends Frame
{
    public textfieldsFrame(String str)
    {
        super (str);
    }

    public boolean handleEvent(Event evt)
    {
        switch (evt.id)
        {
            case Event.WINDOW_DESTROY:
                dispose();
                System.exit(0);
                return true;

            default:
                return super.handleEvent(evt);
        }
    }
}
```

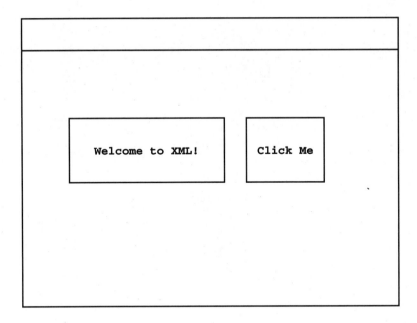

Let's put this to work in a new file named, say, **buttons.java**. We start that file as usual, with a new applet class, which we name **buttons**, and a **main()** method:

```
import java.awt.*;
import java.applet.Applet;

public class buttons extends Applet{

    public static void main(String args[])
    {
        buttonsFrame frame = new buttonsFrame("The buttons
            application");

        frame.resize(400, 300);

        buttons applet = new buttons();

        frame.add("Center", applet);
        applet.init();
        applet.start();
        frame.show();
    }
}
```

Next we add the two controls we need: a text field and a button; the button will be an object of the **Java Button** class:

```
import java.awt.*;
import java.applet.Applet;

public class buttons extends Applet{

    TextField text1;
    Button button1;

    public static void main(String args[])
    {
            .
            .
            .
    }
}
```

As in the previous example, we initialize our controls in the **init()** method; this time, however, we add two controls, not just one: an empty text field and a button with the caption **Click Me**:

```
import java.awt.*;
import java.applet.Applet;

public class buttons extends Applet{

    TextField text1;
    Button button1;

    public static void main(String args[])
    {
            .
            .
            .
    }

    public void init(){
        text1 = new TextField(20);
        add(text1);
        button1 = new Button("Click Me");
        add(button1);
    }
}
```

Now our two new controls are added to the applet's display, but how do we make the button active? That is, how do we display the message we want in the text field when the user clicks the button? We do that in the applet's **action()** method.

The Java `action()` Method

When the user clicks a button, the Java framework calls the applet's
`action()` method, so we add that method now:

```java
import java.awt.*;
import java.applet.Applet;

public class buttons extends Applet{

    TextField text1;
    Button button1;

    public static void main(String args[])
    {
        .
        .
        .
    }

    public void init(){
        .
        .
        .
    }

    public boolean action (Event e, Object o){
        .
        .
        .
    }
}
```

We are passed two arguments in `action()`—an `Event` class object we
name `e` and a simple Java object we name `o`. We can determine which control the user clicked by examining the *target* member object of the `e` Event
object: `e.target`. The target object is the control that caused the Java
framework to call the `action()` method, and if that control is equal to
`button1`, the user clicked the button. We can compare `e.target` with
`button1` with the target object's `equals()` method:

```java
import java.awt.*;
import java.applet.Applet;

public class buttons extends Applet{

    TextField text1;
    Button button1;
```

```
        public static void main(String args[])
        {
                    .
                    .
                    .
        }

        public void init(){
                .
                .
                .
        }

        public boolean action (Event e, Object o){
            if(e.target.equals(button1)){
                        .
                        .
                        .
            }
        }
    }
```

If the user did indeed click the button, we want to place the text
Welcome to XML! in the text field, which we do with the text field's setText()
method:

```
import java.awt.*;
import java.applet.Applet;

public class buttons extends Applet{

    TextField text1;
    Button button1;

    public static void main(String args[])
    {
            .
            .
            .
    }

    public void init(){
            .
            .
            .
    }

    public boolean action (Event e, Object o){
        if(e.target.equals(button1)){
            text1.setText("Welcome to XML!");
        }
    }
}
```

Finally, we have to return a **boolean** value (that is, a value of **true** or **false**) from the **action()** method. We return a value of **true** to indicate that we handled the interface event:

```java
import java.awt.*;
import java.applet.Applet;

public class buttons extends Applet{

    TextField text1;
    Button button1;

    public static void main(String args[])
    {
        .
        .
        .
    }

    public void init(){
        .
        .
        .
    }

    public boolean action (Event e, Object o){
        if(e.target.equals(button1)){
            text1.setText("Welcome to XML!");
        }
        return true;
    }
}
```

Now the example is ready to run—compile and run it, as shown in Figure 1-4. You can see our text field and button in that figure already.

Figure 1-4.
Our buttons
application.

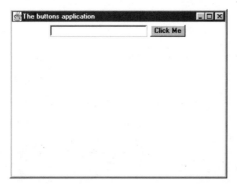

When the user clicks the button, the program displays the **Welcome to XML!** message, as shown in Figure 1-5. Our program is a success—now we're using Java buttons.

The code for this example, **buttons.java**, appears in Listing 1-3.

Figure 1-5.
Clicking the button displays our message.

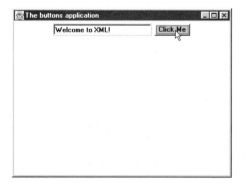

Listing 1-3.
buttons.java.

```java
import java.awt.*;
import java.applet.Applet;

public class buttons extends Applet{

    TextField text1;
    Button button1;

    public static void main(String args[])
    {
        buttonsFrame frame = new buttonsFrame("The buttons
            application");

        frame.resize(400, 300);

        buttons applet = new buttons();

        frame.add("Center", applet);
        applet.init();
        applet.start();
        frame.show();
    }

    public void init(){
        text1 = new TextField(20);
        add(text1);
        button1 = new Button("Click Me");
```

Listing 1-3.
Continued.

```
            add(button1);
        }

    public boolean action (Event e, Object o){
        if(e.target.equals(button1)){
            text1.setText("Welcome to XML!");
        }
        return true;
    }
}

class buttonsFrame extends Frame
{
    public buttonsFrame(String str)
    {
        super (str);
    }

    public boolean handleEvent(Event evt)
    {
        switch (evt.id)
        {
            case Event.WINDOW_DESTROY:
                dispose();
                System.exit(0);
                return true;

            default:
                return super.handleEvent(evt);
        }
    }
}
```

SUMMARY

That's it for our first chapter. In this chapter, we've gotten an introduction to XML and learned—or reviewed—the Java we'll need to use the available XML software (in particular, XML parsers). Let's turn to the next chapter now in which we start seeing how to put XML to work.

Working with XML

This is the chapter where it really begins—where we start dissecting XML and putting it to work for us. To start, we'll work through the formal rules of XML—the XML grammar specification—in this chapter and the next one. Examining the grammar of XML is crucial to creating and using XML documents.

Then, to actually make use of XML documents, we'll see how to use the Microsoft XML parser (written in Java) to read in XML documents, check them for validity, and parse them into their component elements. After that, we'll start seeing how to make use of the data in XML documents.

Let's start now by working through the XML grammar specification.

The XML Grammar Specification

We'll start our exploration of the XML specification with two important XML definitions: *valid* and *well-formed* XML documents. Because we'll refer back to these concepts throughout this chapter, we will start by defining these two terms.

Valid and Well-Formed XML Documents

An XML document is considered valid if there is a *document type declaration* (DTD) associated with it and if the document complies with the DTD. That's all there is to making a document valid.

An XML document is considered well-formed if it contains one or more elements, there is precisely one element (the root or document element) for which neither the start nor the end tag is inside any other element, and all other tags nest within each other correctly. In addition, all *entities* used in the document must either be predefined in XML or in the DTD. As we'll see in the next chapter, an *entity* is a term that represents certain data; the parser will substitute that data for the entity. The predefined entities in XML are: **amp**, **lt**, **gt**, **apos**, **quot**; these entities stand for the following characters respectively: **&, <, >, ', "**. When you place an entity in an XML document, you enclose it in the characters **&** and **;** like this: **&**.

As an example, this XML document is both valid and well-formed:

```
<?XML version = "1.0" ?>
<!DOCTYPE DOCUMENT [
<!ELEMENT DOCUMENT (CUSTOMER)*>
<!ELEMENT CUSTOMER (NAME,DATE,ORDERS)>
<!ELEMENT NAME (LASTNAME,FIRSTNAME)>
<!ELEMENT LASTNAME (#PCDATA)>
<!ELEMENT FIRSTNAME (#PCDATA)>
<!ELEMENT DATE (#PCDATA)>
<!ELEMENT ORDERS (ITEM)*>
<!ELEMENT ITEM (PRODUCT,NUMBER,PRICE)>
<!ELEMENT PRODUCT (#PCDATA)>
<!ELEMENT NUMBER (#PCDATA)>
<!ELEMENT PRICE (#PCDATA)>
]>
<DOCUMENT>
<CUSTOMER>
    <NAME>
        <LASTNAME>Edwards</LASTNAME>
        <FIRSTNAME>Britta</FIRSTNAME>
    </NAME>
```

```
            <DATE>April 17, 1998</DATE>
            <ORDERS>
                <ITEM>
                    <PRODUCT>Cucumber</PRODUCT>
                    <NUMBER>5</NUMBER>
                    <PRICE>$1.25</PRICE>
                </ITEM>
                <ITEM>
                    <PRODUCT>Lettuce</PRODUCT>
                    <NUMBER>2</NUMBER>
                    <PRICE>$.98</PRICE>
                </ITEM>
            </ORDERS>
        </CUSTOMER>
        <CUSTOMER>
            <NAME>
                <LASTNAME>Thompson</LASTNAME>
                <FIRSTNAME>Phoebe</FIRSTNAME>
            </NAME>
            <DATE>May 27, 1998</DATE>
            <ORDERS>
                <ITEM>
                    <PRODUCT>Banana</PRODUCT>
                    <NUMBER>12</NUMBER>
                    <PRICE>$2.95</PRICE>
                </ITEM>
                <ITEM>
                    <PRODUCT>Apple</PRODUCT>
                    <NUMBER>6</NUMBER>
                    <PRICE>$1.50</PRICE>
                </ITEM>
            </ORDERS>
        </CUSTOMER>
    </DOCUMENT>
```

Here's a document that is well-formed but not valid (no DTD):

```
<?XML version="1.0"?>
<TITLE>The Rain in Spain</TITLE>
```

Here is a document that contains a nesting error and no DTD, so it is neither valid nor well-formed:

```
<?XML version="1.0"?>
<TITLE>
The Rain in Spain
<HEADING>
</TITLE>
Falls Mainly on the Plain
</HEADING>
```

Most XML parsers require XML documents to be well-formed but not necessarily valid (many XML parsers do not require a DTD, but if there is one, the parser will use it to check the XML document). The formal specification recommends that your XML documents be both. As we work through the XML grammar specification, we'll see a number of conditions that you need to satisfy to make your documents well-formed and valid.

Now that we've gotten an idea of what constitutes a good XML construction, let's continue with the XML grammar specification. We will base our examination of the XML Grammar in this chapter on the W3C standard draft document "WD-xml-lang-970630" (W3C is the organization that produces standards for the World Wide Web). This document is called a "work in progress" because the XML standard is changing. The latest version of this document may be found at **http://www.w3.org/pub/WWW/ TR/WD-xml-lang.html**.

NOTE   *The "WD-xml-lang-970630" document represents Part I of the XML standard. Part II has to do with XML links, and we'll take a look at that in Chapter 6, "XML Links." Part II also has to do with XML stylesheets.*

To represent the XML grammar, W3C uses a special notation called Extended Backus-Naur notation, and we'll take a look at that notation now.

Extended Backus-Naur Notation

Extended Backus-Naur notation is actually pretty simple and consists of statements like this:

```
symbol ::= expression
```

Here, *symbol* is the symbol we're defining and *expression* is an expression in Extended Backus-Naur Notation. Expressions in this notation are written in the following terminology (adapted from "WD-xml-lang-970630")—take note of the terms that follow, because we'll be using them throughout this and the next chapter:

#xNNNN   **NNNN** is a hexadecimal integer, and the expression represents the character in ISO 10646 whose canonical (UCS-4) bit string, when interpreted as an unsigned binary number, has the value indicated.

`[a-zA-Z]`, `[#xNNNN-#xNNNN]`	Represents any character with a value in the range(s) indicated (inclusive).
`[^a-z]`, `[^#xNNNN-#xNNNN]`	Represents any character with a value outside the range indicated.
`[^abc]`, `[^#xNNNN#xNNNN#xNNNN]`	Represents any character with a value not among the characters given.
`"string"`	Represents a literal string matching that given inside the double quotes.
`'string'`	Represents a literal string matching that given inside the single quotes.
`a b`	**a** followed by **b**.
`a	b`	**a** or **b** but not both.
`a - b`	The set of strings represented by **a** but not represented by **b**.
`a?`	**a** or nothing.
`a+`	One or more occurrences of **a**.
`a*`	Zero or more occurrences of **a**.
`%a`	Indicates that a **parameter** entity may occur in the text at the position where **a** may occur.
`(expression)`	Surrounding expression with parentheses means it is treated as a unit and may carry the **%** prefix operator or a suffix operator: **?**, *****, or **+**.
`/* ... */`	A comment.

Now we will continue with an overview of legal symbols that you can use in XML.

Names, Characters, and White Spaces

The character set of XML is specified by the Unicode standard and "ISO/IEC 10646" (All the characters in ISO 10646 are also available with the same 16-bit values in Unicode). Certain types of characters are given names in the XML specification, such as white spaces, which are referred to with the symbol **s**. Legal white space characters include standard spaces, tabs, carriage returns, and so on; in formal (Extended Backus-

Naur Notation) terms, white spaces are specified to mean this (where each hex value stands for the corresponding ISO 10646 character, such as #x0020, which is a space character):

```
S::= (#x0020 | #x0009 | #x000d | #x000a | #x3000)+
```

Legal characters are defined this way:

```
Char::= #x09 | #x0A | #x0D | [ #x20-#xFFFD] |
        [#x00010000-#x7FFFFFFF]
```

Here are some other definitions that will be useful throughout the XML grammar specification. Refer back to this list as needed:

```
PCData::= [^<&]*

MiscName::= '.' | '-' | '_' | CombiningChar | Ignorable |
        Extender

NameChar::= Letter | Digit | MiscName

Name::= (Letter | '_') (NameChar)*

Names::= Name (S Name)*

Nmtoken::= (NameChar)+

Nmtokens::= Nmtoken ( S Nmtoken)*

Ignorable::= [#x200C-#x200F] | [#x202A-#x202E] |
        [#x206A-#x206F] | #xFEFF

Extender::= #x00B7 | #x02D0 | #x02D1 | #x0387 | #x0640 |
        #x0E46 | #x0EC6 | #x3005 | [#x3031-#x3035] |
        [#x309B-#x309E] | [#x30FC-#x30FE] | #xFF70 | #xFF9E |
        #xFF9F

CombiningChar::= [#x0300-#x0345] | [#x0360-#x0361] |
        [#x0483-#x0486] | [#x0591-#x05A1] | [#x05A3-#x05B9] |
        [#x05BB-#x05BD] | #x05BF | [#x05C1-#x05C2] | #x05C4 |
        [#x064B-#x0652] | #x0670 | [#x06D6-#x06DC] |
        [#x06DD-#x06DF] | [#x06E0-#x06E4] | [#x06E7-#x06E8] |
        [#x06EA-#x06ED] | [#x0901-#x0903] | #x093C |
        [#x093E-#x094C] | #x094D | [#x0951-#x0954] |
        [#x0962-#x0963] | [#x0981-#x0983] | #x09BC | #x09BE |
        #x09BF | [#x09C0-#x09C4] | [#x09C7-#x09C8] |
        [#x09CB-#x09CD] | #x09D7 | [#x09E2-#x09E3] | # x0A02
        | #x0A3C | #x0A3E | #x0A3F | [#x0A40-#x0A42] |
        [#x0A47-#x0A48] | [#x0A4B-#x0A4D] | [#x0A70-#x0A71] |
        [#x0A81-#x0A83] | #x0ABC | [#x0ABE-#x0AC5] |
```

```
[#x0AC7-#x0AC9] | [#x0ACB-#x0ACD] | [#x0B01-#x0B03] |
#x0B3C | [#x0B3E-# x0B43] | [#x0B47-#x0B48] |
[#x0B4B-#x0B4D] | [#x0B56-#x0B57] | [#x0B82-#x0B83] |
[#x0BBE-#x0BC2] | [#x0BC6-#x0BC8] | [#x0BCA-#x0BCD] |
#x0BD7 | [#x0C01-#x0C03] | [#x0C3E-#x0C44] |
[#x0C46-#x0C48] | [#x0C4A-#x0C4D] | [#x0C55-#x0C56] |&
#160;[#x0C82-#x0C83] | [#x0CBE-#x0CC4] |
[#x0CC6-#x0CC8] | [#x0CCA-#x0CCD] | [#x0CD5-#x0CD6] |
[#x0D02-#x0D03] | [#x0D3E-#x0D43] | [#x0D46-#x0D48] |
[#x0D4A-#x0D4D] | #x0D57 | #x0E31| [#x0E34-#x0E3A] |
[#x0E47-#x0E4E] | #x0EB1 | ;[#x0EB4-#x0EB9] |
[#x0EBB-#x0EBC] | [#x0EC8-#x0ECD] | [#x0F18-#x0F19] |
#x0F35 | #x0F37 | #x0F39 | #x0F3E | #x0F3F |
[#x0F71-#x0F84] | [#x0F86-#x0F8B] | [#x0F90-#x0F95] |
#x0F97 | [#x0F99-#x0FAD] | [#x0FB1-#x0FB7] | #x0FB9 |
[#x20D0-#x20DC] | #x20E1 | [#x302A-#x302F] | #x3099 |
#x309A | #xFB1E | [#xFE20-#xFE23]

Hex::= [0-9a-fA-F]

CharRef::= '&#' [0-9]+ ';' | '&#x' Hex+ ';'

EntityRef::= '&' Name ';'

Reference::= EntityRef | CharRef

PEReference::= '%' Name ';'

EntityValue::= '"' ([^% &"] | PEReference | Reference)*
       '"' |   "'" ([^%&'] | PEReference | Reference)* "'"

AttValue::= '"' ([^<&"] | Reference)* '"' | "'" ([^<&'] |
       Reference)* "'"

URLchar::= /* See Document W3C RFC 1738 for definition */

SystemLiteral::= '"' URLchar* '"' | "'" (URLchar - "'")*
       "'"

PubidChar::= #x0020 | #x0009 | #x000d | #x000a | #x3000 |
       [a-zA-Z0-9] | [-'()+,./:=?]

PubidLiteral::= '"' PubidChar * '"' | "'" (PubidChar -
       "'")* "'"

SkipLit::= ('"' [^"]* '"') | ("'" [^']* "'")
```

Now that we've seen some of the terms we'll need, it's time to take a look at what constitutes the formal part of an XML document—the XML markup. It is the XML markup that gives an XML document structure and makes it an XML document.

XML Markup

XML markup is what makes the formal structure of an XML document; it specifies how the data in the document is stored and structured. All text that is not markup is considered the *character data* of the document. In fact, the character data is made up of what we usually consider the real data in an XML document; for example, here the character data is **The Rain in Spain**.

```
<?XML version="1.0"?>
<TITLE>The Rain in Spain</TITLE>
```

Formally, XML markup can consist of these items:

- Comments
- Entity references
- Character references
- Processing instructions
- CDATA sections
- Start tags
- End tags
- Empty elements
- Prolog and Document Type Declarations

Let's work through the list of XML markup items now, item by item, starting with comments.

Comments

You use *comments* to make the structure or content of an XML document clearer. The content of comments is ignored by XML parsers, and it is usually passed to us as an element (as in the example parse tree at the beginning of this chapter).

Here's how comments are defined in "WD-xml-lang-970630":

```
Comment::= '<!-' (Char* - (Char* '-' Char*)) '->'
```

An example of a comment is

```
<?XML version = "1.0" ?>
<!DOCTYPE DOCUMENT [
<!ELEMENT DOCUMENT (CUSTOMER)*>
<!ELEMENT CUSTOMER (NAME,DATE,ORDERS)>
<!ELEMENT NAME (LASTNAME,FIRSTNAME)>
<!ELEMENT LASTNAME (#PCDATA)>
<!ELEMENT FIRSTNAME (#PCDATA)>
<!ELEMENT DATE (#PCDATA)>
<!ELEMENT ORDERS (ITEM)*>
<!ELEMENT ITEM (PRODUCT,NUMBER,PRICE)>
<!ELEMENT PRODUCT (#PCDATA)>
<!ELEMENT NUMBER (#PCDATA)>
<!ELEMENT PRICE (#PCDATA)>
]>
<DOCUMENT>
<!-The first customer's data->
<CUSTOMER>
    <NAME>
        <LASTNAME>Edwards</LASTNAME>
        <FIRSTNAME>Britta</FIRSTNAME>
    </NAME>
    <DATE>April 17, 1998</DATE>
    <ORDERS>
        <ITEM>
            <PRODUCT>Cucumber</PRODUCT>
            <NUMBER>5</NUMBER>
            <PRICE>$1.25</PRICE>
                .
                .
                .
```

Entity References

The next markup type is an *entity reference*. We've already mentioned entity references; an entity is a term that represents certain data; the XML parser will substitute that data for the entity.

Here's how entity references are defined formally. (Note that you preface an entity name with & and end it with ;):

```
EntityRef::= '&' Name ';'
```

The predefined entities in XML are **amp**, **lt**, **gt**, **apos**, **quot**; these entities stand for the following characters respectively: &, <, >, ', ". When you place an entity in an XML document, you enclose them in the characters & and ; like this: **&**, as in

```
<?XML version = "1.0" ?>
<!DOCTYPE DOCUMENT [
```

```
<!ELEMENT DOCUMENT (CUSTOMER)*>
<!ELEMENT CUSTOMER (NAME,DATE,ORDERS)>
<!ELEMENT NAME (LASTNAME,FIRSTNAME)>
<!ELEMENT LASTNAME (#PCDATA)>
<!ELEMENT FIRSTNAME (#PCDATA)>
<!ELEMENT DATE (#PCDATA)>
<!ELEMENT ORDERS (ITEM)*>
<!ELEMENT ITEM (PRODUCT,NUMBER,PRICE)>
<!ELEMENT PRODUCT (#PCDATA)>
<!ELEMENT NUMBER (#PCDATA)>
<!ELEMENT PRICE (#PCDATA)>
]>
<DOCUMENT>
<CUSTOMER>
  <NAME>
->  <LASTNAME>This data is enclosed in the &lt; LASTNAME
      &gt; tag</LASTNAME>
          .
          .
          .
```

When the XML parser comes across an entity reference, it substitutes the entity itself for that reference, as we'll see in the next chapter. Although we've only discussed the character set used in XML, you can also store binary data in an XML entity, as we'll also see in the next chapter.

Character References

A *character reference* is just a character in the ISO 10646 character set not readily entered into an XML document as character data (such as a carriage return). A character reference is the hexadecimal code for a character, and it's defined this way in the "WD-xml-lang-970630" document:

```
Hex::= [0-9a-fA-F]
CharRef::= '&#' [0-9]+ ';' | '&#x' Hex+ ';'
```

For example, a carriage return is **#x000d**.

Processing Instructions

The next markup type, the *processing instruction* (PI), holds processing directions and information passed to XML parsers and programs. Processing instructions are defined this way formally (note that PIs begin with **<?** and end with **?>**):

```
PI::= '<?' Name S (Char* - (Char* '?>' Char*)) '?>'
```

An example of a processing instruction is the `<?XML ?>` tag we have used to specify the XML version, like this:

```
<?XML version = "1.0" ?>
<!DOCTYPE DOCUMENT [
<!ELEMENT DOCUMENT (CUSTOMER)*>
<!ELEMENT CUSTOMER (NAME,DATE,ORDERS)>
<!ELEMENT NAME (LASTNAME,FIRSTNAME)>
<!ELEMENT LASTNAME (#PCDATA)>
<!ELEMENT FIRSTNAME (#PCDATA)>
<!ELEMENT DATE (#PCDATA)>
<!ELEMENT ORDERS (ITEM)*>
        .
        .
        .
```

CDATA Sections

You use a CDATA section to store marked-up text so that the markup is not evaluated; that is, CDATA sections provide a way of making sure specific markup is not interpreted as markup. CDATA sections begin with the string `<![CDATA[` and end with the string `]]>`:

```
CDSect::= CDStart CData CDEnd
CDStart::= '<![CDATA['
CData::= (Char* - (Char* ']]>' Char*))
CDEnd::= ']]>'
```

Here's an example of a CDATA section:

```
<![CDATA[<TITLE>This is the title!</TITLE>]]>
```

You can use a CDATA section when you have XML markup that you want to store as data.

Start Tags and End Tags

Start tags and end tags make up the essence of an XML document's structure. We've already seen start tags and end tags in the last chapter. A start tag looks like this: <TAGNAME> and an end tag like this: </TAGNAME>. You enclose character data or markup between start and end tags, as we've already seen:

```
<?XML version = "1.0" ?>
<!DOCTYPE DOCUMENT [
<!ELEMENT DOCUMENT (CUSTOMER)*>
<!ELEMENT CUSTOMER (NAME,DATE,ORDERS)>
<!ELEMENT NAME (LASTNAME,FIRSTNAME)>
<!ELEMENT LASTNAME (#PCDATA)>
<!ELEMENT FIRSTNAME (#PCDATA)>
<!ELEMENT DATE (#PCDATA)>
<!ELEMENT ORDERS (ITEM)*>
<!ELEMENT ITEM (PRODUCT,NUMBER,PRICE)>
<!ELEMENT PRODUCT (#PCDATA)>
<!ELEMENT NUMBER (#PCDATA)>
<!ELEMENT PRICE (#PCDATA)>
]>
<DOCUMENT>
<CUSTOMER>
    <NAME>
        <LASTNAME>Edwards</LASTNAME>
        <FIRSTNAME>Britta</FIRSTNAME>
    </NAME>
    <DATE>April 17, 1998</DATE>
    <ORDERS>
        <ITEM>
            <PRODUCT>Cucumber</PRODUCT>
            <NUMBER>5</NUMBER>
            <PRICE>$1.25</PRICE>
        </ITEM>
        <ITEM>
            <PRODUCT>Lettuce</PRODUCT>
            <NUMBER>2</NUMBER>
            <PRICE>$.98</PRICE>
        </ITEM>
    </ORDERS>
</CUSTOMER>
<CUSTOMER>
    <NAME>
        <LASTNAME>Thompson</LASTNAME>
        <FIRSTNAME>Phoebe</FIRSTNAME>
    </NAME>
    <DATE>May 27, 1998</DATE>
    <ORDERS>
        <ITEM>
            <PRODUCT>Banana</PRODUCT>
            <NUMBER>12</NUMBER>
            <PRICE>$2.95</PRICE>
        </ITEM>
        <ITEM>
            <PRODUCT>Apple</PRODUCT>
            <NUMBER>6</NUMBER>
            <PRICE>$1.50</PRICE>
        </ITEM>
    </ORDERS>
```

```
</CUSTOMER>
</DOCUMENT>
```

Here's how you define a start tag grammatically:

```
STag::= '<' Name (S Attribute)* S? '>'
Attribute::= Name Eq AttValue
Eq::= S? '=' S?
```

Start tags can also contain *attributes*, as we'll see in the next chapter. In this case, we include an attribute named **Deadbeat** and set the value of that attribute to the string **"no"**:

```
<CUSTOMER Deadbeat = "no">
    <NAME>
        <LASTNAME>Thompson</LASTNAME>
        <FIRSTNAME>Phoebe</FIRSTNAME>
    </NAME>
        .
        .
        .
```

To be well-formed, each start tag's attribute must be unique and can't contain any references to any entities external to the present document. End tags are defined this way:

```
ETag::= '</' Name S? '>'
```

The text between the start tag and end tag is called the *content*, and the entire construct: start tag, content, and end tag, is defined as an *element*:

```
content::= (element | PCData | Reference | CDSect | PI | Comment)*
element::= EmptyElement| STag content ETag
```

Empty Elements

In empty elements, the start tag makes up the whole element. An empty element takes a special form:

```
EmptyElement::= '<' Name (S Attribute)* S? '/>'
```

Here's an example of an empty element:

```
<IMG SRC="image.jpg" />
```

Prolog and Document Type Declaration

Now we've seen many of the XML markup elements that you can place in an XML document; all that's left are Prologs and DTDs.

Formally, an XML document usually consists of a prolog, DTD (the DTD can be internal or external, as we'll see in the next chapter), and the body of the document as shown on the next page.

In fact, here's how "WD-xml-lang-970630" defines a document (the element here is the root element of the document, and it can contain other elements):

```
document::= Prolog element Misc*
```

The prolog, which starts the XML document, is defined this way:

```
Prolog::= XMLDecl? Misc* (doctypedecl Misc*)?
```

Here, XMLDecl, the XML declaration, is defined this way:

```
XMLDecl::= '<?XML' VersionInfo EncodingDecl? RMDecl? S?
      '?>'
VersionInfo::= S 'version' Eq ('"1.0"' | "'1.0'")
Misc::= Comment | PI | S
EncodingDecl::= S 'encoding' Eq QEncoding
EncodingPI::= '<?XML' S 'encoding' Eq QEncoding S? ?>
QEncoding::= '"' Encoding '"' | "' " Encoding "'"
Encoding::= LatinName
LatinName::= [A-Za-z] ([A-Za-z0-9._] | '-')*
```

For example, a valid **XMLDecl** term is: **<?XML version="1.0"?>**.

The **doctypedecl** term in the preceding Prolog is the DTD, and that's defined this way formally:

```
doctypedecl::= '<!DOCTYPE' S Name (S ExternalID)? S? ('['
     markupdecl* ']'
        S?)? '>'
ExternalID::= 'SYSTEM' S SystemLiteral| 'PUBLIC' S
     PubidLiteral S
        SystemLiteral
markupdecl::= %( ( %elementdecl | %AttlistDecl |
     %EntityDecl |
        %NotationDecl | %conditionalSect | %PI | %S |
           %Comment )* )
```

The DTD section of a document may include a pointer (the **ExternalID** item above) to an external DTD (technically speaking, the internal and external portions of the DTD—if there is an external portion—are together called the DTD).

Web Browser

```
┌─────────────────────────────────────────┐
│                                         │
│   ┌─────────────────────────────────┐   │
│   │                                 │   │
│   │   Prolog                        │   │
│   │                                 │   │
│   │   ┌─────────────────────────┐   │   │
│   │   │                         │   │   │
│   │   │   DTD                   │   │   │
│   │   │                         │   │   │
│   │   └─────────────────────────┘   │   │
│   │                                 │   │
│   └─────────────────────────────────┘   │
│                                         │
│   ┌─────────────────────────────────┐   │
│   │                                 │   │
│   │                                 │   │
│   │                                 │   │
│   │   Body                          │   │
│   │                                 │   │
│   │                                 │   │
│   │                                 │   │
│   └─────────────────────────────────┘   │
│                                         │
└─────────────────────────────────────────┘
```

Note the various markup declarations you can include in the DTD—
elementdecl, **AttlistDecl**, **EntityDecl**, and **NotationDecl**. In this
chapter, we'll examine the first of these—element declarations; and in
the next chapter, where we cover DTDs more thoroughly, we'll examine
the other types of declarations you can make in the DTD. To finish our

discussion of DTD for the moment, then, let's take a look at how element declarations (the most common type of declarations) work in the DTD now.

DTD ELEMENT DECLARATIONS An element declaration indicates the element's type and its content. You can also use an element declaration to constrain which element types can appear as children (i.e., subelements) of the element. Here's how element declarations are defined formally:

```
elementdecl::= '<!ELEMENT' S %Name %S %contentspec S? '>'
contentspec::= 'EMPTY' | 'ANY' | Mixed | elements
```

The content of an element declaration can contain either other elements only or other elements and character data (called mixed content). If you want to include only other elements in this element, the `contentspec` term in the preceding element declaration is defined this way:

```
elements::= (choice | seq) ('?' | '*' | '+')?
cp::= (Name | choice | seq) ('?' | '*' | '+')?
cps::= S? %cp S?
choice::= '(' S? %(cps ('|' cps)+) S? ')'
seq::= '(' S? %(cps (', ' cps)*) S? ')'
```

In this case, `Name` gives the name of the element that can appear inside the element you are declaring. If you want to give an element mixed content —both elements and character data—you must define the `contentspec` term in the element declaration above as `Mixed`:

```
Mixed::= '(' S? %( %'#PCDATA' ( S? '|' S? %(%Name
         (S? '|' S? %Name)*) )* ) S? ')*' | '(' S?
                %('#PCDATA') S? ')' '*'?
```

Here, `Name` refers to the types of elements that may appear as children. For example, this is how you declare a `<p>` (for paragraph) tag that can contain character data and these elements: `<underline>`, `<bold>`, and `<italics>`:

```
<!ELEMENT p (#PCDATA|underline|bold|italics)*>
```

Here we indicate that the `<p>` tag can contain character data, or any of the preceding tags, repeated indefinitely. You can also specify which elements must appear inside an element, and in what order, when you use commas to separate the elements this way:

```
<?XML version = "1.0" ?>
<!DOCTYPE DOCUMENT [
<!ELEMENT DOCUMENT (CUSTOMER)*>
<!ELEMENT CUSTOMER (NAME,DATE,ORDERS)>
<!ELEMENT NAME (LASTNAME,FIRSTNAME)>
<!ELEMENT LASTNAME (#PCDATA)>
<!ELEMENT FIRSTNAME (#PCDATA)>
<!ELEMENT DATE (#PCDATA)>
<!ELEMENT ORDERS (ITEM)*>
<!ELEMENT ITEM (PRODUCT,NUMBER,PRICE)>
<!ELEMENT PRODUCT (#PCDATA)>
<!ELEMENT NUMBER (#PCDATA)>
<!ELEMENT PRICE (#PCDATA)>
]>
          .
          .
          .
```

We will see more about element declarations like these in the next chapter; this chapter is just to provide an overview of XML grammar and parsing.

You can declare elements either internally or externally. That is to say, the DTD of an XML document can be either internal or external. Here is an XML document that makes reference to an external DTD named **format.dtd**:

```
<?XML version="1.0"?>
<!DOCTYPE document SYSTEM "format.dtd">
<document>
    Now is the time...
</document>
```

The SYSTEM identifier **format.dtd** indicates the location of a DTD for the document, giving the name of a file. That file gives the appropriate element declaration(s), like this (this is the full contents of **format.dtd**):

```
<!ELEMENT document (#PCDATA)>
```

That completes our look at element declarations and DTDs for this chapter. We're well on our way now with our exploration of XML grammar: we've seen the kinds of characters you can place in an XML document, explored the legal types of markup (including elements from comments to start and end tags), and seen what valid and well-formed XML documents are.

Now it's time to turn all this learning to practical use. We are ready to start writing and using some actual XML documents, so let's turn to some concrete examples and put XML to work. We'll write XML documents following the rules we've learned and then use the Microsoft XML parser to interpret and use those documents.

Parsing XML To Decipher XML Documents

We've already seen what an XML document looks like, such as this representative example (we'll see how to construct XML documents like this one in this chapter):

```
<?XML version = "1.0" ?>
<!DOCTYPE DOCUMENT [
<!ELEMENT DOCUMENT (CUSTOMER)*>
<!ELEMENT CUSTOMER (NAME,DATE,ORDERS)>
<!ELEMENT NAME (LASTNAME,FIRSTNAME)>
<!ELEMENT LASTNAME (#PCDATA)>
<!ELEMENT FIRSTNAME (#PCDATA)>
<!ELEMENT DATE (#PCDATA)>
<!ELEMENT ORDERS (ITEM)*>
<!ELEMENT ITEM (PRODUCT,NUMBER,PRICE)>
<!ELEMENT PRODUCT (#PCDATA)>
<!ELEMENT NUMBER (#PCDATA)>
<!ELEMENT PRICE (#PCDATA)>
]>
<DOCUMENT>
<CUSTOMER>
    <NAME>
        <LASTNAME>Edwards</LASTNAME>
        <FIRSTNAME>Britta</FIRSTNAME>
    </NAME>
    <DATE>April 17, 1998</DATE>
    <ORDERS>
        <ITEM>
            <PRODUCT>Cucumber</PRODUCT>
            <NUMBER>5</NUMBER>
            <PRICE>$1.25</PRICE>
        </ITEM>
        <ITEM>
            <PRODUCT>Lettuce</PRODUCT>
            <NUMBER>2</NUMBER>
            <PRICE>$.98</PRICE>
        </ITEM>
    </ORDERS>
</CUSTOMER>
<CUSTOMER>
    <NAME>
        <LASTNAME>Thompson</LASTNAME>
        <FIRSTNAME>Phoebe</FIRSTNAME>
    </NAME>
    <DATE>May 27, 1998</DATE>
    <ORDERS>
        <ITEM>
```

```
            <PRODUCT>Banana</PRODUCT>
            <NUMBER>12</NUMBER>
            <PRICE>$2.95</PRICE>
        </ITEM>
        <ITEM>
            <PRODUCT>Apple</PRODUCT>
            <NUMBER>6</NUMBER>
            <PRICE>$1.50</PRICE>
        </ITEM>
      </ORDERS>
   </CUSTOMER>
</DOCUMENT>
```

As you can see, all the information in an XML document like this one is packed pretty densely. To make use of that information, we have to unpack it, and that process is known as parsing.

Parsing an XML document is the first step in working with that document. To work with an XML document in code, we have to be able to access the elements in that document, and we do that by parsing the document, which breaks the XML document up into a *logical tree*. This tree represents the structure of the XML document, as we'll see. It is this tree that we'll work with when we work with XML documents.

For example, we can parse this small XML document:

```
<CUSTOMER>
<!- I am a comment ->
<NAME>Britta Edwards</NAME>
</CUSTOMER>
```

When we parse this document, this is the tree generated—note that the text **Britta Edwards** is considered a child of the <NAME> element (as mentioned in the last chapter, **PCDATA** stands for parsed character data— XML data that has no child data beneath it):

```
Document
 |
  —Element(type=ELEMENT, name=CUSTOMER, numChildren=2)
        |
        |—Element(type=COMMENT, text="I am a comment")
        |
        —Element(type=ELEMENT, name=NAME, numChildren=1)
             |
               —Element(type=PCDATA, text="Britta Edwards")
```

After parsing an XML document, we can work through it element by element, looping over each element's child elements, as we'll see.

Using the Microsoft XML Parser

We are ready to start loading XML documents into Java programs and parsing those documents. We'll use the Microsoft XML parser in this book; you can get a copy of this parser at **http://www.microsoft.com/standards/xml/xmlparse.htm**. (Please be aware that net addresses change, so you might have to search the Microsoft site, **http://microsoft.com** for the XML parser.) We'll refer to this parser as the MSXML parser.

Installing the MSXML parser depends on your installation of Java and the version of Java you're using. You download the file **xmlinst.exe** and run it, which extracts the Microsoft COM Java package. Typically, you place this package (e.g., drag the COM folder in the Windows 95 Explorer) into your **java\classes** directory, so the Java programs you write can find the parser class files easily. Then, for example, the MSXML Document class, **com.ms.xml.Document**, will be stored as **java\classes\com\xml\Document.class**. Here are the major MSXML classes and what they do:

Microsoft Parser Class	Does This
com.ms.xml.Element	Handles XML elements
com.ms.xml.ElementFactory	Internal to the parser
com.ms.xml.Attribute	Stores an element's attributes
com.ms.xml.Document	Loads and handles XML documents
com.ms.xml.ParseException	Handles parsing exceptions

To load in an XML document, you use the Document class' **load()** method. Let's put that to work at once as we see how to load in an XML document into a working Java program.

The showtext Application

Our first MSXML parser application will get us started with using the MSXML parser. In this example, we'll see how to load in an XML document and print the character data (i.e., the text) of that document. We'll write this program as a console-oriented program first and then as a window-oriented program. This will give us experience with the MSXML parser in both console-oriented and window-oriented programming (we'll use window-oriented programming for the most part in this book).

Start the new file, **showtext.java**, now, and add a **main()** method this way:

```
class showtext
{
    public static void main(String args[])
    {

    }

}
```

The next step is to load in an XML document, and to do that, we'll need an MSXML Document object.

Creating a Document Object

The XML document we'll work with is named **showtext.xml**:

```
<?XML version = "1.0" ?>
<!DOCTYPE DOCUMENT [
<!ELEMENT DOCUMENT (CUSTOMER)*>
<!ELEMENT CUSTOMER (NAME,DATE,ORDERS)>
<!ELEMENT NAME (LASTNAME,FIRSTNAME)>
<!ELEMENT LASTNAME (#PCDATA)>
<!ELEMENT FIRSTNAME (#PCDATA)>
<!ELEMENT DATE (#PCDATA)>
<!ELEMENT ORDERS (ITEM)*>
<!ELEMENT ITEM (PRODUCT,NUMBER,PRICE)>
<!ELEMENT PRODUCT (#PCDATA)>
<!ELEMENT NUMBER (#PCDATA)>
<!ELEMENT PRICE (#PCDATA)>
]>
<DOCUMENT>
<CUSTOMER>
    <NAME>
        <LASTNAME>Edwards</LASTNAME>
        <FIRSTNAME>Britta</FIRSTNAME>
    </NAME>
    <DATE>April 17, 1998</DATE>
    <ORDERS>
        <ITEM>
            <PRODUCT>Cucumber</PRODUCT>
            <NUMBER>5</NUMBER>
            <PRICE>$1.25</PRICE>
        </ITEM>
        <ITEM>
            <PRODUCT>Lettuce</PRODUCT>
            <NUMBER>2</NUMBER>
```

```
            <PRICE>$.98</PRICE>
        </ITEM>
    </ORDERS>
</CUSTOMER>
<CUSTOMER>
    <NAME>
        <LASTNAME>Thompson</LASTNAME>
        <FIRSTNAME>Phoebe</FIRSTNAME>
    </NAME>
    <DATE>May 27, 1998</DATE>
    <ORDERS>
        <ITEM>
            <PRODUCT>Banana</PRODUCT>
            <NUMBER>12</NUMBER>
            <PRICE>$2.95</PRICE>
        </ITEM>
        <ITEM>
            <PRODUCT>Apple</PRODUCT>
            <NUMBER>6</NUMBER>
            <PRICE>$1.50</PRICE>
        </ITEM>
    </ORDERS>
</CUSTOMER>
</DOCUMENT>
```

We will load this document with the MSXML Document class' **load()** method and display the text in the document with the Document class' **getText()** method. The MSXML Document class' methods appear in Table 2-1.

Table 2-1.

The Document
Class' Methods

Method	Does This
addChild(Element, Element)	Override of the Element method that makes it possible to find the root node via **Document.getRoot**.
createElement(String, int)	Creates a new element for a given tag and element type using the **ElementFactory** for this document.
Document()	Constructs a new empty document.
Document(ElementFactory)	Constructs a new empty document and uses the given **ElementFactory** when loading XML documents.
getAttribute(String)	Returns null.
getAttributes()	Returns an enumeration that will never have any attributes because the Document class doesn't support attributes.
getChildren()	Returns enumeration for root node.

Table 2-1.

Continued.

Method	Does This
`getId()`	Returns the external id specified in the <!DOCTYPE> tag.
`getName()`	Returns the name specified in the <!DOCTYPE> tag.
`getParent()`	Returns null.
`getRoot()`	Returns the root node of the XML parse tree.
`getTagName()`	Returns null.
`getText()`	Returns unmarked-up text representation of entire document.
`getType()`	Returns **Element.DOCUMENT**.
`getURL()`	Returns the URL specified in the <!DOCTYPE> tag or null.
`getXML()`	Returns the information stored in the <?XML ...?> tag as an Element hierarchy.
`load(InputStream)`	Loads the document using the given input stream.
`load(URL)`	Loads the document from the given URL.
`numAttributes()`	Returns zero.
`numElements()`	Returns zero or one.
`removeAttribute(String)`	The Document class doesn't support attributes.
`removeChild(Element)`	Removes the root node, if given element is the root node.
`reportError (ParseException, OutputStream)`	Returns information about the given parse exception that was generated during load.
`save(OutputStream)`	Saves document to given output stream.
`setAttribute(String, String)`	Returns null.
`setText(String)`	Passes the text through to the root node, if any.

We start the document-loading process by storing the document's path and name in a new string named **filename**:

```
class showtext
{
    static String filename;
```

```
public static void main(String args[])
{
    filename = "file:////c://xml//showtext//
        showtext.xml";
        .
        .
        .
}

}
```

Here we store the reference to the file as an URL. (If the file was on the Internet, we would have started the URL with **http://**)—note that because forward slashes have special formatting meaning in Java strings, we need to store each forward slash, as two forward slashes, //, in the filename string:

```
filename = "file:////c://xml//showtext//showtext.xml";
```

NOTE   *Note the path of this example:* **c:\xml\showtext\showtext.xml**. *In this book, we'll give each example its own subdirectory of the* **c:\xml** *directory.*

The next step is to construct a Java URL object for this file. We do that with the Java URL class, which is in the java.net package:

```
import java.net.*;

class showtext
{
    static String filename;

    public static void main(String args[])
    {
        filename = "file:////c://xml//showtext//
            showtext.xml";

        URL url = null;
        try {
            url = new URL(filename);
        }
            .
            .
            .
    }

}
```

Note that we enclose the URL creation statement above in a try block:

```
try {
    url = new URL(filename);
}
```

Creating a new URL object in Java is an operation that can lead to run-time errors called *exceptions*; by enclosing that code in a try block, we indicate that we want to catch any exceptions. We handle the exceptions in a catch block, where we indicate that we could not create the needed URL object, and quit:

```
import com.ms.xml.ParseException;
import com.ms.xml.Document;
import com.ms.xml.Element;

import java.net.*;

class showtext
{
    static String filename;

    public static void main(String args[])
    {
        filename = "file:////c://xml//showtext//
            showtext.xml";

        URL url = null;
        try {
            url = new URL(filename);
        }
        catch (MalformedURLException ex) {
            System.out.println("Cannot create URL for
                file: " + filename);
            System.exit(0);
        }
                      .
                      .
                      .

    }

}
```

If, however, we were successful in creating the URL object, we declare and create a new MSXML Document class object that we name d:

```
import com.ms.xml.Document;

import java.net.*;

class showtext
{
    static String filename;
```

```
     public static void main(String args[])
     {
         filename = "file://///c://xml//showtext//
             showtext.xml";

         URL url = null;
         try {
             url = new URL(filename);
         }
         catch (MalformedURLException ex) {
             System.out.println("Cannot create URL for
                 file: " + filename);
             System.exit(0);
         }

->   Document d = new Document();
                 .
                 .
                 .
     }

}
```

Now that our URL object is ready and our Document object is ready, we're ready to load in the XML document.

Loading in an XML Document

To load in the XML document, we use the Document class' **load()** method. This is another operation that's prone to error, so we enclose it in a try block:

```
import com.ms.xml.Document;

import java.net.*;

class showtext
{
    static String filename;

    public static void main(String args[])
    {
        filename = "file://///c://xml//showtext//
            showtext.xml";

        URL url = null;
        try {
            url = new URL(filename);
        }
        catch (MalformedURLException ex) {
```

```
                    System.out.println("Cannot create URL for
                        file: " + filename);
                    System.exit(0);
                }

                Document d = new Document();

                try {
                    d.load(url);
                }
                          .
                          .
                          .
            }

        }
```

The MSXML parser checks each XML document to make sure it's well-formed (and, if a DTD is present, that it complies with the DTD). If the document is not well-formed, the **load()** operation generates an exception of MSXML class **ParseException**. We can catch that exception with a catch block and report the error with the Document class **reportError()** method:

```java
import com.ms.xml.ParseException;
import com.ms.xml.Document;

import java.net.*;

class showtext
{
    static String filename;

    public static void main(String args[])
    {
        filename = "file:////c://xml//showtext//
            showtext.xml";

        URL url = null;
        try {
            url = new URL(filename);
        }
        catch (MalformedURLException ex) {
            System.out.println("Cannot create URL for
                file: " + filename);
            System.exit(0);
        }

        Document d = new Document();

        try {
            d.load(url);
```

```
        }
        catch (ParseException e) {
            d.reportError(e, System.out);
        }
                        .
                        .
                        .

    }

}
```

If everything has gone smoothly so far, we've loaded in the XML document and now we can display its text.

Displaying an XML Document's Text

We can get the text of a document (stripped of all markup) with the Document class' `getText()` method and display that text with the `println()` method. Note that we first check to make sure the document was in fact loaded in by making sure **d** is a valid object:

```
import com.ms.xml.ParseException;
import com.ms.xml.Document;

import java.net.*;

class showtext
{
    static String filename;

    public static void main(String args[])
    {
        filename = "file:////c://xml//showtext//
            showtext.xml";

        URL url = null;
        try {
            url = new URL(filename);
        }
        catch (MalformedURLException ex) {
            System.out.println("Cannot create URL for
                file: " + filename);
            System.exit(0);
        }

        Document d = new Document();

        try {
```

```
                            d.load(url);
                    }
                    catch (ParseException e) {
                        d.reportError(e, System.out);
                    }

                    if (d != null) {
                        System.out.println(d.getText());
                    }
            }

    }
```

And that's it—compile and run the program now; when you do, you see this text appear in the DOS window:

```
C:\xml\showtext>c:\jdk1-0\java\bin\java showtext
Edwards Britta April 17, 1998 Cucumber 5 $1.25 Lettuce 2
        $.98 Thompson
Phoebe May 27, 1998 Banana 12 $2.95 Apple 6 $1.50
```

That's just what we expected to see—the XML document's text, stripped of markup. As mentioned, the MSXML parser checks to make sure XML documents are well-formed (and, if the document has a DTD, the parser checks to make sure the document complies with the DTD). If the document contains an error of some kind, our program will indicate that; for example, if we change one of the end tags from </NAME> to </NAMES>, the parser will point out the error:

```
<?XML version = "1.0" ?>
<!DOCTYPE DOCUMENT [
<!ELEMENT DOCUMENT (CUSTOMER)*>
<!ELEMENT CUSTOMER (NAME,DATE,ORDERS)>
<!ELEMENT NAME (LASTNAME,FIRSTNAME)>
<!ELEMENT LASTNAME (#PCDATA)>
<!ELEMENT FIRSTNAME (#PCDATA)>
<!ELEMENT DATE (#PCDATA)>
<!ELEMENT ORDERS (ITEM)*>
<!ELEMENT ITEM (PRODUCT,NUMBER,PRICE)>
<!ELEMENT PRODUCT (#PCDATA)>
<!ELEMENT NUMBER (#PCDATA)>
<!ELEMENT PRICE (#PCDATA)>
]>
<DOCUMENT>
<CUSTOMER>
    <NAME>
        <LASTNAME>Edwards</LASTNAME>
        <FIRSTNAME>Britta</FIRSTNAME>
    </NAMES>
    <DATE>April 17, 1998</DATE>
```

```
<ORDERS>
    <ITEM>
        <PRODUCT>Cucumber</PRODUCT>
            .
            .
            .
```

Here's what you see when you run **showtext** now. (Note that the parser pinpoints the error, indicating that an error was found at line 20, character 12, in **showtext.xml** and that the error was **Close tag mismatch: NAMES instead of NAME.**)

```
C:\xml\showtext>c:\jdk1-0\java\bin\java showtext
Error: file://c://xml//showtext//showtext.xml(20,12)
Context:  - <null> - <DOCUMENT> - <CUSTOMER> - <NAME>
com.ms.xml.ParseException: Close tag mismatch: NAMES
     instead of NAME
     com.ms.xml.Parser.error(Parser.java:110)
     com.ms.xml.Parser.parseElement(Parser.java:1100)
     at com.ms.xml.Parser.parseDocument(Parser.java:643)
     at com.ms.xml.Parser.parse(Parser.java:47)
     at com.ms.xml.Document.load(Document.java:171)
     at showtext.main(showtext.java:27)
```

That's it, then, for this example: now we've seen how to load in an XML document and display its text. The code for this program, **showtext.java**, appears in Listing 2-1, and the XML document it reads in, **showtext.xml**, appears in Listing 2-2.

▬ ▬ ▬ ▬

Listing 2-1.
showtext.java.

```
import com.ms.xml.ParseException;
import com.ms.xml.Document;

import java.net.*;

class showtext
{
    static String filename;

    public static void main(String args[])
    {
        filename = "file:////c://xml//showtext//
            showtext.xml";

        URL url = null;
        try {
            url = new URL(filename);
        }
```

Listing 2-1.
Continued.

```
    catch (MalformedURLException ex) {
        System.out.println("Cannot create URL for
            file: " + filename);
        System.exit(0);
    }

    Document d = new Document();

    try {
        d.load(url);
    }
    catch (ParseException e) {
        d.reportError(e, System.out);
    }

    if (d != null) {
        System.out.println(d.getText());
    }
    }

}
```

Listing 2-2.
showtext.xml.

```
<?XML version = "1.0" ?>
<!DOCTYPE DOCUMENT [
<!ELEMENT DOCUMENT (CUSTOMER)*>
<!ELEMENT CUSTOMER (NAME,DATE,ORDERS)>
<!ELEMENT NAME (LASTNAME,FIRSTNAME)>
<!ELEMENT LASTNAME (#PCDATA)>
<!ELEMENT FIRSTNAME (#PCDATA)>
<!ELEMENT DATE (#PCDATA)>
<!ELEMENT ORDERS (ITEM)*>
<!ELEMENT ITEM (PRODUCT,NUMBER,PRICE)>
<!ELEMENT PRODUCT (#PCDATA)>
<!ELEMENT NUMBER (#PCDATA)>
<!ELEMENT PRICE (#PCDATA)>
]>
<DOCUMENT>
<CUSTOMER>
    <NAME>
        <LASTNAME>Edwards</LASTNAME>
        <FIRSTNAME>Britta</FIRSTNAME>
    </NAME>
    <DATE>April 17, 1998</DATE>
    <ORDERS>
        <ITEM>
            <PRODUCT>Cucumber</PRODUCT>
```

Continues

Listing 2-2.
Continued.

```
                    <NUMBER>5</NUMBER>
                    <PRICE>$1.25</PRICE>
            </ITEM>
            <ITEM>
                    <PRODUCT>Lettuce</PRODUCT>
                    <NUMBER>2</NUMBER>
                    <PRICE>$.98</PRICE>
            </ITEM>
        </ORDERS>
    </CUSTOMER>
    <CUSTOMER>
        <NAME>
                <LASTNAME>Thompson</LASTNAME>
                <FIRSTNAME>Phoebe</FIRSTNAME>
        </NAME>
        <DATE>May 27, 1998</DATE>
        <ORDERS>
            <ITEM>
                    <PRODUCT>Banana</PRODUCT>
                    <NUMBER>12</NUMBER>
                    <PRICE>$2.95</PRICE>
            </ITEM>
            <ITEM>
                    <PRODUCT>Apple</PRODUCT>
                    <NUMBER>6</NUMBER>
                    <PRICE>$1.50</PRICE>
            </ITEM>
        </ORDERS>
    </CUSTOMER>
</DOCUMENT>
```

Now we've gotten started with parsing XML documents. These days, however, its rare to have console-oriented programs, so let's take a look at the same document-reading process as before but this time with the idea of displaying the XML document's text in a window.

The `showtextwin` Example

In this next example, we'll display a window with a text field and a button marked `Click Me`:

```
┌─────────────────────────────────────────────┐
│                                             │
├─────────────────────────────────────────────┤
│                    ┌─────────────────┐      │
│   The XML file:    │                 │      │
│                    │                 │      │
│                    └─────────────────┘      │
│                                             │
│              ┌──────────────┐               │
│              │              │               │
│              │   Click Me   │               │
│              │              │               │
│              └──────────────┘               │
│                                             │
└─────────────────────────────────────────────┘
```

When the user clicks the Click Me button, we can read in the XML document **showtextwin.xml**. This document is the same as the document in Listing 2.2, **showtext.xml**, and displays the text of that document in the text field:

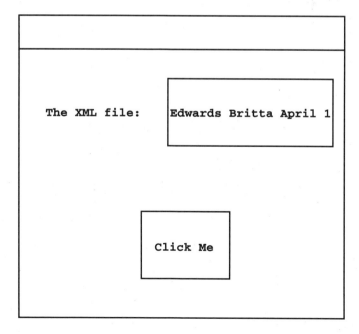

We start this new example, `showtextwin.java`, with a `main()` method that creates and displays a new window of class `showtextwin` (we'll write the code for this class next):

```java
import java.applet.Applet;

public class showtextwin extends Applet{

    public static void main(String args[])
    {
        showtextwinFrame frame = new showtextwinFrame("The
            showtextwin application");

        frame.resize(450, 300);

        showtextwin applet = new showtextwin();

        frame.add("Center", applet);
        applet.init();
        applet.start();
        frame.show();
    }
}
```

We also add the window class `showtextwinFrame` to the end of the `showtextwin.java` file:

```java
class showtextwinFrame extends Frame
{
    public showtextwinFrame(String str)
    {
        super (str);
    }

    public boolean handleEvent(Event evt)
    {
        switch (evt.id)
        {
            case Event.WINDOW_DESTROY:
                dispose();
                System.exit(0);
                return true;

            default:
                return super.handleEvent(evt);
        }
    }
}
```

Now our window is created and we're ready to add the controls we need. We do that in the `init()` method:

```
import java.awt.*;
import java.applet.Applet;


public class showtextwin extends Applet{

    Label label1;
    TextField text1;
    Button button1;

    public static void main(String args[])
    {
        showtextwinFrame frame = new showtextwinFrame("The
            showtextwin application");

        frame.resize(450, 300);

        showtextwin applet = new showtextwin();

        frame.add("Center", applet);
        applet.init();
        applet.start();
        frame.show();
    }

    public void init(){
        label1 = new Label("The XML file:");
        add(label1);
        text1 = new TextField(35);
        add(text1);
        button1 = new Button("Click Me");
        add(button1);
    }
        .
        .
        .
}
```

The controls we need are installed at this point. We can create a new URL object for the XML document we want read in when the user clicks the Click Me button:

```
import java.awt.*;
import java.net.*;
import java.applet.Applet;

public class showtextwin extends Applet{

    Label label1;
    TextField text1;
    Button button1;
    static String filename;
```

```
public static void main(String args[])
{
  .
  .
  .
}

public void init()
{
  .
  .
  .
}

public boolean action (Event e, Object o){

    if(e.target.equals(button1)){

        URL url = null;
        try {
            url = new URL("file:////c://xml//
                showtextwin//showtextwin.xml");
        } catch (MalformedURLException e1) {
            System.out.println("Cannot create URL for:
                " + filename);
            System.exit(0);
        }
          .
          .
          .

    }
    return true;
}

}
```

Next, we will create a new Document object and load the XML document into that document:

```
import com.ms.xml.ParseException;
import com.ms.xml.Document;

import java.awt.*;
import java.net.*;
import java.applet.Applet;


public class showtextwin extends Applet{

    Label label1;
    TextField text1;
    Button button1;
    static String filename;
```

```
                public static void main(String args[])
                {
                   .
                   .
                   .
                }

                public void init()
                {
                   .
                   .
                   .
                }

                public boolean action (Event e, Object o){

                     if(e.target.equals(button1)){

                          URL url = null;
                          try {
                              url = new URL("file:////c://xml//
                                   showtextwin//showtextwin.xml");
                          } catch (MalformedURLException e1) {
                              System.out.println("Cannot create URL for:
                                   " + filename);
                              System.exit(0);
                          }

                          Document d = new Document();

                          try {
                              d.load(url);
                          }
                          catch (ParseException e2) {
                              d.reportError(e2, System.out);
                          }
                             .
                             .
                             .
                          }
                     }
                     return true;
                }

        }
```

Finally, we display the document's text in the text field:

```
import com.ms.xml.ParseException;
import com.ms.xml.Document;

import java.awt.*;
import java.net.*;
import java.applet.Applet;
```

```
public class showtextwin extends Applet{

    Label label1;
    TextField text1;
    Button button1;
    static String filename;

    public static void main(String args[])
    {
        .
        .
        .
    }

    public void init()
    {
        .
        .
        .
    }

    public boolean action (Event e, Object o){

        if(e.target.equals(button1)){

            URL url = null;
            try {
                url = new URL("file:////c://xml//
                    showtextwin//showtextwin.xml");
        } catch (MalformedURLException e1) {
                System.out.println("Cannot create URL for:
                    " + filename);
                System.exit(0);
            }

            Document d = new Document();

            try {
                d.load(url);
            }
            catch (ParseException e2) {
                d.reportError(e2, System.out);
            }

            if(d != null){
                text1.setText(d.getText());
            }
        }
        return true;
    }

}
```

That's it—now run the application, as shown in Figure 2.1.

When you click the Click Me button, the program reads in the **showtextwin.xml** file and displays its text in the text field, as shown in Figure 2-2. Our program is a success.

The code for this application, **showtextwin.java**, appears in Listing 2-3, and the XML document it reads in, **showtextwin.xml,** appears in Listing 2-4.

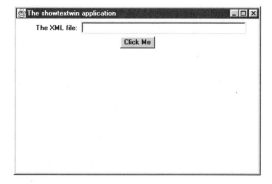

Figure 2-1.
The **showtextwin** application.

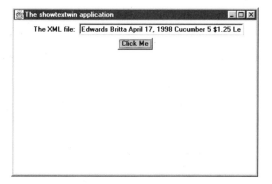

Figure 2-2.
Reading in an XML document.

Listing 2-3.
showtextwin.java

```
import com.ms.xml.ParseException;
import com.ms.xml.Document;

import java.awt.*;
import java.net.*;
import java.applet.Applet;

public class showtextwin extends Applet{

    Label label1;
    TextField text1;
    Button button1;
```

Listing 2-3.
Continued.

```
static String filename;

public static void main(String args[])
{
    showtextwinFrame frame = new showtextwinFrame("The
        showtextwin application");

    frame.resize(450, 300);

    showtextwin applet = new showtextwin();

    frame.add("Center", applet);
    applet.init();
    applet.start();
    frame.show();
}

public void init(){
    label1 = new Label("The XML file:");
    add(label1);
    text1 = new TextField(35);
    add(text1);
    button1 = new Button("Click Me");
    add(button1);
}

public boolean action (Event e, Object o){

    if(e.target.equals(button1)){

        URL url = null;
        try {
            url = new URL("file:////c://xml//
                showtextwin//showtextwin.xml");
        } catch (MalformedURLException e1) {
            System.out.println("Cannot create URL for:
                " + filename);
            System.exit(0);
        }

        Document d = new Document();

        try {
            d.load(url);
        }
        catch (ParseException e2) {
            d.reportError(e2, System.out);
        }

        if(d != null){
            text1.setText(d.getText());
```

Continues

```
                }
            }
            return true;
        }
    }

    class showtextwinFrame extends Frame
    {
        public showtextwinFrame(String str)
        {
            super (str);
        }

        public boolean handleEvent(Event evt)
        {
            switch (evt.id)
            {
                case Event.WINDOW_DESTROY:
                    dispose();
                    System.exit(0);
                    return true;

                default:
                    return super.handleEvent(evt);
            }
        }
    }
```

```
<?XML version = "1.0" ?>
<!DOCTYPE DOCUMENT [
<!ELEMENT DOCUMENT (CUSTOMER)*>
<!ELEMENT CUSTOMER (NAME,DATE,ORDERS)>
<!ELEMENT NAME (LASTNAME,FIRSTNAME)>
<!ELEMENT LASTNAME (#PCDATA)>
<!ELEMENT FIRSTNAME (#PCDATA)>
<!ELEMENT DATE (#PCDATA)>
<!ELEMENT ORDERS (ITEM)*>
<!ELEMENT ITEM (PRODUCT,NUMBER,PRICE)>
<!ELEMENT PRODUCT (#PCDATA)>
<!ELEMENT NUMBER (#PCDATA)>
<!ELEMENT PRICE (#PCDATA)>
]>
<DOCUMENT>
<CUSTOMER>
    <NAME>
        <LASTNAME>Edwards</LASTNAME>
        <FIRSTNAME>Britta</FIRSTNAME>
    </NAME>
```

Listing 2-4.
Continued.

```
        <DATE>April 17, 1998</DATE>
        <ORDERS>
            <ITEM>
                <PRODUCT>Cucumber</PRODUCT>
                <NUMBER>5</NUMBER>
                <PRICE>$1.25</PRICE>
            </ITEM>
            <ITEM>
                <PRODUCT>Lettuce</PRODUCT>
                <NUMBER>2</NUMBER>
                <PRICE>$.98</PRICE>
            </ITEM>
        </ORDERS>
    </CUSTOMER>
    <CUSTOMER>
        <NAME>
            <LASTNAME>Thompson</LASTNAME>
            <FIRSTNAME>Phoebe</FIRSTNAME>
        </NAME>
        <DATE>May 27, 1998</DATE>
        <ORDERS>
            <ITEM>
                <PRODUCT>Banana</PRODUCT>
                <NUMBER>12</NUMBER>
                <PRICE>$2.95</PRICE>
            </ITEM>
            <ITEM>
                <PRODUCT>Apple</PRODUCT>
                <NUMBER>6</NUMBER>
                <PRICE>$1.50</PRICE>
            </ITEM>
        </ORDERS>
    </CUSTOMER>
</DOCUMENT>
```

At this point, we have some experience with reading in XML documents, but no experience working with the content of those documents besides simply printing them all out.

Let's start digging deeper now as we see how to search through an XML document for one particular tag, the <TITLE> tag, so we can display the title we've given to the document. This will give us experience working with the content of XML documents.

NOTE   *Unlike HTML, there is no predefined <TITLE> tag in XML. We are creating one for the purposes of this example.*

The gettitle Example

The **gettitle** application will read in the XML document **gettitle.xml** and retrieve the character data—that is, the text—of one particular tag, the <TITLE> tag. That title is: **The Get Title Example**:

```
<?XML version = "1.0"?>
<DOCUMENT>
<TITLE>The Get Title Example</TITLE>
<CUSTOMER>
    <NAME>
        <LASTNAME>Edwards</LASTNAME>
        <FIRSTNAME>Britta</FIRSTNAME>
    </NAME>
    <DATE>April 17, 1998</DATE>
    <ORDERS>
        <ITEM>
            <PRODUCT>Cucumber</PRODUCT>
            <NUMBER>5</NUMBER>
            <PRICE>$1.25</PRICE>
        </ITEM>
        <ITEM>
            <PRODUCT>Lettuce</PRODUCT>
            <NUMBER>2</NUMBER>
            <PRICE>$.98</PRICE>
        </ITEM>
    </ORDERS>
</CUSTOMER>
<CUSTOMER>
    <NAME>
        <LASTNAME>Thompson</LASTNAME>
        <FIRSTNAME>Phoebe</FIRSTNAME>
    </NAME>
    <DATE>May 27, 1998</DATE>
    <ORDERS>
        <ITEM>
            <PRODUCT>Banana</PRODUCT>
            <NUMBER>12</NUMBER>
            <PRICE>$2.95</PRICE>
        </ITEM>
        <ITEM>
            <PRODUCT>Apple</PRODUCT>
            <NUMBER>6</NUMBER>
            <PRICE>$1.50</PRICE>
        </ITEM>
    </ORDERS>
</CUSTOMER>
</DOCUMENT>
_H
```

Constructing this example will give us some introductory experience in working with the data in an XML document. In this case, we'll see how to retrieve all the tags, in order, from an XML document and loop through them, searching for the tag we want.

Our program will display a text field and a button marked Click Me:

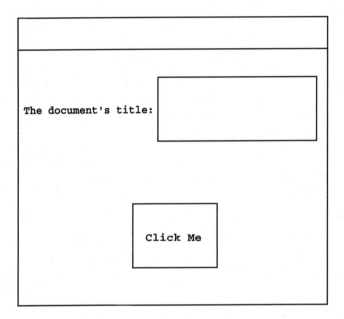

When the user clicks the Click Me button, the program reads in **gettitle.xml**, finds the title element, and displays the text in that element in the text field as shown on the following page.

We start this program with the usual **main()** method and window class. In this case, the window class is named **gettitleFrame**:

```java
import java.applet.Applet;

public class gettitle extends Applet{
    public static void main(String args[])
    {
        gettitleFrame frame = new gettitleFrame("The
            gettitle application");

        frame.resize(400, 300);

        gettitle applet = new gettitle();
```

```
        frame.add("Center", applet);
        applet.init();
        applet.start();
        frame.show();
    }
}

class gettitleFrame extends Frame
{
    public gettitleFrame(String str)
    {
        super (str);
    }

    public boolean handleEvent(Event evt)
    {
        switch (evt.id)
        {
            case Event.WINDOW_DESTROY:
                dispose();
                System.exit(0);
                return true;

            default:
                return super.handleEvent(evt);
        }
    }
}
```

Next, we add the control's we'll need in the `init()` method:

```java
import java.awt.*;
import java.applet.Applet;

public class gettitle extends Applet{

    Label label1;
    TextField text1;
    Button button1;

    public static void main(String args[])
    {
        .
        .
        .
    }

    public void init(){
        label1 = new Label("The document's title:");
        add(label1);
        text1 = new TextField(20);
        add(text1);
        button1 = new Button("Click Me");
        add(button1);
    }
}
```

The next step is to load in the XML document, `gettitle.xml`, and we do that when the user clicks the Click Me button. The code to read in `gettitle.xml` goes into the action method like this:

```java
import com.ms.xml.ParseException;
import com.ms.xml.Document;
import com.ms.xml.Element;

import java.util.Enumeration;
import java.awt.*;
import java.net.*;
import java.applet.Applet;

public class gettitle extends Applet{

    static String filename;

    public static void main(String args[])
    {
        .
        .
        .
    }

    public void init(){
```

```
          .
          .
          .
    }

    public boolean action (Event e, Object o){

        if(e.target.equals(button1)){

            URL url = null;
            try {
                url = new URL("file:////c://xml//
                    gettitle//gettitle.xml");
            } catch (MalformedURLException e1) {
                System.out.println("Cannot create URL for:
                    " + filename);
                System.exit(0);
            }

            Document d = new Document();

            try {
                d.load(url);
            }
            catch (ParseException e2) {
                d.reportError(e2, System.out);
            }
                .
                .
                .
        }
        return true;
    }

}
```

At this point, then, we've read in **gettitle.xml** into the Document object **d**. The next step is to step through the elements in that document, searching for the <TITLE> element.

Accessing an XML Document's Elements

To reach the elements of the XML document, we'll use the MSXML Element class. The MSXML parser recognizes and names seven types of XML elements: DOCUMENT, ELEMENT, PCDATA, PI (processing instruction), META (an element containing information about the tree), COMMENT, and CDATA. The methods of this class appear in Table 2-2.

Table 2-2.

The Element class' methods.

Method	Does This
`addChild(Element,Element)`	Adds a child to this element.
`getAttribute(String)`	Allows for the retrieval of an attribute's value.
`getAttributes()`	Returns an enumeration for the element attributes.
`getChildren()`	Returns an enumeration of this element's children.
`getParent()`	Every element in the tree except the Document itself, has a parent.
`getTagName()`	Returns the name of the tag as a string.
`getText()`	Returns the nonmarked-up text contained by this element.
`getType()`	Gets the type of the element.
`numAttributes()`	Returns the number of attributes.
`numElements()`	Returns the number of child Elements.
`removeAttribute(String)`	Deletes an attribute from an element using this method.
`removeChild(Element)`	Removes a child element from the tree.
`setAttribute(String, String)`	Allows the setting of an attribute of this element.
`setParent(Element)`	Sets the parent of this element.
`setText(String)`	Sets the text for this element.

TIP *The names of the preceding element types, DOCUMENT, ELEMENT, PC-DATA, and so on, correspond to constants returned by the Element class'* `getType()` *method,* `Element.DOCUMENT`, `Element.ELEMENT`, *and so on.*

Now we're going to step our way through the XML document, element by element, until we find the <TITLE> tag. We start by getting the root element of the document; as we've set up our XML document **gettitle.xml**, that's the <DOCUMENT> element:

```
<?XML version = "1.0"?>
<DOCUMENT>
<TITLE>The Get Title Example</TITLE>
<CUSTOMER>
    <NAME>
        <LASTNAME>Edwards</LASTNAME>
        <FIRSTNAME>Britta</FIRSTNAME>
    </NAME>
    <DATE>April 17, 1998</DATE>
    <ORDERS>
        .
        .
        .
```

We get the root element with the MSXML Document class `getRoot()` method:

```
import com.ms.xml.ParseException;
import com.ms.xml.Document;
import com.ms.xml.Element;

import java.util.Enumeration;
import java.awt.*;
import java.net.*;
import java.applet.Applet;

public class gettitle extends Applet{

    public boolean action (Event e, Object o){

        if(e.target.equals(button1)){
            .
            .
            .

            if (d != null) {
                Element root = d.getRoot();
                .
                .
                .
            }
        }
    }
    return true;
}
}
```

Now we have an element corresponding to the root of our document; to search for the <TITLE> tag, we need to examine the child elements of the root element.

Accessing Child Elements

You get the child elements of an element with the Element class' **getChildren()** method. This method returns a Java Enumeration object. An enumeration object handles lists of objects, and it has just two methods: **hasMoreElements()**, which returns true if there are more elements in the enumeration, and **nextElement()**, which returns the next element. Here's how we get our enumeration object, **enum**, which holds the children of the root element:

```java
import com.ms.xml.ParseException;
import com.ms.xml.Document;
import com.ms.xml.Element;

import java.util.Enumeration;
import java.awt.*;
import java.net.*;
import java.applet.Applet;

public class gettitle extends Applet{

    public boolean action (Event e, Object o){

        if(e.target.equals(button1)){
                .
                .
                .
            if (d != null) {
                Element root = d.getRoot();
                Enumeration enum = root.getChildren();
                .
                .
                .
            }
        }
        return true;
    }
}
```

Now we can loop over the child elements using a Java **while** loop, which keeps looping while the condition in its parentheses is true; in this case, we'll keep looping while there are more child elements in the enumeration:

```java
import com.ms.xml.ParseException;
import com.ms.xml.Document;
import com.ms.xml.Element;

import java.util.Enumeration;
import java.awt.*;
```

```
import java.net.*;
import java.applet.Applet;

public class gettitle extends Applet{

    public boolean action (Event e, Object o){

        if(e.target.equals(button1)){
                    .
                    .
                    .
            if (d != null) {
                Element root = d.getRoot();
                Enumeration enum = root.getChildren();
                while (enum.hasMoreElements()) {
                            .
                            .
                            .
                }
            }
        }
        return true;
    }
}
```

Now we are looping over the root element's child elements (note that
that does not mean we are looping over all elements. Some of the root's
children themselves have children). We can get the current element from
the enumeration this way, with **nextElement()**:

```
import com.ms.xml.ParseException;
import com.ms.xml.Document;
import com.ms.xml.Element;

import java.util.Enumeration;
import java.awt.*;
import java.net.*;
import java.applet.Applet;

public class gettitle extends Applet{

    public boolean action (Event e, Object o){

        if(e.target.equals(button1)){
                    .
                    .
                    .
            if (d != null) {
                Element root = d.getRoot();
                Enumeration enum = root.getChildren();
                while (enum.hasMoreElements()) {
                    Element elem =
```

```
                                    (Element)enum.nextElement();

                                .
                                .
                                .
                    }
                }
            }
        }
        return true;
    }
}
```

We can check with the Element class' **getTagName()** whether the current element is the <TITLE> tag. If the current element *is* the <TITLE> tag, we display that element's text with the **getText()** method:

```
import com.ms.xml.ParseException;
import com.ms.xml.Document;
import com.ms.xml.Element;

import java.util.Enumeration;
import java.awt.*;
import java.net.*;
import java.applet.Applet;

public class gettitle extends Applet{

    public boolean action (Event e, Object o){

        if(e.target.equals(button1)){
                    .
                    .
                    .
            if (d != null) {
                Element root = d.getRoot();
                Enumeration enum = root.getChildren();
                while (enum.hasMoreElements()) {
                    Element elem =
                            (Element)enum.nextElement();
                    if (elem.getTagName().equals
                        ("TITLE")) {
                            text1.setText(elem.getText());
                    }
                }
            }
        }
        return true;
    }
}
```

NOTE *The* `getText()` *method sometimes does more than you want; not only does it return the text of the current element, it also returns the text of all the children of the current element.*

That's all we need—now we're able to find the <TITLE> element in an XML document. Compile and run the program, as shown in Figure 2-3.

When you click the Click Me button, the program reads in the **gettitle.xml** document and finds the document's title, displaying it in the text field, as shown in Figure 2-4. Our **gettitle** program is a success.

The code for this program, **gettitle.java**, appears in Listing 2-5, and **gettitle.xml** appears in Listing 2-6.

Figure 2-3.
The **gettitle**
application.

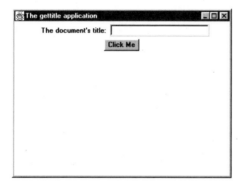

Figure 2-4.
Retrieving the text of
the <TITLE> tag.

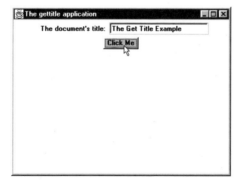

Listing 2-5.
gettitle.java

```java
import com.ms.xml.ParseException;
import com.ms.xml.Document;
import com.ms.xml.Element;

import java.util.Enumeration;
import java.awt.*;
import java.net.*;
import java.applet.Applet;

public class gettitle extends Applet{

    Label label1;
    TextField text1;
    Button button1;
    static String filename;

    public static void main(String args[])
    {
        gettitleFrame frame = new gettitleFrame("The
            gettitle application");

        frame.resize(400, 300);

        gettitle applet = new gettitle();

        frame.add("Center", applet);
        applet.init();
        applet.start();
        frame.show();
    }

    public void init(){
        label1 = new Label("The document's title:");
        add(label1);
        text1 = new TextField(20);
        add(text1);
        button1 = new Button("Click Me");
        add(button1);
    }

    public boolean action (Event e, Object o){

        if(e.target.equals(button1)){

            URL url = null;
            try {
                url = new URL("file:////c://xml//
                    gettitle//gettitle.xml");
            } catch (MalformedURLException e1) {
                System.out.println("Cannot create URL for:
                    " + filename);
```

Listing 2-5.
Continued.

```
                                    System.exit(0);
                            }

                            Document d = new Document();

                            try {
                                    d.load(url);
                            }
                            catch (ParseException e2) {
                                    d.reportError(e2, System.out);
                            }

                            if (d != null) {
                                    Element root = d.getRoot();
                                    Enumeration enum = root.getChildren();
                                    while (enum.hasMoreElements()) {
                                            Element elem =
                                                    (Element)enum.nextElement();
                                            if (elem.getTagName().equals
                                                    ("TITLE")) {
                                                    text1.setText(elem.getText());
                                            }
                                    }
                            }
                    }
                    return true;
            }

    }

    class gettitleFrame extends Frame
    {
            public gettitleFrame(String str)
            {
                    super (str);
            }

            public boolean handleEvent(Event evt)
            {
                    switch (evt.id)
                    {
                            case Event.WINDOW_DESTROY:
                                    dispose();
                                    System.exit(0);
                                    return true;

                            default:
                                    return super.handleEvent(evt);
                    }
            }
    }
```

```
<?XML version = "1.0"?>
<DOCUMENT>
<TITLE>The Get Title Example</TITLE>
<CUSTOMER>
    <NAME>
        <LASTNAME>Edwards</LASTNAME>
        <FIRSTNAME>Britta</FIRSTNAME>
    </NAME>
    <DATE>April 17, 1998</DATE>
    <ORDERS>
        <ITEM>
            <PRODUCT>Cucumber</PRODUCT>
            <NUMBER>5</NUMBER>
            <PRICE>$1.25</PRICE>
        </ITEM>
        <ITEM>
            <PRODUCT>Lettuce</PRODUCT>
            <NUMBER>2</NUMBER>
            <PRICE>$.98</PRICE>
        </ITEM>
    </ORDERS>
</CUSTOMER>
<CUSTOMER>
    <NAME>
        <LASTNAME>Thompson</LASTNAME>
        <FIRSTNAME>Phoebe</FIRSTNAME>
    </NAME>
    <DATE>May 27, 1998</DATE>
    <ORDERS>
        <ITEM>
            <PRODUCT>Banana</PRODUCT>
            <NUMBER>12</NUMBER>
            <PRICE>$2.95</PRICE>
        </ITEM>
        <ITEM>
            <PRODUCT>Apple</PRODUCT>
            <NUMBER>6</NUMBER>
            <PRICE>$1.50</PRICE>
        </ITEM>
    </ORDERS>
</CUSTOMER>
</DOCUMENT>
```

SUMMARY

That's it for this chapter. Here, we have gotten an introduction to the XML specification, seen what constitutes valid and well-formed XML documents, and started to put the MSXML parser to work by reading in XML documents and printing their text, as well as searching for a particular tag. We've already come far.

In the next chapter, we'll continue our exploration of XML as we examine DTDs, attributes, and entities in depth. Let's turn to that now.

3

Document Type Declarations, Attributes, and Entities

In the last chapter, we got an overview of the formal definition of an XML document:

```
document::= Prolog element Misc*
Prolog::= XMLDecl? Misc* (doctypedecl Misc*)?
XMLDecl::= '<?XML' VersionInfo EncodingDecl?
     RMDecl? S? '?>'
VersionInfo::= S 'version' Eq ('"1.0"' |
     "'1.0'")
Misc::= Comment | PI | S
```

We saw that XML documents consist of a prolog (which is optional with most XML parsers) and a root element (which is required and which can include child elements; if there are child elements, they must all be included in the root element). We also saw that in the prolog, you can declare markup this way:

```
doctypedecl::= '<!DOCTYPE' S Name (S ExternalID)?
    S? ('[' markupdecl* ']' S?)? '>'
markupdecl::= %( ( %elementdecl | %AttlistDecl |
    %EntityDecl |
    %NotationDecl | %conditionalSect | %PI | %S | %Comment
        )* )
```

To start working with functioning XML documents in the last chapter, we saw how to declare XML elements, but haven't yet worked with other XML declarations, such as entity declarations or attribute lists. In this chapter, we'll work with the preceding XML definitions in more depth, filling out our XML skills. We'll see how what the **EncodingDecl** and **RMDecl** terms do in the XML declaration:

```
XMLDecl::= '<?XML' VersionInfo EncodingDecl? RMDecl? S?
    '?>'
```

We'll also examine the other large part of the XML specification in more detail than we have before—how to declare elements, attribute lists, entities, notations, and conditional sections:

```
doctypedecl::= '<!DOCTYPE' S Name (S ExternalID)?
    S? ('[' markupdecl* ']' S?)? '>'
markupdecl::= %( ( %elementdecl | %AttlistDecl |
    %EntityDecl |
    %NotationDecl | %conditionalSect | %PI | %S |
        %Comment )* )
```

When we're done with this chapter, we will have completed our coverage of Part I of the XML specification. Let's start by examining the **EncodingDecl** term, which specifies the legal character encodings in XML.

Character Encoding in XML

The character encoding of a document specifies the character set you want to use; you can specify the character encoding you want to use in an XML document. In fact, each text entity in an XML document can use a different encoding. You can specify the character encoding for the whole document in the **XMLDecl** part of the Prolog (note that specifying the character encoding is optional):

```
document::= Prolog element Misc*
Prolog::= XMLDecl? Misc* (doctypedecl Misc*)?
XMLDecl::= '<?XML' VersionInfo EncodingDecl? RMDecl? S?
     '?>'
```

All XML parsers must be able to read text in either the standard UTF-8 or UCS-2 formats (XML entities encoded in UCS-2 must begin with the UCS-2 Byte Order Mark). Here's how the encoding declaration works, in case you want to make use of it:

```
EncodingDecl::= S 'encoding' Eq QEncoding
EncodingPI::= '<?XML' S 'encoding' Eq QEncoding S? ?>
QEncoding::= '"' Encoding '"' | "' " Encoding "'"
Encoding::= LatinName
LatinName::= [A-Za-z] ([A-Za-z0-9._] | '-')*
```

The most common encodings are values **UTF-8**, **UTF-16**, **ISO-10646-UCS-2**, and **ISO-10646-UCS-4**. Here's an example of an encoding declaration:

```
<?XML ENCODING='UTF-8'?>
```

The character encoding is one (optional) part of the XML declaration; another part is the (also optional) required markup declaration.

Required Markup Declarations

In the **RMDecl** part of the XML declaration, you can specify whether a DTD is required to work with your XML document:

```
document::= Prolog element Misc*
Prolog::= XMLDecl? Misc* (doctypedecl Misc*)?
XMLDecl::= '<?XML' VersionInfo EncodingDecl? RMDecl? S?
     '?>'
```

This is the *Required Markup Declaration* (RMD) section of the XML declaration, and you can specify whether there is no DTD, whether it's internal, or whether the parser should use both internal and external DTDs (if provided):

```
RMDecl::= S 'RMD' Eq "'" ('NONE' | 'INTERNAL' |
        'ALL') "'" | S 'RMD' Eq '"' ('NONE' | 'INTERNAL' |
        'ALL') '"'
```

The value **NONE** means the parser doesn't need the DTD to read the document; **INTERNAL** means the parser must read the internal DTD (if there is one); if the value is **ALL**, the parser must read both internal and external DTDs, if provided.

TIP *If there is no* **RMDecl**, *the parser defaults to a value of* **ALL**.

Here's an example XML declaration with a Required Markup Declaration:

```
<?XML version="1.0" RMD='INTERNAL'?>
```

That completes the **XMLDecl** section of the Prolog:

```
Prolog::= XMLDecl? Misc* (doctypedecl Misc*)?
```

However, we still have a great deal to cover in the **doctypedecl** section of the Prolog—that is, the DTD. In the rest of this chapter, we'll examine how DTDs work and the types of declarations you can use in them:

```
doctypedecl::= '<!DOCTYPE' S Name (S ExternalID)?
    S? ('[' markupdecl* ']' S?)? '>'
markupdecl::= %( ( %elementdecl | %AttlistDecl |
    %EntityDecl |
    %NotationDecl | %conditionalSect | %PI | %S |
        %Comment )* )
```

Document Type Declarations

We already know what a DTD is for: using a DTD, you can specify a grammar for your XML document, indicating to the XML parser what tags you allow in your document, what order they come in, and what tags other tags can enclose. The MSXML parser does not require a DTD, but if you include one, it will use it to make sure the XML document is valid. Here's how the DTD is defined:

```
doctypedecl::= '<!DOCTYPE' S Name (S ExternalID)?
    S? ('[' markupdecl* ']' S?)? '>'
markupdecl::= %( ( %elementdecl | %AttlistDecl |
    %EntityDecl |
```

```
%NotationDecl | %conditionalSect | %PI | %S |
    %Comment )* )
```

Because XML is a free-form markup language, it's usually a good idea to include a DTD with your XML documents, so the parser can check it for validity. In fact, many XML programmers believe you should only use an XML editor—which can check your XML against a DTD as you write your document—to write XML.

We'll work through the DTD specification in the rest of this chapter, examining such items as attribute lists and entity declarations. We'll start with the first item in the DTD—the document name.

Document Names

You can specify the name of the document in the beginning of the DTD:

```
doctypedecl::= '<!DOCTYPE' S Name (S ExternalID)?
        S? ('[' markupdecl* ']' S?)? '>'
markupdecl::= %( ( %elementdecl | %AttlistDecl |
    %EntityDecl |
        %NotationDecl | %conditionalSect | %PI | %S |
            %Comment )* )
```

For example, in this XML document, the document's name is **Thesis**:

```
<?XML version="1.0"?>
<!doctype Thesis [
    <!ELEMENT Thesis (p*)>
    <!ELEMENT p (#PCDATA)>
]>
<Thesis>
<p>
In this thesis, I hope to get my Ph.D.
</p>
<p>
A Ph.D. is great to impress friends.
</p>
<p>
Hopefully I'll get a job.
</p>
</Thesis>
```

You can retrieve the document's name using the MSXML classes. Let's see this at work: we will get and display the name of the preceding document in this example.

The getname **Example**

Create a new Java application now called **getname.java**. We can use the above XML document in this example, so put that document into the file **getname.xml**. In **getname.java**, we can start by reading in **getname.xml**:

```java
import com.ms.xml.ParseException;
import com.ms.xml.Document;
import com.ms.xml.Element;

import java.net.*;

class getname
{
    static String filename;

    public static void main(String args[])
    {
        filename = "file:////c://xml/getname//getname.xml";

        URL url = null;
        try {
            url = new URL(filename);
        }
        catch (MalformedURLException ex) {
            System.out.println("Cannot create URL for: "
                    + filename);
            System.exit(0);
        }

        Document d = new Document();

        try {
            d.load(url);
        }
        catch (ParseException e) {
            d.reportError(e, System.out);
        }
            .
            .
            .
```

To actually display the name of the document, we just use the Document class' **getName()** method this way:

```java
import com.ms.xml.ParseException;
import com.ms.xml.Document;
import com.ms.xml.Element;

import java.net.*;

class getname
```

```
{
    static String filename;
        .
        .
        .
    try {
        d.load(url);
    }
    catch (ParseException e) {
        d.reportError(e, System.out);
    }

    if (d != null) {
        System.out.println("The document's name is: "
            + d.getName());
    }
    }
}
```

That's it—that's all we need. When you run this program, it creates the following output:

The document's name is: THESIS

Our example works as intended. The code for this example, **getname.java**, is in Listing 3-1.

Besides giving a document a name, we can also specify a name for an external DTD, and we'll take a look at that next.

External DTDs

The **doctypedecl** section of the document allows us to give the name of an external DTD this way:

```
doctypedecl::= '<!DOCTYPE' S Name (S ExternalID)?
        S? ('[' markupdecl* ']' S?)? '>'
markupdecl::= %( ( %elementdecl | %AttlistDecl |
    %EntityDecl |
        %NotationDecl | %conditionalSect | %PI | %S |
            %Comment )* )
```

Here, **ExternalID** is defined this way:

```
ExternalID::= 'SYSTEM' S SystemLiteral|  'PUBLIC' S
    PubidLiteral S
        SystemLiteral
```

Let's take a look at an example, which we might call **dtdexternal.xml**:

Listing 3-1.
getname.java.

```java
import com.ms.xml.ParseException;

import com.ms.xml.Document;
import com.ms.xml.Element;

import java.net.*;

class getname
{
    static String filename;

    public static void main(String args[])
    {
        filename = "file:////c://xml/getname//getname.xml";

        URL url = null;
        try {
            url = new URL(filename);
        }
        catch (MalformedURLException ex) {
            System.out.println("Cannot create URL for: " +
                    filename);
            System.exit(0);
        }

        Document d = new Document();

        try {
            d.load(url);
        }
        catch (ParseException e) {
            d.reportError(e, System.out);
        }

        if (d != null) {
            System.out.println("The document's name is: "
                    + d.getName());
        }
    }
}
```

```xml
<?XML version="1.0"?>
<!DOCTYPE Thesis SYSTEM "dtdexternal.dtd">
<Thesis>
<p>
In this thesis, I hope to get my Ph.D.
</p>
<p>
A Ph.D. is great to impress friends.
</p>
```

```
<p>
Hopefully I'll get a job.
</p>
</Thesis>
```

In this example, we indicate that the system identifier for the DTD file is **dtdexternal.dtd**; note the **SYSTEM** keyword, which we use to indicate that the following term is a system identifier:

```
<?XML version="1.0"?>
<!DOCTYPE Thesis SYSTEM "dtdexternal.dtd">
<Thesis>
   .
   .
   .
```

That file, **dtdexternal.dtd**, contains the declaration of the two elements we use in **dtdexternal.xml**:

```
<!ELEMENT Thesis (p*)>
<!ELEMENT p (#PCDATA)>
```

Here, we indicate that the **Thesis** element (which is the root element for the XML document) can include zero or more occurrences of the <p> (for paragraph) tag by including a * after the p symbol:

```
<!ELEMENT Thesis (p*)>
<!ELEMENT p (#PCDATA)>
```

Using the + symbol, on the other hand, would mean one or more occurrences of the **p** tag.

The **dtdexternal** Example

We can check whether **dtdexternal.dtd** is a valid XML document by parsing it. Create a new Java application named dtdexternal.java now. In that application, we can read in the **dtdexternal.xml** file this way:

```
import com.ms.xml.ParseException;
import com.ms.xml.Document;
import com.ms.xml.Element;

import java.util.Enumeration;
import java.net.*;

class dtdexternal
{
```

```
        static String filename;

        public static void main(String args[])
        {
            filename = "file:////c://xml//dtdexternal//
                dtdexternal.xml";

            URL url = null;

            try {
                url = new URL(filename);
            }
            catch (MalformedURLException ex) {
                System.out.println("Cannot create URL for: "
                    + filename);
                System.exit(0);
            }

            Document d = new Document();

            try {
                d.load(url);
            }
            catch (ParseException e) {
                d.reportError(e, System.out);
                System.exit(0);
            }
                    .
                    .
                    .

        }
    }
```

If the document did not cause a parse exception and end the program, we can assume that it parsed without problems and indicate that to the user:

```
import com.ms.xml.ParseException;
import com.ms.xml.Document;
import com.ms.xml.Element;

import java.util.Enumeration;
import java.net.*;

class dtdexternal
{
    static String filename;
            .
            .
            .
        if (d != null) {
            System.out.println(filename + " parsed OK.");
        }
    }
}
```

Running this program gives us this output:

```
file:////c://xml//dtdexternal//dtdexternal.xml parsed OK.
```

Our example is a success. In this way, you can use the MSXML parser to check the validity of your XML documents. The listing for this application, **dtdexternal.java**, appears in Listing 3-2.

**Listing 3-2.
dtdexternal.
java.**

```
import com.ms.xml.ParseException;
import com.ms.xml.Document;
import com.ms.xml.Element;

import java.util.Enumeration;
import java.net.*;

class dtdexternal
{
    static String filename;

    public static void main(String args[])
    {
        filename = "file:////c://xml//dtdexternal//
            dtdexternal.xml";

        URL url = null;

        try {
            url = new URL(filename);
        }
        catch (MalformedURLException ex) {
            System.out.println("Cannot create URL for: " +
                filename);
            System.exit(0);
        }

        Document d = new Document();

        try {
            d.load(url);
        }
        catch (ParseException e) {
            d.reportError(e, System.out);
            System.exit(0);
        }

        if (d != null) {
            System.out.println(filename + " parsed OK.");
        }
    }
}
```

Now that we've taken a look at naming XML documents and specifying an external filename for the DTD, we will start looking at the actual markup declarations in the DTD:

```
doctypedecl::= '<!DOCTYPE' S Name (S ExternalID)?
    S? ('[' markupdecl* ']' S?)? '>'
markupdecl::= %( ( %elementdecl | %AttlistDecl |
    %EntityDecl |
    %NotationDecl | %conditionalSect | %PI | %S |
        %Comment )* )
```

We'll start our exploration of markup declarations with a topic we got an introduction to in the last chapter—element declarations.

Element Declarations

You declare XML elements in the **markupdecl** section of the DTD:

```
doctypedecl::= '<!DOCTYPE' S Name (S ExternalID)?
    S? ('[' markupdecl* ']' S?)? '>'
markupdecl::= %( ( %elementdecl | %AttlistDecl |
    %EntityDecl |
    %NotationDecl | %conditionalSect | %PI | %S |
        %Comment )* )
```

Here's how you declare elements formally:

```
elementdecl::= '<!ELEMENT' S %Name %S %contentspec S? '>'
contentspec::= 'EMPTY' | 'ANY' | Mixed | elements
```

If your elements can contain both other elements and character data, you declare them with mixed content:

```
Mixed::= '(' S? %( %'#PCDATA' ( S? '|' S? %(%Name
        (S? '|' S? %Name)*) )* ) S? ')*' | '(' S?
            %('#PCDATA') S? ')' '*'?
```

If your elements can only contain other elements, you declare them this way:

```
elements::= (choice | seq) ('?' | '*' | '+')?
cp::= (Name | choice | seq) ('?' | '*' | '+')?
cps::= S? %cp S?
choice::= '(' S? %(cps ('|' cps)+) S? ')'
seq::= '(' S? %(cps (', ' cps)*) S? ')'
```

Let's take a look at a few examples to make this clearer.

The DTD Example

We saw an example of a DTD earlier in this chapter when we discussed external DTDs. Let's put that DTD inside the document now to create a new file, **dtd.xml**, so we can dissect this new example.

We start the DTD in **dtd.xml** with the DOCTYPE keyword and enclose the actual declarations inside square braces, [and]:

```
<?XML version="1.0"?>
<!DOCTYPE Thesis [
    <!ELEMENT Thesis (p*)>
    <!ELEMENT p (#PCDATA)>
]>
<Thesis>
<p>
In this thesis, I hope to get my Ph.D.
</p>
<p>
A Ph.D. is great to impress friends.
</p>
<p>
Hopefully I'll get a job.
</p>
</Thesis>
```

In this case, we're declaring an element of type **Thesis** that can contain zero or more **<p>** tags. We also declare the **<p>** tag to contain character data. That's an example of a simple DTD. Let's go on now to a more complex example.

The dtd2 Example

Here's another example which is called **dtd2.xml** on the CD-ROM:

```
<?XML version = "1.0"?>
<!DOCTYPE DOCUMENT [
    <!ELEMENT DOCUMENT (CUSTOMER)*>
    <!ELEMENT CUSTOMER (NAME,DATE,ORDERS)>
    <!ELEMENT NAME (LASTNAME,FIRSTNAME)>
    <!ELEMENT LASTNAME (#PCDATA)>
    <!ELEMENT FIRSTNAME (#PCDATA)>
    <!ELEMENT DATE (#PCDATA)>
    <!ELEMENT ORDERS (ITEM)*>
    <!ELEMENT ITEM (PRODUCT,NUMBER,PRICE)>
    <!ELEMENT PRODUCT (#PCDATA)>
    <!ELEMENT NUMBER (#PCDATA)>
    <!ELEMENT PRICE (#PCDATA)>
]>
```

```
<DOCUMENT>
<CUSTOMER>
    <NAME>
        <LASTNAME>Edwards</LASTNAME>
        <FIRSTNAME>Britta</FIRSTNAME>
    </NAME>
    <DATE>April 17, 1998</DATE>
    <ORDERS>
        <ITEM>
            <PRODUCT>Cucumber</PRODUCT>
            <NUMBER>5</NUMBER>
            <PRICE>$1.25</PRICE>
        </ITEM>
        <ITEM>
            <PRODUCT>Lettuce</PRODUCT>
            <NUMBER>2</NUMBER>
            <PRICE>$.98</PRICE>
        </ITEM>
    </ORDERS>
</CUSTOMER>
<CUSTOMER>
    <NAME>
        <LASTNAME>Thompson</LASTNAME>
        <FIRSTNAME>Phoebe</FIRSTNAME>
    </NAME>
    <DATE>May 27, 1998</DATE>
    <ORDERS>
        <ITEM>
            <PRODUCT>Banana</PRODUCT>
            <NUMBER>12</NUMBER>
            <PRICE>$2.95</PRICE>
        </ITEM>
        <ITEM>
            <PRODUCT>Apple</PRODUCT>
            <NUMBER>6</NUMBER>
            <PRICE>$1.50</PRICE>
        </ITEM>
    </ORDERS>
</CUSTOMER>
</DOCUMENT>
```

Let's take a closer look at the DTD of this document now. To start, we declare the root element, <DOCUMENT>, which can contain zero or more <CUSTOMER> tags:

```
<!DOCTYPE DOCUMENT [
    <!ELEMENT DOCUMENT (CUSTOMER)*>
            .
            .
            .
```

Now we declare the <CUSTOMER> tag, which contains, in this order, the following tags: <NAME>, <DATE>, and <ORDERS>:

```
<!DOCTYPE DOCUMENT [
    <!ELEMENT DOCUMENT (CUSTOMER)*>
    <!ELEMENT CUSTOMER (NAME,DATE,ORDERS)>
        .
        .
        .
]>
```

Then we declare the <NAME> tag and indicate that this tag contains <LASTNAME> and <FIRSTNAME> tags, again in that order:

```
<!DOCTYPE DOCUMENT [
    <!ELEMENT DOCUMENT (CUSTOMER)*>
    <!ELEMENT CUSTOMER (NAME,DATE,ORDERS)>
    <!ELEMENT NAME (LASTNAME,FIRSTNAME)>
        .
        .
        .
```

We also declare the <LASTNAME>, <FIRSTNAME>, and <DATE> tags to contain character data:

```
<!DOCTYPE DOCUMENT [
    <!ELEMENT DOCUMENT (CUSTOMER)*>
    <!ELEMENT CUSTOMER (NAME,DATE,ORDERS)>
    <!ELEMENT NAME (LASTNAME,FIRSTNAME)>
    <!ELEMENT LASTNAME (#PCDATA)>
    <!ELEMENT FIRSTNAME (#PCDATA)>
    <!ELEMENT DATE (#PCDATA)>
        .
        .
        .
]>
```

The <ORDERS> tag is next, and it contains zero or one <ITEM> tags:

```
<!DOCTYPE DOCUMENT [
    <!ELEMENT DOCUMENT (CUSTOMER)*>
    <!ELEMENT CUSTOMER (NAME,DATE,ORDERS)>
    <!ELEMENT NAME (LASTNAME,FIRSTNAME)>
    <!ELEMENT LASTNAME (#PCDATA)>
    <!ELEMENT FIRSTNAME (#PCDATA)>
    <!ELEMENT DATE (#PCDATA)>
    <!ELEMENT ORDERS (ITEM)*>
        .
        .
        .
]>
```

The <ITEM> tag contains a <PRODUCT>, <NUMBER>, and <PRICE> tag in that order:

```
<!DOCTYPE DOCUMENT [
    <!ELEMENT DOCUMENT (CUSTOMER)*>
    <!ELEMENT CUSTOMER (NAME,DATE,ORDERS)>
    <!ELEMENT NAME (LASTNAME,FIRSTNAME)>
    <!ELEMENT LASTNAME (#PCDATA)>
    <!ELEMENT FIRSTNAME (#PCDATA)>
    <!ELEMENT DATE (#PCDATA)>
    <!ELEMENT ORDERS (ITEM)*>
    <!ELEMENT ITEM (PRODUCT,NUMBER,PRICE)>
         .
         .
         .
]>
```

The <PRODUCT>, <NUMBER>, and <PRICE> tags contain character data:

```
<!DOCTYPE DOCUMENT [
    <!ELEMENT DOCUMENT (CUSTOMER)*>
    <!ELEMENT CUSTOMER (NAME,DATE,ORDERS)>
    <!ELEMENT NAME (LASTNAME,FIRSTNAME)>
    <!ELEMENT LASTNAME (#PCDATA)>
    <!ELEMENT FIRSTNAME (#PCDATA)>
    <!ELEMENT DATE (#PCDATA)>
    <!ELEMENT ORDERS (ITEM)*>
    <!ELEMENT ITEM (PRODUCT,NUMBER,PRICE)>
    <!ELEMENT PRODUCT (#PCDATA)>
    <!ELEMENT NUMBER (#PCDATA)>
    <!ELEMENT PRICE (#PCDATA)>
]>
```

We can write an application—**dtd2.java** on the CD-ROM—that parses this example, **dtd2.xml**, like this:

```
import com.ms.xml.ParseException;
import com.ms.xml.Document;
import com.ms.xml.Element;

import java.util.Enumeration;
import java.net.*;

class dtdexternal
{
    static String filename;

    public static void main(String args[])
    {
        filename = "file:////c://xml//dtd2//dtd2.xml";

        URL url = null;

        try {
            url = new URL(filename);
```

```
            }
        catch (MalformedURLException ex) {
            System.out.println("Cannot create URL for: " +
                filename);
            System.exit(0);
        }

        Document d = new Document();

        try {
            d.load(url);
        }
        catch (ParseException e) {
            d.reportError(e, System.out);
            System.exit(0);
        }

        if (d != null) {
            System.out.println(filename + " parsed OK.");
        }
    }
}
```

When you run this program, it parses the document and its DTD, indicating that the document parsed without trouble. That's it—now our **dtd2.xml** example is complete. Let's take a look at one more—and still more complex—DTD example now.

The DTD3 Example

Here's another example XML document, **dtd3.xml**:

```
<?XML version="1.0"?>
<!DOCTYPE tstmt SYSTEM "file:////xml//dtd3//dtd3.dtd">
<DOCUMENT>
<TITLE>Thesis</TITLE>
<PART>
<HEADING>Ice Cream Consumption</HEADING>
<CHAPTER>
<CHAPTERTITLE>CHAPTER 1</CHAPTERTITLE>
<p>I like chocolate ice cream.</p>
<p>I like vanilla ice cream.</p>
<p>I like strawberry ice cream.</p>
</CHAPTER>
</PART>
</DOCUMENT>
```

In this case, we have a number of elements: <DOCUMENT>, <TITLE>, <PART>, <HEADING>, and so on. The DTD for this file will be **dtd3.dtd**, and we start that file by declaring the **<p>** element:

```
<!ELEMENT p                 (#PCDATA)>
                      .
                      .
                      .
```

Next, we declare the root element, <DOCUMENT>. We declare the <DOCUMENT> element to contain a <TITLE> tag, possibly a <SUBTITLE> tag (by placing a ? after the SUBTITLE declaration), possibly a <PREFACE> tag, and one or more sections or parts as declared with the <SECTION> or <PART> tags this way:

```
<!ELEMENT p                 (#PCDATA)>
<!ELEMENT DOCUMENT          (TITLE,SUBTITLE?,PREFACE?,(SECTION
   | PART)+)>
                      .
                      .
                      .
```

Next, we declare a <TITLE> tag that contains zero or more occurrences of character data and <TITLE2> tags:

```
<!ELEMENT p                 (#PCDATA)>
<!ELEMENT DOCUMENT          (TITLE,SUBTITLE?,PREFACE?,(SECTION
   | PART)+)>
<!ELEMENT TITLE             ((#PCDATA),TITLE2?)*>
                      .
                      .
                      .
```

The <TITLE2> element can contain character data:

```
<!ELEMENT p                 (#PCDATA)>
<!ELEMENT DOCUMENT          (TITLE,SUBTITLE?,PREFACE?,(SECTION
   | PART)+)>
<!ELEMENT TITLE             ((#PCDATA),TITLE2?)*>
<!ELEMENT TITLE2            (#PCDATA)>
                      .
                      .
                      .
```

Next, we declare the <SUBTITLE> tag, which can contain one or more paragraph elements:

```
<!ELEMENT p                 (#PCDATA)>
<!ELEMENT DOCUMENT          (TITLE,SUBTITLE?,PREFACE?,(SECTION
   | PART)+)>
<!ELEMENT TITLE             ((#PCDATA),TITLE2?)*>
<!ELEMENT TITLE2            (#PCDATA)>
<!ELEMENT SUBTITLE          (p)+>
                      .
```

.
.

The <PREFACE> element can contain one or more <HEADING> or <p> elements:

```
<!ELEMENT p            (#PCDATA)>
<!ELEMENT DOCUMENT     (TITLE,SUBTITLE?,PREFACE?,(SECTION |
PART)+)>
<!ELEMENT TITLE        ((#PCDATA),TITLE2?)*>
<!ELEMENT TITLE2       (#PCDATA)>
<!ELEMENT SUBTITLE     (p)+>
<!ELEMENT PREFACE      (HEADING, p+)+>
```
.
.
.

The <PART> element can contain <HEADING> and <CHAPTER> elements:

```
<!ELEMENT p            (#PCDATA)>
<!ELEMENT DOCUMENT     (TITLE,SUBTITLE?,PREFACE?,(SECTION |
PART)+)>
<!ELEMENT TITLE        ((#PCDATA),TITLE2?)*>
<!ELEMENT TITLE2       (#PCDATA)>
<!ELEMENT SUBTITLE     (p)+>
<!ELEMENT PREFACE      (HEADING, p+)+>
<!ELEMENT PART         (HEADING, CHAPTER+)>
```
.
.
.

The <CHAPTER> element can contain <CHAPTERTITLE> and <p> elements:

```
<!ELEMENT p            (#PCDATA)>
<!ELEMENT DOCUMENT     (TITLE,SUBTITLE?,PREFACE?,(SECTION |
PART)+)>
<!ELEMENT TITLE        ((#PCDATA),TITLE2?)*>
<!ELEMENT TITLE2       (#PCDATA)>
<!ELEMENT SUBTITLE     (p)+>
<!ELEMENT PREFACE      (HEADING, p+)+>
<!ELEMENT PART         (HEADING, CHAPTER+)>
<!ELEMENT SECTION      (HEADING, p+)>
<!ELEMENT HEADING      (#PCDATA)>
<!ELEMENT CHAPTER      (CHAPTERTITLE, p+)>
```
.
.
.

Finally, the <CHAPTERTITLE> element contains parsed character data:

```
<!ELEMENT p              (#PCDATA)>
<!ELEMENT DOCUMENT       (TITLE,SUBTITLE?,PREFACE?,(SECTION
    | PART)+)>
<!ELEMENT TITLE          ((#PCDATA),TITLE2?)*>
<!ELEMENT TITLE2         (#PCDATA)>
<!ELEMENT SUBTITLE       (p)+>
<!ELEMENT PREFACE        (HEADING, p+)+>
<!ELEMENT PART           (HEADING, CHAPTER+)>
<!ELEMENT SECTION        (HEADING, p+)>
<!ELEMENT HEADING        (#PCDATA)>
<!ELEMENT CHAPTER        (CHAPTERTITLE, p+)>
<!ELEMENT CHAPTERTITLE (#PCDATA)>
```

We can write an application, **dtd3.java** on the CD-ROM, that makes sure **dtd3.xml** is valid, like this:

```java
import com.ms.xml.ParseException;
import com.ms.xml.Document;
import com.ms.xml.Element;

import java.util.Enumeration;
import java.net.*;

class dtdexternal
{
    static String filename;

    public static void main(String args[])
    {
        filename = "file:////c://xml//dtd3//dtd3.xml";

        URL url = null;

        try {
            url = new URL(filename);
        }
        catch (MalformedURLException ex) {
            System.out.println("Cannot create URL for: "
                    + filename);
            System.exit(0);
        }

        Document d = new Document();

        try {
            d.load(url);
        }
        catch (ParseException e) {
            d.reportError(e, System.out);
            System.exit(0);
        }

        if (d != null) {
            System.out.println(filename + " parsed OK.");
```

```
            }
        }
    }
```

That completes our element declaration examples. As you can see, element declarations can get fairly complex, but by using the DTD, you can specify the exact grammar for the elements in your XML documents.

Next, we'll take a look at XML *attributes* and *attribute lists*.

Attribute Lists

Attributes represent data that you can include in start tags. You can use an attribute to store more data about an element; for example, here are some attributes that we add to the following start tags:

```
<?XML version = "1.0"?>
<DOCUMENT>
<CUSTOMER>
    <NAME>
        <LASTNAME>Edwards</LASTNAME>
        <FIRSTNAME>Britta</FIRSTNAME>
    </NAME>
    <DATE>April 17, 1998</DATE>
    <ORDERS>
        <ITEM>
            <PRODUCT>Cucumber</PRODUCT>
            <NUMBER>5</NUMBER>
            <PRICE>$1.25</PRICE>
        </ITEM>
        <ITEM>
            <PRODUCT>Lettuce</PRODUCT>
            <NUMBER>2</NUMBER>
            <PRICE>$.98</PRICE>
        </ITEM>
    </ORDERS>
</CUSTOMER>
<CUSTOMER>
    <NAME>
        <LASTNAME>Thompson</LASTNAME>
        <FIRSTNAME>Phoebe</FIRSTNAME>
    </NAME>
    <DATE>May 27, 1998</DATE>
    <ORDERS>
        <ITEM>
            <PRODUCT ATTRIBUTE1 = "Hello there!">
                Banana
            </PRODUCT>
            <NUMBER>12</NUMBER>
            <PRICE>$2.95</PRICE>
```

```
        </ITEM>
        <ITEM ATTRIBUTE2 = "Hello there again!">
            <PRODUCT>Apple</PRODUCT>
            <NUMBER>6</NUMBER>
            <PRICE>$1.50</PRICE>
        </ITEM>
    </ORDERS>
  </CUSTOMER>
</DOCUMENT>
```

Using attributes, you can associate data that your program needs to process the tag correctly. For example, you can store the width and height of an image as attributes in an <IMAGE> tag:

```
<IMAGE SRC = "figure.jpg" WIDTH = "244" HEIGHT = "150">
```

Note that we didn't include a DTD in the preceding XML document example. That's because if you use attributes and include a DTD, you must declare the attributes in an attribute list, the `AttlistDecl` item here:

```
doctypedecl::= '<!DOCTYPE' S Name (S ExternalID)?
    S? ('[' markupdecl* ']' S?)? '>'
markupdecl::= %( ( %elementdecl | %AttlistDecl |
    %EntityDecl |
    %NotationDecl | %conditionalSect | %PI | %S |
        %Comment )* )
```

Formally, attribute lists are declared this way:

```
AttlistDecl::= '<!ATTLIST' S %Name S? (%AttDef+)+ S? '>'
```

Here, **Name** is the element whose attributes you are listing. **AttDef** represents the specific attribute you are defining, as we'll see. You specify the **AttDef** value this way:

```
AttDef::= S %Name S %AttType S %Default
```

In other words, to define an attribute, you specify the attribute's name, its type, and a default. The name of the attribute is simply that—its name. The other two items, the attribute type and default specification, take a little more exploration. Let's take a look at these two items now, starting with the attribute type—the AttType item.

Attribute Types

There are three XML attribute types: a string type, a set of tokenized types, and enumerated types.

The string attribute type may take any literal string as a value, the tokenized types can be various types as noted, and the enumerated type can consist of either a notation type or an enumeration type:

```
AttType::= StringType | TokenizedType | EnumeratedType
StringType::= 'CDATA'
TokenizedType::= 'ID' | 'IDREF' | 'IDREFS' | 'ENTITY' |
    'ENTITIES'
        | 'NMTOKEN' | 'NMTOKENS'
EnumeratedType::= NotationType | Enumeration
```

The **string** attribute type can be made up of any valid CDATA data.

TIP   *If there is no DTD available, the parser treats all attributes as CDATA data.*

The **Tokenized** attribute type can only be one of the following: **ID** (a valid and unique Name symbol), **IDREF** (a reference to an ID value), **IDREFS** (one or more references to an ID value), **ENTITY** (the name of an entity), **ENTITIES** (one or more entity names), and **NMTOKEN** or **NMTOKENS** (one or more **Nmtokens**).

TIP   *Terms like* Nmtokens, Names, *and so on are defined in the previous chapter.*

The **Enumerated** attribute type can be either a Notation or an Enumeration:

```
NotationType::= %'NOTATION' S '(' S? %Ntoks (S? '|' S?
%Ntoks)* S? ')'
Ntoks::= %Name (S? '|' S? %Name)*
Enumeration::= '(' S? %Etoks (S? '|' S? %Etoks)* S? ')'
Etoks::= %Nmtoken (S? '|' S? %Nmtoken)*
```

We'll see how to declare attributes of these types in a moment, but before we do, we must take a look at how to specify *attribute defaults*.

Specifying Attribute Defaults

Besides the attribute type, you can also give a default attribute specification in the attribute list for each attribute; this specification is listed as the **Default** item here:

```
AttlistDecl::= '<!ATTLIST' S %Name S? (%AttDef+)+ S? '>'
AttDef::= S %Name S %AttType S %Default
```

Here's how you give the default specification:

```
Default::= '#REQUIRED' | '#IMPLIED' | ((%'#FIXED' S)?
    %AttValue)
```

This specification gives you considerable control over how a XML parser makes use of the attributes in the attribute list.

If you declare an attribute as **#REQUIRED**, the XML document is invalid (recall that an XML document must comply with its DTD to be valid) if the parser finds a start tag that supports this attribute but where the attribute is not present. That is, if you skip this attribute (such as the WIDTH and HEIGHT attributes of an image in an <IMAGE> tag), the document is invalid.

If you declare an attribute as **#IMPLIED**, the XML parser should inform us that no value was given for this attribute. However, the document is not considered invalid.

If the attribute is considered neither **#REQUIRED** nor **#IMPLIED**, the **AttValue** value contains the declared default value:

```
Default::= '#REQUIRED' | '#IMPLIED' | ((%'#FIXED' S)?
    %AttValue)
```

On the other hand, if you declare an attribute as **#FIXED**, the parser must consider the document invalid if the declared attribute is present in the document with a different value from the default. Let's take a look at some attribute list examples now.

Some Sample Attribute Lists

Here's an attribute list for an element named **RECORD**. This element has three required attributes, name (of type **CDATA**), date (also of type **CDATA**), and id (of type **ID**):

```
<!ATTLIST RECORD
    name      CDATA      #REQUIRED>
    date      CDATA      #REQUIRED>
    id        ID         #REQUIRED
```

Here's how you would use that attribute list in a DTD. (Note that we declare the element itself, the **RECORD** element, and then add a list of its attributes):

```
<!DOCTYPE DOCUMENT [
    <!ELEMENT RECORD (#PCDATA)>
    <!ATTLIST RECORD
        name    CDATA    #REQUIRED>
        date    CDATA    #REQUIRED>
        id      ID       #REQUIRED
]>
```

Besides **Token**ized attribute types, we can also declare attributes of the **String** type like this:

```
<!ATTLIST CUSTOMER
        type   CDATA   #FIXED "solvent">
```

Here, we make sure the <CUSTOMER> tag has a type **attribute** whose value must be **solvent**. You use this new attribute list in the DTD this way:

```
<!DOCTYPE DOCUMENT [
    <!ELEMENT RECORD (#PCDATA)>
    <!ELEMENT CUSTOMER (#PCDATA)>
    <!ATTLIST RECORD
        name    CDATA    #REQUIRED>
        date    CDATA    #REQUIRED>
        id      ID       #REQUIRED
    <!ATTLIST CUSTOMER
        type    CDATA    #FIXED "solvent">
]>
```

In addition, you can declare attributes of the enumerated type this way:

```
<!ATTLIST figure
        kind    (circle|square|star)   "square">
```

Let's take a look at an example program now that will read in an XML document that has a DTD and examine the elements for attributes, displaying what attributes they have. This will give us experience with the process of reading in an element's attributes.

The **attlist** Example

Let's see how to use an attribute list in code now. In this example, we'll come close to creating an XML browser (we'll create true browsers in the next chapter) as we loop over the elements of an XML document and display the attributes of those elements.

In this example, we'll add a list of attributes to the <CUSTOMER> tag this way:

```
<?XML version = "1.0"?>
<!DOCTYPE DOCUMENT [
<!ELEMENT DOCUMENT (CUSTOMER)*>
<!ELEMENT CUSTOMER (NAME,DATE,ORDERS)>
<!ELEMENT NAME (LASTNAME,FIRSTNAME)>
<!ELEMENT LASTNAME (#PCDATA)>
<!ELEMENT FIRSTNAME (#PCDATA)>
<!ELEMENT DATE (#PCDATA)>
<!ELEMENT ORDERS (ITEM)*>
<!ELEMENT ITEM (PRODUCT,NUMBER,PRICE)>
<!ELEMENT PRODUCT (#PCDATA)>
<!ELEMENT NUMBER (#PCDATA)>
<!ELEMENT PRICE (#PCDATA)>
<!ATTLIST CUSTOMER
     TYPE CDATA #IMPLIED>
]>
<DOCUMENT>
<CUSTOMER>
    <NAME>
        <LASTNAME>Edwards</LASTNAME>
        <FIRSTNAME>Britta</FIRSTNAME>
    </NAME>
    <DATE>April 17, 1998</DATE>
    <ORDERS>
        <ITEM>
            <PRODUCT>Cucumber</PRODUCT>
            <NUMBER>5</NUMBER>
            <PRICE>$1.25</PRICE>
        </ITEM>
        <ITEM>
            <PRODUCT>Lettuce</PRODUCT>
            <NUMBER>2</NUMBER>
            <PRICE>$.98</PRICE>
        </ITEM>
    </ORDERS>
</CUSTOMER>
<CUSTOMER>
    <NAME>
        <LASTNAME>Thompson</LASTNAME>
        <FIRSTNAME>Phoebe</FIRSTNAME>
    </NAME>
    <DATE>May 27, 1998</DATE>
    <ORDERS>
        <ITEM>
            <PRODUCT>Banana</PRODUCT>
            <NUMBER>12</NUMBER>
            <PRICE>$2.95</PRICE>
        </ITEM>
        <ITEM>
            <PRODUCT>Apple</PRODUCT>
            <NUMBER>6</NUMBER>
            <PRICE>$1.50</PRICE>
        </ITEM>
```

```
        </ORDERS>
    </CUSTOMER>
</DOCUMENT>
```

Here, the TYPE attribute indicates what type of customer we're deal-
ing with: excellent, good, or poor. We can give this attribute a value this
way:

```
<?XML version = "1.0"?>
<!DOCTYPE DOCUMENT [
<!ELEMENT DOCUMENT (CUSTOMER)*>
<!ELEMENT CUSTOMER (NAME,DATE,ORDERS)>
<!ELEMENT NAME (LASTNAME,FIRSTNAME)>
<!ELEMENT LASTNAME (#PCDATA)>
<!ELEMENT FIRSTNAME (#PCDATA)>
<!ELEMENT DATE (#PCDATA)>
<!ELEMENT ORDERS (ITEM)*>
<!ELEMENT ITEM (PRODUCT,NUMBER,PRICE)>
<!ELEMENT PRODUCT (#PCDATA)>
<!ELEMENT NUMBER (#PCDATA)>
<!ELEMENT PRICE (#PCDATA)>
<!ATTLIST CUSTOMER
     TYPE CDATA #IMPLIED>
]>
<DOCUMENT>
<CUSTOMER TYPE = "Excellent">
    <NAME>
         <LASTNAME>Edwards</LASTNAME>
         <FIRSTNAME>Britta</FIRSTNAME>
    </NAME>
    <DATE>April 17, 1998</DATE>
    <ORDERS>
         <ITEM>
              <PRODUCT>Cucumber</PRODUCT>
              <NUMBER>5</NUMBER>
              <PRICE>$1.25</PRICE>
         </ITEM>
         <ITEM>
              <PRODUCT>Lettuce</PRODUCT>
              <NUMBER>2</NUMBER>
              <PRICE>$.98</PRICE>
         </ITEM>
    </ORDERS>
</CUSTOMER>
<CUSTOMER TYPE = "Good">
    <NAME>
         <LASTNAME>Thompson</LASTNAME>
         <FIRSTNAME>Phoebe</FIRSTNAME>
    </NAME>
    <DATE>May 27, 1998</DATE>
    <ORDERS>
         <ITEM>
```

```
                    <PRODUCT>Banana</PRODUCT>
                    <NUMBER>12</NUMBER>
                    <PRICE>$2.95</PRICE>
                </ITEM>
                <ITEM>
                    <PRODUCT>Apple</PRODUCT>
                    <NUMBER>6</NUMBER>
                    <PRICE>$1.50</PRICE>
                </ITEM>
            </ORDERS>
        </CUSTOMER>
    </DOCUMENT>
```

That completes the XML file we'll use in this example—**attlist.xml**.
Let's put together the Java application we'll use, attlist.java, to read in
the attributes in this file now. Create a new file named **attlist.java** now.
First, we read in the XML document, **attlist.xml**:

```java
import com.ms.xml.ParseException;
import com.ms.xml.Document;
import com.ms.xml.Element;

import java.util.Enumeration;
import java.io.*;
import java.io.PrintStream;
import java.net.*;

class attlist
{
    static String filename;

    public static void main(String args[])
    {
        filename = "file:////c://xml//attlist//
            attlist.xml";

        URL url = null;
        try {
            url = new URL(filename);
        }
        catch (MalformedURLException e) {
            System.out.println("Cannot create URL for: "
                + filename);
            System.exit(0);
        }

        Document d = new Document();

        try {
            d.load(url);
        }
        catch (ParseException e) {
```

```
            d.reportError(e, System.out);
    }
                    .
                    .
                    .
```

Next, we will work through the elements in the XML file. Note, however, that many elements have children, and some of the child elements have child elements themselves:

```
<?XML version = "1.0"?>
<!DOCTYPE DOCUMENT [
<!ELEMENT DOCUMENT (CUSTOMER)*>
<!ELEMENT CUSTOMER (NAME,DATE,ORDERS)>
<!ELEMENT NAME (LASTNAME,FIRSTNAME)>
<!ELEMENT LASTNAME (#PCDATA)>
<!ELEMENT FIRSTNAME (#PCDATA)>
<!ELEMENT DATE (#PCDATA)>
<!ELEMENT ORDERS (ITEM)*>
<!ELEMENT ITEM (PRODUCT,NUMBER,PRICE)>
<!ELEMENT PRODUCT (#PCDATA)>
<!ELEMENT NUMBER (#PCDATA)>
<!ELEMENT PRICE (#PCDATA)>
<!ATTLIST CUSTOMER
     TYPE CDATA #IMPLIED>
]>
<DOCUMENT>
<CUSTOMER TYPE = "Excellent">
    <NAME>
        <LASTNAME>Edwards</LASTNAME>
        <FIRSTNAME>Britta</FIRSTNAME>
    </NAME>
    <DATE>April 17, 1998</DATE>
    <ORDERS>
        <ITEM>
            <PRODUCT>Cucumber</PRODUCT>
            <NUMBER>5</NUMBER>
            <PRICE>$1.25</PRICE>
        </ITEM>
        <ITEM>
            <PRODUCT>Lettuce</PRODUCT>
            <NUMBER>2</NUMBER>
            <PRICE>$.98</PRICE>
        </ITEM>
    </ORDERS>
</CUSTOMER>
            .
            .
            .
```

This means we can't just loop over the root element's children like this:

```
Element root = d.getRoot();
Enumeration enum = root.getChildren();

while (enum.hasMoreElements()) {
    Element elem2 = (Element)enum.nextElement();
        .
        .
        .

}
```

If we used the above code, we'd just loop over the root element's immediate children. Instead, we want to loop over all children in the document, and that will take a little thought. We start with the root element, <DOCUMENT>:

```
<DOCUMENT>
    .
    .
    .
```

Then we examine the root element's first child and print its attribute:

```
<DOCUMENT>
    <CUSTOMER TYPE = "Excellent">
        .
        .
        .
```

This element itself has a child element, and we have to check that element as well:

```
<DOCUMENT>
    <CUSTOMER TYPE = "Excellent">
        <NAME>
            .
            .
            .
```

This element, however, also has child elements—in fact, two of them:

```
<DOCUMENT>
    <CUSTOMER TYPE = "Excellent">
        <NAME>
            <LASTNAME>Edwards</LASTNAME>
            <FIRSTNAME>Britta</FIRSTNAME>
            .
            .
            .
```

None of those elements have attributes, however, so we go back up the tree to find the next tag, <DATE>:

```
<DOCUMENT>
    <CUSTOMER TYPE = "Excellent">
        <NAME>
            <LASTNAME>Edwards</LASTNAME>
            <FIRSTNAME>Britta</FIRSTNAME>
        </NAME>
        <DATE>April 17, 1998</DATE>
                    .
                    .
                    .
```

This element has no children, so we move on to the next element:

```
<DOCUMENT>
    <CUSTOMER TYPE = "Excellent">
        <NAME>
            <LASTNAME>Edwards</LASTNAME>
            <FIRSTNAME>Britta</FIRSTNAME>
        </NAME>
        <DATE>April 17, 1998</DATE>
        <ORDERS>
                    .
                    .
                    .
```

This element has a child element that has children itself:

```
<DOCUMENT>
    <CUSTOMER TYPE = "Excellent">
        <NAME>
            <LASTNAME>Edwards</LASTNAME>
            <FIRSTNAME>Britta</FIRSTNAME>
        </NAME>
        <DATE>April 17, 1998</DATE>
        <ORDERS>
            <ITEM>
                <PRODUCT>Cucumber</PRODUCT>
                <NUMBER>5</NUMBER>
                <PRICE>$1.25</PRICE>
                    .
                    .
                    .
```

When we're done with those elements, we move back one level and examine the elements of the next branch of the tree:

```
<DOCUMENT>
    <CUSTOMER TYPE = "Excellent">
        <NAME>
            <LASTNAME>Edwards</LASTNAME>
            <FIRSTNAME>Britta</FIRSTNAME>
        </NAME>
        <DATE>April 17, 1998</DATE>
```

```
<ORDERS>
    <ITEM>
        <PRODUCT>Cucumber</PRODUCT>
        <NUMBER>5</NUMBER>
        <PRICE>$1.25</PRICE>
    </ITEM>
    <ITEM>
        <PRODUCT>Lettuce</PRODUCT>
        <NUMBER>2</NUMBER>
        <PRICE>$.98</PRICE>
    </ITEM>
        .
        .
        .
```

The pattern is clear: we start at a particular element, display its attributes (if any), and then loop over all its children. If we reach a child element that has children itself, we have to loop over those children.

How will we do this in code? We'll set up a new method named **doTree()** to handle this process. This method displays the current element's attributes and then loops over the element's children, calling *itself* (i.e., the **doTree()** method) for the each child. The **doTree()** method handles each child by printing the child's attributes. And if the child has children, it loops over the children as well. After all the children have been examined, we return to the original element and then return to the code that called the method, which may itself have been the same method calling itself from a higher level.

This process—a method calling itself—is called *recursion*, and it's a fundamental technique of XML browsers, as we'll see in the next chapter. Using recursion, we can work through the entire element tree, traveling down one branch to its end, moving back up that branch, and continuing to the next one. All we have to do is handle the current element by displaying its attributes, and then loop over all its children, having the method call itself. That's how **doTree()** will work.

We will add another refinement to **doTree()**: to make the structure of the tree more evident, we'll indent the elements as we display them, just as they appear in the **attlist.xml** file:

```
<DOCUMENT>
    <CUSTOMER TYPE = "Excellent">
        <NAME>
            <LASTNAME>Edwards</LASTNAME>
            <FIRSTNAME>Britta</FIRSTNAME>
        </NAME>
        <DATE>April 17, 1998</DATE>
        <ORDERS>
            <ITEM>
                <PRODUCT>Cucumber</PRODUCT>
                <NUMBER>5</NUMBER>
```

```
        <PRICE>$1.25</PRICE>
    </ITEM>
    <ITEM>
        <PRODUCT>Lettuce</PRODUCT>
        <NUMBER>2</NUMBER>
        <PRICE>$.98</PRICE>
    </ITEM>
            .
            .
            .
```

We do this by passing an *indentation string* consisting of spaces to **doTree()**, and every time we call **doTree()**, we simply add four more spaces to the indentation string. When we print the attributes of each element, we'll simply preface those attributes' text with the indentation string.

Let's see this in action. Our first step is to call **doTree()** with the root element to start things off. Note that we pass an empty string (**""**) as the indentation string for the root element, because we don't want that element to appear indented:

```
import com.ms.xml.ParseException;
import com.ms.xml.Document;
import com.ms.xml.Element;

import java.util.Enumeration;
import java.io.*;
import java.io.PrintStream;
import java.net.*;

class attlist
{
    static String filename;

    public static void main(String args[])
    {
        filename = "file:////c://xml//attlist//
            attlist.xml";
                .
                .
                .

        catch (ParseException e) {
            d.reportError(e, System.out);
        }

        if (d != null) {
            doTree(d.getRoot(), "");
        }
    }
        .
        .
        .
```

Now let's write our recursive method, `doTree()`.

Writing the `doTree()` Method

The `doTree()` method takes an `Element` and a `String`:

```
import com.ms.xml.ParseException;
import com.ms.xml.Document;
import com.ms.xml.Element;

import java.util.Enumeration;
import java.io.*;
import java.io.PrintStream;
import java.net.*;

class attlist
{
    static String filename;

    public static void main(String args[])
    {
        .
        .
        .
    }

    static void doTree(Element elem, String indent)
    {
        .
        .
        .
    }
}
```

This method has two purposes: to display the attributes of the current element and to loop over its children (if any), calling itself again and again as needed to process the children.

We'll start by displaying the current element's attributes, and the first step in doing so is to get an enumeration of those attributes. We do that with the Element class' `getAttributes()` method, which returns an enumeration of the current element's attributes:

```
import com.ms.xml.ParseException;
import com.ms.xml.Document;
import com.ms.xml.Element;

import java.util.Enumeration;
import java.io.*;
```

```
import java.io.PrintStream;
import java.net.*;

class attlist
{
    static String filename;

    public static void main(String args[])
    {
        .
        .
        .
    }

    static void doTree(Element elem, String indent)
    {
        Enumeration attribEnum = elem.getAttributes();
        .
        .
        .
    }
}
```

Next, we loop over all the attributes in the attribute enumeration:

```
import com.ms.xml.Attribute;
import com.ms.xml.ParseException;
import com.ms.xml.Document;
import com.ms.xml.Element;

import java.util.Enumeration;
import java.io.*;
import java.io.PrintStream;
import java.net.*;

class attlist
{
    static String filename;

    public static void main(String args[])
    {
        .
        .
        .
    }

    static void doTree(Element elem, String indent)
    {
        Enumeration attribEnum = elem.getAttributes();
        while (attribEnum.hasMoreElements()) {
            .
            .
            .
```

```
        }
    }
}
```

And we get the current attribute from the enumeration:

```
import com.ms.xml.Attribute;

import com.ms.xml.ParseException;

import com.ms.xml.Document;

import com.ms.xml.Element;

import java.util.Enumeration;
import java.io.*;
import java.io.PrintStream;
import java.net.*;

class attlist
{
    static String filename;

    public static void main(String args[])
    {
        .
        .
        .

    }

    static void doTree(Element elem, String indent)
    {
        Enumeration attribEnum = elem.getAttributes();
        while (attribEnum.hasMoreElements()) {
            Attribute attrib =
                ((Attribute)attribEnum.nextElement());
                .
                .
                .

        }

        System.out.println(indent + elem.getTagName() +
            attribString);

        if(elem.numElements() > 1){
            Enumeration enum = elem.getChildren();
            while (enum.hasMoreElements()) {
                Element elem2 =
                    (Element)enum.nextElement();
                doTree(elem2, indent + "    ");
            }
        }
    }
}
```

We can get the name of the current attribute with the Attribute class' **getAttribute()** method and the value of the attribute with the **getValue()** method. We add those strings—the attribute's name and value—to a string named **attribString** this way:

```java
import com.ms.xml.Attribute;
import com.ms.xml.ParseException;
import com.ms.xml.Document;
import com.ms.xml.Element;

import java.util.Enumeration;
import java.io.*;
import java.io.PrintStream;
import java.net.*;

class attlist
{
    static String filename;

    public static void main(String args[])
    {
        .
        .
        .
    }

    static void doTree(Element elem, String indent)
    {
        String attribString = " Attributes: ";
        Enumeration attribEnum = elem.getAttributes();
        while (attribEnum.hasMoreElements()) {
            Attribute attrib =
                ((Attribute)attribEnum.nextElement());
            attribString += attrib.getName() + " = " +
                attrib.getValue() + " ";
        }
        .
        .
        .
    }
}
```

NOTE *If you haven't seen the **+=** operator before, here's how it works: this operator just condenses the + and = operators into one operation. For example, x += 3 is the same as x = x + 3.*

When the string holding the attribute names and values is complete, we can display it with **System.out.println()**:

```
import com.ms.xml.Attribute;
import com.ms.xml.ParseException;
import com.ms.xml.Document;
import com.ms.xml.Element;

import java.util.Enumeration;
import java.io.*;
import java.io.PrintStream;
import java.net.*;

class attlist
{
    static String filename;

    public static void main(String args[])
    {
        .
        .
        .
    }

    static void doTree(Element elem, String indent)
    {
        String attribString = " Attributes: ";
        Enumeration attribEnum = elem.getAttributes();
        while (attribEnum.hasMoreElements()) {
            Attribute attrib =
                ((Attribute)attribEnum.nextElement());
            attribString += attrib.getName() + " = " +
                attrib.getValue() + " ";
        }

        System.out.println(indent + elem.getTagName() +
            attribString);
        .
        .
        .
    }
}
```

That completes the process of printing the attributes of the current element.

If the element has children, we should repeat the process by calling **doTree()** again for each child. First, we check whether there *are* children:

```
import com.ms.xml.Attribute;
import com.ms.xml.ParseException;
import com.ms.xml.Document;
import com.ms.xml.Element;

import java.util.Enumeration;
import java.io.*;
```

```
import java.io.PrintStream;
import java.net.*;

class attlist
{
    static String filename;

    public static void main(String args[])
    {
        .
        .
        .
    }

    static void doTree(Element elem, String indent)
    {
        String attribString = " Attributes: ";
        Enumeration attribEnum = elem.getAttributes();
        while (attribEnum.hasMoreElements()) {
            Attribute attrib =
                ((Attribute)attribEnum.nextElement());
            attribString += attrib.getName() + " = " +
                attrib.getValue() + " ";
        }

        System.out.println(indent + elem.getTagName() +
            attribString);

        if(elem.numElements() > 1){
            .
            .
            .
        }
    }
}
```

If there are child elements, we get an enumeration of those child elements this way:

```
import com.ms.xml.Attribute;
import com.ms.xml.ParseException;
import com.ms.xml.Document;
import com.ms.xml.Element;


import java.util.Enumeration;
import java.io.*;
import java.io.PrintStream;
import java.net.*;

class attlist
{
    static String filename;
```

```
public static void main(String args[])
{
    .
    .
    .

}

static void doTree(Element elem, String indent)
{
    String attribString = " Attributes: ";
    Enumeration attribEnum = elem.getAttributes();
    while (attribEnum.hasMoreElements()) {
        Attribute attrib =
                ((Attribute)attribEnum.nextElement());
        attribString += attrib.getName() + " = " +
                attrib.getValue() + " ";
    }

    System.out.println(indent + elem.getTagName() +
        attribString);

    if(elem.numElements() > 1){
        Enumeration enum = elem.getChildren();
            .
            .
            .

    }
}
}
```

Then we loop over those children this way:

```
static void doTree(Element elem, String indent)
{
    String attribString = " Attributes: ";
    Enumeration attribEnum = elem.getAttributes();
    while (attribEnum.hasMoreElements()) {
        Attribute attrib =
                ((Attribute)attribEnum.nextElement());
        attribString += attrib.getName() + " = " +
                attrib.getValue() + " ";
    }

    System.out.println(indent + elem.getTagName() +
        attribString);

    if(elem.numElements() > 1){
        Enumeration enum = elem.getChildren();
        while (enum.hasMoreElements()) {
            .
            .
            .

        }
```

```
        }
    }
}
```

Finally, we get the next child and call `doTree()` again. Note that we add four more spaces to the indentation string each time we call `doTree()`:

```
static void doTree(Element elem, String indent)
{
    String attribString = " Attributes: ";
    Enumeration attribEnum = elem.getAttributes();
    while (attribEnum.hasMoreElements()) {
        Attribute attrib =
            ((Attribute)attribEnum.nextElement());
        attribString += attrib.getName() + " = " +
            attrib.getValue() + " ";
    }

    System.out.println(indent + elem.getTagName() +
        attribString);

    if(elem.numElements() > 1){
        Enumeration enum = elem.getChildren();
        while (enum.hasMoreElements()) {
            Element elem2 =
                (Element)enum.nextElement();
            doTree(elem2, indent + "    ");
        }
    }
}
```

And that's it; now run the program, giving us the following result. Note that we display the attributes of the two customer elements.

```
DOCUMENT Attributes:
    CUSTOMER Attributes: TYPE = excellent
        NAME Attributes:
            LASTNAME Attributes:
            FIRSTNAME Attributes:
        DATE Attributes:
        ORDERS Attributes:
            ITEM Attributes:
                PRODUCT Attributes:
                NUMBER Attributes:
                PRICE Attributes:
            ITEM Attributes:
                PRODUCT Attributes:
                NUMBER Attributes:
                PRICE Attributes:
    CUSTOMER Attributes: TYPE = Good
        NAME Attributes:
```

```
        LASTNAME Attributes:
        FIRSTNAME Attributes:
    DATE Attributes:
ORDERS Attributes:
    ITEM Attributes:
        PRODUCT Attributes:
        NUMBER Attributes:
        PRICE Attributes:
    ITEM Attributes:
        PRODUCT Attributes:
        NUMBER Attributes:
        PRICE Attributes:
```

Our `attlist.java` program is a success. The code for this program appears in Listing 3-3, and `attlist.xml` appears in Listing 3-4. We've started the process of creating with true XML browsers, and we'll see more about this topic in the next chapter.

Listing 3-3.
`attlist.java`.

```java
import com.ms.xml.Attribute;
import com.ms.xml.ParseException;
import com.ms.xml.Document;
import com.ms.xml.Element;

import java.util.Enumeration;
import java.io.*;
import java.io.PrintStream;
import java.net.*;

class attlist
{
    static String filename;

    public static void main(String args[])
    {
        filename = "file:////c://xml//attlist//
            attlist.xml";

        URL url = null;
        try {
            url = new URL(filename);
        }
        catch (MalformedURLException e) {
            System.out.println("Cannot create URL for: " +
                    filename);
            System.exit(0);
        }

        Document d = new Document();
```

Listing 3-3.
Continued.

```
        try {
            d.load(url);
        }
        catch (ParseException e) {
            d.reportError(e, System.out);
        }

        if (d != null) {
            doTree(d.getRoot(), "");
        }
    }

    static void doTree(Element elem, String indent)
    {
        String attribString = " Attributes: ";
        Enumeration attribEnum = elem.getAttributes();
        while (attribEnum.hasMoreElements()) {
            Attribute attrib =
                    ((Attribute)attribEnum.nextElement());
            attribString += attrib.getName() + " = " +
                attrib.getValue() + " ";
        }

        System.out.println(indent + elem.getTagName() +
            attribString);

        if(elem.numElements() > 1){
            Enumeration enum = elem.getChildren();
            while (enum.hasMoreElements()) {
                Element elem2 =
                        (Element)enum.nextElement();
                doTree(elem2, indent + "    ");
            }
        }
    }
}
```

Listing 3-4.
attlist.xml.

```
<?XML version = "1.0"?>
<!DOCTYPE DOCUMENT [
<!ELEMENT DOCUMENT (CUSTOMER)*>
<!ELEMENT CUSTOMER (NAME,DATE,ORDERS)>
<!ELEMENT NAME (LASTNAME,FIRSTNAME)>
<!ELEMENT LASTNAME (#PCDATA)>

<!ELEMENT FIRSTNAME (#PCDATA)>
<!ELEMENT DATE (#PCDATA)>
```

Continues

Listing 3-4.
Continued.

```
<!ELEMENT ORDERS (ITEM)*>
<!ELEMENT ITEM (PRODUCT,NUMBER,PRICE)>
<!ELEMENT PRODUCT (#PCDATA)>
<!ELEMENT NUMBER (#PCDATA)>
<!ELEMENT PRICE (#PCDATA)>
<!ATTLIST CUSTOMER
    TYPE CDATA #IMPLIED>
]>
<DOCUMENT>
    <CUSTOMER TYPE = "Excellent">
        <NAME>
            <LASTNAME>Edwards</LASTNAME>
            <FIRSTNAME>Britta</FIRSTNAME>
        </NAME>
        <DATE>April 17, 1998</DATE>
        <ORDERS>
            <ITEM>
                <PRODUCT>Cucumber</PRODUCT>
                <NUMBER>5</NUMBER>
                <PRICE>$1.25</PRICE>
            </ITEM>
            <ITEM>
                <PRODUCT>Lettuce</PRODUCT>
                <NUMBER>2</NUMBER>
                <PRICE>$.98</PRICE>
            </ITEM>
        </ORDERS>
    </CUSTOMER>
    <CUSTOMER TYPE = "Good">
        <NAME>
            <LASTNAME>Thompson</LASTNAME>
            <FIRSTNAME>Phoebe</FIRSTNAME>
        </NAME>
        <DATE>May 27, 1998</DATE>
        <ORDERS>
            <ITEM>
                <PRODUCT>Banana</PRODUCT>
                <NUMBER>12</NUMBER>
                <PRICE>$2.95</PRICE>
            </ITEM>
            <ITEM>
                <PRODUCT>Apple</PRODUCT>
                <NUMBER>6</NUMBER>
                <PRICE>$1.50</PRICE>
            </ITEM>
        </ORDERS>
    </CUSTOMER>
</DOCUMENT>
```

Next, we'll take a look at *entity declarations*.

Entity Declarations

Entities are made to be replaced; that is, when you include a reference to an entity in a document, you expect the parser to replace it with either other text or binary data. For example, if you declare an entity named **Number5** this way in the DTD

```
<!ENTITY  Number5 '5'>
```

then you can use that entity in the document like the following. (Note that we surround the entity reference with the characters **&** and **;**.)

```
<text>We have &Number5; bananas left.</text>
```

The parser will replace the entity reference, **&Number5;**, with the character **'5'**:

```
<text>We have 5 bananas left.</text>
```

In this way, you expect entities to be replaced when you place them in a document.

You declare entities in the DTD. See the **EntityDecl** term that follows:

```
doctypedecl::= '<!DOCTYPE' S Name (S ExternalID)?
    S? ('[' markupdecl* ']' S?)? '>'
markupdecl::= %( ( %elementdecl | %AttlistDecl |
    %EntityDecl |
    %NotationDecl | %conditionalSect | %PI | %S |
        %Comment )* )
```

An entity can be either text or binary (the parser tells them apart by how they're declared). There are two types of entities—**general** and **parameter** entities. You use **general** entities as we've just seen previously, enclosing references to them between **&** and **;**. **Parameter** entities may be used in the external part of the DTD, and in conditional sections (we'll examine conditional sections at the end of this chapter), you enclose references to parameter entities between **%** and **;**.

Here's how you declare and use entities: **EntityRef** below is a reference to a general entity, and **PEReference** is a reference to a **parameter** entity:

```
EntityDecl::= '<!ENTITY' S %Name S %EntityDef S? '>'/*
    General entities */
            | '<!ENTITY' S '%' S %Name S %EntityDef S? '>'/*
                Parameter entities */
EntityDef::= EntityValue | ExternalDef
EntityValue::= '"' ([^%&"] | PEReference | Reference)* '"'
```

```
          |    "'"
               ([^%&'] | PEReference | Reference)* "'"
     ExternalDef::= ExternalID %NDataDecl?
     ExternalID::= 'SYSTEM' S SystemLiteral|  'PUBLIC' S
          PubidLiteral S
               SystemLiteral
     NDataDecl::= S %'NDATA' S %Name
     Hex::= [0-9a-fA-F]
     CharRef::= '&#' [0-9]+ ';' | '&#x' Hex+ ';'
     Reference::= EntityRef | CharRef
     EntityRef::= '&' Name ';'                     /* General
                                                      entities */

     PEReference::= '%' Name ';'                   /* Parameter
                                                      entities */
```

NOTE *As mentioned in the last chapter, any time you've seen a* **%** *in the declarations we've been working through, it means that a parameter entity can be used at that point.*

TIP *If you use a* **parameter** *reference, the entity declaration must precede the reference to that entity. Also, for all entity references, the reference must not include recursive reference to itself. If you declare an entity more than once, only the first declaration is binding.*

Internal Entities

If the entity is defined without any separate storage file, and the replacement text is given in its declaration, the entity is called an *internal entity*. In the **EntityValue** term above, **parameter** entity references are recognized and expanded immediately. **General** entity references are not recognized at the time the entity declaration is parsed (they are expanded when you refer to the entity).

In the replacement text of an internal entity, **parameter** entity references are expanded, but references to **general** entities are not expanded before the replacement text is stored in the parser's symbol table. Also, it's worth noting that when a reference to a **general** entity is expanded in the document, the replacement text is parsed.

External Entities

If an entity is not internal, it must be external, and you declare it this way:

```
ExternalDef::= ExternalID NDataDecl?
ExternalID::= 'SYSTEM' S SystemLiteral | 'PUBLIC' S
        PubidLiteral S
            SystemLiteral
NDataDecl::= S %'NDATA' S %Name
```

If you supply a **NDataDecl** term, this entity is a binary data entity (otherwise it's a text entity). You can refer to binary entities only in attribute values declared to be of type **ENTITY** or **ENTITIES**.

Here's an example of a external entity declaration, where we declare the entity **dataFFile** to refer to the external file **data.xml**:

```
<!ENTITY dataFile  SYSTEM "data.xml">
```

Here's a declaration of an external binary entity, a **.gif** file:

```
<!ENTITY dataGraph SYSTEM "graph.gif" NDATA gif>
```

NOTE *If you use binary entities as above, you should declare the binary format—*.gif *in the above example—with a notation declaration (coming up next).*

Predefined Entities

As mentioned in the last chapter, there are several predefined entities in XML. The predefined entities are: **amp**, **lt**, **gt**, **apos**, and **quot**. These entities stand for the following characters respectively: &, <, >, ', and ". If you use one of those entities in a document, and you want to keep the document valid, you must declare the entity, even though it's already predefined. Here's how you declare these entities:

```
<!ENTITY lt        "<">
<!ENTITY gt        ">">
<!ENTITY amp       "&">
<!ENTITY apos      "'">
<!ENTITY quot      '"'>
```

When you use one of these predefined entities in an XML document, they are replaced with the corresponding replacement text. Now that we've covered the theory, let's see example of entities at work with the MSXML parser.

The entities **Example**

In this example, we'll use this XML document, `entities.xml`:

```
<?XML version="1.0"?>
<!DOCTYPE Note system "entities.dtd" >
<text>We have &Number5; bananas left.</text>
```

This document uses an external DTD, stored in `entities.dtd`:

```
<!ENTITY Number5 '5'>
<!ELEMENT text   (#PCDATA) >
```

In the DTD, we declare an entity named **Number5** with the replacement text `'5'`. When we refer to that entity in the document, the parser should replace that reference with the replacement text:

```
<?XML version="1.0"?>
<!DOCTYPE Note system "entities.dtd" >
<text>We have &Number5; bananas left.</text>
```

When we display the text of this document, this is what we should see, where the entity is replaced with its replacement text:

```
We have 5 bananas left.
```

Let's write this program now. We start the program, entities.java, by reading in the `entities.xml` file:

```
import com.ms.xml.ParseException;
import com.ms.xml.Document;
import com.ms.xml.Element;
import java.util.Enumeration;
import java.net.*;

class entities
{
    static String filename;
    static URL url;

    public static void main(String args[])
    {
        filename = "file:////c://xml//entities//
            entities.xml";

        try {
            url = new URL(filename);
        }
        catch (MalformedURLException ex) {
```

```
                        System.out.println("Cannot create URL for: "
                            + filename);
                        System.exit(0);
                }

            Document d = new Document();

            try {
                    d.load(url);
            }
            catch (ParseException e) {
                    d.reportError(e, System.out);
            }
                .
                .
                .
```

The parser does all the work for us, replacing the entity reference with the entity's replacement text when we call **getText()**. That means that to see the text of the document—with the replacement text already in place—we just have to display the document's text with **getText()**:

```
import com.ms.xml.ParseException;
import com.ms.xml.Document;
import com.ms.xml.Element;

import java.util.Enumeration;
import java.net.*;

class entities
{
    static String filename;
    static URL url;

    public static void main(String args[])
    {
        filename = "file:////c://xml//entities//
            entities.xml";
            .
            .
            .
        if (d != null) {
            System.out.println(d.getText());
        }
    }
}
```

That's all there is to it. Run the program now. When you do, you see the result:

```
We have 5 bananas left.
```

As you can see, the entity **Number5** has been replaced with its replacement text. Our entities program is a success. The code for this example, **entities.java**, appears in Listing 3-5, **entities.xml** appears in Listing 3-6, and **entities.dtd** appears in Listing 3-7.

Next, we'll take a look at notation declarations.

**Listing 3-5.
entities.java.**

```java
import com.ms.xml.ParseException;
import com.ms.xml.Document;
import com.ms.xml.Element;

import java.util.Enumeration;
import java.net.*;

class entities

{

    static String filename;

    static URL url;

    public static void main(String args[])
    {
        filename = "file:////c://xml//entities//
            entities.xml";

        try {
            url = new URL(filename);
        }
        catch (MalformedURLException ex) {
            System.out.println("Cannot create URL for: " +
                filename);
            System.exit(0);
        }

        Document d = new Document();

        try {
            d.load(url);
        }
        catch (ParseException e) {
            d.reportError(e, System.out);
        }

        if (d != null) {
            System.out.println(d.getText());
        }
    }
}
```

Listing 3-6.
entities.xml.

```
<?XML version="1.0"?>

<!DOCTYPE Note system "entities.dtd" >

<text>We have &Number5; bananas left.</text>
```

Listing 3-7.
entities.dtd.

```
<!ENTITY   Number5 '5'>
<!ELEMENT   text   (#PCDATA) >
```

Notation Declarations

You use a notation to identify an external binary entity format; notation declarations are part of the DTD:

```
doctypedecl::= '<!DOCTYPE' S Name (S ExternalID)?
        S? ('[' markupdecl* ']' S?)? '>'
markupdecl::= %( ( %elementdecl | %AttlistDecl |
      %EntityDecl |
          %NotationDecl | %conditionalSect | %PI | %S |
              %Comment )* )
```

By declaring a notation, you identify the format of external binary entities; in this way, you can think of a notation declaration as a format declaration. Here's how you make a notation declaration:

```
NotationDecl::= '<!NOTATION' S %Name S %ExternalID S? '>'
```

Besides listing the format by name, you can also specify the name of a helper application that the parser might use to launch or process the binary entity. Here's an example that lists Microsoft's Word for Windows as a helper application, connecting it to the notation **doc**:

```
<!NOTATION doc SYSTEM "winword.exe" >
```

The last topic we'll cover in this chapter is *conditional sections*.

Conditional Sections

You can use a conditional section to explicitly include or exclude a part of the DTD. This is a good idea if your document is under development or has several different versions that you want to switch among.

Here's how conditional sections are defined:

```
conditionalSect::= includeSect | ignoreSect
includeSect::= '<![' %'INCLUDE' '[' (%markupdecl*)* ']]>'
ignoreSect::= '<![' %'IGNORE' '[' ( ((SkipLit | Comment |
     PI) -
        (Char* ']]>' Char*)) | ignoreSect | (Char - ([<'"]
            | ']'))*
        | ('<!' (Char - ('-' | '['))* ) ) ']]>'
```

You can place anything in a conditional section that you would normally place in a DTD. If the keyword is **INCLUDE**, the text in the conditional section is included in the DTD. If the keyword is **IGNORE**, the text is ignored.

Here's an example of a conditional section: the included sections are parsed, and the ignored sections are not:

```
<![IGNORE[
<!ELEMENT researchPaper (header, body, appendix?)>
]]>

<![INCLUDE[
<!ELEMENT researchPaper (comments*,  header, body,
     appendix?)>
]]>

<![INCLUDE[
<!ELEMENT comments (#PCDATA)>
]]>
```

Using conditional sections, you can tailor a DTD the way you want it to match different versions of your document, switching between versions easily by simply having the parser include or ignore sections as you like.

You can use entities, but only **parameter** entities, in a conditional section, like the following. (Note that we declare the entities with a **%** symbol to make them **parameter** entities.)

```
<!ENTITY % proposed 'IGNORE' >
<!ENTITY % reviewed 'INCLUDE' >

<![%proposed;[
<!ELEMENT researchPaper (header, body, appendix?)>
]]>

<![%reviewed;[
<!ELEMENT researchPaper (comments*,  header, body,
     appendix?)>
]]>

<![%reviewed;[
<!ELEMENT comments (#PCDATA)>
]]>
```

NOTE   *The MSXML parser does not yet support conditional sections.*

SUMMARY

That's it for conditional sections, and that's it for this chapter.

In this chapter, we've examined the DTD in depth, seeing how to declare elements, attributes and attribute lists, entities, notations, and conditional sections. We've finished our coverage of Part I of the XML specification. In the next chapter, we'll continue our exploration of XML when we build XML *browsers*.

4

Creating XML Browsers: Four Complete Examples

In this chapter, we'll see how to create XML browsers, which we'll use to read and interpret XML tags in XML documents. XML is a free-form language, which means that we design it ourselves, so we can't expect a prewritten browser to know how we want to handle the markup correctly.

For example, let's say we had a document whose text could appear colored either red or blue and that we set up a <RED> tag and a <BLUE> tag to indicate the text colorings we wanted in this XML document:

```
<?XML VERSION = "1.0" ?>
<!DOCTYPE COLORDOCUMENT [
<!ELEMENT COLORDOCUMENT (BLUE|RED)*>
<!ELEMENT BLUE (#PCDATA|BLUE)*>
<!ELEMENT RED (#PCDATA|RED)*>
]>
<COLORDOCUMENT>
    <RED>Britta</RED>
    <RED>
        Adam
    </RED>
    <BLUE>
        Christina
        <BLUE>Phoebe</BLUE>
        <BLUE>Fred</BLUE>
        Edward
    </BLUE>
    <RED>
        Sammy
    </RED>
</COLORDOCUMENT>
```

If you opened this document in a commercial HTML browser, that browser would have no idea what to do with the <RED> and <BLUE> tags (and would probably display them as text).

We'll have to interpret tags like <RED> and <BLUE> ourselves, making use of them in Java applications and coloring the text ourselves. And that's what our XML browsers will be—Java applications that use the MSXML parser to read in and parse XML documents, making use of the tags in that document as we have designed them to.

In this chapter, then, we'll see how to create XML browser applications. This will involve some detailed work in dissecting XML document trees using recursion—a process we've had a little experience with in the last chapter. We'll create a number of examples in this chapter—a tree example that will display the tree structure of an XML document; an example named **browser** that displays the character data of an XML document; an example named **indenter** that lets us use two tags: <INDENT> and <INDENTDOUBLE> to format text; and an example named caps that lets us display text in lower- or uppercase with the tags <LOWER> and <UPPER>. Let's start now with the tree example.

The tree Example

Our first XML browser will display the tree structure of an XML document. For example, we might pass this XML document to the tree application:

```
<?XML version = "1.0" ?>
<!DOCTYPE DOCUMENT [
<!ELEMENT DOCUMENT (CUSTOMER)*>
<!ELEMENT CUSTOMER (NAME,DATE,ORDERS)>
<!ELEMENT NAME (LASTNAME,FIRSTNAME)>
<!ELEMENT LASTNAME (#PCDATA)>
<!ELEMENT FIRSTNAME (#PCDATA)>
<!ELEMENT DATE (#PCDATA)>
<!ELEMENT ORDERS (ITEM)*>
<!ELEMENT ITEM (PRODUCT,NUMBER,PRICE)>
<!ELEMENT PRODUCT (#PCDATA)>
<!ELEMENT NUMBER (#PCDATA)>
<!ELEMENT PRICE (#PCDATA)>
]>
<DOCUMENT>
    <CUSTOMER>
        <NAME>
            <LASTNAME>Edwards</LASTNAME>
            <FIRSTNAME>Britta</FIRSTNAME>
        </NAME>
        <DATE>April 17, 1998</DATE>
        <ORDERS>
            <ITEM>
                <PRODUCT>Cucumber</PRODUCT>
                <NUMBER>5</NUMBER>
                <PRICE>$1.25</PRICE>
            </ITEM>
            <ITEM>
                <PRODUCT>Lettuce</PRODUCT>
                <NUMBER>2</NUMBER>
                <PRICE>$.98</PRICE>
            </ITEM>
        </ORDERS>
    </CUSTOMER>
    <CUSTOMER>
        <NAME>
            <LASTNAME>Thompson</LASTNAME>
            <FIRSTNAME>Phoebe</FIRSTNAME>
        </NAME>
        <DATE>May 27, 1998</DATE>
        <ORDERS>
            <ITEM>
                <PRODUCT>Banana</PRODUCT>
                <NUMBER>12</NUMBER>
                <PRICE>$2.95</PRICE>
            </ITEM>
            <ITEM>
                <PRODUCT>Apple</PRODUCT>
                <NUMBER>6</NUMBER>
                <PRICE>$1.50</PRICE>
            </ITEM>
        </ORDERS>
    </CUSTOMER>
</DOCUMENT>
```

The tree application will take the preceding document and display the element tree of that document like this, displaying the start tag and end tag structure of the document and indenting it properly:

```
<DOCUMENT>
    <CUSTOMER>
        <NAME>
            <LASTNAME>
            </LASTNAME>
            <FIRSTNAME>
            </FIRSTNAME>
        </NAME>
        <DATE>
        </DATE>
        <ORDERS>
            <ITEM>
                <PRODUCT>
                </PRODUCT>
                <NUMBER>
                </NUMBER>
                <PRICE>
                </PRICE>
            </ITEM>
            <ITEM>
                <PRODUCT>
                </PRODUCT>
                <NUMBER>
                </NUMBER>
                <PRICE>
                </PRICE>
            </ITEM>
        </ORDERS>
    </CUSTOMER>
    <CUSTOMER>
        <NAME>
            <LASTNAME>
            </LASTNAME>
            <FIRSTNAME>
            </FIRSTNAME>
        </NAME>
        <DATE>
        </DATE>
        <ORDERS>
            <ITEM>
                <PRODUCT>
                </PRODUCT>
                <NUMBER>
                </NUMBER>
                <PRICE>
                </PRICE>
            </ITEM>
            <ITEM>
```

```
                    <PRODUCT>
                    </PRODUCT>
                    <NUMBER>
                    </NUMBER>
                    <PRICE>
                    </PRICE>
                </ITEM>
            </ORDERS>
        </CUSTOMER>
    </DOCUMENT>
```

Let's start this example now; the code in this example will give us experience with the process of dissecting and displaying the data in XML documents, which is what XML browsers are all about.

We start by creating the Java file for this application, **tree.java**, and adding code to that file to read in the document **tree.xml**:

```java
import com.ms.xml.ParseException;
import com.ms.xml.Document;

import java.net.*;

class tree
{
    static String filename;

    public static void main(String args[])
    {
        URL url = null;

        try {
            url = new URL("file:////c://xml//tree//
                tree.xml");
        }
        catch (MalformedURLException e) {
            System.out.println("Cannot create URL for:
                " + filename);
            System.exit(0);
        }

        Document d = new Document();

        try {
            d.load(url);
        }
        catch (ParseException e) {
            d.reportError(e, System.out);
        }
            .
            .
            .
```

TIP   *Browser applications would be of limited utility if they could only read in one file (such as the tree example, which is written to read in only the* `tree.xml` *file). In windowed applications, you can read the name—and URL— of the document the user wants to read in using a text field. If the user specifies only a local filename in the same directory as the application without giving the file's path (which you need to create an URL), you can create a File object using the Java File class, passing it the filename, then use the File class' getAbsolutePath() method to get the file's whole path. Use the* `http://` *prefix for files on the Web and the* `file://` *prefix for files on the local computer when you create an URL object for the file.*

We'll use recursion to work through the branches of the tree, so we set up a method we might call **doTree()** for that purpose, and pass it an indentation string (as we did in our **attlist** example in the last chapter) so that we can indent successive levels of the document's tree. We start by calling the **doTree()** method with the document's root element, passing **doTree()** empty string (**""**) for the indentation string since the root element should not be indented:

```
import com.ms.xml.ParseException;
import com.ms.xml.Document;
import com.ms.xml.Element;

import java.net.*;

class tree
{
    static String filename;

    public static void main(String args[])
    {
        .
        .
        .
        .
        if (d != null) {
            doTree(d.getRoot(), "");
        }
    }
}
```

Now we're ready to write the **doTree()** method. The **doTree()** method works by displaying the current element's start tag, then adding four spaces to the indentation string and looping over the tag's children. After it's processed the children, it displays the current element's end tag.

We start by displaying the current element's start tag, which we get with the `getTagName()` method:

```
import com.ms.xml.ParseException;
import com.ms.xml.Document;
import com.ms.xml.Element;

import java.io.*;
import java.io.PrintStream;
import java.net.*;

class tree
{
    static String filename;

    public static void main(String args[])
    {
        .
        .
        .
    }

    static void doTree(Element elem, String indent)
    {
        System.out.println(indent + "<" +
            elem.getTagName() + ">");
        .
        .
        .
    }
}
```

If this element has children, we loop over those children, starting by getting an enumeration of those children this way:

```
import com.ms.xml.ParseException;
import com.ms.xml.Document;
import com.ms.xml.Element;

import java.util.Enumeration;
import java.io.*;
import java.io.PrintStream;
import java.net.*;

class tree
{
    static String filename;

    public static void main(String args[])
    {
        .
```

```
          .
          .
     }

     static void doTree(Element elem, String indent)
     {
         System.out.println(indent + "<" +
             elem.getTagName() + ">");
->    if(elem.numElements() > 1){
->        Enumeration enum = elem.getChildren();
              .
              .
              .

->    }
     }
}
```

Then we loop over the child elements in the enumeration and call
doTree() again to handle each child—note that we add four spaces to the
indentation string to indent each deeper level of the tree correctly:

```
import com.ms.xml.ParseException;
import com.ms.xml.Document;
import com.ms.xml.Element;

import java.util.Enumeration;
import java.io.*;
import java.io.PrintStream;
import java.net.*;

class tree
{
    static String filename;

    public static void main(String args[])
    {
          .
          .
          .
    }

    static void doTree(Element elem, String indent)
    {
        System.out.println(indent + "<" +
            elem.getTagName() + ">");
        if(elem.numElements() > 1){
            Enumeration enum = elem.getChildren();
->          while (enum.hasMoreElements()) {
->              Element elem2 =
                    (Element)enum.nextElement();
->              doTree(elem2, indent + "    ");
```

```
    ->           }
              }
          }
      }
```

Finally, after looping over all the element's children, we display the close tag for the element:

```java
import com.ms.xml.ParseException;
import com.ms.xml.Document;
import com.ms.xml.Element;

import java.util.Enumeration;
import java.io.*;
import java.io.PrintStream;
import java.net.*;

class tree
{
    static String filename;

    public static void main(String args[])
    {
        .
        .
        .
    }

    static void doTree(Element elem, String indent)
    {
        System.out.println(indent + "<" +
            elem.getTagName() + ">");
        if(elem.numElements() > 1){
            Enumeration enum = elem.getChildren();
            while (enum.hasMoreElements()) {
                Element elem2 =
                    (Element)enum.nextElement();
                doTree(elem2, indent + "    ");
            }
        }
->      System.out.println(indent + "</" +
            elem.getTagName() + ">");
    }
}
```

And that's it—using recursion, we're able to dissect an XML document's tree and display it.

Running the tree example on the preceding XML document gives us that document's tree structure as created by its start and end tags; here's the console output of the tree program:

```
<DOCUMENT>
    <CUSTOMER>
        <NAME>
            <LASTNAME>
            </LASTNAME>
            <FIRSTNAME>
            </FIRSTNAME>
        </NAME>
        <DATE>
        </DATE>
        <ORDERS>
            <ITEM>
                <PRODUCT>
                </PRODUCT>
                <NUMBER>
                </NUMBER>
                <PRICE>
                </PRICE>
            </ITEM>
            <ITEM>
                <PRODUCT>
                </PRODUCT>
                <NUMBER>
                </NUMBER>
                <PRICE>
                </PRICE>
            </ITEM>
        </ORDERS>
    </CUSTOMER>
    <CUSTOMER>
        <NAME>
            <LASTNAME>
            </LASTNAME>
            <FIRSTNAME>
            </FIRSTNAME>
        </NAME>
        <DATE>
        </DATE>
        <ORDERS>
            <ITEM>
                <PRODUCT>
                </PRODUCT>
                <NUMBER>
                </NUMBER>
                <PRICE>
                </PRICE>
            </ITEM>
            <ITEM>
                <PRODUCT>
                </PRODUCT>
                <NUMBER>
                </NUMBER>
                <PRICE>
```

```
                    </PRICE>
                  </ITEM>
                </ORDERS>
              </CUSTOMER>
            </DOCUMENT>
```

That's it—now we've dissected the **tree.xml** file and displayed the tree structure of that file using a simple recursion algorithm. The tree example is a success—the code for this example, **tree.java**, appears in Listing 4-1, and the XML file we read in, **tree.xml**, appears in Listing 4-2.

Listing 4-1.
tree.java.

```java
import com.ms.xml.ParseException;
import com.ms.xml.Document;
import com.ms.xml.Element;

import java.util.Enumeration;
import java.io.*;
import java.io.PrintStream;
import java.net.*;

class tree
{
    static String filename;

    public static void main(String args[])
    {
        URL url = null;

        try {
            url = new URL("file:////c://xml//tree//
                    tree.xml");
        }
        catch (MalformedURLException e) {
            System.out.println("Cannot create URL for: " +
                    filename);
            System.exit(0);
        }

        Document d = new Document();

        try {
            d.load(url);
        }
        catch (ParseException e) {
            d.reportError(e, System.out);
        }
```

Continues

Listing 4-1.
Continued.

```java
        if (d != null) {
            doTree(d.getRoot(), "");
        }
    }

    static void doTree(Element elem, String indent)
    {
        System.out.println(indent + "<" +
            elem.getTagName() + ">");
        if(elem.numElements() > 1){
            Enumeration enum = elem.getChildren();
            while (enum.hasMoreElements()) {
                Element elem2 =
                        (Element)enum.nextElement();
                doTree(elem2, indent + "    ");
            }
        }
        System.out.println(indent + "</" +
            elem.getTagName() + ">");
    }
}
```

Listing 4-2.
tree.xml.

```xml
<?XML version = "1.0" ?>
<!DOCTYPE DOCUMENT [
<!ELEMENT DOCUMENT (CUSTOMER)*>
<!ELEMENT CUSTOMER (NAME,DATE,ORDERS)>
<!ELEMENT NAME (LASTNAME,FIRSTNAME)>
<!ELEMENT LASTNAME (#PCDATA)>
<!ELEMENT FIRSTNAME (#PCDATA)>
<!ELEMENT DATE (#PCDATA)>
<!ELEMENT ORDERS (ITEM)*>
<!ELEMENT ITEM (PRODUCT,NUMBER,PRICE)>
<!ELEMENT PRODUCT (#PCDATA)>
<!ELEMENT NUMBER (#PCDATA)>
<!ELEMENT PRICE (#PCDATA)>
]>
<DOCUMENT>
    <CUSTOMER>
        <NAME>
            <LASTNAME>Edwards</LASTNAME>
            <FIRSTNAME>Britta</FIRSTNAME>
        </NAME>
        <DATE>April 17, 1998</DATE>
        <ORDERS>
            <ITEM>
                <PRODUCT>Cucumber</PRODUCT>
                <NUMBER>5</NUMBER>
                <PRICE>$1.25</PRICE>
```

Listing 4-2.
Continued.

```
                </ITEM>
                <ITEM>
                    <PRODUCT>Lettuce</PRODUCT>
                    <NUMBER>2</NUMBER>
                    <PRICE>$.98</PRICE>
                </ITEM>
            </ORDERS>
        </CUSTOMER>
        <CUSTOMER>
            <NAME>
                <LASTNAME>Thompson</LASTNAME>
                <FIRSTNAME>Phoebe</FIRSTNAME>
            </NAME>
            <DATE>May 27, 1998</DATE>
            <ORDERS>
                <ITEM>
                    <PRODUCT>Banana</PRODUCT>
                    <NUMBER>12</NUMBER>
                    <PRICE>$2.95</PRICE>
                </ITEM>
                <ITEM>
                    <PRODUCT>Apple</PRODUCT>
                    <NUMBER>6</NUMBER>
                    <PRICE>$1.50</PRICE>
                </ITEM>
            </ORDERS>
        </CUSTOMER>
</DOCUMENT>
```

The tree example has given us some experience in dissecting an XML document, but it's a console-oriented example. When you say "browser," people think of a window-oriented application that displays its documents in a graphical way. Our next example does just that.

The browser Example

Our next example will be a windowed browser named **browser.java**. When the user runs this application, we'll present them with a window with a button in it labeled Browse:

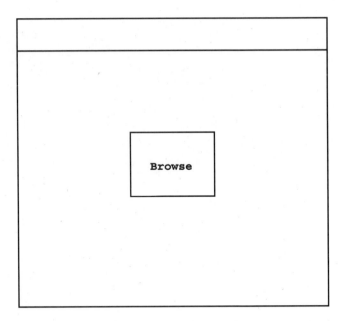

When the user clicks the Browse button, we'll read in our example document, which we'll call **browser.xml** here:

```
<?XML version = "1.0" ?>
<!DOCTYPE DOCUMENT [
<!ELEMENT DOCUMENT (CUSTOMER)*>
<!ELEMENT CUSTOMER (NAME,DATE,ORDERS)>
<!ELEMENT NAME (LASTNAME,FIRSTNAME)>
<!ELEMENT LASTNAME (#PCDATA)>
<!ELEMENT FIRSTNAME (#PCDATA)>
<!ELEMENT DATE (#PCDATA)>
<!ELEMENT ORDERS (ITEM)*>
<!ELEMENT ITEM (PRODUCT,NUMBER,PRICE)>
<!ELEMENT PRODUCT (#PCDATA)>
<!ELEMENT NUMBER (#PCDATA)>
<!ELEMENT PRICE (#PCDATA)>
]>
<DOCUMENT>
<CUSTOMER>
    <NAME>
        <LASTNAME>Edwards</LASTNAME>
        <FIRSTNAME>Britta</FIRSTNAME>
    </NAME>
    <DATE>April 17, 1998</DATE>
    <ORDERS>
        <ITEM>
            <PRODUCT>Cucumber</PRODUCT>
            <NUMBER>5</NUMBER>
```

```
                    <PRICE>$1.25</PRICE>
              </ITEM>
              <ITEM>
                    <PRODUCT>Lettuce</PRODUCT>
                    <NUMBER>2</NUMBER>
                    <PRICE>$.98</PRICE>
              </ITEM>
        </ORDERS>
  </CUSTOMER>
  <CUSTOMER>
        <NAME>
              <LASTNAME>Thompson</LASTNAME>
              <FIRSTNAME>Phoebe</FIRSTNAME>
        </NAME>
        <DATE>May 27, 1998</DATE>
        <ORDERS>
              <ITEM>
                    <PRODUCT>Banana</PRODUCT>
                    <NUMBER>12</NUMBER>
                    <PRICE>$2.95</PRICE>
              </ITEM>
              <ITEM>
                    <PRODUCT>Apple</PRODUCT>
                    <NUMBER>6</NUMBER>
                    <PRICE>$1.50</PRICE>
              </ITEM>
        </ORDERS>
  </CUSTOMER>
  </DOCUMENT>
```

The browser will then display the content of the document (as opposed to the document's tags, as in the last example), just as any browser might as shown on the following page.

Here we'll indent each successive line of the document's content to indicate the document's structure. This will be our first windowed browser, so let's get started immediately.

We begin by declaring a new applet class named browser in the **browser.java** file:

```
import java.applet.Applet;

public class browser extends Applet{
      .
      .
      .
}
```

Then, in the **main()** method, we create a new window of the browser-Frame class (which we'll write in a moment), install the applet in that window, and call the applet's **init()** method:

Edwards

Britta

April 17, 1

Cucumber

| Browse |

5

$1.25

Lettuce

2

$.98

Thompson

Phoebe

May 27, 1988

Banana

12

$2.95

Apple

```
import java.applet.Applet;

public class browser extends Applet{

    public static void main(String args[])
    {
        browserFrame frame = new browserFrame("XML
Browser");
```

```
            frame.show();
            frame.hide();
            frame.resize(320, 240);

            browser applet = new browser();

            frame.add("Center", applet);
            applet.init();
            applet.start();
            frame.show();
        }
    }
```

The browserFrame class is just a standard window of the kind we've created before:

```
class browserFrame extends Frame
{
    public browserFrame(String str)
    {
        super (str);
    }

    public boolean handleEvent(Event evt)
    {
        switch (evt.id)
        {
            case Event.WINDOW_DESTROY:
                dispose();
                System.exit(0);
                return true;

            default:
                return super.handleEvent(evt);
        }
    }
}
```

In the applet's init() method, we add the button we'll use, giving it the caption "Browse":

```
import java.awt.*;
import java.applet.Applet;

public class browser extends Applet{

    Button button1;

    public static void main(String args[])
    {
        .
        .
```

```
        }

        public void init(){
            button1 = new Button("Browse");
            add(button1);
        }
    }
```

In the **action()** method, we read in the **browser.xml** document and call the recursive method **doTree()**. The **doTree()** method will place the content of the XML document in a String array named displayLines[ ], which we'll display in the applet's **paint()** method (each string in this array corresponds to one line on the screen). To make sure that array is displayed, we call the **repaint()** method (to force Java to call the **paint()** method) after calling **doTree()**:

```
import com.ms.xml.ParseException;
import com.ms.xml.Document;
import com.ms.xml.Element;

import java.awt.*;
import java.net.*;
import java.applet.Applet;

public class browser extends Applet{

    Button button1;
    static String filename;

    public static void main(String args[])
    {
        .
        .
        .
    }

    public void init(){
        .
        .
        .
    }

    public boolean action (Event e, Object o){

        URL url = null;
        try {
            url = new
URL("file:////c://xml//browser//browser.xml");
        }
        catch (MalformedURLException e1) {
```

```
                    System.out.println("Cannot create URL for: " +
        filename);
                    System.exit(0);
            }

            Document d = new Document();

            try {
                d.load(url);
            }
            catch (ParseException e3) {
                d.reportError(e3, System.out);
            }

            if (d != null) {
                doTree(d.getRoot(), "");
                repaint();
            }
            return true;
        }
```

Now we can write the doTree() method:

```
import com.ms.xml.ParseException;
import com.ms.xml.Document;
import com.ms.xml.Element;

import java.util.Enumeration;
import java.awt.*;
import java.net.*;
import java.applet.Applet;

public class browser extends Applet{

    Button button1;
    static String filename;

    public static void main(String args[])
    {
        .
        .
        .
    }

    public void init(){
        .
        .
        .
    }

    public boolean action (Event e, Object o)
    {
```

```
                .
                .
                .
        }


    void doTree(Element elem, String indent)
    {

        }
    }
```

The `doTree()` method here has two tasks: to loop over the current element's children, calling `doTree()` again for each of them, or to add the current element's character data to the array of Strings we've named displayStrings[ ] (this is the array we'll print out in the `paint()` method).

We start `doTree()`, then, by checking whether there are any child elements in the current element (the `numElements()` method always returns at least a value of 1, for the current element—if it returns more than 1, there are child elements):

```
void doTree(Element elem, String indent)
{
    if(elem.numElements() > 1){
                .
                .
                .

    }
}
```

We continue by looping over the element's children, if there are any:

```
void doTree(Element elem, String indent)
{
    if(elem.numElements() > 1){
        Enumeration enum = elem.getChildren();
        while (enum.hasMoreElements()) {
                .
                .
                .

        }
    }
}
```

In this loop, we first get the next child element, calling it elem2:

```
void doTree(Element elem, String indent)
{
```

```
if(elem.numElements() > 1){
    Enumeration enum = elem.getChildren();
    while (enum.hasMoreElements()) {
        Element elem2 = (Element)enum.nextElement();
                    .
                    .
                    .
    }
}
}
```

Then we call **doTree()** again for that child element, adding four spaces to the indent string to indent each successive level correctly:

```
void doTree(Element elem, String indent)
{
    if(elem.numElements() > 1){
        Enumeration enum = elem.getChildren();
        while (enum.hasMoreElements()) {
            Element elem2 = (Element)enum.nextElement();
            doTree(elem2, indent + "    ");
        }
    }
}
```

That takes care of the child elements. On the other hand, if the element doesn't have any child elements, we'll assume this element holds character data that we should display in our browser's window.

NOTE *In our next example, we'll start handling more sophisticated documents where elements can contain both character data and child elements; in this simple example, we'll restrict elements to containing one or the other type of content: child elements or character data.*

We'll place the element's character data in the displayStrings[ ] array and use an integer index into that array named numberDisplayLines; here's how we set up those two new items in our program:

```
import com.ms.xml.ParseException;
import com.ms.xml.Document;
import com.ms.xml.Element;

import java.util.Enumeration;
import java.awt.*;
import java.net.*;
import java.applet.Applet;
```

```
public class browser extends Applet{

    Button button1;
    static String filename;
->  static String displayStrings[] = new String[100];
->  static int numberDisplayLines = 0;

    public static void main(String args[])
    {
        .
        .
        .
```

We add the current element's character data to the displayStrings[ ] array this way—note that we include the indentation string as well to indent the current entry properly:

```
void doTree(Element elem, String indent)
{
    if(elem.numElements() > 1){
        Enumeration enum = elem.getChildren();
        while (enum.hasMoreElements()) {
            Element elem2 = (Element)enum.nextElement();
            doTree(elem2, indent + "    ");
        }
    }else{
        displayStrings[numberDisplayLines++] = indent +
            elem.getText();
    }
}
```

That completes `doTree()`. The last step in completing our example is to add the `paint()` method to display the content of the XML document as stored in the displayStrings[ ] array:

```
import com.ms.xml.ParseException;
import com.ms.xml.Document;
import com.ms.xml.Element;

import java.util.Enumeration;
import java.awt.*;
import java.net.*;
import java.applet.Applet;

public class browser extends Applet{

    Button button1;
    static String filename;
    static String displayStrings[] = new String[100];
    static int numberDisplayLines = 0;
```

```
            public static void main(String args[])
            {
                    .
                    .
                    .
            }

            public void init(){
                    .
                    .
                    .
            }

            public boolean action (Event e, Object o)
            {
                    .
                    .
                    .
            }


            void doTree(Element elem, String indent)
            {
                    .
                    .
                    .
            }

            public void paint(Graphics g)
            {
                    .
                    .
                    .
    -> }
    }
```

In the **paint()** method, we want to display the strings in the array displayStrings[ ] in the browser's window. We've already seen that we can use the Java Graphics class' **drawString()** method to display a line of text in a window, but we'll have multiple lines of text here—how do we handle that? We will have to find the height of each line and move down to the next line ourselves in order to display each successive line.

Using the FontMetrics Class

We can find the height of each text line on the screen with the Java Font-Metrics class. This class holds a great deal of information about a font—to use it, we start by creating an object of that class using the getFont-

`Metrics()` method and passing to that method the applet's current font, which we get with the `getFont()` method:

```
public void paint(Graphics g)
{
    FontMetrics fontmetrics = getFontMetrics(getFont());
        .
        .
        .
}
```

Now we can get the height of text lines using the FontMetrics class' `getHeight()` method.

To display our text, then, we set up a loop that will loop over all the entries in the displayStrings[ ] array:

```
public void paint(Graphics g)
{
    FontMetrics fontmetrics = getFontMetrics(getFont());

    for(int index = 0; index < numberDisplayLines;
        index++){
            .
            .
            .
    }
}
```

Then we set up a variable, y, to hold the vertical location of our current text line, adding the height of a text line to that variable each time through the loop:

```
public void paint(Graphics g)
{
    int y = 0;
    FontMetrics fontmetrics = getFontMetrics(getFont());

    for(int index = 0; index < numberDisplayLines; in-
dex++){
        y += fontmetrics.getHeight();
            .
            .
            .
    }
}
```

Finally, we can display the current line of text in the displayStrings[ ] array at the location (0, y) using the drawString() method:

```
public void paint(Graphics g)
{
```

```
int y = 0;
FontMetrics fontmetrics = getFontMetrics(getFont());

for(int index = 0; index < numberDisplayLines; in-
dex++){
        y += fontmetrics.getHeight();
        g.drawString(displayStrings[index], 0, y);
    }
}
```

The browser application is ready to run now—when you do run it, you see the window in Figure 4-1, which presents the user with the Browse button.

When the user clicks the Browse button, the program reads in the browser.xml file and displays the content of that file, indenting for each level, as shown in Figure 4-2.

The browser application is a success—now we've created a rudimentary XML graphical browser.

The code for this application, **browser.java**, appears in Listing 4-3, and the XML document it reads in, **browser.xml**, appears in Listing 4-4.

Figure 4-1.
The browser application.

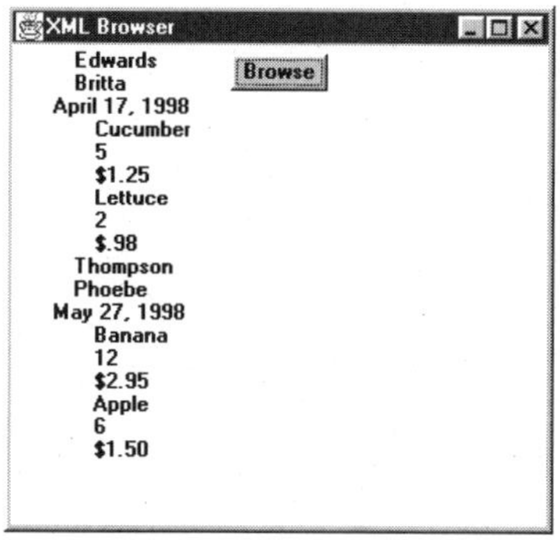

Figure 4-2.
Reading in and displaying an XML file.

Listing 4-3.
browser.java.

```
import com.ms.xml.ParseException;

import com.ms.xml.Document;
import com.ms.xml.Element;

import java.util.Enumeration;
import java.awt.*;
import java.net.*;
import java.applet.Applet;


public class browser extends Applet{

    Button button1;
    static String filename;
    static String displayStrings[] = new String[100];
    static int numberDisplayLines = 0;

    public static void main(String args[])
    {
        browserFrame frame = new browserFrame("XML
            Browser");

        frame.show();
        frame.hide();
        frame.resize(320, 240);

        browser applet = new browser();

        frame.add("Center", applet);
        applet.init();
        applet.start();
        frame.show();
    }

    public void init(){
        button1 = new Button("Browse");
        add(button1);
    }

    public boolean action (Event e, Object o){

        URL url = null;
        try {
            url = new URL("file:////c://xml//browser//
                browser.xml");
        }
        catch (MalformedURLException e1) {
            System.out.println("Cannot create URL for: " +
                filename);
            System.exit(0);
        }
```

Listing 4-3.
Continued.

```
        Document d = new Document();

        try {
            d.load(url);
        }
        catch (ParseException e3) {
            d.reportError(e3, System.out);
        }

        if (d != null) {
            doTree(d.getRoot(), "");
            repaint();
        }
        return true;
    }


    void doTree(Element elem, String indent)
    {
        if(elem.numElements() > 1){
            Enumeration enum = elem.getChildren();
            while (enum.hasMoreElements()) {
                Element elem2 =
                    (Element)enum.nextElement();
                doTree(elem2, indent + "    ");
            }
        }else{
            displayStrings[numberDisplayLines++] = indent
                + elem.getText();
        }
    }

    public void paint(Graphics g)
    {
        int y = 0;
        FontMetrics fontmetrics =
            getFontMetrics(getFont());

        for(int index = 0; index < numberDisplayLines;
            index++){
            y += fontmetrics.getHeight();
            g.drawString(displayStrings[index], 0, y);
        }
    }

}

class browserFrame extends Frame
{
    public browserFrame(String str)
```

Continues

Listing 4-3.
Continued.

```
    {
        super (str);
    }

    public boolean handleEvent(Event evt)
    {
        switch (evt.id)
        {
            case Event.WINDOW_DESTROY:
                dispose();
                System.exit(0);
                return true;

            default:
                return super.handleEvent(evt);
        }
    }

}
```

Listing 4-4.
browser.xml.

```
<?XML version = "1.0" ?>
<!DOCTYPE DOCUMENT [
<!ELEMENT DOCUMENT (CUSTOMER)*>
<!ELEMENT CUSTOMER (NAME,DATE,ORDERS)>
<!ELEMENT NAME (LASTNAME,FIRSTNAME)>
<!ELEMENT LASTNAME (#PCDATA)>
<!ELEMENT FIRSTNAME (#PCDATA)>
<!ELEMENT DATE (#PCDATA)>
<!ELEMENT ORDERS (ITEM)*>
<!ELEMENT ITEM (PRODUCT,NUMBER,PRICE)>
<!ELEMENT PRODUCT (#PCDATA)>
<!ELEMENT NUMBER (#PCDATA)>
<!ELEMENT PRICE (#PCDATA)>
]>
<DOCUMENT>
<CUSTOMER>
    <NAME>
        <LASTNAME>Edwards</LASTNAME>
        <FIRSTNAME>Britta</FIRSTNAME>
    </NAME>
    <DATE>April 17, 1998</DATE>
    <ORDERS>
        <ITEM>
            <PRODUCT>Cucumber</PRODUCT>
            <NUMBER>5</NUMBER>
            <PRICE>$1.25</PRICE>
        </ITEM>
        <ITEM>
            <PRODUCT>Lettuce</PRODUCT>
```

Listing 4-4.
Continued.

```
                <NUMBER>2</NUMBER>
                <PRICE>$.98</PRICE>
            </ITEM>
        </ORDERS>
    </CUSTOMER>
    <CUSTOMER>
        <NAME>
            <LASTNAME>Thompson</LASTNAME>
            <FIRSTNAME>Phoebe</FIRSTNAME>
        </NAME>
        <DATE>May 27, 1998</DATE>
        <ORDERS>
            <ITEM>
                <PRODUCT>Banana</PRODUCT>
                <NUMBER>12</NUMBER>
                <PRICE>$2.95</PRICE>
            </ITEM>
            <ITEM>
                <PRODUCT>Apple</PRODUCT>
                <NUMBER>6</NUMBER>
                <PRICE>$1.50</PRICE>
            </ITEM>
        </ORDERS>
    </CUSTOMER>
</DOCUMENT>
```

Our first two examples have been a little simplistic in two ways: first, we haven't interpreted the tags in our XML documents yet—so far, a tag has been only an indication to indent another level in the document.

Second, we've only been able to handle documents whose elements contain only other elements *or* character data, but not both, as you might note by taking a look at the DTDs from the preceding documents:

```
<?XML version = "1.0" ?>
<!DOCTYPE DOCUMENT [
<!ELEMENT DOCUMENT (CUSTOMER)*>
<!ELEMENT CUSTOMER (NAME,DATE,ORDERS)>
<!ELEMENT NAME (LASTNAME,FIRSTNAME)>
<!ELEMENT LASTNAME (#PCDATA)>
<!ELEMENT FIRSTNAME (#PCDATA)>
<!ELEMENT DATE (#PCDATA)>
<!ELEMENT ORDERS (ITEM)*>
<!ELEMENT ITEM (PRODUCT,NUMBER,PRICE)>
<!ELEMENT PRODUCT (#PCDATA)>
<!ELEMENT NUMBER (#PCDATA)>
<!ELEMENT PRICE (#PCDATA)>
]>
```

In real XML documents, however, we can't have any such restrictions. In our next example, indenter, we'll allow the user to write documents with mixed content ("mixed" is the XML term for both character data and element content). Let's look into that now.

The `indenter` Example

In this next example, we'll construct a browser that indents text as the user directs, supporting both an <INDENT> (indents two spaces) and <DOUBLEINDENT> (indents four spaces) tag. In this way, we'll read and interpret each tag, taking the correct action depending on the tag type.

We'll also allow mixed content, so elements may contain both character data and other elements like this:

```
<?XML VERSION = "1.0" ?>
<!DOCTYPE DOCUMENT [
<!ELEMENT DOCUMENT (INDENT|INDENTDOUBLE)*>
<!ELEMENT INDENT (#PCDATA|INDENT|INDENTDOUBLE)*>
<!ELEMENT INDENTDOUBLE (#PCDATA|INDENT|INDENTDOUBLE)*>
]>
<DOCUMENT>
    <INDENTDOUBLE>Britta</INDENTDOUBLE>
    <INDENTDOUBLE>
        <INDENTDOUBLE>
            Adam
        </INDENTDOUBLE>
        <INDENT>
            Christina
            <INDENTDOUBLE>
                <INDENT>Phoebe</INDENT>
                <INDENT>Fred</INDENT>
                Edward
            </INDENTDOUBLE>
        </INDENT>
    </INDENTDOUBLE>
    <INDENT>
        Sammy
    </INDENT>
</DOCUMENT>
```

When properly interpreted, the preceding XML document should produce this output:

```
        Britta

          Adam

       Christina

              Phoebe

            Fred

          Edward

   Sammy
```

Let's write the code now. In this example, we'll present the user with a window with a button labelled Browse:

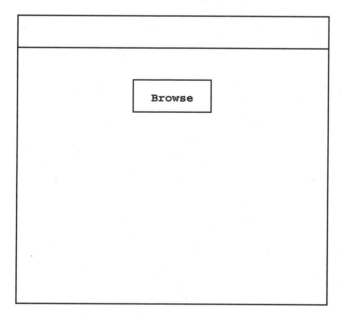

When the user clicks the Browse button, the program will read in the **indenter.xml** document, format it, and display it correctly as shown on the following page.

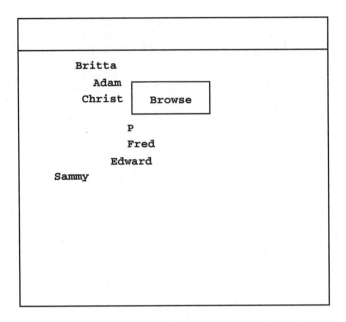

We place the code in this new example, **indenter.java**, to create the application's window, install the applet in it, and call the applet's **init()** method:

```java
import java.applet.Applet;

public class indenter extends Applet{

    public static void main(String args[])
    {
        indenterFrame frame = new indenterFrame("The
            indenter application");

        frame.show();
        frame.hide();
        frame.resize(400, 400);

        indenter applet = new indenter();

        frame.add("Center", applet);
        applet.init();
        applet.start();
        frame.show();
    }
        .
        .
        .
```

In the **init()** method, we install the Browse button, and in the **action()** method, we call the recursive method we'll use, **doTree()**. As in the previous example, **browser.java**, we'll place the lines we want to display in an array named displayStrings[ ] and display that array in the **paint()** method; so after we call **doTree()**, we call **repaint()**:

```java
import com.ms.xml.ParseException;
import com.ms.xml.Document;
import com.ms.xml.Element;

import java.awt.*;
import java.net.*;
import java.applet.Applet;

public class indenter extends Applet{

    Button button1;
    static String filename;
    static String displayStrings[] = new String[100];
    static int numberDisplayLines = 0;

    public static void main(String args[])
    {
        .
        .
        .
    }

    public void init(){
        button1 = new Button("Browse");
        add(button1);
    }

    public boolean action (Event e, Object o){

        URL url = null;
        try {
            url = new URL("file:////c://xml//indenter//
                indenter.xml");
        }
        catch (MalformedURLException e1) {
            System.out.println("Cannot create URL for: " +
                filename);
            System.exit(0);
        }

        Document d = new Document();

        try {
            d.load(url);
        }
        catch (ParseException e3) {
            d.reportError(e3, System.out);
        }

        if (d != null) {
```

```
                doTree(d.getRoot(), "");
                repaint();
        }

            return true;
        }
    }
```

We also add the window class we'll use in this example, indenterFrame, to the **indenter.java** file:

```
class indenterFrame extends Frame
{
    public indenterFrame(String str)
    {
        super (str);
    }

    public boolean handleEvent(Event evt)
    {
        switch (evt.id)
        {
            case Event.WINDOW_DESTROY:
                dispose();
                System.exit(0);
                return true;

            default:
                return super.handleEvent(evt);
        }
    }
}
```

Now we come to the core of the indenter example—the **doTree()** method.

Writing the **doTree()** Method

In this example's **doTree()** method, we want to do several things, elaborating on our previous examples. Here, we want to allow elements to have mixed content—both character data and child elements. We also want to interpret the tags and act on their content (i.e., indent two spaces or four spaces).

We have to assume, then, that the current element in **doTree()** can have both characterr data and child elements, so we will loop over all children in this element—the MSXML parser treats character data as a child element, but only true XML elements have the type Element.ELEMENT; if the child element's type is not Element.ELEMENT, we will assume it holds character data. We start **doTree()**, then, by looping over all the child elements of this element:

```
    void doTree(Element elem, String indent)
    {
        Enumeration enum = elem.getChildren();

        while (enum.hasMoreElements()) {
            Element elem2 = (Element)enum.nextElement();
               .
               .
               .
        }
    }
```

If the current child element is not of type Element.ELEMENT, we will assume it is character data, and so we will add its text to the displayStrings[] array. First, we check to make sure the element's type is not Element.ELEMENT:

```
    void doTree(Element elem, String indent)
    {
        Enumeration enum = elem.getChildren();

        while (enum.hasMoreElements()) {
            Element elem2 = (Element)enum.nextElement();

            if(elem2.getType() != com.ms.xml.Element.ELEMENT){
                  .
                  .
                  .
            }
        }
    }
```

Then we add the character data to the displayStrings[] array:

```
    void doTree(Element elem, String indent)
    {
        Enumeration enum = elem.getChildren();

        while (enum.hasMoreElements()) {
            Element elem2 = (Element)enum.nextElement();
            if(elem2.getType() != com.ms.xml.Element.ELEMENT){
                displayStrings[numberDisplayLines++] = indent
                    + elem2.getText();
            }
        }
    }
```

In the element's type *is* Element.ELEMENT, however, it can be a <INDENT> or <INDENTDOUBLE> element, so we should indent the text accordingly.

We can get the tag's name with the Element class' **getTagName()** method; if the tag is <INDENTDOUBLE>, we fill a new String, **ind**, with the current indentation string plus four spaces (we use a new indentation string here, **ind**, so we can preserve the value in the original indentation string, **indent**, for the other elements in the while loop):

```
void doTree(Element elem, String indent)
{
    String ind = "";

    Enumeration enum = elem.getChildren();

    while (enum.hasMoreElements()) {
        Element elem2 = (Element)enum.nextElement();
        if(elem2.getType() != com.ms.xml.Element.ELEMENT){
            int textLength = elem2.getText().length();
            displayStrings[numberDisplayLines++] = indent
                + elem2.getText();
        }
        else{
            if(elem2.getTagName().equals("INDENTDOUBLE")){
                ind = indent + "        ";
            }
                        .
                        .
                        .

        }
    }
}
```

If the tag is <INDENT>, we set the **ind** string to the current indentation string plus two spaces:

```
void doTree(Element elem, String indent)
{
    String ind = "";

    Enumeration enum = elem.getChildren();

    while (enum.hasMoreElements()) {
        Element elem2 = (Element)enum.nextElement();
        if(elem2.getType() != com.ms.xml.Element.ELEMENT){
            int textLength = elem2.getText().length();
            displayStrings[numberDisplayLines++] = indent
                + elem2.getText();
        }
        else{
            if(elem2.getTagName().equals("INDENTDOUBLE")){
                ind = indent + "        ";
            }
            if(elem2.getTagName().equals("INDENT")){
                ind = indent + "    ";
            }
        }
    }
```

```
        }
    }
```

Now that we've filled the new indentation string correctly, we can call **doTree()** again for the current element:

```
void doTree(Element elem, String indent)
{
    String ind = "";

    Enumeration enum = elem.getChildren();

    while (enum.hasMoreElements()) {
        Element elem2 = (Element)enum.nextElement();
        if(elem2.getType() != com.ms.xml.Element.ELEMENT){
            int textLength = elem2.getText().length();
            displayStrings[numberDisplayLines++] = indent
                + elem2.getText();
        }
        else{
            if(elem2.getTagName().equals("INDENTDOUBLE")){
                ind = indent + "        ";
            }
            if(elem2.getTagName().equals("INDENT")){
                ind = indent + "    ";
            }
            doTree(elem2, ind);
        }
    }
}
```

And that's it for **doTree()**. All that remains is to display the strings in the displayStrings[ ] array in the **paint()** method. That method looks like this:

```
public void paint(Graphics g)
{
    int y = 0;
    FontMetrics fontmetrics = getFontMetrics(getFont());

    for(int index = 0; index < numberDisplayLines;
        index++){
        y += fontmetrics.getHeight();
        g.drawString(displayStrings[index], 0, y);
    }
}
```

That's it—run the indenter application now, as shown in Figure 4-3. As you can see in that figure, we present the user with a window holding one button marked Browse.

When the user clicks the Browse button, the program reads the **indenter.xml** file in and displays that text indented properly, as you see in Figure 4-4.

Figure 4-3.
The **indenter**
application.

Figure 4-4.
Indenting an XML
document using its
tags to format the
document.

To make the action of this program clearer, we might have indenter use **x**es instead of spaces to indent; the result appears in Figure 4-5, where we display the formatted **indenter.xml** document.

The indenter application is a success—now we've added considerable power to our browser applications. We've not only started interpreting XML tags, but also have handled mixed content. The code for this application, **indenter.java**, appears in Listing 4-5. The XML document it reads in, **indenter.xml**, appears in Listing 4-6.

We'll take a look at one more example in this chapter—the **caps.java** XML browser, which will capitalize text using XML tags.

Figure 4-5.
The **indenter**
application using
xes.

Listing 4-5.
indenter.java.

```java
import com.ms.xml.ParseException;
import com.ms.xml.Document;
import com.ms.xml.Element;

import java.util.Enumeration;
import java.awt.*;
import java.net.*;
import java.applet.Applet;

public class indenter extends Applet{

    Button button1;
    static String filename;
    static String displayStrings[] = new String[100];
    static int numberDisplayLines = 0;

    public static void main(String args[])
    {
        indenterFrame frame = new indenterFrame("The
            indenter application");

        frame.show();
        frame.hide();
        frame.resize(400, 400);

        indenter applet = new indenter();

        frame.add("Center", applet);
        applet.init();
        applet.start();
        frame.show();
    }
```

Continues

Listing 4-5.
Continued.

```java
public void init(){
    button1 = new Button("Browse");
    add(button1);
}

public boolean action (Event e, Object o){

    URL url = null;
    try {
        url = new URL("file:////c://xml//indenter//
            indenter.xml");
    }
    catch (MalformedURLException e1) {
        System.out.println("Cannot create URL for: " +
            filename);
        System.exit(0);
    }

    Document d = new Document();

    try {
        d.load(url);
    }
    catch (ParseException e3) {
        d.reportError(e3, System.out);
    }

    if (d != null) {
        doTree(d.getRoot(), "");
        repaint();
    }
        return true;
}

void doTree(Element elem, String indent)
{
    String ind = "";

    Enumeration enum = elem.getChildren();

    while (enum.hasMoreElements()) {
        Element elem2 = (Element)enum.nextElement();
        if(elem2.getType() !=
            com.ms.xml.Element.ELEMENT){
            displayStrings[numberDisplayLines++] =
                indent + elem2.getText();
        }
        else{
            if(elem2.getTagName().equals
```

Listing 4-5.
Continued.

```
                                ("INDENTDOUBLE")){
                        ind = indent + "    ";
                    }
                    if(elem2.getTagName().equals("INDENT")){
                        ind = indent + "  ";
                    }
                    doTree(elem2, ind);
                }
            }
        }

    public void paint(Graphics g)
    {
        int y = 0;
        FontMetrics fontmetrics =
            getFontMetrics(getFont());

        for(int index = 0; index < numberDisplayLines;
            index++){
            y += fontmetrics.getHeight();
            g.drawString(displayStrings[index], 0, y);
        }
    }
}

class indenterFrame extends Frame
{
    public indenterFrame(String str)
    {
        super (str);
    }

    public boolean handleEvent(Event evt)
    {
        switch (evt.id)
        {
            case Event.WINDOW_DESTROY:
                dispose();
                System.exit(0);
                return true;

            default:
                return super.handleEvent(evt);
        }
    }
}
```

```
<?XML VERSION = "1.0" ?>
<!DOCTYPE DOCUMENT [
<!ELEMENT DOCUMENT (INDENT|INDENTDOUBLE)*>
<!ELEMENT INDENT (#PCDATA|INDENT|INDENTDOUBLE)*>
<!ELEMENT INDENTDOUBLE (#PCDATA|INDENT|INDENTDOUBLE)*>
]>
<DOCUMENT>
    <INDENTDOUBLE>Britta</INDENTDOUBLE>
    <INDENTDOUBLE>
        <INDENTDOUBLE>
            Adam
        </INDENTDOUBLE>
        <INDENT>
            Christina
            <INDENTDOUBLE>
                <INDENT>Phoebe</INDENT>
                <INDENT>Fred</INDENT>
                Edward
            </INDENTDOUBLE>
        </INDENT>
    </INDENTDOUBLE>
    <INDENT>
        Sammy
    </INDENT>
</DOCUMENT>
```

The caps Example

In this next example, we'll let the user specify the capitalization of text with two new tags: <UPPER> and <LOWER>. The <UPPER> tag converts its enclosed text to uppercase, and the <LOWER> tag converts its text to lowercase. Here's how a document that uses those tags, caps.xml, looks:

```
<?XML version = "1.0" ?>
<!DOCTYPE DOCUMENT [
<!ELEMENT DOCUMENT (UPPER|LOWER)*>
<!ELEMENT UPPER (#PCDATA|UPPER|LOWER)*>
<!ELEMENT LOWER (#PCDATA|UPPER|LOWER)*>
]>
<DOCUMENT>
<UPPER>Britta</UPPER>
<UPPER>
<UPPER>
Adam
</UPPER>
<LOWER>
Christine
```

```
<UPPER>
<LOWER>Phoebe</LOWER>
<UPPER>Fred</UPPER>
Edward
</UPPER>
</LOWER>
</UPPER>
<LOWER>
Sammy
</LOWER>
</DOCUMENT>
_H
```

And here's the result of interpreting those tags and formatting the document:

```
BRITTA
ADAM
christine
phoebe
FRED
EDWARD
sammy
```

When we start this application, we can present the user with a window holding the Browse button, as we have done with previous browsers:

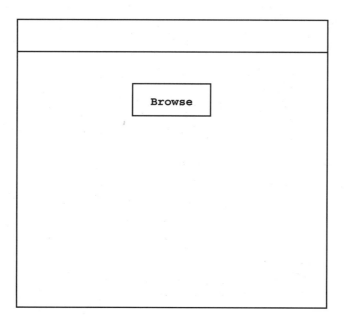

When the user clicks the Browse button, we can read in, format, and display the **caps.xml** file:

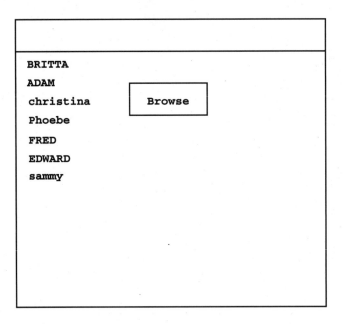

Let's write this example, **caps.java**, now. We start by adding the caps applet to a window in the **main()** method:

```java
import java.applet.Applet;

public class caps extends Applet{

    public static void main(String args[])
    {
        capsFrame frame = new capsFrame("The caps
            application");

        frame.show();
        frame.hide();
        frame.resize(400, 400);

        caps applet = new caps();

        frame.add("Center", applet);
        applet.init();
        applet.start();
        frame.show();
    }
```

We define our window class, capsFrame, as usual:

```
class capsFrame extends Frame
{
    public capsFrame(String str)
    {
        super (str);
    }

    public boolean handleEvent(Event evt)
    {
        switch (evt.id)
        {
            case Event.WINDOW_DESTROY:
                dispose();
                System.exit(0);
                return true;

            default:
                return super.handleEvent(evt);
        }
    }
}
```

Next, we write the **init()** and **action()** methods to add the Browse button to the browser's window and to handle button clicks. In the **action()** method, we'll call our recursive method, naming it **doTree()** again—but this time, we won't pass an indentation string to **doTree()**, because we won't need to indent the output (note that we also call **repaint()** after calling **doTree()** to refresh the screen display):

```
import com.ms.xml.ParseException;
import com.ms.xml.Document;
import com.ms.xml.Element;

import java.util.Enumeration;
import java.awt.*;
import java.net.*;
import java.applet.Applet;

public class caps extends Applet{

    Button button1;
    static String fileName;
    static String displayStrings[] = new String[100];
    static int numberDisplayLines = 0;

    public static void main(String args[])
    {
        .
```

```
        .
        .
    }

    public void init(){
        button1 = new Button("Browse");
        add(button1);
    }

    public boolean action (Event e, Object o){

        URL url = null;
        try {
            url = new URL("file:////c://xml//caps//
                caps.xml");
        }
        catch (MalformedURLException e1) {
            System.out.println("Cannot create url for: " +
                fileName);
            System.exit(0);
        }

        Document d = new Document();

        try {
            d.load(url);
        }
        catch (ParseException e3) {
            d.reportError(e3, System.out);
        }

        if (d != null) {
            doTree(d.getRoot());
            repaint();
        }
        return true;
    }
}
```

Now we're ready to write the **doTree()** method. Here, we will allow mixed content for elements and interpret both the <UPPER> and <LOWER> tags. We'll write the code for doTree() now; first, we loop over all the children of the current element:

```
void doTree(Element elem)
{
    Enumeration enum = elem.getChildren();

    while (enum.hasMoreElements()) {
        Element elem2 = (Element)enum.nextElement();
            .
            .
```

```
        }
    }
```

Now we check to see whether the current child element is of type Element.ELEMENT; if not, we assume it's character data:

```
void doTree(Element elem)
{
    Enumeration enum = elem.getChildren();

    while (enum.hasMoreElements()) {
        Element elem2 = (Element)enum.nextElement();

        if(elem2.getType() != com.ms.xml.Element.ELEMENT){
            .
            .
            .
        }
    }
}
```

At this point, then, we should add this element's character data to an array of strings to display (we'll name this array displayStrings[ ]). The question is: should we capitalize the character data before storing it or convert it to lowercase? We'll use a boolean flag to indicate if we should capitalize the current character data or not, and we'll call this flag doCaps:

```
import com.ms.xml.ParseException;
import com.ms.xml.Document;
import com.ms.xml.Element;

import java.util.Enumeration;
import java.awt.*;
import java.net.*;
import java.applet.Applet;

public class caps extends Applet{

    Button button1;
    static String fileName;
    static String displayStrings[] = new String[100];
    static int numberDisplayLines = 0;
    boolean doCaps = false;
        .
        .
        .
```

If doCaps is set to true, we should capitalize the current character data before storing it in the displayStrings[] array, and we do that with the Java String class' **toUpperCase()** method:

```
void doTree(Element elem)
{
    Enumeration enum = elem.getChildren();

    while (enum.hasMoreElements()) {
        Element elem2 = (Element)enum.nextElement();

        if(elem2.getType() != com.ms.xml.Element.ELEMENT){

            if(doCaps){
                displayStrings[numberDisplayLines++] =
                    elem2.getText().toUpperCase();
            }
                    .
                    .
                    .

        }
    }
}
```

If doCaps is *not* true, on the other hand, we should convert the current character data to lowercase, and we can do that with the Java String class' **toLowerCase()** method:

```
void doTree(Element elem)
{
    Enumeration enum = elem.getChildren();

    while (enum.hasMoreElements()) {
        Element elem2 = (Element)enum.nextElement();

        if(elem2.getType() != com.ms.xml.Element.ELEMENT){

            if(doCaps){
                displayStrings[numberDisplayLines++] =
                    elem2.getText().toUpperCase();
            }
            else{
                displayStrings[numberDisplayLines++] =
                    elem2.getText().toLowerCase();
            }
        }
    }
}
```

That handles the character data—although we have yet to see how to set the doCaps flag. How do we set that flag? We set that flag when we handle the start tag for the current character data. In the **doTree()** method, that works like this: if current element is not character data but is an <UPPER> tag, we set doCaps to true:

```
void doTree(Element elem)
{
    Enumeration enum = elem.getChildren();

    while (enum.hasMoreElements()) {
        Element elem2 = (Element)enum.nextElement();

        if(elem2.getType() != com.ms.xml.Element.ELEMENT){

            if(doCaps){
                displayStrings[numberDisplayLines++] =
                    elem2.getText().toUpperCase();
            }
            else{
                displayStrings[numberDisplayLines++] =
                    elem2.getText().toLowerCase();
            }

        }
        else{
            if(elem2.getTagName().equals("UPPER")){
                doCaps = true;
            }
        }
    }
}
```

If the current tag is a <LOWER> tag, we should set the doCaps boolean flag to false:

```
void doTree(Element elem)
{
    Enumeration enum = elem.getChildren();

    while (enum.hasMoreElements()) {
        Element elem2 = (Element)enum.nextElement();

        if(elem2.getType() != com.ms.xml.Element.ELEMENT){

            if(doCaps){
                displayStrings[numberDisplayLines++] =
                    elem2.getText().toUpperCase();
            }
            else{
                displayStrings[numberDisplayLines++] =
                    elem2.getText().toLowerCase();
            }

        }
        else{
            boolean doCapsOld = doCaps;
```

```
            if(elem2.getTagName().equals("UPPER")){
                doCaps = true;
            }
            if(elem2.getTagName().equals("LOWER")){
                doCaps = false;
            }
        }
    }
}
```

Then we can call **doTree()** again to handle the character data enclosed in this element:

```
void doTree(Element elem)
{
    Enumeration enum = elem.getChildren();

    while (enum.hasMoreElements()) {
        Element elem2 = (Element)enum.nextElement();

        if(elem2.getType() != com.ms.xml.Element.ELEMENT){

            if(doCaps){
                displayStrings[numberDisplayLines++] =
                    elem2.getText().toUpperCase();
            }
            else{
                displayStrings[numberDisplayLines++] =
                    elem2.getText().toLowerCase();
            }

        }
        else{
            boolean doCapsOld = doCaps;

            if(elem2.getTagName().equals("UPPER")){
                doCaps = true;
            }
            if(elem2.getTagName().equals("LOWER")){
                doCaps = false;
            }

            doTree(elem2);
            doCaps = doCapsOld;
        }
    }
}
```

Note also that before we call **doTree()**, we save the old doCaps setting, and after we return from the **doTree()** call, we restore that setting to its original value. That's because the <UPPER> and <LOWER> tags are not cumulative (as the indentation in the previous example, **indenter.java** was)—they are absolute. In other words, <UPPER>, when encountered, overrides the <LOWER> tag, and <LOWER>, when encountered, overrides the <UPPER> tag. For example, this text will be formatted to lowercase:

```
<UPPER>
<LOWER>
Here is the text.
</LOWER>
<UPPER>
```

That completes the **doTree()** method. Finally, we need a **paint()** method to display the array of strings, displayString[]:

```
public void paint(Graphics g)
{
    int y = 0;
    FontMetrics fontmetrics = getFontMetrics(getFont());

    for(int index = 0; index < numberDisplayLines; index++){
        y += fontmetrics.getHeight();
        g.drawString(displayStrings[index], 0, y);
    }
}
```

And that's it—run the program now, as shown in Figure 4-6.

When you click the Browse button, the program reads in the XML document **caps.xml** and formats it, displaying the result as in Figure 4-7.

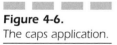

Figure 4-6.
The caps application.

Figure 4-7.
Using the <UPPER>
and <LOWER>
tags in an XML
document.

Our `caps.java` application works as we designed it—now we're supporting the <UPPER> and <LOWER> tags. The code for this application appears in Listing 4-7, and the XML document it reads in, `caps.xml`, appears in Listing 4-8.

Listing 4-7.
`caps.java`.

```
import com.ms.xml.ParseException;
import com.ms.xml.Document;
import com.ms.xml.Element;

import java.util.Enumeration;
import java.awt.*;
import java.net.*;
import java.applet.Applet;

public class caps extends Applet{

    Button button1;
    static String fileName;
    static String displayStrings[] = new String[100];
    static int numberDisplayLines = 0;
    boolean doCaps = false;

    public static void main(String args[])
    {
        capsFrame frame = new capsFrame("The caps
            application");

        frame.show();
        frame.hide();
        frame.resize(400, 400);
```

Listing 4-7.
Continued.

```
        caps applet = new caps();

        frame.add("Center", applet);
        applet.init();
        applet.start();
        frame.show();
    }

    public void init(){
        button1 = new Button("Browse");
        add(button1);
    }

    public boolean action (Event e, Object o){

        URL url = null;
        try {
            url = new URL("file:////c://xml//caps//
                    caps.xml");
        }
        catch (MalformedURLException e1) {
            System.out.println("Cannot create url for: " +
                    fileName);
            System.exit(0);
        }

        Document d = new Document();

        try {
            d.load(url);
        }
        catch (ParseException e3) {
            d.reportError(e3, System.out);
        }

        if (d != null) {
            doTree(d.getRoot());
            repaint();
        }
        return true;
    }


void doTree(Element elem)
{
    Enumeration enum = elem.getChildren();

    while (enum.hasMoreElements()) {
        Element elem2 = (Element)enum.nextElement();
```

Continues

Listing 4-7.
Continued.

```
                if(elem2.getType() !=
                    com.ms.xml.Element.ELEMENT){

                if(doCaps){
                    displayStrings[numberDisplayLines++]
                        =
                        elem2.getText().toUpperCase();
                }
                else{
                    displayStrings[numberDisplayLines++]
                        =
                        elem2.getText().toLowerCase();
                }

            }
            else{
                boolean doCapsOld = doCaps;

                if(elem2.getTagName().equals("UPPER")){
                    doCaps = true;
                }
                if(elem2.getTagName().equals("LOWER")){
                    doCaps = false;
                }

                doTree(elem2);
                doCaps = doCapsOld;
            }
        }
    }

    public void paint(Graphics g)
    {
        int y = 0;
        FontMetrics fontmetrics =
            getFontMetrics(getFont());

        for(int index = 0; index < numberDisplayLines;
            index++){
            y += fontmetrics.getHeight();
            g.drawString(displayStrings[index], 0, y);
        }
    }
}

class capsFrame extends Frame
{
    public capsFrame(String str)
    {
        super (str);
    }
```

Listing 4-7.
Continued.

```java
public boolean handleEvent(Event evt)
{
    switch (evt.id)
    {
        case Event.WINDOW_DESTROY:
            dispose();
            System.exit(0);
            return true;

        default:
            return super.handleEvent(evt);
    }
}

}
```

Listing 4-8.
caps.xml.

```xml
<?XML version = "1.0" ?>
<!DOCTYPE DOCUMENT [
<!ELEMENT DOCUMENT (UPPER|LOWER)*>
<!ELEMENT UPPER (#PCDATA|UPPER|LOWER)*>
<!ELEMENT LOWER (#PCDATA|UPPER|LOWER)*>
]>
<DOCUMENT>
<UPPER>Britta</UPPER>
<UPPER>
<UPPER>
Adam
</UPPER>
<LOWER>
Christine
<UPPER>
<LOWER>Phoebe</LOWER>
<UPPER>Fred</UPPER>
Edward
</UPPER>
</LOWER>
</UPPER>
<LOWER>
Sammy
</LOWER>
</DOCUMENT>
```

SUMMARY

That's it for our coverage of creating simple XML browsers for the moment. As you can see, there are some powerful techniques here that we can use to create XML browsers and display XML documents with, now that we've started interpreting the XML tags we place in XML documents.

In the next chapter, we'll continue working with the content of XML tags as we start to create database applications that work with XML documents.

CHAPTER **5**

XML and Databases

In this chapter, we're going to take a look at one of the things that XML does best—storing data. In particular, we'll see how to set up XML documents to use with database applications.

This topic is a large one, and database work can get very complex, as anyone who has worked with database programs is aware. In fact, Microsoft has already proposed a new data-handling standard for XML named *discuss XML-Data* that allows for involved data storage and structuring. You can find a copy of the XML-Data proposal at the Microsoft Web site. This proposal includes many specifications for handling graphs of data, data description techniques, schema, and more.

In this chapter, we will go as far as the MSXML parser lets us go with databases. We will see how to move through the records of a database, how to add records to a database, how to search the records of a database, and how to handle variable-length records. There's a lot going on here, so we will get started at once, seeing how to set up a database and work through that database's records now.

The employees Example

In the first example of this chapter, we'll set up a database of employees. Here are the employees we want to include in our database:

```
Tom Franklin
Phoebe Guertin
Frank Johnson
Brenda Tomlin
Tina Edwards
```

We can include these employees in an XML document, **employees.xml**, this way:

```
<?XML version = "1.0" ?>
<!DOCTYPE DOCUMENT [
<!ELEMENT DOCUMENT (NAME)*>
<!ELEMENT NAME (LASTNAME, FIRSTNAME)>
<!ELEMENT LASTNAME (#PCDATA)>
<!ELEMENT FIRSTNAME (#PCDATA)>
]>
<DOCUMENT>
<NAME>
     <LASTNAME>Franklin</LASTNAME>
     <FIRSTNAME>Tom</FIRSTNAME>
</NAME>
<NAME>
     <LASTNAME>Guertin</LASTNAME>
     <FIRSTNAME>Phoebe</FIRSTNAME>
</NAME>
<NAME>
     <LASTNAME>Johnson</LASTNAME>
     <FIRSTNAME>Frank</FIRSTNAME>
</NAME>
<NAME>
```

```
     <LASTNAME>Tomlin</LASTNAME>
     <FIRSTNAME>Brenda</FIRSTNAME>
</NAME>
<NAME>
     <LASTNAME>Edwards</LASTNAME>
     <FIRSTNAME>Tina</FIRSTNAME>
</NAME>
</DOCUMENT>
```

Here, we set up an individual record for each employee using the <NAME> tag. Each <NAME> tag is allowed to hold one <LASTNAME> tag and one <FIRSTNAME> tag in that order:

```
<?XML version = "1.0" ?>
<!DOCTYPE DOCUMENT [
<!ELEMENT DOCUMENT (NAME)*>
<!ELEMENT NAME (LASTNAME, FIRSTNAME)>
<!ELEMENT LASTNAME (#PCDATA)>
<!ELEMENT FIRSTNAME (#PCDATA)>
]>
<DOCUMENT>
<NAME>
     <LASTNAME>Franklin</LASTNAME>
     <FIRSTNAME>Tom</FIRSTNAME>
</NAME>
<NAME>
     <LASTNAME>Guertin</LASTNAME>
     <FIRSTNAME>Phoebe</FIRSTNAME>
</NAME>
           .
           .
           .
```

If you include a DTD with your database file, the XML parser can check to make sure your database file is valid, which is a good check on its internal structure. This is one of the main reasons for XML, in fact—handling and structuring your data. Being able to check the validity of documents is one reason XML and database handling is a natural combination.

In this first example, we can let the user work through the records in the **employees.xml** file using forward and back navigation buttons. When the application starts, we display the first record in the database:

```
┌─────────────────────────────────────────────┐
│                                             │
├─────────────────────────────────────────────┤
│                                             │
│                   ┌─────────────────────┐   │
│   First Name:     │  Tom                │   │
│                   └─────────────────────┘   │
│                                             │
│                                             │
│                   ┌─────────────────────┐   │
│   Last Name:      │  Franklin           │   │
│                   └─────────────────────┘   │
│                                             │
│                   ┌─────┐   ┌─────┐         │
│                   │  <  │   │  >  │         │
│                   └─────┘   └─────┘         │
│                                             │
│                                             │
└─────────────────────────────────────────────┘
```

When the user clicks the forward navigation button, we display the next record:

```
┌─────────────────────────────────────────────┐
│                                             │
├─────────────────────────────────────────────┤
│                                             │
│                   ┌─────────────────────┐   │
│   First Name:     │  Phoebe             │   │
│                   └─────────────────────┘   │
│                                             │
│                                             │
│                   ┌─────────────────────┐   │
│   Last Name:      │  Guertin            │   │
│                   └─────────────────────┘   │
│                                             │
│                   ┌─────┐   ┌─────┐         │
│                   │  <  │   │  >  │         │
│                   └─────┘   └─────┘         │
│                                             │
│                                             │
└─────────────────────────────────────────────┘
```

Using the forward and back button, the user can move through the records of the database as they like. We will see how to create this example, `employees.java`, now.

We start as usual, with a `main()` method, where we set the application up, including calling the applet's `init()` method:

```java
import java.applet.Applet;

public class employees extends Applet{

    public static void main(String args[])
    {
        employeesFrame frame = new employeesFrame("The
            employees application");

        frame.show();
        frame.hide();
        frame.resize(320, 400);

        employees applet = new employees();

        frame.add("Center", applet);
        applet.init();
        applet.start();
        frame.show();
    }
```

In the *init()* method, we add the two text fields—text1 and text2—and two buttons—button1 and button2—we need. In addition, we want to display the database's first record when the program first starts, so we read the database file, `employees.xml`, in `init()`. To maneuver easily through the database, we'll set up a method named `showRecord()`, to which we will pass a record number (starting at 0); this method will then display that record in the text fields. When the application first runs, we call `showRecord(0)` to display the first record:

```java
import com.ms.xml.ParseException;
import com.ms.xml.Document;
import com.ms.xml.Element;

import java.util.Enumeration;
import java.awt.*;
import java.net.*;
import java.applet.Applet;

public class employees extends Applet{

    static String filename;
    Label firstNameLabel, lastNameLabel;
    TextField text1, text2;
```

```
Button button1, button2;
Document d;

public static void main(String args[])
{
    .
    .
    .
}

public void init()
{
    firstNameLabel = new Label("First Name:");
    add(firstNameLabel);
    text1 = new TextField(24);
    add(text1);
    lastNameLabel = new Label("Last Name:");
    add(lastNameLabel);
    text2 = new TextField(24);
    add(text2);
    button1 = new Button("<");
    add(button1);
    button2 = new Button(">");
    add(button2);

    URL url = null;
    try {
        url = new URL("file:////c://xml//employees//
            employees.xml");
    }
    catch (MalformedURLException e1) {
        System.out.println("Cannot create URL for: " +
            filename);
        System.exit(0);
    }

    d = new Document();

    try {
        d.load(url);
    }
    catch (ParseException e3) {
        d.reportError(e3, System.out);
    }

    if (d != null) {
        showRecord(0);
    }
}
```

Next we will make the two buttons, the forward and back buttons, active, and we do that in the **action()** method. Now that we're moving through the database records, we should keep track of the current record number so that we don't try to move past the end of the database or before its beginning. We will add a new variable `currentRecordNumber` to keep track of the current record number:

```
import com.ms.xml.ParseException;
import com.ms.xml.Document;
import com.ms.xml.Element;

import java.util.Enumeration;
import java.awt.*;
import java.net.*;
import java.applet.Applet;

public class employees extends Applet{

    static String filename;
    Label firstNameLabel, lastNameLabel;
    TextField text1, text2;
    Button button1, button2;
    Document d;
    int currentRecordNumber = 0;
        .
        .
        .
```

If the user presses the back button, button1, we decrement `currentRecordNumber` (and check to make sure it's not less than 0); if the user clicks the forward button we increment `currentRecordNumber` (and check to make sure it's not greater than the last record number). Then we show the new record with the `showRecord()` method:

```
public boolean action (Event e, Object o)
{

    if(e.target.equals(button1)){   //The < button
        if(currentRecordNumber > 0){
            currentRecordNumber-;
        }
        showRecord(currentRecordNumber);
    }

    if(e.target.equals(button2)){   //The > button
        if(currentRecordNumber < 4){
            currentRecordNumber++;
        }
        showRecord(currentRecordNumber);
    }

    return true;
}
```

The `showRecord()` Method

All that remains is to write the `showRecord()` method. We pass the number of the record we want to display to this method, and it displays the record's <FIRSTNAME> and <LASTNAME> data—called the record's *fields*—in the two text fields. We will write this method now.

We start the `showRecord()` method by getting the XML document's `root` element (here, **d** is the document variable; we've made that variable global so that we can reach it in different methods throughout the `applet` class):

```
void showRecord(int recordNumber)
{
    Element root = d.getRoot();
        .
        .
        .
}
```

Next, we get an enumeration of the root's children, which are the records in the database:

```
void showRecord(int recordNumber)
{
    Element root = d.getRoot();
    Enumeration enum = root.getChildren();
        .
        .
        .
```

Now we can simply loop through the database until we come to the correct record:

```
void showRecord(int recordNumber)
{
    Element root = d.getRoot();
    Element elem = null, elem2 = null;
    Enumeration enum = root.getChildren();

    for(int index = 0; index <= recordNumber; index++){
        elem = (Element)enum.nextElement();
    }
        .
        .
        .
}
```

At this point, the `elem` element holds the record we want; if we wanted record number 1, we'd be pointing at this data:

```
<?XML version = "1.0" ?>
<!DOCTYPE DOCUMENT [
<!ELEMENT DOCUMENT (NAME)*>
<!ELEMENT NAME (LASTNAME, FIRSTNAME)>
<!ELEMENT LASTNAME (#PCDATA)>
<!ELEMENT FIRSTNAME (#PCDATA)>
]>
<DOCUMENT>
<NAME>
    <LASTNAME>Franklin</LASTNAME>
    <FIRSTNAME>Tom</FIRSTNAME>
</NAME>
<NAME>
    <LASTNAME>Guertin</LASTNAME>
    <FIRSTNAME>Phoebe</FIRSTNAME>
</NAME>
      .
      .
      .
```

Note that the actual data is stored as **child** elements of the <NAME> element in the <LASTNAME> and <FIRSTNAME> elements, so we have to get an enumeration of the current record's children. We can loop over those children this way:

```
void showRecord(int recordNumber)
{
    Element root = d.getRoot();
    Element elem = null, elem2 = null;
    Enumeration enum = root.getChildren();

    for(int index = 0; index <= recordNumber;
          index++){
        elem = (Element)enum.nextElement();
    }

    Enumeration enum2 = elem.getChildren();
    for(int index = 0; index < 2; index++){
            .
            .
            .

    }
  }
}
```

All that remains is to display the first and last names of the employee. We do that as we loop over the **<FIRSTNAME>** and **<LASTNAME>** elements:

```
void showRecord(int recordNumber)
{
    Element root = d.getRoot();
```

```
Element elem = null, elem2 = null;
Enumeration enum = root.getChildren();

for(int index = 0; index <= recordNumber;
        index++){
    elem = (Element)enum.nextElement();
}

Enumeration enum2 = elem.getChildren();
for(int index = 0; index < 2; index++){

    elem2 = (Element)enum2.nextElement();

    if (elem2.getTagName().equals("FIRSTNAME")) {
        text1.setText(elem2.getText());
    }

    if (elem2.getTagName().equals("LASTNAME")) {
        text2.setText(elem2.getText());
    }
}
    }
}
```

Run the program now, as shown in Figure 5-1. As you can see, the program already displays the first record of the database, as also shown in Figure 5-1.

When the user clicks the forward and back buttons, we can move through the database, as shown in Figure 5-2.

That's it—the employees program is a success. Now we've gotten started with databases in XML, setting up a database document and allowing the user to navigate through it. The listing for this program,

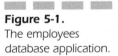

Figure 5-1.

The employees database application.

employees.java, appears in Listing 5-1, and the XML document it reads in, employees.xml, appears in Listing 5-2.

Figure 5-2.
Moving through the employees database.

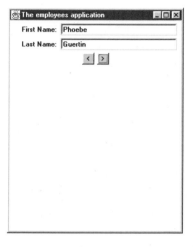

Listing 5-1.
employees.java.

```
import com.ms.xml.ParseException;
import com.ms.xml.Document;
import com.ms.xml.Element;

import java.util.Enumeration;
import java.awt.*;
import java.net.*;
import java.applet.Applet;

public class employees extends Applet{

    static String filename;
    Label firstNameLabel, lastNameLabel;
    TextField text1, text2;
    Button button1, button2;
    Document d;
    int currentRecordNumber = 0;

    public static void main(String args[])
    {
        employeesFrame frame = new employeesFrame("The
            employees application");

        frame.show();
        frame.hide();
        frame.resize(320, 400);
```

Continues

Listing 5-1.
Continued.

```
    employees applet = new employees();

    frame.add("Center", applet);
    applet.init();
    applet.start();
    frame.show();
}

public void init()
{
    firstNameLabel = new Label("First Name:");
    add(firstNameLabel);
    text1 = new TextField(24);
    add(text1);
    lastNameLabel = new Label("Last Name:");
    add(lastNameLabel);
    text2 = new TextField(24);
    add(text2);
    button1 = new Button("<");
    add(button1);
    button2 = new Button(">");
    add(button2);

    URL url = null;
    try {
        url = new URL("file:////c://xml//employees//
            employees.xml");
    }
    catch (MalformedURLException e1) {
        System.out.println("Cannot create URL for: " +
            filename);
        System.exit(0);
    }

    d = new Document();

    try {
        d.load(url);
    }
    catch (ParseException e3) {
        d.reportError(e3, System.out);
    }

    if (d != null) {
        showRecord(0);
    }
}

public boolean action (Event e, Object o)
{

    if(e.target.equals(button1)){  //The < button
```

Listing 5-1.
Continued.

```
                        if(currentRecordNumber > 0){
                            currentRecordNumber-;
                        }
                        showRecord(currentRecordNumber);
                    }

                    if(e.target.equals(button2)){   //The > button
                        if(currentRecordNumber < 4){
                            currentRecordNumber++;
                        }
                        showRecord(currentRecordNumber);
                    }

                    return true;
                }

                void showRecord(int recordNumber)
                {
                    Element root = d.getRoot();
                    Element elem = null, elem2 = null;
                    Enumeration enum = root.getChildren();

                    for(int index = 0; index <= recordNumber;
                        index++){
                        elem = (Element)enum.nextElement();
                    }

                    Enumeration enum2 = elem.getChildren();
                    for(int index = 0; index < 2; index++){

                        elem2 = (Element)enum2.nextElement();

                        if (elem2.getTagName().equals("FIRSTNAME")) {
                            text1.setText(elem2.getText());
                        }

                        if (elem2.getTagName().equals("LASTNAME")) {
                            text2.setText(elem2.getText());
                        }
                    }
                }
            }

            class employeesFrame extends Frame
            {
                public employeesFrame(String str)
                {
                    super (str);
                }

                public boolean handleEvent(Event evt)
```

Continues

Listing 5-1.
Continued.

```
    {
        switch (evt.id)
        {
            case Event.WINDOW_DESTROY:
                dispose();
                System.exit(0);
                return true;

            default:
                return super.handleEvent(evt);
        }
    }
}
```

Listing 5-2.
employees.xml.

```
<?XML version = "1.0" ?>
<!DOCTYPE DOCUMENT [
<!ELEMENT DOCUMENT (NAME)*>
<!ELEMENT NAME (LASTNAME, FIRSTNAME)>
<!ELEMENT LASTNAME (#PCDATA)>
<!ELEMENT FIRSTNAME (#PCDATA)>
]>
<DOCUMENT>
<NAME>
    <LASTNAME>Franklin</LASTNAME>
    <FIRSTNAME>Tom</FIRSTNAME>
</NAME>
<NAME>
    <LASTNAME>Guertin</LASTNAME>
    <FIRSTNAME>Phoebe</FIRSTNAME>
</NAME>
<NAME>
    <LASTNAME>Johnson</LASTNAME>
    <FIRSTNAME>Frank</FIRSTNAME>
</NAME>
<NAME>
    <LASTNAME>Tomlin</LASTNAME>
    <FIRSTNAME>Brenda</FIRSTNAME>
</NAME>
<NAME>
    <LASTNAME>Edwards</LASTNAME>
    <FIRSTNAME>Tina</FIRSTNAME>
</NAME>
</DOCUMENT>
_H
```

We will extend our database expertise now. In the next example, we'll
see how to manipulate databases by adding records to them on the fly.

The `birds` Example

In this next example, we'll set up a database for birdwatchers, **birds.java**, recording the birds they've seen and allowing them to *add* new records to the database as they sight more birds.

Here's how the database file, **birds.xml**, might look—note that for each record (called a *sighting* here), we record the name of the bird seen and the date of the sighting:

```
<?XML version = "1.0" ?>
<!DOCTYPE DOCUMENT [
<!ELEMENT DOCUMENT (SIGHTING)*>
<!ELEMENT SIGHTING (BIRD,DATE)>
<!ELEMENT BIRD (#PCDATA)>
<!ELEMENT DATE (#PCDATA)>
]>
<DOCUMENT>
    <SIGHTING>
        <BIRD>
            Robin
        </BIRD>
        <DATE>
            March 2
        </DATE>
    </SIGHTING>
    <SIGHTING>
        <BIRD>
            Sparrow
        </BIRD>
        <DATE>
            April 10
        </DATE>
    </SIGHTING>
    <SIGHTING>
        <BIRD>
            Eagle
        </BIRD>
        <DATE>
            June 23
        </DATE>
    </SIGHTING>
    <SIGHTING>
        <BIRD>
            Owl
        </BIRD>
        <DATE>
            July 11
        </DATE>
    </SIGHTING>
    <SIGHTING>
```

```
<BIRD>
        Finch
</BIRD>
<DATE>
        August 3
</DATE>
</SIGHTING>
</DOCUMENT>
```

When the program starts, we will display the first record of the **birds.xml** database:

Using the < and > buttons, the user can move through the database. If they see a new bird, they can simply type the new bird name and the date of the sighting into the text fields like this and click the Add record button:

Clicking the Add record button adds the new record to the database. When the user clicks the Save database button, we'll save the new version of the XML file to disk, including the new record:

```
<?XML version = "1.0" ?>
<!DOCTYPE DOCUMENT [
<!ELEMENT DOCUMENT (SIGHTING)*>
<!ELEMENT SIGHTING (BIRD,DATE)>
<!ELEMENT BIRD (#PCDATA)>
<!ELEMENT DATE (#PCDATA)>
]>
<DOCUMENT>
    <SIGHTING>
        <BIRD>
            Robin
        </BIRD>
        <DATE>
            March 2
        </DATE>
    </SIGHTING>
    <SIGHTING>
        <BIRD>
            Sparrow
        </BIRD>
        <DATE>
            April 10
```

```
        </DATE>
    </SIGHTING>
    <SIGHTING>
        <BIRD>
            Eagle
        </BIRD>
        <DATE>
            June 23
        </DATE>
    </SIGHTING>
    <SIGHTING>
        <BIRD>
            Owl
        </BIRD>
        <DATE>
            July 11
        </DATE>
    </SIGHTING>
    <SIGHTING>
        <BIRD>
            Finch
        </BIRD>
        <DATE>
            August 3
        </DATE>
    </SIGHTING>
    <SIGHTING>
        <BIRD>
            Falcon
        </BIRD>
        <DATE>
            June 7
        </DATE>
    </SIGHTING>
</DOCUMENT>
```

Let's put this program to work now. We start as we did in the last example, **employees**, by creating the applet we'll need, the window we'll use, and installing the applet in the window. In addition, we add the controls we'll need—the forward and back buttons and the Add record and Save database buttons—in the **init()** method. Note also that the number of records in the database can change as the user edits it, so we keep track of the total number of records in a new integer named **maxRecordNumber**. We fill that variable with the number of records in the database we're reading in by using the **root** element's **numElements()** method:

```
import com.ms.xml.ParseException;
import com.ms.xml.Document;
import com.ms.xml.Element;

import java.io.*;
```

```
import java.awt.*;
import java.net.*;
import java.applet.Applet;

public class birds extends Applet{

    static String filename;
    Label birdLabel, dateLabel;
    TextField text1, text2;
    Button button1, button2, button3, button4;
    Document d;
    int currentRecordNumber = 0;
    int maxRecordNumber = 4;

    public static void main(String args[])
    {
        birdsFrame frame = new birdsFrame("The birds
            application");

        frame.show();
        frame.hide();
        frame.resize(330, 320);

        birds applet = new birds();

        frame.add("Center", applet);
        applet.init();
        applet.start();
        frame.show();
    }

    public void init()
    {
        birdLabel = new Label("Bird:");
        add(birdLabel);
        text1 = new TextField(30);
        add(text1);
        dateLabel = new Label("Date:");
        add(dateLabel);
        text2 = new TextField(30);
        add(text2);
        button1 = new Button("<");
        add(button1);
        button2 = new Button("Add record");
        add(button2);
        button3 = new Button("Save database");
        add(button3);
        button4 = new Button(">");
        add(button4);

        URL url = null;
        try {
            url = new URL("file:////c://xml//birds//
                birds.xml");
```

```
    }
    catch (MalformedURLException el) {
        System.out.println("Cannot create url for:
            " + filename);
        System.exit(0);
    }

    d = new Document();

    try {
        d.load(url);
    }
    catch (ParseException e3) {
        d.reportError(e3, System.out);
    }

    if (d != null) {
        maxRecordNumber = d.getRoot().numElements()
            - 1;
        showRecord(0);
    }
}
```

At the end of the init() method, we show the first record, using the
showRecord() method. That method is the same as in the employees example, except that we search for <BIRD> and <DATE> tags, not <LASTNAME>
and <FIRSTNAME>:

```
void showRecord(int recordNumber)
{
    Element root = d.getRoot();
    Element elem = null, elem2 = null;
    Enumeration enum = root.getChildren();
    for(int index = 0; index <= recordNumber;
            index++){
        elem = (Element)enum.nextElement();
    }

    Enumeration enum2 = elem.getChildren();
    for(int index = 0; index < 2; index++){

        elem2 = (Element)enum2.nextElement();

        if (elem2.getTagName().equals("BIRD")) {
            text1.setText(elem2.getText());
        }

        if (elem2.getTagName().equals("DATE")) {
            text2.setText(elem2.getText());
        }
    }
}
}
```

Now we'll handle the four buttons in the application in the `action()` method. We start with the back button, which moves us back a record in the birds database. Here, we simply decrement the current record number and (if we haven't tried to move back before the database's first record), display the new record:

```
public boolean action (Event e, Object o){

    if(e.target.equals(button1)){   //The < button
        if(currentRecordNumber > 0){
            currentRecordNumber-;
        }
        showRecord(currentRecordNumber);
    }
    .
    .
    .
```

On the other hand, if the user pressed the Add record button (button2), we should take the text strings in the text fields text1 and text2 and create a new record in the database like this:

```
<SIGHTING>
    <BIRD>
        Falcon
    </BIRD>
    <DATE>
        June 7
    </DATE>
</SIGHTING>
```

Creating a New XML Element

We start the element-creation process like this, where we use the `createElement()` method to create a new <SIGHTINGS> element that the program will add to the end of the database:

```
public boolean action (Event e, Object o){

    if(e.target.equals(button1)){   //The < button
        .
        .
        .
    }

    if(e.target.equals(button2)){   //The Add record button

        Element elem = d.createElement(new
```

```
            String("SIGHTING"),
        Element.ELEMENT);
            .
            .
            .

    }
```

Now we create the <BIRD> element, which has one child, the character data from the text field text1:

```
<SIGHTING>
    <BIRD>
        Falcon
    </BIRD>
    <DATE>
        June 7
    </DATE>
</SIGHTING>
```

Here's how we create the <BIRD> element, give it a **child** element of type **PCDATA**, set the text of the **child** element to the text now in text1, and use the **addChild()** method to add the **child** element to the <BIRD> element:

```
public boolean action (Event e, Object o){

    if(e.target.equals(button1)){   //The < button
            .
            .
            .

    }

    if(e.target.equals(button2)){   //The Add record button

        Element elem = d.createElement(new
            String("SIGHTING"),
            Element.ELEMENT);

        Element t1 = d.createElement(new String("BIRD"),
            Element.ELEMENT);
        Element x1 = d.createElement(null,
            Element.PCDATA);
        x1.setText(text1.getText());
        t1.addChild(x1, null);
            .
            .
            .

    }
```

You pass two arguments to **addChild()**; the first argument is the element you want to add, and the second argument is the element you want to add the new element after. Passing **null** as the second argument adds the child to the end of the list, passing **this** as the second argument adds the element to the beginning of the list.

TIP *If you want to remove a* **child** *element from a document instead of adding one, use the* **removeChild()** *method.*

Next, we create the <DATE> element using the date in the second text field, text2:

```
<SIGHTING>
        <BIRD>
            Falcon
        </BIRD>
        <DATE>
            June 7
        </DATE>
</SIGHTING>
```

Here's how we create a new <DATE> element, just as we created the <BIRD> element:

```
public boolean action (Event e, Object o){

    if(e.target.equals(button1)){   //The < button
            .
            .
            .
    }

    if(e.target.equals(button2)){   //The Add record button

        Element elem = d.createElement(new
            String("SIGHTING"),
            Element.ELEMENT);

        Element t1 = d.createElement(new String("BIRD"),
            Element.ELEMENT);
        Element x1 = d.createElement(null,
            Element.PCDATA);
        x1.setText(text1.getText());
        t1.addChild(x1, null);

        Element t2 = d.createElement(new String("DATE"),
            Element.ELEMENT);
        Element x2 = d.createElement(null,
            Element.PCDATA);
        x2.setText(text2.getText());
        t2.addChild(x2, null);
```

.
.
.

```
    }
```

Adding a New XML Element to a Document

All that remains is to add the <BIRD> and <DATE> elements to the new <SIGHTING> element, add the new <SIGHTING> element to the document itself (by adding it to the **root** element), and increment the maximum number of records:

```
public boolean action (Event e, Object o){

    if(e.target.equals(button1)){   //The < button
        .
        .
        .

    }

    if(e.target.equals(button2)){   //The Add record button

        Element elem = d.createElement(new
            String("SIGHTING"),
            Element.ELEMENT);

        Element t1 = d.createElement(new String("BIRD"),
            Element.ELEMENT);
        Element x1 = d.createElement(null,
            Element.PCDATA);
        x1.setText(text1.getText());
        t1.addChild(x1, null);

        Element t2 = d.createElement(new String("DATE"),
            Element.ELEMENT);
        Element x2 = d.createElement(null,
            Element.PCDATA);
        x2.setText(text2.getText());
        t2.addChild(x2, null);

        elem.addChild(t1,null);
        elem.addChild(t2,null);
        d.getRoot().addChild(elem, null);
        maxRecordNumber++;
    }
```

That's it—now we've added a new record to the database.

However, we haven't made the change permanent yet. If the user wants to update the **birds.xml** document on disk, we will let them do so.

Writing a New XML Document

If the user clicks the Save database button, we will save the new version of the document in the **birds.xml** file. We do that by first declaring a Java **FileOutputStream** object, **outstream**, in the **action()** method:

```
public boolean action (Event e, Object o){

    if(e.target.equals(button1)){   //The < button
        .
        .
        .
    }

    if(e.target.equals(button2)){   //The Add record button
        .
        .
        .
    }

    if(e.target.equals(button3)){   //The Save database
        button

        FileOutputStream outstream = null;
        .
        .
        .
```

Now we try to open the **birds.xml** file in order to write to it; if there's an error, we let the user know:

```
public boolean action (Event e, Object o){

    if(e.target.equals(button1)){   //The < button
        .
        .
        .
    }

    if(e.target.equals(button2)){   //The Add record button
        .
        .
        .
    }

    if(e.target.equals(button3)){   //The Save database
        button

        FileOutputStream outstream = null;

        try {
```

```
                      outstream = new FileOutputStream("birds.xml");
              }
              catch (java.io.IOException ex) {
                  System.out.println("Could not create file
                      input stream.");
              }
                .
                .
                .

         }
}
```

Finally, we use the Document class' **save()** method to write the new version of **birds.xml** to disk. All that's left is to close the file output stream this way:

```
public boolean action (Event e, Object o){

    if(e.target.equals(button1)){   //The < button
            .
            .
            .
    }

    if(e.target.equals(button2)){   //The Add record button
            .
            .
            .
    }

    if(e.target.equals(button3)){   //The Save database
            button

        FileOutputStream outstream = null;

        try {
            outstream = new FileOutputStream("birds.xml");
        }
        catch (java.io.IOException ex) {
            System.out.println("Could not create file
                input stream.");
        }

        d.save(outstream);

        try {
            outstream.close();
        }
        catch (java.io.IOException ex) {
            System.out.println("IO exception");
        }
    }
}
```

That completes the file-writing process. We've seen how to load documents with the **Document** class' **load()** method, and now we've seen how to save them to disk using the **save()** method.

 TIP *The document* **load()** *method can take a Java file input stream as an argument instead of an URL object.*

Finally, we make the forward navigation button active as we did in the previous example, **employees**:

```
public boolean action (Event e, Object o){

    if(e.target.equals(button1)){   //The < button
            .
            .
            .
    }

    if(e.target.equals(button2)){   //The Add record button
            .
            .
            .
    }

    if(e.target.equals(button3)){   //The Save database
        button
            .
            .
            .
    }

    if(e.target.equals(button4)){   //The > button
        if(currentRecordNumber < maxRecordNumber){
            currentRecordNumber++;
        }
        showRecord(currentRecordNumber);
    }

    return true;
}
```

That's it—the **birds.java** program is complete. Run this program now, as shown in Figure 5-3. As you can see in that figure, the program displays the first record in the database.

The user can add a new record to the database by filling in the text fields, as shown in Figure 5-4, and by clicking the Add record and Save database buttons.

When the user does add a new record to the database and writes out that database, the **birds.xml** file is updated with the new record:

Figure 5-3.
The birds application.

Figure 5-4.
Adding a new record
to the birds
database.

```
<?XML version = "1.0" ?>

<!DOCTYPE DOCUMENT [
<!ELEMENT DOCUMENT (SIGHTING)*>
<!ELEMENT SIGHTING (BIRD,DATE)>
<!ELEMENT BIRD (#PCDATA)>
<!ELEMENT DATE (#PCDATA)>
]>
<DOCUMENT>
    <SIGHTING>
        <BIRD>
            Robin
        </BIRD>
        <DATE>
            March 2
        </DATE>
    </SIGHTING>
    <SIGHTING>
        <BIRD>
            Sparrow
        </BIRD>
```

```
                    <DATE>
                        April 10
                    </DATE>
                </SIGHTING>
                <SIGHTING>
                    <BIRD>
                        Eagle
                    </BIRD>
                    <DATE>
                        June 23
                    </DATE>
                </SIGHTING>
                <SIGHTING>
                    <BIRD>
                        Owl
                    </BIRD>
                    <DATE>
                        July 11
                    </DATE>
                </SIGHTING>
                <SIGHTING>
                    <BIRD>
                        Finch
                    </BIRD>
                    <DATE>
                        August 3
                    </DATE>
                </SIGHTING>
                <SIGHTING>
                    <BIRD>
                        Falcon
                    </BIRD>
                    <DATE>
                        June 7
                    </DATE>
                </SIGHTING>
            </DOCUMENT>
```

And that's it—the **birds.java** program is a success. Now we've seen how to add new records to a database and save them to a file. The listing for this, **birds.java**, appears in Listing 5-3, and the XML document it reads in—and writes out—appears in Listing 5-4.

**Listing 5-3.
birds.java**.

```java
import com.ms.xml.ParseException;
import com.ms.xml.Document;
import com.ms.xml.Element;

import java.util.Enumeration;
import java.io.*;
```
                                                              Continues

Listing 5-3.
Continued.

```java
import java.awt.*;
import java.net.*;
import java.applet.Applet;

public class birds extends Applet{

    static String filename;
    Label birdLabel, dateLabel;
    TextField text1, text2;
    Button button1, button2, button3, button4;
    Document d;
    int currentRecordNumber = 0;
    int maxRecordNumber = 4;
    public static void main(String args[])
    {
        birdsFrame frame = new birdsFrame("The birds
            application");

        frame.show();
        frame.hide();
        frame.resize(330, 320);

        birds applet = new birds();

        frame.add("Center", applet);
        applet.init();
        applet.start();
        frame.show();
    }

    public void init()
    {
        birdLabel = new Label("Bird:");
        add(birdLabel);
        text1 = new TextField(30);
        add(text1);
        dateLabel = new Label("Date:");
        add(dateLabel);
        text2 = new TextField(30);
        add(text2);
        button1 = new Button("<");
        add(button1);
        button2 = new Button("Add record");
        add(button2);
        button3 = new Button("Save database");
        add(button3);
        button4 = new Button(">");
        add(button4);

        URL url = null;
        try {
            url = new URL("file:////c://xml//birds//
        birds.xml");
```

Listing 5-3.
Continued.

```
        }
        catch (MalformedURLException e1) {
            System.out.println("Cannot create url for: " +
                    filename);
            System.exit(0);
        }

        d = new Document();

        try {
            d.load(url);
        }
        catch (ParseException e3) {
            d.reportError(e3, System.out);
        }

        if (d != null) {
            maxRecordNumber = d.getRoot().numElements() -
                    1;
            showRecord(0);
        }
    }

    public boolean action (Event e, Object o){

        if(e.target.equals(button1)){   //The < button
            if(currentRecordNumber > 0){
                currentRecordNumber-;
            }
            showRecord(currentRecordNumber);
        }

        if(e.target.equals(button2)){   //The Add record
            button

            Element elem = d.createElement(new
                    String("SIGHTING"), Element.ELEMENT);

            Element t1 = d.createElement(new
                    String("BIRD"), Element.ELEMENT);
            Element x1 = d.createElement(null,
                    Element.PCDATA);
            x1.setText(text1.getText());
            t1.addChild(x1, null);

            Element t2 = d.createElement(new
                    String("DATE"), Element.ELEMENT);
            Element x2 = d.createElement(null,
                    Element.PCDATA);
            x2.setText(text2.getText());
            t2.addChild(x2, null);
```

Continues

Listing 5-3.
Continued.

```
            elem.addChild(t1,null);
            elem.addChild(t2,null);
            d.getRoot().addChild(elem, null);
            maxRecordNumber++;
    }

    if(e.target.equals(button3)){   //The Save database
        button

        FileOutputStream outstream = null;

        try {
            outstream = new
                FileOutputStream("birds.xml");
        }
        catch (java.io.IOException ex) {
            System.out.println("Could not create file
                input stream.");
        }

        d.save(outstream);

        try {
            outstream.close();
        }
        catch (java.io.IOException ex) {
            System.out.println("IO exception");
        }

    }

    if(e.target.equals(button4)){   //The > button
        if(currentRecordNumber < maxRecordNumber){
            currentRecordNumber++;
        }
        showRecord(currentRecordNumber);
    }

    return true;
}

void showRecord(int recordNumber)
{
    Element root = d.getRoot();
    Element elem = null, elem2 = null;
    Enumeration enum = root.getChildren();
    for(int index = 0; index <= recordNumber;
        index++){
        elem = (Element)enum.nextElement();
    }

    Enumeration enum2 = elem.getChildren();
    for(int index = 0; index < 2; index++){
```

Listing 5-3.
Continued.

```
                elem2 = (Element)enum2.nextElement();

                if (elem2.getTagName().equals("BIRD")) {
                    text1.setText(elem2.getText());
                }

                if (elem2.getTagName().equals("DATE")) {
                    text2.setText(elem2.getText());
                }
            }
        }
}
class birdsFrame extends Frame
{
    public birdsFrame(String str)
    {
        super (str);
    }

    public boolean handleEvent(Event evt)
    {
        switch (evt.id)
        {
            case Event.WINDOW_DESTROY:
                dispose();
                System.exit(0);
                return true;

            default:
                return super.handleEvent(evt);
        }
    }
}
```

Listing 5-4.
birds.xml

```
<?XML version = "1.0" ?>
<!DOCTYPE DOCUMENT [
<!ELEMENT DOCUMENT (SIGHTING)*>
<!ELEMENT SIGHTING (BIRD,DATE)>
<!ELEMENT BIRD (#PCDATA)>
<!ELEMENT DATE (#PCDATA)>
]>
<DOCUMENT>
    <SIGHTING>
        <BIRD>
            Robin
        </BIRD>
        <DATE>
```

Continues

Listing 5-4.
Continued.

```
                    March 2
            </DATE>
        </SIGHTING>
        <SIGHTING>
            <BIRD>
                Sparrow
            </BIRD>
            <DATE>
                April 10
            </DATE>
        </SIGHTING>
        <SIGHTING>
            <BIRD>
                Eagle
            </BIRD>
            <DATE>
                June 23
            </DATE>
        </SIGHTING>
        <SIGHTING>
            <BIRD>
                Owl
            </BIRD>
            <DATE>
                July 11
            </DATE>
        </SIGHTING>
        <SIGHTING>
            <BIRD>
                Finch
            </BIRD>
            <DATE>
                August 3
            </DATE>
        </SIGHTING>
</DOCUMENT>
```

In the next database example, we'll see how to search through a database for a particular record; searching for records is an important database function, and we'll take a look at the process now.

The searcher Example

In this example, **searcher**, we'll see how to search through a database XML document for a particular record. We can use the **employees.xml** document we developed earlier (renamed **searcher.xml** for this example):

```
<?XML version = "1.0" ?>
<!DOCTYPE DOCUMENT [
<!ELEMENT DOCUMENT (NAME)*>
<!ELEMENT NAME (LASTNAME, FIRSTNAME)>
<!ELEMENT LASTNAME (#PCDATA)>
<!ELEMENT FIRSTNAME (#PCDATA)>
]>
<DOCUMENT>
<NAME>
     <LASTNAME>Franklin</LASTNAME>
     <FIRSTNAME>Tom</FIRSTNAME>
</NAME>
<NAME>
     <LASTNAME>Guertin</LASTNAME>
     <FIRSTNAME>Phoebe</FIRSTNAME>
</NAME>
<NAME>
     <LASTNAME>Johnson</LASTNAME>
     <FIRSTNAME>Frank</FIRSTNAME>
</NAME>
<NAME>
     <LASTNAME>Tomlin</LASTNAME>
     <FIRSTNAME>Brenda</FIRSTNAME>
</NAME>
<NAME>
     <LASTNAME>Edwards</LASTNAME>
     <FIRSTNAME>Tina</FIRSTNAME>
</NAME>
</DOCUMENT>
_H
```

We can let the user search through this database for a match to one of the fields, such as the <FIRSTNAME> field. When the user starts the application, we present them with this window:

```
┌─────────────────────────────────────────────┐
│                                             │
├─────────────────────────────────────────────┤
│                                             │
│   First Name:    ┌──────────────────────┐   │
│                  │                      │   │
│                  └──────────────────────┘   │
│                                             │
│                                             │
│   Last Name:     ┌──────────────────────┐   │
│                  │                      │   │
│                  └──────────────────────┘   │
│                                             │
│   ┌───────────────────────────────┐ ┌─────┐ │
│   │ Search for this first name:   │ │     │ │
│   └───────────────────────────────┘ └─────┘ │
│                                             │
│                                             │
│                                             │
└─────────────────────────────────────────────┘
```

If the user is searching for a record in which the first name is **Tom**, they can enter that name in the lower text field this way:

```
┌─────────────────────────────────────────────┐
│                                             │
├─────────────────────────────────────────────┤
│                                             │
│                                             │
│   First Name:    ┌──────────────────────┐   │
│                  │                      │   │
│                  └──────────────────────┘   │
│                                             │
│                                             │
│   Last Name:     ┌──────────────────────┐   │
│                  │                      │   │
│                  └──────────────────────┘   │
│                                             │
│   ┌───────────────────────────────┐ ┌─────┐ │
│   │ Search for this first name:   │ │ Tom │ │
│   └───────────────────────────────┘ └─────┘ │
│                                             │
│                                             │
└─────────────────────────────────────────────┘
```

When they press the Search for this first name button, we find the record in which the first name is Tom and display that record this way:

We will put this example to work now. As in the previous two examples, we start by creating the window we'll use, the applet we'll insert in the window, install the applet, call its **init()** method, and add the controls we'll use in the **init()** method. Finally, we read in the **searcher.xml** document. Note that we set the variable **maxRecordNumber** to the number of records in the XML document when we load the document:

```
import com.ms.xml.ParseException;
import com.ms.xml.Document;
import com.ms.xml.Element;

import java.awt.*;
import java.net.*;
import java.applet.Applet;

public class searcher extends Applet{

    static String fileName;
    Label firstNameLabel, lastNameLabel;
    TextField text1, text2, text3;
    Button button1;
    Document d;
```

```
int maxRecordNumber = 0;

public static void main(String args[])
{
    searcherFrame frame = new searcherFrame("The
        searcher application");

    frame.show();
    frame.hide();
    frame.resize(320, 300);

    searcher applet = new searcher();

    frame.add("Center", applet);
    applet.init();
    applet.start();
    frame.show();
}

public void init(){
    firstNameLabel = new Label("First Name:");
    add(firstNameLabel);
    text1 = new TextField(24);
    add(text1);
    lastNameLabel = new Label("Last Name:");
    add(lastNameLabel);
    text2 = new TextField(24);
    add(text2);
    button1 = new Button("Search for this first
        name:");
    add(button1);
    text3 = new TextField(10);
    add(text3);

    URL url = null;
    try {
        url = new URL("file:////c://xml//searcher//
            searcher.xml");
    }
    catch (MalformedURLException e1) {
        System.out.println("Cannot create url for: "
            + fileName);
        System.exit(0);
    }

    d = new Document();

    try {
        d.load(url);
    }
    catch (ParseException e3) {
        d.reportError(e3, System.out);
    }
```

```
        if (d != null) {
            maxRecordNumber = d.getRoot().numElements()
                - 1;
        }
    }
```

Now we'll write the **action()** method to handle the actual search process. First, we make sure the user has pressed the Search button, button1:

```
public boolean action (Event e, Object o){

    if(e.target.equals(button1)){   //The Find button
        .
        .
        .
    }
}
```

If the user has pressed button1 and wants to search for a particular first name, we will loop over all the records until we find a matching record (if there is one):

```
public boolean action (Event e, Object o){

    if(e.target.equals(button1)){   //The Find button

        Element root = d.getRoot();
        Enumeration enum = root.getChildren();

        for(int index = 0; index <= maxRecordNumber;
            index++){
            elem = (Element)enum.nextElement();
            .
            .
            .
        }
    }
}
```

The actual <FIRSTNAME> element is the second **child** element in each record:

```
<NAME>
    <LASTNAME>Edwards</LASTNAME>
    <FIRSTNAME>Tina</FIRSTNAME>
</NAME>
```

Because the element we're looking for is the second **child** element, we have to get an enumeration of the current record's children and call `nextElement()` twice to get the <FIRSTNAME> element, which we place in the variable `elem3`:

```
public boolean action (Event e, Object o){

    if(e.target.equals(button1)){   //The Find button

        Element root = d.getRoot();
        Element elem = null, elem2 = null, elem3 =
            null;
        Enumeration enum = root.getChildren();

        for(int index = 0; index <= maxRecordNumber;
            index++){
            elem = (Element)enum.nextElement();

            Enumeration enum2 = elem.getChildren();

            elem2 = (Element)enum2.nextElement();
            elem3 = (Element)enum2.nextElement();
                         .
                         .
                         .

        }
    }
}
```

Now we have the current record's <FIRSTNAME> element in the `elem3` variable. If the text in that element matches the text in the text field (text3) that holds the name we're looking for, we fill the top two text fields (text1 and text2) with the first and last names from this record:

```
public boolean action (Event e, Object o){

    if(e.target.equals(button1)){   //The Find button

        Element root = d.getRoot();
        Element elem = null, elem2 = null, elem3 =
            null;
        Enumeration enum = root.getChildren();

        for(int index = 0; index <= maxRecordNumber;
            index++){
            elem = (Element)enum.nextElement();

            Enumeration enum2 = elem.getChildren();

            elem2 = (Element)enum2.nextElement();
            elem3 = (Element)enum2.nextElement();

            if (elem3.getTagName().equals("FIRSTNAME")
                &&
```

```
                                elem3.getText()
                                        .equals(text3.getText()) ) {
                            text1.setText(elem3.getText());
                            text2.setText(elem2.getText());
                        }
                    }
                }
                return true;
            }
        }
```

That's it—run the searcher program now, as shown in Figure 5-5.

If you place a first name in the lower text field that matches one of the first names in a record in the **searcher.xml** document and click the Search button, the program will display that record in the upper text fields, as shown in Figure 5-6.

The **searcher.java** application is a success—using this program, we've gotten a start on searching through databases. Of course, you can elaborate this topic endlessly, organizing your XML documents into binary trees and other formal data structures to make the searching process more efficient. The code for this program, **searcher.java**, appears in List-

Figure 5-5.
The searcher application.

Figure 5-6.
Finding a record in the searcher application.

ing 5-5, and the XML document that program reads in, `searcher.xml`, appears in Listing 5-6.

```java
import com.ms.xml.ParseException;
import com.ms.xml.Document;
import com.ms.xml.Element;

import java.util.Enumeration;
import java.awt.*;
import java.net.*;
import java.applet.Applet;

public class searcher extends Applet{

    static String fileName;
    Label firstNameLabel, lastNameLabel;
    TextField text1, text2, text3;
    Button button1;
    Document d;
    int maxRecordNumber = 0;

    public static void main(String args[])
    {
        searcherFrame frame =
            new searcherFrame("The searcher application");

        frame.show();
        frame.hide();
        frame.resize(320, 300);

        searcher applet = new searcher();

        frame.add("Center", applet);
        applet.init();
        applet.start();
        frame.show();
    }

    public void init(){
        firstNameLabel = new Label("First Name:");
        add(firstNameLabel);
        text1 = new TextField(24);
        add(text1);
        lastNameLabel = new Label("Last Name:");
        add(lastNameLabel);
        text2 = new TextField(24);
        add(text2);
        button1 = new Button("Search for this first
            name:");
```

Listing 5-5.
Continued.

```
    add(button1);
text3 = new TextField(10);
add(text3);

URL url = null;
try {
    url = new URL("file:////c://xml//searcher//
        searcher.xml");
}
catch (MalformedURLException e1) {
    System.out.println("Cannot create url for: "
        + fileName);
    System.exit(0);
}

d = new Document();

try {
    d.load(url);
}
catch (ParseException e3) {
    d.reportError(e3, System.out);
}

if (d != null) {
    maxRecordNumber = d.getRoot().numElements()
        - 1;
}
}

public boolean action (Event e, Object o){

    if(e.target.equals(button1)){   //The Find button

        Element root = d.getRoot();
        Element elem = null, elem2 = null, elem3 =
            null;
        Enumeration enum = root.getChildren();

        for(int index = 0; index <= maxRecordNumber;
            index++){
            elem = (Element)enum.nextElement();

            Enumeration enum2 = elem.getChildren();

            elem2 = (Element)enum2.nextElement();
            elem3 = (Element)enum2.nextElement();

            if (elem3.getTagName().equals("FIRSTNAME")
                && elem3.getText().equals(text3
                .getText()) ) {
```

Continues

Listing 5-5.
Continued.

```java
                        text1.setText(elem3.getText());
                        text2.setText(elem2.getText());
                }
            }
        }
        return true;
    }

}
class searcherFrame extends Frame
{
    public searcherFrame(String str)
    {
        super (str);
    }

    public boolean handleEvent(Event evt)
    {
        switch (evt.id)
        {
            case Event.WINDOW_DESTROY:
                dispose();
                System.exit(0);
                return true;

            default:
                return super.handleEvent(evt);
        }
    }
}
```

Listing 5-6.
searcher.xml.

```xml
<?XML version = "1.0" ?>
<!DOCTYPE DOCUMENT [
<!ELEMENT DOCUMENT (NAME)*>
<!ELEMENT NAME (LASTNAME, FIRSTNAME)>
<!ELEMENT LASTNAME (#PCDATA)>
<!ELEMENT FIRSTNAME (#PCDATA)>
]>
<DOCUMENT>
<NAME>
    <LASTNAME>Franklin</LASTNAME>
    <FIRSTNAME>Tom</FIRSTNAME>
</NAME>
<NAME>
    <LASTNAME>Guertin</LASTNAME>
    <FIRSTNAME>Phoebe</FIRSTNAME>
</NAME>
<NAME>
    <LASTNAME>Johnson</LASTNAME>
```

Listing 5-6.
Continued.

```
        <FIRSTNAME>Frank</FIRSTNAME>
    </NAME>
    <NAME>
        <LASTNAME>Tomlin</LASTNAME>
        <FIRSTNAME>Brenda</FIRSTNAME>
    </NAME>
    <NAME>
        <LASTNAME>Edwards</LASTNAME>
        <FIRSTNAME>Tina</FIRSTNAME>
    </NAME>
</DOCUMENT>
```

The last example in this chapter will have to do with something we haven't yet encountered—variable length records.

The medicines Example

Many databases require some flexibility on the part of the database application. For example, we might put together a database application that keeps track of the medicines a set of patients is taking. Not every patient will take the same number of medicines, so we must allow for variable-length records; some patients may be taking three medications, some only one.

XML is up to the task: the variable-length nature of our records is reflected in the DTD of our new example's XML file, **medicines.xml**, where we indicate that each record can contain exactly one <LASTNAME> element, exactly one <FIRSTNAME> element, but zero or more occurrences of the <MEDICINE> element:

```
<?XML version = "1.0" ?>
<!DOCTYPE DOCUMENT [
<!ELEMENT DOCUMENT (NAME)*>
<!ELEMENT NAME (LASTNAME,FIRSTNAME,MEDICINE*)>
<!ELEMENT LASTNAME (#PCDATA)>
<!ELEMENT FIRSTNAME (#PCDATA)>
<!ELEMENT MEDICINE (#PCDATA)>
]>
```

Here's the whole database for this example, **medicines.xml**:

```
<?XML version = "1.0" ?>
<!DOCTYPE DOCUMENT [
<!ELEMENT DOCUMENT (NAME)*>
<!ELEMENT NAME (LASTNAME,FIRSTNAME,MEDICINE*)>
```

```
<!ELEMENT LASTNAME (#PCDATA)>
<!ELEMENT FIRSTNAME (#PCDATA)>
<!ELEMENT MEDICINE (#PCDATA)>
]>
<DOCUMENT>
<NAME>
     <LASTNAME>Franklin</LASTNAME>
     <FIRSTNAME>Tom</FIRSTNAME>
     <MEDICINE>
     Medicine 1
     </MEDICINE>
     <MEDICINE>
     Medicine 2
     </MEDICINE>
     <MEDICINE>
     Medicine 3
     </MEDICINE>
</NAME>
<NAME>
     <LASTNAME>Johnson</LASTNAME>
     <FIRSTNAME>Ed</FIRSTNAME>
     <MEDICINE>
     Medicine 1
     </MEDICINE>
     <MEDICINE>
     Medicine 2
     </MEDICINE>
</NAME>
<NAME>
     <LASTNAME>Edwards</LASTNAME>
     <FIRSTNAME>Phoebe</FIRSTNAME>
     <MEDICINE>
     Medicine 1
     </MEDICINE>
</NAME>
<NAME>
     <LASTNAME>Parnell</LASTNAME>
     <FIRSTNAME>Britta</FIRSTNAME>
     <MEDICINE>
     Medicine 1
     </MEDICINE>
     <MEDICINE>
     Medicine 2
     </MEDICINE>
     <MEDICINE>
     Medicine 3
     </MEDICINE>
</NAME>
<NAME>
     <LASTNAME>Tompkins</LASTNAME>
     <FIRSTNAME>Tina</FIRSTNAME>
     <MEDICINE>
     Medicine 1
```

```
        </MEDICINE>
        <MEDICINE>
        Medicine 2
        </MEDICINE>
    </NAME>
    </DOCUMENT>
```

Our application for this example will display each record, including the person's name and the medications they take:

```
┌─────────────────────────────────────────┐
│                                         │
├─────────────────────────────────────────┤
│                                         │
│                                         │
│                  ┌───────────────────┐  │
│  First Name:     │ Tom               │  │
│                  └───────────────────┘  │
│                                         │
│                  ┌───────────────────┐  │
│  Last Name:      │ Franklin          │  │
│                  └───────────────────┘  │
│                                         │
│  ┌───────────────────────────────────┐  │
│  │ Medicine 1                        │  │
│  └───────────────────────────────────┘  │
│  ┌───────────────────────────────────┐  │
│  │ Medicine 2                        │  │
│  └───────────────────────────────────┘  │
│  ┌───────────────────────────────────┐  │
│  │ Medicine 3                        │  │
│  └───────────────────────────────────┘  │
│           ┌─────┐   ┌─────┐             │
│           │  <  │   │  >  │             │
│           └─────┘   └─────┘             │
└─────────────────────────────────────────┘
```

Using the forward and back navigation buttons, the user can move through the database displaying record after record, including the medications the patient is taking, whether that's one, two, or three medications:

```
┌─────────────────────────────────────────┐
│                                         │
├─────────────────────────────────────────┤
│                                         │
│                    ┌──────────────────┐ │
│   First Name:      │ Ed               │ │
│                    └──────────────────┘ │
│                                         │
│                    ┌──────────────────┐ │
│   Last Name:       │ Johnson          │ │
│                    └──────────────────┘ │
│                                         │
│   ┌─────────────────────────────────┐   │
│   │ Medicine 1                      │   │
│   └─────────────────────────────────┘   │
│                                         │
│   ┌─────────────────────────────────┐   │
│   │ Medicine 2                      │   │
│   └─────────────────────────────────┘   │
│                                         │
│   ┌─────────────────────────────────┐   │
│   │                                 │   │
│   └─────────────────────────────────┘   │
│           ┌─────┐   ┌─────┐             │
│           │  <  │   │  >  │             │
│           └─────┘   └─────┘             │
└─────────────────────────────────────────┘
```

We begin this example as we have with the previous examples in this chapter—by setting up the applet in a window, displaying the controls we'll need, as well as loading in the document (**medicines.xml** here) and displaying the first record:

```java
import com.ms.xml.ParseException;
import com.ms.xml.Document;
import com.ms.xml.Element;

import java.awt.*;
import java.net.*;
import java.applet.Applet;


public class medicines extends Applet{

    static String filename;
    Label firstNameLabel, lastNameLabel;
    TextField text1, text2;
    TextField medicine1, medicine2, medicine3;
    Button button1, button2;
    Document d;
```

```
    int currentRecordNumber = 0;

public static void main(String args[])
{
    medicinesFrame frame = new medicinesFrame("The
        medicines application");

    frame.show();
    frame.hide();
    frame.resize(320, 240);

    medicines applet = new medicines();

    frame.add("Center", applet);
    applet.init();
    applet.start();
    frame.show();
}

public void init(){
    firstNameLabel = new Label("First Name:");
    add(firstNameLabel);
    text1 = new TextField(24);
    add(text1);
    lastNameLabel = new Label("Last Name:");
    add(lastNameLabel);
    text2 = new TextField(24);
    add(text2);
    medicine1 = new TextField(35);
    add(medicine1);
    medicine2 = new TextField(35);
    add(medicine2);
    medicine3 = new TextField(35);
    add(medicine3);
    button1 = new Button("<");
    add(button1);
    button2 = new Button(">");
    add(button2);

    URL url = null;
    try {
        url = new URL("file:////c://xml//medicines//
            medicines.xml");
    }
    catch (MalformedURLException e1) {
        System.out.println("Cannot create URL for: "
            + filename);
        System.exit(0);
    }

    d = new Document();

    try {
        d.load(url);
    }
```

```
        catch (ParseException e3) {
            d.reportError(e3, System.out);
        }
        if (d != null) {
            showRecord(0);
        }
    }
```

We also enable the forward and back buttons as we have before, incrementing or decrementing the current record number and calling the method we'll name `showRecord()`:

```
public boolean action (Event e, Object o){

    if(e.target.equals(button1)){   //The < button
        if(currentRecordNumber > 0){
            currentRecordNumber-;
        }
        showRecord(currentRecordNumber);
    }
    if(e.target.equals(button2)){   //The > button
        if(currentRecordNumber < 4){
            currentRecordNumber++;
        }
        showRecord(currentRecordNumber);
    }

    return true;
}
```

Writing the `showRecord()` Method

The `showRecord()` method is where we have to allow for a variable number of medicine fields in each record. We start that method by getting the **root** element of the document and looping over an enumeration of the root's **child** elements until we get to the record we're supposed to display:

```
void showRecord(int recordNumber)
{
    Element root = d.getRoot();
    Element elem = null, elem2 = null;
    Enumeration enum = root.getChildren();

    for(int index = 0; index <= recordNumber; index++){
        elem = (Element)enum.nextElement();
    }
     .
     .
     .
```

Next, we clear all the text fields that display the medicines the person is taking (because although this person may only be taking one medicine, the last record displayed may have included two or three medicines, and we don't want to leave any data left over in the medicine text fields from the last record displayed):

```
void showRecord(int recordNumber)
{
    Element root = d.getRoot();
    Element elem = null, elem2 = null;
    Enumeration enum = root.getChildren();

    for(int index = 0; index <= recordNumber;
        index++){
        elem = (Element)enum.nextElement();
    }

    medicine1.setText("");
    medicine2.setText("");
    medicine3.setText("");
                      .
                      .
                      .

    }
}
```

Now we get the **child** elements of the current record, looping over those **child** elements and filling the text1 and text2 text fields with the patient's first and last names:

```
void showRecord(int recordNumber)
{
    Element root = d.getRoot();
    Element elem = null, elem2 = null;
    Enumeration enum = root.getChildren();

    for(int index = 0; index <= recordNumber;
        index++){
        elem = (Element)enum.nextElement();
    }

    medicine1.setText("");
    medicine2.setText("");
    medicine3.setText("");

    Enumeration enum2 = elem.getChildren();
    while(enum2.hasMoreElements()){

        elem2 = (Element)enum2.nextElement();

        if (elem2.getTagName().equals("FIRSTNAME")) {
```

```
                    text1.setText(elem2.getText());
                }

                if (elem2.getTagName().equals("LASTNAME")) {
                    text2.setText(elem2.getText());
                }
                         .
                         .
                         .

            }
        }
    }
```

Finally, if the element is a <MEDICINE> element, we want to display its text in the medicine text fields, which we have declared as medicine1, medicine2, and medicine3. Before placing the medicine name into one of those text fields, we check to make sure that text field is empty, and if it is, we display the medicine name in that text field this way:

```
    void showRecord(int recordNumber)
    {
        Element root = d.getRoot();
        Element elem = null, elem2 = null;
        Enumeration enum = root.getChildren();

        for(int index = 0; index <= recordNumber;
               index++){
            elem = (Element)enum.nextElement();
        }

        medicine1.setText("");
        medicine2.setText("");
        medicine3.setText("");

        Enumeration enum2 = elem.getChildren();
        while(enum2.hasMoreElements()){

            elem2 = (Element)enum2.nextElement();

            if (elem2.getTagName().equals("FIRSTNAME")) {
                text1.setText(elem2.getText());
            }

            if (elem2.getTagName().equals("LASTNAME")) {
                text2.setText(elem2.getText());
            }

            if (elem2.getTagName().equals("MEDICINE")) {
                if(medicine1.getText().equals("")){
                    medicine1.setText(elem2.getText());
                }
                else if(medicine2.getText().equals("")){
```

```
                            medicine2.setText(elem2.getText());
                        }
                        else if(medicine3.getText().equals("")){
                            medicine3.setText(elem2.getText());
                        }
                    }
                }
            }
        }
```

In this way we're able to fill the medicine text fields successively with entry after entry.

That's it—run the medicines application now, as shown in Figure 5-7. As you can see in that figure, the program is displaying the first record in the **medicines.xml** database.

When the user clicks the forward button, we move to the next record in the database, as shown in Figure 5-8. Here, there are only two medicines, but the program handles the variable-length records as we have designed it.

The **medicines.java** program is a success; now we're handling databases with variable-length records. The code for this application, **medicines.java**, appears in Listing 5-7, and the document it reads in, **medicines.xml**, appears in Listing 5-8.

Figure 5-7.
The medicines application.

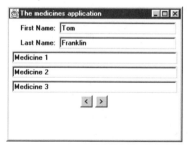

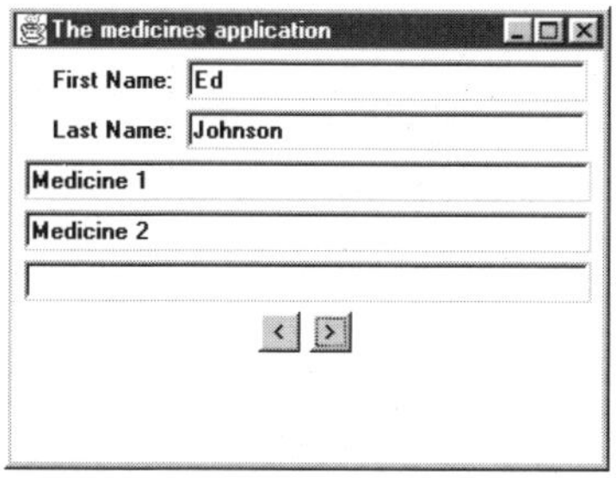

Figure 5-8.
Handling variable-length records in the medicines application.

Listing 5-7.
medicines.java

```java
import com.ms.xml.ParseException;
import com.ms.xml.Document;
import com.ms.xml.Element;

import java.util.Enumeration;
import java.awt.*;
import java.net.*;
import java.applet.Applet;


public class medicines extends Applet{

    static String filename;
    Label firstNameLabel, lastNameLabel;
    TextField text1, text2;
    TextField medicine1, medicine2, medicine3;
    Button button1, button2;
    Document d;
    int currentRecordNumber = 0;

    public static void main(String args[])
    {
        medicinesFrame frame = new
                medicinesFrame("The medicines application");

        frame.show();
        frame.hide();
        frame.resize(320, 240);

        medicines applet = new medicines();

        frame.add("Center", applet);
        applet.init();
        applet.start();
        frame.show();
    }

    public void init(){
        firstNameLabel = new Label("First Name:");
        add(firstNameLabel);
        text1 = new TextField(24);
        add(text1);
        lastNameLabel = new Label("Last Name:");
        add(lastNameLabel);
        text2 = new TextField(24);
        add(text2);
        medicine1 = new TextField(35);
        add(medicine1);
        medicine2 = new TextField(35);
        add(medicine2);
        medicine3 = new TextField(35);
        add(medicine3);
```

Listing 5-7.
Continued.

```
        button1 = new Button("<");
        add(button1);
        button2 = new Button(">");
        add(button2);

        URL url = null;
        try {
            url = new URL("file:////c://xml//medicines//
                medicines.xml");
        }
        catch (MalformedURLException e1) {
            System.out.println("Cannot create URL for: " +
                filename);
            System.exit(0);
        }

        d = new Document();

        try {
            d.load(url);
        }
        catch (ParseException e3) {
            d.reportError(e3, System.out);
        }
        if (d != null) {
            showRecord(0);
        }
    }

    public boolean action (Event e, Object o){

        if(e.target.equals(button1)){   //The < button
            if(currentRecordNumber > 0){
                currentRecordNumber-;
            }
            showRecord(currentRecordNumber);
        }
        if(e.target.equals(button2)){   //The > button
            if(currentRecordNumber < 4){
                currentRecordNumber++;
            }
            showRecord(currentRecordNumber);
        }

        return true;
    }

    void showRecord(int recordNumber)
    {
        Element root = d.getRoot();
        Element elem = null, elem2 = null;
```

Continues

Listing 5-7.
Continued.

```
        Enumeration enum = root.getChildren();
        for(int index = 0; index <= recordNumber;
                index++){
            elem = (Element)enum.nextElement();
        }
        medicine1.setText("");
        medicine2.setText("");
        medicine3.setText("");

        Enumeration enum2 = elem.getChildren();
        while(enum2.hasMoreElements()){

            elem2 = (Element)enum2.nextElement();

            if (elem2.getTagName().equals("FIRSTNAME")) {
                text1.setText(elem2.getText());
            }

            if (elem2.getTagName().equals("LASTNAME")) {
                text2.setText(elem2.getText());
            }

            if (elem2.getTagName().equals("MEDICINE")) {
                if(medicine1.getText().equals("")){
                    medicine1.setText(elem2.getText());
                }
                else if(medicine2.getText().equals("")){
                    medicine2.setText(elem2.getText());
                }
                else if(medicine3.getText().equals("")){
                    medicine3.setText(elem2.getText());
                }
            }
        }
    }
}

class medicinesFrame extends Frame
{
    public medicinesFrame(String str)
    {
        super (str);
    }

    public boolean handleEvent(Event evt)
    {
        switch (evt.id)
        {
            case Event.WINDOW_DESTROY:
                dispose();
```

Listing 5-7.
Continued.

```
                                System.exit(0);
                                return true;

                        default:
                                return super.handleEvent(evt);
                }
        }
}
```

Listing 5-8.
`medicines.xml`.

```xml
<?XML version = "1.0" ?>
<!DOCTYPE DOCUMENT [
<!ELEMENT DOCUMENT (NAME)*>
<!ELEMENT NAME (LASTNAME,FIRSTNAME,MEDICINE*)>
<!ELEMENT LASTNAME (#PCDATA)>
<!ELEMENT FIRSTNAME (#PCDATA)>
<!ELEMENT MEDICINE (#PCDATA)>
]>
<DOCUMENT>
<NAME>
        <LASTNAME>Franklin</LASTNAME>
        <FIRSTNAME>Tom</FIRSTNAME>
        <MEDICINE>
        Medicine 1
        </MEDICINE>
        <MEDICINE>
        Medicine 2
        </MEDICINE>
        <MEDICINE>
        Medicine 3
        </MEDICINE>
</NAME>
<NAME>
        <LASTNAME>Johnson</LASTNAME>
        <FIRSTNAME>Ed</FIRSTNAME>
        <MEDICINE>
        Medicine 1
        </MEDICINE>
        <MEDICINE>
        Medicine 2
        </MEDICINE>
</NAME>
<NAME>
        <LASTNAME>Edwards</LASTNAME>
        <FIRSTNAME>Phoebe</FIRSTNAME>
        <MEDICINE>
        Medicine 1
        </MEDICINE>
</NAME>
```

Continues

Listing 5-8.
Continued.

```xml
<NAME>
    <LASTNAME>Parnell</LASTNAME>
    <FIRSTNAME>Britta</FIRSTNAME>
    <MEDICINE>
    Medicine 1
    </MEDICINE>
    <MEDICINE>
    Medicine 2
    </MEDICINE>
    <MEDICINE>
    Medicine 3
    </MEDICINE>
</NAME>
<NAME>
    <LASTNAME>Tompkins</LASTNAME>
    <FIRSTNAME>Tina</FIRSTNAME>
    <MEDICINE>
    Medicine 1
    </MEDICINE>
    <MEDICINE>
    Medicine 2
    </MEDICINE>
</NAME>
</DOCUMENT>
```

SUMMARY

That completes our exploration of XML database handling for the moment. We've seen how to move through the records in a database while displaying each record's data, how to add records to a database and save the new database file, how to search through a database for a record that matches a specific criterion, and now how to handle variable-length records. We've come far in this chapter.

In the next chapter, we'll continue our exploration of XML as we look at Part II of the XML specification—XML links.

6

XML Links

In this chapter, we'll explore part II of the XML specification—XML links. XML links expand the idea of the simple links you find in specifications like HTML. This chapter is based on the W3C document "WD-xml-link-970731," which you can find at `http://www.w3.org/TR/WD-xml-link-970731`; the most up-to-date version of the XML link specification may be found at `http://www.w3.org/TR/WD-xml-link`.

XML can support not only the unidirectional links of HTML, but also more sophisticated multidirectional and self-describing links. A multidirectional link is a link that you can move along—a process called *traversing*—starting at more than one of the data items that it links; these data items are called the link's *resources*. We are going to examine the XML link specification in this chapter, including simple links, extended links, inline links, out-of-line links, keyword-driven links, extended link groups, the show and actuate link axes, and more. There's a great deal coming up in this chapter, so we will start at once with an overview of XML links.

What Is an XML Link?

As you might expect, you specify an XML link with an XML element. However, unlike HTML, there is no specific XML link tag (like the <A> tag in HTML). Instead, you use the XML-LINK *attribute* to specify a link; this attribute can take the values SIMPLE, EXTENDED, LOCATOR, GROUP, or DOCUMENT corresponding to the various types of XML links and linking elements. The actual target of the link or the link element is stored in the HREF attribute. Here's an example of the simplest type of XML link, which we can model after the HTML <A> element:

```
<A XML-LINK="SIMPLE" HREF="http://microsoft.com/
    ">Microsoft</A>
```

TIP *Because XML links rely on using attributes, there may be a conflict between the attributes you are already using for a tag and the XML link attributes (which are ROLE, HREF, TITLE, SHOW, INLINE, CONTENT-ROLE, CONTENT-TITLE, ACTUATE, BEHAVIOR, and STEPS). To remove the conflict, you can rename (this process is called* remapping*) the XML attributes to new names, like this, where we rename the XML link TITLE attribute to XML-TITLE and the XML link attribute SHOW to XML-SHOW:*

```
<!ATTLIST DOCUMENT XML-LINK          CDATA #FIXED "SIMPLE"
                   XML-ATTRIBUTES CDATA #FIXED
                       "TITLE XML-TITLE SHOW XML-SHOW">
```

The two main types of XML links are *simple* and *extended,* and we'll get an overview of those types now.

Simple XML Links

Simple XML links are very much like HTML links. Here's how you can set up an <A> tag in a document so that it acts like an HTML link (note that you can give the tag any tag name, not just <A>, because XML checks the XML-LINK attribute to find links, not the tag name):

```
<!ELEMENT A ANY>
<!ATTLIST A
           XML-LINK        CDATA               #FIXED
                                               "SIMPLE"
```

```
        ROLE            CDATA                       #IMPLIED
        HREF            CDATA                       #REQUIRED
        TITLE           CDATA                       #IMPLIED
        INLINE          (TRUE|FALSE)                "TRUE"
        CONTENT-ROLE    CDATA                       #IMPLIED
        CONTENT-TITLE   CDATA                       #IMPLIED
        SHOW            (EMBED|REPLACE|NEW)         "REPLACE"
        ACTUATE         (AUTO|USER)                 "USER"
        BEHAVIOR        CDATA                       #IMPLIED
    >
```

What do all the preceding attributes—ROLE, TITLE, and so on—mean?

We've seen the XML-LINK attribute; this is the attribute that indicates this element is a link. Possible values are SIMPLE, EXTENDED, LOCATOR, GROUP, or DOCUMENT. The ROLE attribute is a string that indicates the role of the link; for example, you could keep track of cross-references or a list of appendixes by filling in the ROLE attribute.

We've also seen the HREF attribute; this attribute holds the locator for the resource we're linking to. This attribute can contain URLs or other pointers, as we'll see. The TITLE attribute holds the link's title—the text the link is known by. It's optional to give the link a title.

The INLINE attribute can take values of TRUE or FALSE and indicates if the link is *inline* or *out-of-line*. If a link is inline (which is the default), all the content of this element is to be considered a resource of the link—except for any child locator elements, if there are any. If INLINE is FALSE, the link is out-of-line, which means the link instructs applications where to look for links. (This will make more sense when we examine link groups at the end of the chapter.)

TIP *Out-of-line links are needed to support multidirectional links, because such out-of-line elements indicate where to look for links. You also use them to set up links to and from read-only resources where you can't embed a link.*

When the link is inline, you can use the CONTENT-ROLE and CONTENT-TITLE attributes to provide the title and role for the content of this link.

The SHOW *axis* indicates what traversal to the new resource should do. The value of SHOW indicates if the new resource should be embedded in the present resource (SHOW = EMBED), replace the present resource (SHOW = REPLACE, the default), or be processed in an entirely new context (SHOW = NEW).

You use the ACTUATE axis to indicate when the application activates the link. You can indicate that the program should traverse the link as soon as it comes upon that link (ACTUATE = AUTO), or when the user directs (ACTUATE = USER, the default). You use the BEHAVIOR attribute to hold a text string that is made up of instructions for traversal behavior. This attribute is added to make linking as general as possible in XML, but XML does not dictate the contents of this attribute; you can place application and system-specific information in this attribute and make use of it in your application.

That's what the various attributes do in a simple XML link. We will put this declaration to use now as we create an example with a simple XML link built-in.

The `link` Example

In the first example of this chapter, we'll present the user with a window like this:

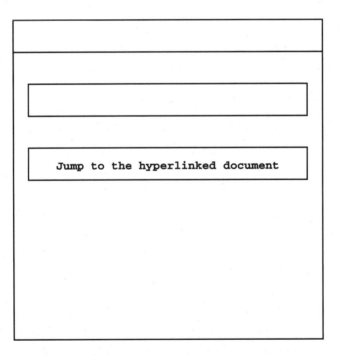

When the user clicks the Jump to the hyperlinked document button, we'll load in the document `link.xml`:

```
<?XML VERSION = "1.0" ?>
<!DOCTYPE DOCUMENT [
```

```
<!ELEMENT DOCUMENT (#PCDATA|A)*>
<!ELEMENT A (#PCDATA)>
<!ATTLIST A
          XML-LINK          CDATA              #FIXED
                                               "SIMPLE"
          ROLE              CDATA              #IMPLIED
          HREF              CDATA              #REQUIRED
          TITLE             CDATA              #IMPLIED
          INLINE            (TRUE|FALSE)       "TRUE"
          CONTENT-ROLE      CDATA              #IMPLIED
          CONTENT-TITLE     CDATA              #IMPLIED
          SHOW              (EMBED|REPLACE|NEW) "REPLACE"
          ACTUATE           (AUTO|USER)        "USER"
          BEHAVIOR          CDATA              #IMPLIED
>
]>
<DOCUMENT>
    <A XML-LINK="SIMPLE"
HREF="FILE:////C://XML//LINK//LINK2.XML">The
    new document.</A>
</DOCUMENT>
```

NOTE   *In the examples in this chapter, we'll double each forward slash in HREF strings so that we can pass those strings directly to the Java URL class constructor. In practice, you are free to set up HREF strings as you like in your applications; usually, you use single, not double, slashes.*

We'll search through `link.xml` until we find the element with the XML-LINK attribute and then jump to the linked document as specified in the HREF attribute. Here, that's `link2.xml`, which looks like this:

```
<?XML version = "1.0" ?>
<!DOCTYPE DOCUMENT [
<!ELEMENT DOCUMENT (CUSTOMER)*>
<!ELEMENT CUSTOMER (NAME,DATE,ORDERS)>
<!ELEMENT NAME (LASTNAME,FIRSTNAME)>
<!ELEMENT LASTNAME (#PCDATA)>
<!ELEMENT FIRSTNAME (#PCDATA)>
<!ELEMENT DATE (#PCDATA)>
<!ELEMENT ORDERS (ITEM)*>
<!ELEMENT ITEM (PRODUCT,NUMBER,PRICE)>
<!ELEMENT PRODUCT (#PCDATA)>
<!ELEMENT NUMBER (#PCDATA)>
<!ELEMENT PRICE (#PCDATA)>
]>
<DOCUMENT>
<CUSTOMER>
    <NAME>
        <LASTNAME>Edwards</LASTNAME>
        <FIRSTNAME>Britta</FIRSTNAME>
```

```
        </NAME>
        <DATE>April 17, 1998</DATE>
        <ORDERS>
            <ITEM>
                <PRODUCT>Cucumber</PRODUCT>
                <NUMBER>5</NUMBER>
                <PRICE>$1.25</PRICE>
            </ITEM>
            <ITEM>
                <PRODUCT>Lettuce</PRODUCT>
                <NUMBER>2</NUMBER>
                <PRICE>$.98</PRICE>
            </ITEM>
        </ORDERS>
    </CUSTOMER>
    <CUSTOMER>
        <NAME>
            <LASTNAME>Thompson</LASTNAME>
            <FIRSTNAME>Phoebe</FIRSTNAME>
        </NAME>
        <DATE>May 27, 1998</DATE>
        <ORDERS>
            <ITEM>
                <PRODUCT>Banana</PRODUCT>
                <NUMBER>12</NUMBER>
                <PRICE>$2.95</PRICE>
            </ITEM>
            <ITEM>
                <PRODUCT>Apple</PRODUCT>
                <NUMBER>6</NUMBER>
                <PRICE>$1.50</PRICE>
            </ITEM>
        </ORDERS>
    </CUSTOMER>
</DOCUMENT>
```

After loading in **link2.xml**, we'll display that document's text in the text field as shown on the following page.

We start this application by constructing and setting up the application's window and adding the controls we'll need:

```
┌─────────────────────────────────────────┐
│                                         │
├─────────────────────────────────────────┤
│                                         │
│   ┌─────────────────────────────────┐   │
│   │   Edwards Britta April 17, 1998 │   │
│   └─────────────────────────────────┘   │
│                                         │
│   ┌─────────────────────────────────┐   │
│   │  Jump to the hyperlinked document│   │
│   └─────────────────────────────────┘   │
│                                         │
│                                         │
│                                         │
│                                         │
│                                         │
│                                         │
└─────────────────────────────────────────┘
```

```java
import com.ms.xml.ParseException;
import com.ms.xml.Document;
import com.ms.xml.Element;

import java.awt.*;
import java.net.*;
import java.applet.Applet;

public class link extends Applet{

    static String filename;
    TextField text1;
    Button button1;

    public static void main(String args[])
    {
        linkFrame frame = new linkFrame("The link
            application");

        frame.show();
        frame.hide();
        frame.resize(320, 320);
```

```
        link applet = new link();

        frame.add("Center", applet);
        applet.init();
        applet.start();
        frame.show();
    }

public void init(){
        text1 = new TextField(20);
        add(text1);
        button1 = new Button("Jump to the hyperlinked
            document");
        add(button1);
    }
```

When the user clicks the button, we should read in **link.xml**, and we do that this way in the **action()** method:

```
public boolean action (Event e, Object o){

    URL url = null;
    filename = "file:////c://xml//link//link.xml";
    try {
        url = new URL(filename);
    } catch (MalformedURLException e1) {
        System.out.println("Cannot create url for: "
            + filename);
        System.exit(0);
    }

    Document d = new Document();

    try {
        d.load(url);
    }
    catch (ParseException e2) {
        d.reportError(e2, System.out);
    }
        .
        .
        .

}
```

Now we have **link.xml** stored in the document object **d**. The next step is to search for the element we've defined as the link element, <A>, and we do that this way, with an enumeration of the **root** element's children:

```
public boolean action (Event e, Object o){

    URL url = null;
        .
```

```
        .
        .

if (d != null) {
    Element root = d.getRoot();
    Enumeration enum = root.getChildren();
    while (enum.hasMoreElements()) {
        Element elem =
                (Element)enum.nextElement();
        if (elem.getTagName().equals("A")) {
            .
            .
            .

        }
    }
}
}
}
```

Now we will read in the document we are linking to, which we find in the HREF attribute. To get the text of that attribute, we use **getAttribute()** this way, creating a new URL object for the document we're linking to:

```
public boolean action (Event e, Object o){

    URL url = null;
        .
        .
        .

    if (d != null) {
        Element root = d.getRoot();
        Enumeration enum = root.getChildren();
        while (enum.hasMoreElements()) {
            Element elem =
                    (Element)enum.nextElement();
            if (elem.getTagName().equals("A")) {

                URL url2 = null;

                try {
                    url2 = new
                    URL(elem.getAttribute("HREF"));
                }
                catch (MalformedURLException e3) {
                    System.out.println("Cannot create
                    URL for: " +
                    elem.getAttribute("HREF"));
                    System.exit(0);
                }
                    .
                    .
```

```
                     }
                  }
               }
            }
         }
```

Now we have an URL for the document we're linking to; we read in that document and display its text in the text field, text1:

```
public boolean action (Event e, Object o){

    URL url = null;
       .
       .
       .

    if (d != null) {
        Element root = d.getRoot();
        Enumeration enum = root.getChildren();
        while (enum.hasMoreElements()) {
            Element elem =
                (Element)enum.nextElement();
            if (elem.getTagName().equals("A")) {

                URL url2 = null;

                try {
                    url2 = new URL
                        (elem.getAttribute("HREF"));
                }
                catch (MalformedURLException e3) {
                    System.out.println("Cannot create
                        URL for: " +
                        elem.getAttribute("HREF"));
                    System.exit(0);
                }

                Document d2 = new Document();

                try {
                    d2.load(url2);
                }
                catch (ParseException e4) {
                    d2.reportError(e4, System.out);
                }

                text1.setText(d2.getText());
            }
        }
    }
    return true;
    }
}
```

That's it—run the link example now, as shown in Figure 6-1.

When the user clicks the Jump button, we read in the **link.xml** document and jump to the linked document, **link2.xml**, and display that second document's text, as shown in Figure 6-2.

The link example is a success; now we're using simple links in XML. The code for this application, **link.java**, appears in Listing 6-1, and the documents this application uses, **link.xml** and **link2.xml**, appear in Listings 6-2 and 6-3, respectively.

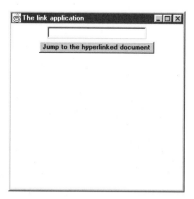

Figure 6-1.
The link application.

Figure 6-2.
Following a simple
XML link.

Listing 6-1.
link.java.

```
import com.ms.xml.ParseException;
import com.ms.xml.Document;
import com.ms.xml.Element;

import java.util.Enumeration;
import java.awt.*;
import java.net.*;
import java.applet.Applet;
```

Continues

Listing 6-1.
Continued.

```java
public class link extends Applet{

    static String filename;
    TextField text1;
    Button button1;

    public static void main(String args[])
    {
        linkFrame frame = new linkFrame("The link
            application");

        frame.show();
        frame.hide();
        frame.resize(320, 320);

        link applet = new link();

        frame.add("Center", applet);
        applet.init();
        applet.start();
        frame.show();
    }

    public void init(){
        text1 = new TextField(20);
        add(text1);
        button1 = new Button("Jump to the hyperlinked
            document");
        add(button1);
    }

    public boolean action (Event e, Object o){

        URL url = null;
        filename = "file:////c://xml//link//link.xml";
        try {
            url = new URL(filename);
        } catch (MalformedURLException e1) {
            System.out.println("Cannot create url for: "
                + filename);
            System.exit(0);
        }

        Document d = new Document();

        try {
            d.load(url);
        }
        catch (ParseException e2) {
            d.reportError(e2, System.out);
        }

        if (d != null) {
```

Listing 6-1.
Continued.

```
                      Element root = d.getRoot();
                      Enumeration enum = root.getChildren();
                      while (enum.hasMoreElements()) {
                          Element elem =
                                (Element)enum.nextElement();
                          if (elem.getTagName().equals("A")) {

                              URL url2 = null;

                              try {
                                  url2 = new URL(elem.getAttribute
                                      ("HREF"));
                              }
                              catch (MalformedURLException e3) {
                                  System.out.println("Cannot create
                                      URL for: " +
                                      elem.getAttribute("HREF"));
                                  System.exit(0);
                              }

                              Document d2 = new Document();

                              try {
                                  d2.load(url2);
                              }
                              catch (ParseException e4) {
                                  d2.reportError(e4, System.out);
                              }

                              text1.setText(d2.getText());
                          }
                      }
                  }
                  return true;
              }
          }

          class linkFrame extends Frame
          {
              public linkFrame(String str)
              {
                  super (str);
              }

              public boolean handleEvent(Event evt)
              {
                  switch (evt.id)
                  {
                      case Event.WINDOW_DESTROY:
                          dispose();
                          System.exit(0);
                          return true;
```

Continues

Listing 6-1.
Continued.

```
                    default:
                        return super.handleEvent(evt);
                }
            }
        }
```

Listing 6-2.
link.xml.

```
<?XML VERSION = "1.0" ?>
<!DOCTYPE DOCUMENT [
<!ELEMENT DOCUMENT (#PCDATA|A)*>
<!ELEMENT A (#PCDATA)>
<!ATTLIST A
            XML-LINK        CDATA                   #FIXED
                                                        "SIMPLE"
            ROLE            CDATA                   #IMPLIED
            HREF            CDATA                   #REQUIRED
            TITLE           CDATA                   #IMPLIED
            INLINE          (TRUE|FALSE)            "TRUE"
            CONTENT-ROLE    CDATA                   #IMPLIED
            CONTENT-TITLE   CDATA                   #IMPLIED
            SHOW            (EMBED|REPLACE|NEW)     "REPLACE"
            ACTUATE         (AUTO|USER)             "USER"
            BEHAVIOR        CDATA                   #IMPLIED
>
]>
<DOCUMENT>
    <A XML-LINK="SIMPLE" HREF="FILE:////C://XML//LINK//
        LINK2.XML">The new document.</A>
</DOCUMENT>
```

Listing 6-3.
link2.xml.

```
<?XML version = "1.0" ?>
<!DOCTYPE DOCUMENT [
<!ELEMENT DOCUMENT (CUSTOMER)*>
<!ELEMENT CUSTOMER (NAME,DATE,ORDERS)>
<!ELEMENT NAME (LASTNAME,FIRSTNAME)>
<!ELEMENT LASTNAME (#PCDATA)>
<!ELEMENT FIRSTNAME (#PCDATA)>
<!ELEMENT DATE (#PCDATA)>
<!ELEMENT ORDERS (ITEM)*>
<!ELEMENT ITEM (PRODUCT,NUMBER,PRICE)>
<!ELEMENT PRODUCT (#PCDATA)>
<!ELEMENT NUMBER (#PCDATA)>
<!ELEMENT PRICE (#PCDATA)>
]>
<DOCUMENT>
<CUSTOMER>
    <NAME>
```

Listing 6-3.
Continued.

```
                    <LASTNAME>Edwards</LASTNAME>
                    <FIRSTNAME>Britta</FIRSTNAME>
            </NAME>
            <DATE>April 17, 1998</DATE>
            <ORDERS>
                <ITEM>
                        <PRODUCT>Cucumber</PRODUCT>
                        <NUMBER>5</NUMBER>
                        <PRICE>$1.25</PRICE>
                </ITEM>
                <ITEM>
                        <PRODUCT>Lettuce</PRODUCT>
                        <NUMBER>2</NUMBER>
                        <PRICE>$.98</PRICE>
                </ITEM>
            </ORDERS>
    </CUSTOMER>
    <CUSTOMER>
        <NAME>
                <LASTNAME>Thompson</LASTNAME>
                <FIRSTNAME>Phoebe</FIRSTNAME>
        </NAME>
        <DATE>May 27, 1998</DATE>
        <ORDERS>
                <ITEM>
                        <PRODUCT>Banana</PRODUCT>
                        <NUMBER>12</NUMBER>
                        <PRICE>$2.95</PRICE>
                </ITEM>
                <ITEM>
                        <PRODUCT>Apple</PRODUCT>
                        <NUMBER>6</NUMBER>
                        <PRICE>$1.50</PRICE>
                </ITEM>
        </ORDERS>
    </CUSTOMER>
</DOCUMENT>
```

Now that we've taken a look at simple XML links, we'll take a look at the other main kind of XML links—extended XML links.

Extended XML Links

Extended links are more complex than simple links, as you might expect. An extended link can involve any number of linked-to resources, and it need not be located with any of them. How you structure extended links is largely up to you, but it's usually the case that you place several *locator* elements in an encompassing extended link element. In this way, one link element can be linked to many other resources—and you can theoretically traverse (i.e., activate the link) these links from any of the linked-to resources.

For example, a single extended link to a large document representing an entire book can link to many different locations in that book, such as all the uses of a specific keyword. Or you might have an extended link embedded in a scientific paper that holds all the references to that paper in other documents.

An extended link's locators are placed in child elements of the linking element, each with its own set of attributes. Here's how you might declare an extended link and its child locator elements (you don't have to declare these elements as <EXTENDED> or <LOCATOR>, because those names are set in the XML-LINK attribute):

```
<!ELEMENT  EXTENDED  ANY>
<!ELEMENT  LOCATOR   ANY>
<!ATTLIST  EXTENDED
           XML-LINK          CDATA                   #FIXED
                                                     "EXTENDED"

           ROLE              CDATA                   #IMPLIED
           TITLE             CDATA                   #IMPLIED
           INLINE            (TRUE|FALSE)            "TRUE"
           CONTENT-ROLE      CDATA                   #IMPLIED
           CONTENT-TITLE     CDATA                   #IMPLIED
           SHOW              (EMBED|REPLACE|NEW)     "REPLACE"
           ACTUATE           (AUTO|USER)             "USER"
           BEHAVIOR          CDATA                   #IMPLIED
>
<!ATTLIST  LOCATOR
           XML-LINK  CDATA                   #FIXED "LOCATOR"
           ROLE      CDATA                   #IMPLIED
           HREF      CDATA                   #REQUIRED
           TITLE     CDATA                   #IMPLIED
           SHOW      (EMBED|REPLACE|NEW)     "REPLACE"
           ACTUATE   (AUTO|USER)             "USER"
           BEHAVIOR  CDATA                   #IMPLIED
>
```

To make this clearer, let's take a look at an example of an extended link now.

The extended Example

In this example, **extended.xml**, we'll support an extended link to three other documents, each of which is specified in a <LOCATOR> element:

```
<?XML version="1.0"?>
<!doctype DOCUMENT [
<!element DOCUMENT (EXTENDED|LOCATOR)*>
<!ELEMENT EXTENDED    (#PCDATA | LOCATOR)*>
<!ELEMENT LOCATOR ANY>
<!ATTLIST EXTENDED
          XML-LINK        CDATA              #FIXED
                                             "EXTENDED"
          ROLE            CDATA              #IMPLIED
          TITLE           CDATA              #IMPLIED
          INLINE          (TRUE|FALSE)       "TRUE"
          CONTENT-ROLE    CDATA              #IMPLIED
          CONTENT-TITLE   CDATA              #IMPLIED
          SHOW            (EMBED|REPLACE|NEW) "REPLACE"
          ACTUATE         (AUTO|USER)        "USER"
          BEHAVIOR        CDATA              #IMPLIED
>
<!ATTLIST LOCATOR
          XML-LINK CDATA                     #FIXED "LOCATOR"
          ROLE       CDATA                   #IMPLIED
          HREF       CDATA                   #REQUIRED
          TITLE      CDATA                   #IMPLIED
          SHOW       (EMBED|REPLACE|NEW)     "REPLACE"
          ACTUATE    (AUTO|USER)             "USER"
          BEHAVIOR CDATA                     #IMPLIED
>
]>
<DOCUMENT>
<EXTENDED>
<LOCATOR
  TITLE = "link1"
  XML-LINK="LOCATOR"
  HREF="FILE:////C://XML//EXTENDED//EXTENDED1.XML">
  Here is an extended link.
</LOCATOR>
<LOCATOR
  TITLE = "link2"
  XML-LINK="LOCATOR"
  HREF="FILE:////C://XML//EXTENDED//EXTENDED2.XML">
  Here is an extended link.
</LOCATOR>
<LOCATOR
  TITLE = "link3"
  XML-LINK="LOCATOR"
  HREF="FILE:////C://XML//EXTENDED//EXTENDED3.XML">
  Here is an extended link.
</LOCATOR>
</EXTENDED>
</DOCUMENT>
```

Note that we give a different title to each locator element: link1, link2, and link3. It's up to our application when to link to those links. In this case, we'll just let the user specify what link to jump to by name (although we could jump to linked resources when the user wants to browse a set of cross references, browse through another document paragraph by paragraph, or set up our application to use the extended link in any other of a hundred ways) in our main window:

```
┌─────────────────────────────────────────────┐
│                                             │
├─────────────────────────────────────────────┤
│                                             │
│   ┌───────────────────────┐  ┌──────────────┐│
│   │  Browse this link:    │  │              ││
│   └───────────────────────┘  └──────────────┘│
│                                             │
│   ┌──────────────────────────────────────┐  │
│   │                                      │  │
│   └──────────────────────────────────────┘  │
│                                             │
│                                             │
│                                             │
│                                             │
│                                             │
│                                             │
└─────────────────────────────────────────────┘
```

When the user gives the title of a link, such as link2, and clicks the Browse button, we'll jump to the resource named in that link and display the text of that resource as shown in the figure on the following page.

We'll need three documents to link to: **extended1.xml**, **extended2.xml**, and **extended3.xml**. We'll use our standard XML example file here, adding a <LINK> element so that we can tell each document apart when we display the document's text:

```
┌─────────────────────────────────────────────────────┐
│                                                       │
├─────────────────────────────────────────────────────┤
│                                                       │
│   ┌──────────────────────────┐  ┌──────────────────┐ │
│   │  Browse this link:       │  │   link2          │ │
│   └──────────────────────────┘  └──────────────────┘ │
│                                                       │
│   ┌─────────────────────────────────────────────┐    │
│   │  Link 2 Edwards Britta April 17, 1997        │    │
│   └─────────────────────────────────────────────┘    │
│                                                       │
│                                                       │
│                                                       │
│                                                       │
│                                                       │
│                                                       │
└─────────────────────────────────────────────────────┘
```

```
<?XML version = "1.0"?>
<!DOCTYPE DOCUMENT [
<!ELEMENT DOCUMENT (CUSTOMER|LINK)*>
<!ELEMENT LINK (#PCDATA)>
<!ELEMENT CUSTOMER (NAME,DATE,ORDERS)>
<!ELEMENT NAME (LASTNAME,FIRSTNAME)>
<!ELEMENT LASTNAME (#PCDATA)>
<!ELEMENT FIRSTNAME (#PCDATA)>
<!ELEMENT DATE (#PCDATA)>
<!ELEMENT ORDERS (ITEM)*>
<!ELEMENT ITEM (PRODUCT,NUMBER,PRICE)>
<!ELEMENT PRODUCT (#PCDATA)>
<!ELEMENT NUMBER (#PCDATA)>
<!ELEMENT PRICE (#PCDATA)>
]>
<DOCUMENT>
<LINK>Link 1</LINK>
    <CUSTOMER>
        <NAME>
            <LASTNAME>Edwards</LASTNAME>
            <FIRSTNAME>Britta</FIRSTNAME>
```

```
        </NAME>
        <DATE>April 17, 1998</DATE>
        <ORDERS>
            <ITEM>
                <PRODUCT>Cucumber</PRODUCT>
                <NUMBER>5</NUMBER>
                <PRICE>$1.25</PRICE>
            </ITEM>
            <ITEM>
                <PRODUCT>Lettuce</PRODUCT>
                <NUMBER>2</NUMBER>
                <PRICE>$.98</PRICE>
            </ITEM>
        </ORDERS>
    </CUSTOMER>
    <CUSTOMER>
        <NAME>
            <LASTNAME>Thompson</LASTNAME>
            <FIRSTNAME>Phoebe</FIRSTNAME>
        </NAME>
        <DATE>May 27, 1998</DATE>
        <ORDERS>
            <ITEM>
                <PRODUCT>Banana</PRODUCT>
                <NUMBER>12</NUMBER>
                <PRICE>$2.95</PRICE>
            </ITEM>
            <ITEM>
                <PRODUCT>Apple</PRODUCT>
                <NUMBER>6</NUMBER>
                <PRICE>$1.50</PRICE>
            </ITEM>
        </ORDERS>
    </CUSTOMER>
</DOCUMENT>
```

We'll know which document we're linking to by examining the <LINK> tag's text in the beginning of the document as shown in the figure on the following page.

We will put this program together now; we start by setting up the application's window and applet and installing the controls we'll use:

```
 _____
|                                           |
|_____|
|                                           |
|                                           |
|    _____   _____  |
|   | Browse this link:     | | link2     | |
|   |_____| |_____| |
|                                           |
|    _____  |
|   | Link 2 Edwards Britta April 17, 199 | |
|   |_____| |
|                                           |
|                                           |
|                                           |
|                                           |
|                                           |
|_____|
```

```java
import com.ms.xml.ParseException;
import com.ms.xml.Document;
import com.ms.xml.Element;

import java.util.Enumeration;
import java.awt.*;
import java.net.*;
import java.applet.Applet;

public class extended extends Applet{

    Button button1;
    String filename;
    TextField text1, text2;

    public static void main(String args[])
    {
        extendedFrame frame = new extendedFrame("The ex-
tended application");

        frame.show();
        frame.hide();
        frame.resize(320, 240);
```

```
            extended applet = new extended();

            frame.add("Center", applet);
            applet.init();
            applet.start();
            frame.show();
        }

    public void init(){
            button1 = new Button("Browse this link:");
            add(button1);
            text1 = new TextField(20);
            text1.setText("link1");
            add(text1);
            text2 = new TextField(30);
            add(text2);
        }
```

Next, we read in the document that holds the extended link,
extended.xml. We will search through this document for locator elements,
so we'll use the recursive **doTree()** method to work through the document's tree structure after reading in the document:

```
public boolean action (Event e, Object o)
{

    URL url = null;
    filename = "file:////c://xml//extended//extended.xml";

    try {
        url = new URL(filename);
    } catch (MalformedURLException e1) {
        System.out.println("Cannot create URL for: "
            + filename);
        System.exit(0);
    }

    Document d = new Document();

    try {
        d.load(url);
    }
    catch (ParseException e3) {
        d.reportError(e3, System.out);
    }

    if (d != null) {
        doTree(d.getRoot());
    }
    return true;
}
```

Finally, we'll write the **doTree()** method. In this method, we'll search the document for a <LOCATOR> element with a TITLE attribute matching the title the user has given (link1, link2, or link3). Because the <LOCATOR> element is a child element, we'll check the current element's child elements to see whether any of them are <LOCATOR> elements; here's how we loop over the current element's children in **doTree()**:

```
void doTree(Element elem)
{
    Enumeration enum = elem.getChildren();

    while (enum.hasMoreElements()) {
        Element elem2 = (Element)enum.nextElement();
            .
            .
            .
    }
}
```

If the current child element is of type **Element.ELEMENT**, we can check whether its tag name is <LOCATOR>. (Note that we have to make sure the current child is an element before using the **equals()** method on the return value from the **getTagName()** method, because **getTagName()** returns null when you use it on character data.) We also check to make sure the <LOCATOR> element's title is the same as the user has specified, and we do so this way:

```
void doTree(Element elem)
{
    Enumeration enum = elem.getChildren();

    while (enum.hasMoreElements()) {
        Element elem2 = (Element)enum.nextElement();
        if(elem2.getType() ==
            com.ms.xml.Element.ELEMENT){

            if(elem2.getTagName().equals("LOCATOR") &&

elem2.getAttribute("TITLE").equals(text1.getText())){
                    .
                    .
                    .
            }
        }
    }
}
```

If the tag name and title match what we we're looking for, we load the linked-to resource specified in the locator's HREF attribute and display it this way:

```
void doTree(Element elem)
{
    Enumeration enum = elem.getChildren();

    while (enum.hasMoreElements()) {
        Element elem2 = (Element)enum.nextElement();
        if(elem2.getType() ==
            com.ms.xml.Element.ELEMENT){

            if(elem2.getTagName().equals("LOCATOR") &&
                elem2.getAttribute("TITLE").equals
                    (text1.getText())){

                URL url = null;

                try {
                    url = new URL(elem2.getAttribute
                        ("HREF"));
                } catch (MalformedURLException e1) {
                    System.out.println("Cannot
                        create url for: " +
                        filename);
                    System.exit(0);
                }

                Document d = new Document();

                try {
                    d.load(url);
                }
                catch (ParseException e3) {
                    d.reportError(e3, System.out);
                }

                if (d != null) {
                    text2.setText(d.getText());
                }
            }
            doTree(elem2);
        }
    }
}
```

The program is complete—run it now, as shown in Figure 6-3.

When the user specifies the title of link to jump to (link1, link2, or link3) and clicks the Browse button, we read in the new document and display its text, as shown in Figure 6-4.

Figure 6-3.
The extended
application.

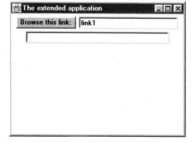

Figure 6-4.
Linking to a resource
with an extended
link.

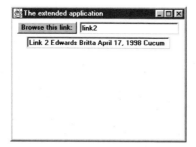

The extended application is a success—now we're using XML extended links. The code for this application, **extended.java**, appears in Listing 6-4, and the document this application reads in, **extended.xml**, appears in Listing 6-5.

Listing 6-4.
extended.java.

```java
import com.ms.xml.ParseException;
import com.ms.xml.Document;
import com.ms.xml.Element;

import java.util.Enumeration;
import java.awt.*;
import java.net.*;
import java.applet.Applet;


public class extended extends Applet{

    Button button1;
    String filename;
    TextField text1, text2;

    public static void main(String args[])
    {
        extendedFrame frame = new extendedFrame("The
```
Continues

Listing 6-4.
Continued.

```
                    extended application");

        frame.show();
        frame.hide();
        frame.resize(320, 240);

        extended applet = new extended();

        frame.add("Center", applet);
        applet.init();
        applet.start();
        frame.show();
    }

public void init(){
        button1 = new Button("Browse this link:");
        add(button1);
        text1 = new TextField(20);
        text1.setText("link1");
        add(text1);
        text2 = new TextField(30);
        add(text2);
    }

public boolean action (Event e, Object o)
{

        URL url = null;
        filename = "file:////c://xml//extended//
            extended.xml";

        try {
            url = new URL(filename);
        } catch (MalformedURLException e1) {
            System.out.println("Cannot create URL for: "
                + filename);
            System.exit(0);
        }

        Document d = new Document();

        try {
            d.load(url);
        }
        catch (ParseException e3) {
            d.reportError(e3, System.out);
        }

        if (d != null) {
            doTree(d.getRoot());
        }
        return true;
```

Listing 6-4.
Continued.

```
    }

    void doTree(Element elem)
    {
        Enumeration enum = elem.getChildren();

        while (enum.hasMoreElements()) {
            Element elem2 = (Element)enum.nextElement();
            if(elem2.getType() ==
                com.ms.xml.Element.ELEMENT){

                if(elem2.getTagName().equals("LOCATOR") &&
                    elem2.getAttribute("TITLE")
                        .equals(text1.getText())){

                    URL url = null;

                    try {
                        url = new URL(elem2.getAttribute
                            ("HREF"));
                    } catch (MalformedURLException e1) {
                        System.out.println("Cannot
                            create URL for: " +
                            filename);
                        System.exit(0);
                    }

                    Document d = new Document();

                    try {
                        d.load(url);
                    }
                    catch (ParseException e3) {
                        d.reportError(e3, System.out);
                    }

                    if (d != null) {
                        text2.setText(d.getText());
                    }
                }
                doTree(elem2);
            }
        }
    }
}

class extendedFrame extends Frame
{
    public extendedFrame(String str)
    {
```

Continues

Listing 6-4.
Continued.

```
        super (str);
    }

    public boolean handleEvent(Event evt)
    {
        switch (evt.id)
        {
            case Event.WINDOW_DESTROY:
                dispose();
                System.exit(0);
                return true;

            default:
                return super.handleEvent(evt);
        }
    }
}
```

Listing 6-5.
extended.xml.

```
<?XML version="1.0"?>
<!doctype DOCUMENT [
<!element DOCUMENT (EXTENDED|LOCATOR)*>
<!ELEMENT EXTENDED    (#PCDATA | LOCATOR)*>
<!ELEMENT LOCATOR ANY>
<!ATTLIST EXTENDED
          XML-LINK         CDATA                    #FIXED
                                                    "EXTENDED"

          ROLE             CDATA                    #IMPLIED
          TITLE            CDATA                    #IMPLIED
          INLINE           (TRUE|FALSE)             "TRUE"
          CONTENT-ROLE     CDATA                    #IMPLIED
          CONTENT-TITLE CDATA                       #IMPLIED
          SHOW             (EMBED|REPLACE|NEW) "REPLACE"
          ACTUATE          (AUTO|USER)             "USER"
          BEHAVIOR         CDATA                    #IMPLIED
>
<!ATTLIST LOCATOR
          XML-LINK CDATA                    #FIXED "LOCATOR"
          ROLE     CDATA                    #IMPLIED
          HREF     CDATA                    #REQUIRED
          TITLE    CDATA                    #IMPLIED
          SHOW     (EMBED|REPLACE|NEW) "REPLACE"
          ACTUATE  (AUTO|USER)             "USER"
          BEHAVIOR CDATA                    #IMPLIED
>
]>
<DOCUMENT>
<EXTENDED>
<LOCATOR
  TITLE = "link1"
```

Listing 6-5.
Continued.

```
    XML-LINK="LOCATOR"
    HREF="FILE:////C://XML//EXTENDED//EXTENDED1.XML">
    Here is an extended link.
</LOCATOR>
<LOCATOR
  TITLE = "link2"
  XML-LINK="LOCATOR"
  HREF="FILE:////C://XML//EXTENDED//EXTENDED2.XML">
  Here is an extended link.
</LOCATOR>
<LOCATOR
  TITLE = "link3"
  XML-LINK="LOCATOR"
  HREF="FILE:////C://XML//EXTENDED//EXTENDED3.XML">
  Here is an extended link.
</LOCATOR>
</EXTENDED>
</DOCUMENT>
```

Now we've taken a first look at both simple and extended XML links, but so far our locator values—placed in the HREF attribute—have been simple URLs. However, there's much more here that we can do.

Addressing XML Links

In general, a locator contains an URL, and you can follow the actual URL text with a **?** and a query string (as in HTML). You can also follow the URL with a **#** and a *fragment identifier*, which narrows down exactly what part of the target document you're linking to. This fragment identifier is an extended pointer called an *XPointer* in XML. (We'll see more about XPointers in a moment; you usually tack an XPointer on the end of an URL to make a locator in XML.)

When you are linking specifically to an XML document (i.e., not an HTML document or some other kind) and are using a fragment identifier —that is, an XPointer—the locator, which you place in the HREF attribute, can contain either or both an URL and a fragment identifier:

```
Locator::= URL | Connector (XPointer | Name)| URL Connector
      (XPointer | Name)
Connector::= '#' | '|'
URL::= URLchar*
```

If you include an URL, it locates a resource called the *containing resource* (usually an XML document). If you don't supply an URL, the containing resource is the document the link is in. If you include an XPointer, which targets a specific location in the containing resource, the specific resource you target is called the *designated* or *target resource*.

If you include a connector and a name (not an XPointer), the name is treated as a reference to the element in the containing resource that has the ID attribute which matches the name you've supplied.

If you use the connector **#**, you expect the application to get the containing resource whole; the target resource inside the containing resource will be extracted on the same system where the linking element is processed. If you use the connector **|**, on the other hand, you are not giving any directions as to how to go about accessing the target resource.

When you link specifically to an XML document (i.e., not an HTML document or some other kind of document) and want to include a query, W3C urges programmers not to use a **?** but the string **'XML-XPTR='** followed by an XPointer:

```
Query::= 'XML-XPTR=' (XPointer | Name)
```

As we've seen, you use XPointers to target a specific part of the containing resource. As you might expect, targeting a specific location in a general document can be an elaborate business, and the XPointer syntax is designed to match. Let's see how to create XPointers, how they work, and what they do, and then we'll work through a few examples using them.

All About XPointers

To reference documents, you use URLs; to reference specific parts of the document, you use XPointers, which you usually add to the end of an URL to make an XML locator.

An XPointer is made up of a series of *location terms*, each of which indicates a location; these locations can be absolute, relative to the last location, or a string-match location. These location terms can include a keyword such as **ID**, **CHILD**, **ANCESTOR**, and so on, and can include parameters such as an instance number, element type, or attribute.

We'll see how to create location terms in a moment, but as a quick example, the relative locator string **CHILD(2,CHAPTER)(4,PART)(6)** refers to the sixth child of the fourth <PART> element within the second <CHAPTER> element in the referenced document.

XPointers usually start with an absolute location term. If the absolute term is followed by relative or string-match terms, the location that it points to is called the *location source*; this source serves as a starting point for the location terms that follow.

An XML locator may also contain two XPointers separated by the string '..'. These XPointers define the beginning and end of a *span*, and it is this span which makes up the target resource:

```
XPointer::= First ('..' Second)?
```

As mentioned, each location term can be either an absolute term (**AbsTerm** as follows), a relative term (**RelTerm** as follows), or a string-match term (**StringTerm** as follows):

```
First::= AbsTerm? RelTerm* StringTerm?
Second::= AbsTermOrDitto? RelTerm* StringTerm?
```

We'll take a look at all three types of location terms now.

Absolute Location Terms

The first type of XPointer location term we'll take a look at is the absolute location term:

```
XPointer::= First ('..' Second)?
First::= AbsTerm? RelTerm* StringTerm?
Second::= AbsTermOrDitto? RelTerm* StringTerm?
AbsTerm::= 'ROOT()' | 'HERE()' | IdLoc | HTMLAddr
AbsTermOrDitto::= 'DITTO()' | AbsTerm
IdLoc::= 'ID(' Name ')'
HTMLAddr::= 'HTML(' SkipLit ')'
```

Absolute location terms specify locations in the containing resource in an absolute manner; the possible absolute location terms are **ROOT()**, **HERE()**, **DITTO()**, ID locators, and HTML addresses. The **ROOT()** location term refers to the containing resource's root.

TIP *If an XPointer does not start with an absolute location term, the application assumes it starts with a* **ROOT()** *location term.*

The **HERE()** location term refers to the location of the linking element containing the locator.

If the second XPointer (**second** in the preceding XPointer specification) is **DITTO()**, the start location for the second XPOINTER is the location pointed to by the first XPointer.

TIP *The **DITTO()** keyword makes specifying a location span easier.*

If an XPointer is preceded by ID(*Name*), the start location is the element in the containing resource with an ID attribute that matches *Name*. In fact, using an ID location is a common XPointer technique. Let's take a look at an example now.

The `idlocator` Example

In this next example, we'll see how to use an ID location term. We start with an XML document, **idlocator.xml**, with an extended link to another document, **idlocator2.xml**:

```
<?XML version="1.0"?>
<!doctype LINK [
<!ELEMENT LINK     (#PCDATA | LOCATOR)*>
<!ELEMENT LOCATOR ANY>
<!ATTLIST LINK
                XML-LINK          CDATA              #FIXED
                                                     "EXTENDED"
                ROLE              CDATA              #IMPLIED
                TITLE             CDATA              #IMPLIED
                INLINE            (TRUE|FALSE)       "TRUE"
                CONTENT-ROLE      CDATA              #IMPLIED
                CONTENT-TITLE     CDATA              #IMPLIED
                SHOW              (EMBED|REPLACE|NEW) "REPLACE"
                ACTUATE           (AUTO|USER)        "USER"
                BEHAVIOR          CDATA              #IMPLIED
>
<!ATTLIST LOCATOR
                XML-LINK CDATA                   #FIXED "LOCATOR"
                ROLE        CDATA                #IMPLIED
                HREF        CDATA                #REQUIRED
                TITLE       CDATA                #IMPLIED
                SHOW        (EMBED|REPLACE|NEW)  "REPLACE"
                ACTUATE     (AUTO|USER)          "USER"
                BEHAVIOR CDATA                   #IMPLIED
>
]>
<LINK XML-LINK = "EXTENDED">
  <LOCATOR
  XML-LINK="LOCATOR"
```

```
HREF="FILE:////C://XML//IDLOCATOR//
      IDLOCATOR2.XML#ROOT()X15">
Here is an extended link.
</LOCATOR>
</LINK>
```

Note the location terms we include here are ROOT() and X15:

```
HREF="FILE:////C://XML//IDLOCATOR//
      IDLOCATOR2.XML#ROOT()X15">
```

ROOT() is the absolute location term that refers to the root of the IDLOCATOR2.XML document, and X15 is a name that refers to the element which has the ID X15. Here's how the IDLOCATOR2.XML document looks (this document is the containing resource)—note that we have to add X15 to the <NAME> element's attribute list before using that attribute:

```
<?XML version = "1.0" ?>
<!DOCTYPE DOCUMENT [
<!ELEMENT DOCUMENT (CUSTOMER|NAME)*>
<!ELEMENT CUSTOMER (NAME,DATE,PRODUCT*)>
<!ELEMENT NAME (LASTNAME?,FIRSTNAME?,#PCDATA?)>
<!ELEMENT LASTNAME (#PCDATA)>
<!ELEMENT FIRSTNAME (#PCDATA)>
<!ELEMENT DATE (#PCDATA)>
<!ELEMENT PRODUCT (NAME,NUMBER,PRICE)>
<!ELEMENT NUMBER (#PCDATA)>
<!ELEMENT PRICE (#PCDATA)>
<!ATTLIST NAME
          ID   CDATA #IMPLIED>
]>
<DOCUMENT>
<CUSTOMER>
    <NAME>
        <LASTNAME>Kennilworth</LASTNAME>
        <FIRSTNAME>Susanne</FIRSTNAME>
    </NAME>
    <DATE>March 23, 1998</DATE>
        <PRODUCT>
            <NAME>Banana</NAME>
            <NUMBER>12</NUMBER>
            <PRICE>4.98</PRICE>
        </PRODUCT>
        <PRODUCT>
            <NAME>Peach</NAME>
            <NUMBER>3</NUMBER>
            <PRICE>.69</PRICE>
        </PRODUCT>
</CUSTOMER>
<NAME ID = "X15">
    Here's the X15 element!
```

```
</NAME>
<CUSTOMER>
    <NAME>
        <LASTNAME>Edwards</LASTNAME>
        <FIRSTNAME>Britta</FIRSTNAME>
    </NAME>
    <DATE>June 17, 1998</DATE>
        <PRODUCT>
            <NAME>Peach</NAME>
            <NUMBER>24</NUMBER>
            <PRICE>3.12</PRICE>
        </PRODUCT>
        <PRODUCT>
            <NAME>Apple</NAME>
            <NUMBER>9</NUMBER>
            <PRICE>.98</PRICE>
        </PRODUCT>
</CUSTOMER>
</DOCUMENT>
```

In this example we present the user with a window and a button labeled Display item with ID = X15:

Display item with ID = X15

When the user clicks the button, we read in the `idlocator.xml` document, find the extended link in that document, read in the linked-to `idlocator2.xml` document, and find the **x15** element in that second document. Finally, we will display the content of the **x15** element in the application's window:

```
Here's the X15 element!


Display item with ID = X15
```

We start this example, `idlocator.java`, by creating a window, an applet, installing the applet in the window, and setting up the controls we'll use:

```java
import com.ms.xml.ParseException;
import com.ms.xml.Document;
import com.ms.xml.Element;

import java.util.Enumeration;
import java.awt.*;
import java.net.*;
import java.applet.Applet;

public class idlocator extends Applet{

    static String filename;
    TextField text1;
    Button button1;

    public static void main(String args[])
    {
        idlocatorFrame frame = new
            idlocatorFrame("The idlocator application");

        frame.show();
        frame.hide();
        frame.resize(320, 320);

        idlocator applet = new idlocator();

        frame.add("Center", applet);
        applet.init();
```

```
        applet.start();
        frame.show();
    }

    public void init(){
        text1 = new TextField(20);
        add(text1);
        button1 = new Button("Display item with ID
            = X15");
        add(button1);
    }
```

When the user clicks the Display button, we read in the `idlocator.xml` document and search for a child element of the <LOCATOR> type:

```
    public boolean action (Event e, Object o)
    {

        String locator = "";
        URL url = null;
        filename = "file:////c://xml//idlocator//
            idlocator.xml";

        try {
            url = new URL(filename);
        } catch (MalformedURLException e1) {
            System.out.println("Cannot create url for: "
                + filename);
            System.exit(0);
        }

        Document d = new Document();

        try {
            d.load(url);
        }
        catch (ParseException e2) {
            d.reportError(e2, System.out);
        }

        if (d != null) {
            Element root = d.getRoot();
            Enumeration enum = root.getChildren();
            while (enum.hasMoreElements()) {
                Element elem =
                    (Element)enum.nextElement();
                if (elem.getTagName().equals("LOCATOR")) {
                    .
                    .
                    .

                }
            }
        }
```

```
        }
    }
```

Next, we get the name of the containing resource from the HREF attribute of the link. Note that we search for the connector "#" as an indication of the end of the URL part of the locator and use the Java String
class **substring()** method to extract substrings from the locator string:

```
public boolean action (Event e, Object o)
{

    String locator = "";
    URL url = null;
    filename = "file:////c://xml//idlocator//
            idlocator.xml";

    try {
        url = new URL(filename);
    } catch (MalformedURLException e1) {
        System.out.println("Cannot create url for: "
                + filename);
        System.exit(0);
    }

    Document d = new Document();

    try {
        d.load(url);
    }
    catch (ParseException e2) {
        d.reportError(e2, System.out);
    }

    if (d != null) {
        Element root = d.getRoot();
        Enumeration enum = root.getChildren();
        while (enum.hasMoreElements()) {
            Element elem =
                (Element)enum.nextElement();
            if (elem.getTagName().equals("LOCATOR")) {

                URL url2 = null;
                try {
                    locator = new String
                        (elem.getAttribute("HREF"));
                    url2 = new
                        URL(locator.substring(0,
                        locator.indexOf("#")));
                } catch (MalformedURLException e3) {
                    System.out.println("Cannot
                        create URL for: " +
                        filename);
```

```
                                        System.exit(0);
                                }

                                Document d2 = new Document();

                                try {
                                        d2.load(url2);
                                }
                                catch (ParseException e4) {
                                        d2.reportError(e4, System.out);
                                }
                                        .
                                        .
                                        .

                        }
                }
        }
        return true;
    }
}
```

Now we've loaded in the containing resource, **idlocator2.xml**. The next step is to find the ID value of the element we're supposed to locate, and we do that by parsing the locator string:

```
HREF="FILE:////C://XML//IDLOCATOR//
      IDLOCATOR2.XML#ROOT()X15">
```

In this case, we will simply extract the term following "**#ROOT**" and treat that as the ID value of the target resource:

```
public class idlocator extends Applet{

        static String filename;
        TextField text1;
        Button button1;
        String rootString = "#ROOT()";
                    .
                    .
                    .

        public boolean action (Event e, Object o)
        {

            String locator = "";
            URL url = null;
            filename = "file:////c://xml//idlocator//idloca-
tor.xml";
                        .
                        .
                        .

                        try {
                                d2.load(url2);
```

```
            }
            catch (ParseException e4) {
                d2.reportError(e4, System.out);
            }

            String IDName =
                locator.substring(locator
                    .indexOf(rootString) +
                rootString.length());
                    .
                    .
                    .
        }
      }
   }
   return true;
 }
}
```

Finally, we loop over the elements of the containing resource until we find the correct element, which has the ID matching the one specified in the locator string. When we find that element, we display its text in the application's text field:

```
public boolean action (Event e, Object o)
{

    String locator = "";
    URL url = null;
    filename = "file:////c://xml//idlocator//
        idlocator.xml";
                .
                .
                .
        try {
            d2.load(url2);
        }
        catch (ParseException e4) {
            d2.reportError(e4, System.out);
        }

        Element newRoot = d2.getRoot();

        String IDName =
            locator.substring(locator
                .indexOf(rootString) +
            rootString.length());

        Element elem2 = null;
        Element target = null;
        Enumeration enum2 =
            newRoot.getChildren();
```

```
            while (enum2.hasMoreElements()) {
                elem2 = (Element)enum2
                    .nextElement();
                if(elem2.getAttribute("ID") !=
                    null){

if(elem2.getAttribute("ID").equals(IDName)){
                        text1.setText(elem2
                            .getText());
                    }
                }
            }
        }
    }
    return true;
}
}
```

That's it—run the application now, as shown in Figure 6-5.

Figure 6-5.
The idlocator
application.

When the user clicks the Display button, the program loads **idlocator.xml** and decodes the locator in that document to extract the target resource. The program then reads in the target resource and displays its character data, as shown in Figure 6-6.

The **idlocator.java** application is a success. Now we're using locator terms in code. The code for this application, **idlocator.java**, appears in Listing 6-6. The two documents the application reads in, **idlocator.xml** and **idlocator2.xml**, appear in Listing 6-7 and 6-8 respectively.

The last absolute XML location term is **HTML()**. The location term **HTML(NAMEVALUE)** selects the first element whose type is **A** (i.e., referring to the HTML <A> tag) and which has a **NAME** attribute with a value that is the same as the supplied **NAMEVALUE**.

Figure 6-6.
Linking using an ID
location term.

Listing 6-6.
`idlocator.java.`

```java
import com.ms.xml.ParseException;
import com.ms.xml.Document;
import com.ms.xml.Element;

import java.util.Enumeration;
import java.awt.*;
import java.net.*;
import java.applet.Applet;

public class idlocator extends Applet{

    static String filename;
    TextField text1;
    Button button1;
    String rootString = "#ROOT()";

    public static void main(String args[])
    {
        idlocatorFrame frame = new idlocatorFrame("The
            idlocator application");

        frame.show();
        frame.hide();
        frame.resize(320, 320);

        idlocator applet = new idlocator();

        frame.add("Center", applet);
        applet.init();
        applet.start();
        frame.show();
    }


    public void init(){
        text1 = new TextField(20);
```

Continues

Listing 6-6.
Continued.

```
        add(text1);
        button1 = new Button("Display item with ID =
            X15");
        add(button1);
    }

    public boolean action (Event e, Object o)
    {

        String locator = "";
        URL url = null;
        filename = "file:////c://xml//idlocator//
            idlocator.xml";

        try {
            url = new URL(filename);
        } catch (MalformedURLException e1) {
            System.out.println("Cannot create url for: "
                + filename);
            System.exit(0);
        }

        Document d = new Document();

        try {
            d.load(url);
        }
        catch (ParseException e2) {
            d.reportError(e2, System.out);
        }

        if (d != null) {
            Element root = d.getRoot();
            Enumeration enum = root.getChildren();
            while (enum.hasMoreElements()) {
                Element elem =
                    (Element)enum.nextElement();
                if (elem.getTagName().equals("LOCATOR")) {

                    URL url2 = null;
                    try {
                        locator = new String(elem
                            .getAttribute("HREF"));
                        url2 = new
                            URL(locator.substring(0,
                            locator.indexOf("#")));
                    } catch (MalformedURLException e3) {
                        System.out.println("Cannot
                            create URL for: " +
                            filename);
                        System.exit(0);
```

Listing 6-6.
Continued.

```
                        }

                        Document d2 = new Document();

                        try {
                            d2.load(url2);
                        }
                        catch (ParseException e4) {
                            d2.reportError(e4, System.out);
                        }

                        Element newRoot = d2.getRoot();

                        String IDName =
                            locator.substring(locator
                                .indexOf(rootString) +
                            rootString.length());

                        Element elem2 = null;
                        Element target = null;
                        Enumeration enum2 =
                            newRoot.getChildren();

                        while (enum2.hasMoreElements()) {
                            elem2 = (Element)
                                enum2.nextElement();
                            if(elem2.getAttribute("ID") !=
                                null){
                                if(elem2.getAttribute("ID")
                                    .equals(IDName)){
                                    text1.setText
                                        (elem2.getText());
                                }
                            }
                        }
                    }
                }
            }
        return true;
    }
}

class idlocatorFrame extends Frame
{
    public idlocatorFrame(String str)
    {
        super (str);
    }
```

Continues

Listing 6-6.
Continued.

```
public boolean handleEvent(Event evt)
{
    switch (evt.id)
    {
        case Event.WINDOW_DESTROY:
            dispose();
            System.exit(0);
            return true;

        default:
            return super.handleEvent(evt);
    }
}
}
```

Listing 6-7.
idlocator.xml.

```
<?XML version="1.0"?>
<!doctype LINK [
<!ELEMENT LINK     (#PCDATA | LOCATOR)*>
<!ELEMENT LOCATOR ANY>
<!ATTLIST LINK
          XML-LINK         CDATA                    #FIXED
                                                    "EXTENDED"

          ROLE             CDATA                    #IMPLIED
          TITLE            CDATA                    #IMPLIED
          INLINE           (TRUE|FALSE)             "TRUE"
          CONTENT-ROLE     CDATA                    #IMPLIED
          CONTENT-TITLE    CDATA                    #IMPLIED
          SHOW             (EMBED|REPLACE|NEW)      "REPLACE"
          ACTUATE          (AUTO|USER)              "USER"
          BEHAVIOR         CDATA                    #IMPLIED
>
<!ATTLIST LOCATOR
          XML-LINK CDATA                       #FIXED "LOCATOR"
          ROLE        CDATA                    #IMPLIED
          HREF        CDATA                    #REQUIRED
          TITLE       CDATA                    #IMPLIED
          SHOW        (EMBED|REPLACE|NEW)      "REPLACE"
          ACTUATE     (AUTO|USER)              "USER"
          BEHAVIOR CDATA                       #IMPLIED
>
]>
<LINK XML-LINK = "EXTENDED">
  <LOCATOR
  XML-LINK="LOCATOR"
  HREF="FILE:////C://XML//IDLOCATOR//
        IDLOCATOR2.XML#ROOT()X15">
  Here is an extended link.
  </LOCATOR>
</LINK>
```

Listing 6-8.
idlocator2.xml

```
<?XML version = "1.0" ?>
<!DOCTYPE DOCUMENT [
<!ELEMENT DOCUMENT (CUSTOMER|NAME)*>
<!ELEMENT CUSTOMER (NAME,DATE,PRODUCT*)>
<!ELEMENT NAME (LASTNAME?,FIRSTNAME?,#PCDATA?)>
<!ELEMENT LASTNAME (#PCDATA)>
<!ELEMENT FIRSTNAME (#PCDATA)>
<!ELEMENT DATE (#PCDATA)>
<!ELEMENT PRODUCT (NAME,NUMBER,PRICE)>
<!ELEMENT NUMBER (#PCDATA)>
<!ELEMENT PRICE (#PCDATA)>
<!ATTLIST NAME
          ID  CDATA #IMPLIED>
]>
<DOCUMENT>
<CUSTOMER>
    <NAME>
         <LASTNAME>Kennilworth</LASTNAME>
         <FIRSTNAME>Susanne</FIRSTNAME>
    </NAME>
    <DATE>March 23, 1998</DATE>
        <PRODUCT>
             <NAME>Banana</NAME>
             <NUMBER>12</NUMBER>
             <PRICE>4.98</PRICE>
        </PRODUCT>
        <PRODUCT>
             <NAME>Peach</NAME>
             <NUMBER>3</NUMBER>
             <PRICE>.69</PRICE>
        </PRODUCT>
</CUSTOMER>
<NAME ID = "X15">
    Here's the X15 element!
</NAME>
<CUSTOMER>
    <NAME>
         <LASTNAME>Edwards</LASTNAME>
         <FIRSTNAME>Britta</FIRSTNAME>
    </NAME>
    <DATE>June 17, 1998</DATE>
        <PRODUCT>
             <NAME>Peach</NAME>
             <NUMBER>24</NUMBER>
             <PRICE>3.12</PRICE>
        </PRODUCT>
        <PRODUCT>
             <NAME>Apple</NAME>
             <NUMBER>9</NUMBER>
             <PRICE>.98</PRICE>
        </PRODUCT>
</CUSTOMER>
</DOCUMENT>
```

That completes our look at the absolute location terms. Next we'll take a look at relative XML location terms.

XPointer Relative Location Terms

You use relative location terms, such as **RelTerm** as follows, to indicate a location with respect to the location source:

```
XPointer::= First ('..' Second)?
First::= AbsTerm? RelTerm* StringTerm?
Second::= AbsTermOrDitto? RelTerm* StringTerm?
RelTerm::= Keyword Arguments+
Keyword::= 'CHILD' | 'DESCENDANT' | 'ANCESTOR' |
     'PRECEDING' |
         'PSIBLING' | 'FOLLOWING' | 'FSIBLING'
Arguments::= '(' Instance ',' ElType (',' Attr ',' Val)*
     ')'
InstanceOrAll::= 'ALL' | Instance
Instance::= ('+' | '-')? Digit+
ElType::= '*CDATA'/* selects text pseudo-elements */
           | '*'/* elements and pseudo-elements */
           | '.'/* elements only */
           | Name/* elements of this type */
Attr::= '*'/* any attribute name */|
NameVal::= '*IMPLIED'/* no value specified, no default */
           | '*'/* any value */
           | Name/* case and space normalized */
           | SkipLit/* exact match */
```

Note the keywords you can use in relative links: **CHILD**, **DESCENDANT**, **ANCESTOR**, **PRECEDING**, **PSIBLING**, **FOLLOWING**, and **FSIBLING**. We'll take a look at those terms, with examples, now.

▓ The **CHILD** keyword allows you to select child elements of the location source. For example, this XPointer selects the second <MENU> element inside the element with an ID that equals X12. We specify the *instance number*—that is, the occurrence—we want (the second occurrence of the element we're looking for) and the element type we want (<MENU>) this way:

ID(X12),CHILD(2,MENU)

There's a shorthand you should be aware of as you use multiple relative keywords. You can skip keywords like **CHILD** if they are repeated; for example, these two XPointers are the same:

CHILD(2,MENU)(1,SUBMENU)

```
CHILD(2,MENU)CHILD(1,SUBMENU)
```

Here's an example that skips the **CHILD** keyword twice; this location specification selects the seventh paragraph of the sixth part of the second section:

```
CHILD(2,SECTION)(6,PART)(7,P)
```

You can give the element's type by name or one of the values: **.**, ***CDATA**, or ***. The **.** term matches any element type, ***CDATA** matches untagged subparts of an element that have mixed content (called *pseudo-elements*), and * matches either child elements or psuedo-elements. For example, if this is the document section we're linking to:

```
<BOOK><SECTION>Natural Phenomena</SECTION>
<TITLE>Thunder and Storms</TITLE>Thunder storms
are loud.<TITLE>Landslides</TITLE>
Landslides are dangerous.<TITLE>Floods</TITLE>
Watch out for floods.</BOOK>
```

Here are a few location term examples, treating the <BOOK> element as the location source: **CHILD(2,TITLE)** selects the second **TITLE** element, "Landslides". **CHILD(2,.)** selects the second **child** element, which is the first **<TITLE>**, "Thunder and Storms". **CHILD(2,*CDATA)** selects the second pseudo-element, "Thunder storms are loud." (The first pseudo-element is the carriage return after the </SECTION> tag.) Finally, **CHILD(3,*)** selects the third element *or* pseudo-element among the children, which is the **<TITLE>** element "Thunder and Storms."

You can also select items using the item's attribute name and value. If you specify the attribute name in quotation marks, the attribute-value parameter is case-sensitive. Otherwise it is not. You can use * for attribute names in location terms; for example, this location term selects the second child of any type for which the attribute TARGET has a value (any value at all):

```
CHILD(2,*,TARGET,*)
```

This location specification selects the second child which is a **P** element for which the ALIGN attribute has been left unspecified:

```
CHILD(2,P,ALIGN,*IMPLIED)
```

Besides **CHILD**, you can also use **DESCENDANT**, which selects among the elements with content in the location source. For example, this location specification selects the second **MENU** element with a CHICKEN attribute that has value of **ROASTED**:

`DESCENDANT(2,MENU,CHICKEN,ROASTED)`

- The **ANCESTOR** keyword selects an element from among the direct ancestors of the location source. For example, this location specification finds the smallest element containing the location source and having the attribute FINDME with value **HEREIAM**:

`ANCESTOR(1,*,FINDME,HEREIAM)`

- The **PRECEDING** keyword selects an element—or a pseudo-element—from all those that precede the location source. For example, this location specification points to the third element or pseudo-element preceding the element with an ID of M15:

`ID(M15)PRECEDING(3,.)`

- You use the **PSIBLING** keyword to select an element or pseudo-element from among those that precede the location source within the same parent element. (A *sibling* is an element or pseudo-element contained by the same parent element.)Those elements or pseudo-elements that precede the current location in the document are *elder siblings*; those that follow it are *younger siblings*. For example, here we point to the element or pseudo-element immediately preceding the element with an ID of M99:

`ID(M99)PSIBLING(1,.)`

TIP *Negative instance numbers point at elder siblings.*

- You use the keyword **FOLLOWING** like the keyword **PRECEDING**, but here you select elements from the part of the document following the location source (not preceding it). In a similar way, the **FSIBLING** keyword works like **PSIBLING** but selects from the younger siblings of the location source, not the elder siblings.

We've covered a lot of relative location terms now, so let's take a look at a longer example that makes use of them. In this example, we'll decode an extended link with the location terms:

`#ROOT()CHILD(2,CUSTOMER)(2,PRODUCT)(1,NAME)`

The `locator` Example

In this next example, we'll read in this XML document, `locator.xml`, and let the user traverse that link:

```
<?XML version="1.0"?>
<!doctype LINK [
<!ELEMENT LINK    (#PCDATA | LOCATOR)*>
<!ELEMENT LOCATOR ANY>
<!ATTLIST LINK
        XML-LINK        CDATA                    #FIXED
                                                 "EXTENDED"
        ROLE            CDATA                    #IMPLIED
        TITLE           CDATA                    #IMPLIED
        INLINE          (TRUE|FALSE)             "TRUE"
        CONTENT-ROLE    CDATA                    #IMPLIED
        CONTENT-TITLE   CDATA                    #IMPLIED
        SHOW            (EMBED|REPLACE|NEW)      "REPLACE"
        ACTUATE         (AUTO|USER)              "USER"
        BEHAVIOR        CDATA                    #IMPLIED
>
<!ATTLIST LOCATOR
        XML-LINK CDATA                   #FIXED "LOCATOR"
        ROLE     CDATA                   #IMPLIED
        HREF     CDATA                   #REQUIRED
        TITLE    CDATA                   #IMPLIED
        SHOW     (EMBED|REPLACE|NEW)     "REPLACE"
        ACTUATE  (AUTO|USER)             "USER"
        BEHAVIOR CDATA                   #IMPLIED
>
]>
<LINK XML-LINK = "EXTENDED">
  <LOCATOR
  XML-LINK="LOCATOR"
  HREF="FILE:////C://XML//LOCATOR//LOCATOR2.XML#ROOT()
        CHILD(2,CUSTOMER)(2,PRODUCT)(1,NAME)">
Here is an extended link.
  </LOCATOR>
</LINK>
```

Here's the document that serves as the containing resource,
`locator2.xml`:

```
<?XML version = "1.0" ?>
<!DOCTYPE DOCUMENT [
<!ELEMENT DOCUMENT (CUSTOMER|NAME)*>
<!ELEMENT CUSTOMER (NAME,DATE,PRODUCT*)>
<!ELEMENT NAME (LASTNAME?,FIRSTNAME?,#PCDATA?)>
<!ELEMENT LASTNAME (#PCDATA)>
<!ELEMENT FIRSTNAME (#PCDATA)>
<!ELEMENT DATE (#PCDATA)>
<!ELEMENT PRODUCT (NAME,NUMBER,PRICE)>
<!ELEMENT NUMBER (#PCDATA)>
<!ELEMENT PRICE (#PCDATA)>
]>
<DOCUMENT>
<CUSTOMER>
    <NAME>
```

```
        <LASTNAME>Kennilworth</LASTNAME>
        <FIRSTNAME>Susanne</FIRSTNAME>
    </NAME>
    <DATE>March 23, 1998</DATE>
        <PRODUCT>
            <NAME>Banana</NAME>
            <NUMBER>12</NUMBER>
            <PRICE>4.98</PRICE>
        </PRODUCT>
        <PRODUCT>
            <NAME>Peach</NAME>
            <NUMBER>3</NUMBER>
            <PRICE>.69</PRICE>
        </PRODUCT>
</CUSTOMER>
<CUSTOMER>
    <NAME>
        <LASTNAME>Edwards</LASTNAME>
        <FIRSTNAME>Britta</FIRSTNAME>
    </NAME>
    <DATE>June 17, 1998</DATE>
        <PRODUCT>
            <NAME>Peach</NAME>
            <NUMBER>24</NUMBER>
            <PRICE>3.12</PRICE>
        </PRODUCT>
        <PRODUCT>
            <NAME>Apple</NAME>
            <NUMBER>9</NUMBER>
            <PRICE>.98</PRICE>
        </PRODUCT>
</CUSTOMER>
</DOCUMENT>
```

The location specification we will decode looks like this: `#ROOT()CHILD(2,CUSTOMER)(2,PRODUCT)(1,NAME)`. That means we're looking for the first `<NAME>` element in the second `<PRODUCT>` element, in the second `<CUSTOMER>` element. Referring to the preceding document, we see that the content of that element is `Apple`, so that's what we'll expect to see when the program runs.

We'll present the user with a window like this, with a button marked Display item with linked-to text and a text field:

```
┌─────────────────────────────────────────────────┐
│                                                 │
├─────────────────────────────────────────────────┤
│                                                 │
│   ┌─────────────────────────────────────────┐   │
│   │                                         │   │
│   └─────────────────────────────────────────┘   │
│                                                 │
│   ┌─────────────────────────────────────────┐   │
│   │  Display item with linked-to text       │   │
│   └─────────────────────────────────────────┘   │
│                                                 │
│                                                 │
│                                                 │
│                                                 │
│                                                 │
└─────────────────────────────────────────────────┘
```

When the user clicks the Display button, we'll read in the **locator.xml** file and decode the locator string in that document. Then we'll read in the target resource and display its character data this way:

```
┌─────────────────────────────────────────────────┐
│                                                 │
├─────────────────────────────────────────────────┤
│                                                 │
│   ┌─────────────────────────────────────────┐   │
│   │  Apple                                   │   │
│   └─────────────────────────────────────────┘   │
│                                                 │
│   ┌─────────────────────────────────────────┐   │
│   │  Display item with linked-to text       │   │
│   └─────────────────────────────────────────┘   │
│                                                 │
│                                                 │
│                                                 │
│                                                 │
│                                                 │
└─────────────────────────────────────────────────┘
```

We start by setting up the application and its applet and adding the controls we'll need:

```
import com.ms.xml.ParseException;
import com.ms.xml.Document;
import com.ms.xml.Element;

import java.util.Enumeration;
import java.awt.*;
import java.net.*;
import java.applet.Applet;


public class locator extends Applet{

    static String filename;
    TextField text1;
    Button button1;
    String rootString = new String("#ROOT()");

    public static void main(String args[])
    {
        locatorFrame frame = new locatorFrame("The
            locator application");

        frame.show();
        frame.hide();
        frame.resize(320, 240);

        locator applet = new locator();

        frame.add("Center", applet);
        applet.init();
        applet.start();
        frame.show();
    }

    public void init(){
        text1 = new TextField(20);
        add(text1);
        button1 = new Button("Display the linked-to
            text");
        add(button1);
    }
```

When the user clicks the Display button, we'll read in the `locator.xml` document:

```
public boolean action (Event e, Object o)
{
    String locator = "";
```

```
        URL url = null;
        filename = "file:////c://xml//locator//locator.xml";

        try {
            url = new URL(filename);
        } catch (MalformedURLException e1) {
            System.out.println("Cannot create url for: "
                + filename);
            System.exit(0);
        }

        Document d = new Document();

        try {
            d.load(url);
        }
        catch (ParseException e2) {
            d.reportError(e2, System.out);
        }
            .
            .
            .
```

Next, we search for the URL of the containing resource, which is the file **locator2.xml,** and read in that file:

```
        public boolean action (Event e, Object o)
        {
            String locator = "";

            URL url = null;
            filename = "file:////c://xml//locator//
                locator.xml";

            try {
                url = new URL(filename);
            } catch (MalformedURLException e1) {
                System.out.println("Cannot create url for: "
                    + filename);
                System.exit(0);
            }

            Document d = new Document();

            try {
                d.load(url);
            }
            catch (ParseException e2) {
                d.reportError(e2, System.out);
            }

            if (d != null) {
                Element root = d.getRoot();
```

```
Enumeration enum = root.getChildren();
while (enum.hasMoreElements()) {
    Element elem =
        (Element)enum.nextElement();
    if (elem.getTagName().equals("LOCATOR")) {
        URL url2 = null;
        try {
            locator = new String(elem
                .getAttribute("HREF"));
            url2 = new URL
                (locator.substring(0,
                locator.indexOf("#")));
        }
        catch (MalformedURLException e3) {
            System.out.println("Cannot
                create URL for: " +
                elem.getAttribute("HREF"));
            System.exit(0);
        }

        Document d2 = new Document();

        try {
            d2.load(url2);
        }
        catch (ParseException e4) {
            d2.reportError(e4, System.out);
        }
            .
            .
            .
    }
    }
}
    return true;
    }
}
```

Now we need to decode the string of location terms, which we've stored in the string named `locator`:

`#ROOT()CHILD(2,CUSTOMER)(2,PRODUCT)(1,NAME)`

We perform the decoding process by stripping off the `#ROOT()` term and by looping over all the remaining terms in the locator string—identifying each successive term by the opening parenthesis, `(`:

```
public class locator extends Applet{

    static String filename;
    TextField text1;
    Button button1;
```

```
            String rootString = new String("#ROOT()");
                .
                .
                .

public boolean action (Event e, Object o)
{
        String locator = "";
                    .
                    .
                    .

                        Element newRoot = d2.getRoot();

                        int number = 0;
                        String tagName = "";

                        locator =
                            locator.substring(locator
                                    .indexOf(rootString) +
                                rootString.length());

                        int begin = locator.indexOf("(", 0);

                        Element elem2 = null;
                        Enumeration enum2 = null;

                        while(begin != -1){
                                .
                                .
                                .
                        }
                    }
                }
            }
        }
}
```

Then we simply read off term-by-term in the location string, converting instance numbers into integers and element types into strings, and work through the entire document until we come to exactly the element we are searching for:

```
public boolean action (Event e, Object o)
{
        String locator = "";
                    .
                    .
                    .

                        Element newRoot = d2.getRoot();

                        int number = 0;
                        String tagName = "";
```

```
locator =
    locator.substring(locator
            .indexOf(rootString) +
    rootString.length());

int begin = locator.indexOf("(", 0);

Element elem2 = null;
Enumeration enum2 = null;

while(begin != -1){
    begin++;
    number =
        Integer.parseInt(locator
                .substring(begin,
            ++begin));
    tagName = locator.substring
        (++begin,
        locator.indexOf(")", begin));

    enum2 = newRoot.getChildren();

    int index = 0;

    while (enum2.hasMoreElements()
            && index <= number) {
        elem2 = (Element)
                enum2.nextElement();
        if(elem2.getTagName().equals
            (tagName)){
            index++;
            newRoot = elem2;
        }
    }
    begin = locator.indexOf("(",
        begin);
}
text1.setText(newRoot.getText());
                }
            }
        }
        return true;
    }
}
```

After we finish working through the locator string, we have reached the resource we are supposed to find and so place its character data into the application's text field. That's all there is to it: we've decoded the locator string by taking it term-by-term, parsing each such term into an instance number and element type, and searching for the correct instance of that element. Run the locator application now, as shown in Figure 6-7.

When the user clicks the Display button, we read in the **locator.xml** document and decode the locator there. That locator string is **#ROOT()CHILD(2,CUSTOMER)(2,PRODUCT)(1,NAME)**, so we search for the first <NAME> element in the second <PRODUCT> element, which is itself in the second <CUSTOMER> element. Finally, we display the text in the target element, as shown in Figure 6-8—**Apple**.

The locator application is a success. Now we're using complex location terms in XML. The code for this program, **locator.xml**, appears in Listing 6-9; the two documents it uses, **locator.xml** and **locator2.xml**, appear in Listings 6-10 and 6-11 respectively.

Figure 6-7.
The locator application.

Figure 6-8.
Decoding and using a complex locator string.

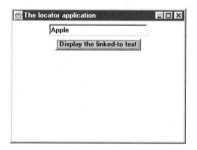

Listing 6-9.
locator.java.

```
import com.ms.xml.ParseException;
import com.ms.xml.Document;
import com.ms.xml.Element;

import java.util.Enumeration;
import java.awt.*;
import java.net.*;
import java.applet.Applet;


public class locator extends Applet{
```
Continues

Listing 6-9.
Continued.

```
static String filename;
TextField text1;
Button button1;
String rootString = new String("#ROOT()");

public static void main(String args[])
{
    locatorFrame frame = new locatorFrame("The
        locator application");

    frame.show();
    frame.hide();
    frame.resize(320, 240);

    locator applet = new locator();

    frame.add("Center", applet);
    applet.init();
    applet.start();
    frame.show();
}

public void init(){
    text1 = new TextField(20);
    add(text1);
    button1 = new Button("Display the linked-to
        text");
    add(button1);
}

public boolean action (Event e, Object o)
{
    String locator = "";

    URL url = null;
    filename = "file:////c://xml//locator//
        locator.xml";

    try {
        url = new URL(filename);
    } catch (MalformedURLException e1) {
        System.out.println("Cannot create url for: "
            + filename);
        System.exit(0);
    }

    Document d = new Document();

    try {
        d.load(url);
    }
    catch (ParseException e2) {
        d.reportError(e2, System.out);
```

Listing 6-9.
Continued.

```
        }

    if (d != null) {
        Element root = d.getRoot();
        Enumeration enum = root.getChildren();
        while (enum.hasMoreElements()) {
            Element elem = (Element)enum
                .nextElement();
            if (elem.getTagName().equals("LOCATOR")) {
                URL url2 = null;
                try {
                    locator = new String(elem
                        .getAttribute("HREF"));
                    url2 = new URL
                        (locator.substring(0,
                        locator.indexOf("#")));
                }
                catch (MalformedURLException e3) {
                    System.out.println("Cannot
                        create URL for: " +
                        elem.getAttribute("HREF"));
                    System.exit(0);
                }

                Document d2 = new Document();

                try {
                    d2.load(url2);
                }
                catch (ParseException e4) {
                    d2.reportError(e4, System.out);
                }

                Element newRoot = d2.getRoot();

                int number = 0;
                String tagName = "";

                locator =
                    locator.substring(locator.
                        indexOf(rootString) +
                    rootString.length());

                int begin = locator.indexOf("(", 0);

                Element elem2 = null;
                Enumeration enum2 = null;

                while(begin != -1){
                    begin++;
                    number =
                        Integer.parseInt
```

Continues

Listing 6-9.
Continued.

```
                                          (locator.substring
                                             (begin,++begin));
                       tagName = locator.substring
                          (++begin,
                           locator.indexOf(")", begin));

                       enum2 = newRoot.getChildren();

                       int index = 0;

                       while (enum2.hasMoreElements()
                             && index <= number) {
                          elem2 = (Element)
                                enum2.nextElement();
                          if(elem2.getTagName()
                                .equals(tagName)){
                             index++;
                             newRoot = elem2;
                          }
                       }
                       begin = locator.indexOf("(",
                          begin);
                    }
                    text1.setText(newRoot.getText());
                }
            }
        }
        return true;
    }
}

class locatorFrame extends Frame
{
    public locatorFrame(String str)
    {
        super (str);
    }

    public boolean handleEvent(Event evt)
    {
        switch (evt.id)
        {
            case Event.WINDOW_DESTROY:
                dispose();
                System.exit(0);
                return true;

            default:
                return super.handleEvent(evt);
        }
    }
}
```

Listing 6-10.
`locator.xml`.

```
<?XML version="1.0"?>
<!doctype LINK [
<!ELEMENT LINK    (#PCDATA | LOCATOR)*>
<!ELEMENT LOCATOR ANY>
<!ATTLIST LINK
            XML-LINK          CDATA                    #FIXED
                                                       "EXTENDED"
            ROLE              CDATA                    #IMPLIED
            TITLE             CDATA                    #IMPLIED
            INLINE            (TRUE|FALSE)             "TRUE"
            CONTENT-ROLE    CDATA                    #IMPLIED
            CONTENT-TITLE   CDATA                    #IMPLIED
            SHOW              (EMBED|REPLACE|NEW)     "REPLACE"
            ACTUATE           (AUTO|USER)             "USER"
            BEHAVIOR          CDATA                    #IMPLIED
>
<!ATTLIST LOCATOR
            XML-LINK  CDATA                  #FIXED "LOCATOR"
            ROLE      CDATA                  #IMPLIED
            HREF      CDATA                  #REQUIRED
            TITLE     CDATA                  #IMPLIED
            SHOW      (EMBED|REPLACE|NEW)    "REPLACE"
            ACTUATE   (AUTO|USER)            "USER"
            BEHAVIOR  CDATA                  #IMPLIED
>
]>
<LINK XML-LINK = "EXTENDED">
  <LOCATOR
  XML-LINK="LOCATOR"
  HREF="FILE:////C://XML//LOCATOR//LOCATOR2.XML#ROOT()
        CHILD(2,CUSTOMER)(2,PRODUCT)(1,NAME)">
Here is an extended link.
  </LOCATOR>
</LINK>
```

Listing 6-11.
`locator2.xml`.

```
<?XML version = "1.0" ?>
<!DOCTYPE DOCUMENT [
<!ELEMENT DOCUMENT (CUSTOMER|NAME)*>
<!ELEMENT CUSTOMER (NAME,DATE,PRODUCT*)>
<!ELEMENT NAME (LASTNAME?,FIRSTNAME?,#PCDATA?)>
<!ELEMENT LASTNAME (#PCDATA)>
<!ELEMENT FIRSTNAME (#PCDATA)>
<!ELEMENT DATE (#PCDATA)>
<!ELEMENT PRODUCT (NAME,NUMBER,PRICE)>
<!ELEMENT NUMBER (#PCDATA)>
<!ELEMENT PRICE (#PCDATA)>
]>
<DOCUMENT>
```

Continues

Listing 6-11.
Continued.

```
<CUSTOMER>
    <NAME>
        <LASTNAME>Kennilworth</LASTNAME>
        <FIRSTNAME>Susanne</FIRSTNAME>
    </NAME>
    <DATE>March 23, 1998</DATE>
        <PRODUCT>
            <NAME>Banana</NAME>
            <NUMBER>12</NUMBER>
            <PRICE>4.98</PRICE>
        </PRODUCT>
        <PRODUCT>
            <NAME>Peach</NAME>
            <NUMBER>3</NUMBER>
            <PRICE>.69</PRICE>
        </PRODUCT>
</CUSTOMER>
<CUSTOMER>
    <NAME>
        <LASTNAME>Edwards</LASTNAME>
        <FIRSTNAME>Britta</FIRSTNAME>
    </NAME>
    <DATE>June 17, 1998</DATE>
        <PRODUCT>
            <NAME>Peach</NAME>
            <NUMBER>24</NUMBER>
            <PRICE>3.12</PRICE>
        </PRODUCT>
        <PRODUCT>
            <NAME>Apple</NAME>
            <NUMBER>9</NUMBER>
            <PRICE>.98</PRICE>
        </PRODUCT>
</CUSTOMER>
</DOCUMENT>
```

Now we've taken a look at both absolute and relative location terms, and there is one more kind to come—string-match location terms.

String-Match Location Terms

Here's how string-match terms are defined in "WD-xml-link-970731":

```
XPointer::= First ('..' Second)?
First::= AbsTerm? RelTerm* StringTerm?
Second::= AbsTermOrDitto? RelTerm* StringTerm?
```

```
StringTerm::= 'STRING(' Instance ',' SkipLit ',' Offset ')'
Offset::= Digit+
```

Here, the target resource is found by searching the text of the location source for a match to the **SkipLit** string. The Index is a number that selects among the matches, and Offset is a number that gives an offset (in characters) from the start of the match to the designated location.

For example, this location specification selects the letter **i** (location 9 from the start of the string) in the fourth occurrence of the string **"Thomas Edison"**:

```
ROOT()STRING(4,"Thomas Edison",9)
```

This location specification selects the character following the sixth **'x'** in the document:

```
ROOT()STRING(6,'x',1)
```

That's it for location terms. We've taken a look at all three possible types: absolute, relative, and string-match. We will continue on with the final topic of this chapter, extended link groups.

Extended Link Groups

Sometimes it's best to work with linked documents in groups. Working with groups, you can indicate the linked nature of a set of resources. If you are using out-of-line links, you'll have to read other documents to get the links you need, and a linked group of documents is perfect for that. You set up a linked group of documents using the GROUP XML link.

Each document in the group is linked to using the HREF attribute in an extended link element; those link elements themselves are the children of a link group. For example, here's how the W3C document "WD-xml-link-970731" declares link groups and the links to documents in them:

```
<!ELEMENT GROUP (DOCUMENT*)>
<!ATTLIST GROUP
          XML-LINK CDATA #FIXED "GROUP"
          STEPS    CDATA #IMPLIED
>
<!ELEMENT DOCUMENT EMPTY>
<!ATTLIST DOCUMENT
          XML-LINK CDATA #FIXED "DOCUMENT"
          HREF     CDATA #REQUIRED
>
```

You use the STEPS attribute when an extended link group directs the application to another document, which contains an extended link group of its own. In such cases, the STEPS attribute can hold a value that indicates how many steps of extended link group processing should be undertaken.

SUMMARY

That's it for our coverage of link groups, and that's it for our coverage of XML links. We've seen a great deal in this chapter, from simple links to extended links, from absolute location terms to relative and string-match location terms, from the many location keywords and how they work to extended link groups. There's a great deal of power here, as you can see.

In the next chapter, we'll continue our exploration when we develop our skills by using XML with text and graphics.

XML with Text and Graphics

In this chapter, we'll integrate XML and Java as we work creating XML browsers with some powerful features. We'll see how to work with text in XML browsers as we create examples that let the user specify the text's font weight (bold or plain), as well as how to select the font size. We'll also see how to create XML browsers that display nontext graphical displays when we create XML documents that produce circles, lines, and rectangles in browsers. The techniques in this chapter will extend what we can do with XML as we learn how to support what XML can do in Java. For example, there's no reason XML browsers have to display text documents only; you can use XML documents to construct any kind of graphically oriented figures as well.

There's a lot coming up in this chapter, so let's get started at once with our first example.

The `textbrowser` Example

In our first example, `textbrowser`, we'll let the user specify what text should appear bold and what text should appear plain when we display a document. To do that, we'll support two new XML tags: <BOLD> and <PLAIN>; here's a document that uses those tags—`textbrowser.xml`:

```
<?XML version = "1.0" ?>
<!DOCTYPE DOCUMENT [
<!ELEMENT DOCUMENT (BOLD|PLAIN)*>
<!ELEMENT BOLD (#PCDATA|BOLD|PLAIN)*>
<!ELEMENT PLAIN (#PCDATA|BOLD|PLAIN)*>
]>
<DOCUMENT>
<BOLD>Britta</BOLD>
<BOLD>
<BOLD>
Adam
</BOLD>
<PLAIN>
Phoebe
<BOLD>
<PLAIN>Tom</PLAIN>
<BOLD>Fred</BOLD>
Edward
</BOLD>
</PLAIN>
</BOLD>
<PLAIN>
Sammy
</PLAIN>
</DOCUMENT>
```

When the user starts the textbrowser application, the program displays a window with a button in it labeled Browse as shown at the top of the following page.

When the user clicks the Browse button, we read in the `textbrowser.xml` document and display the text in that document as shown at the bottom of the following page.

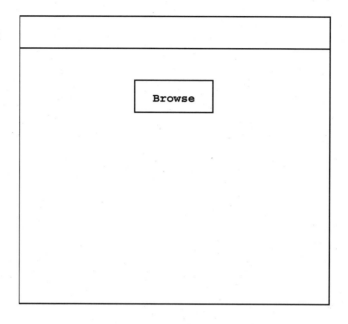

The text enclosed in <BOLD> tags will appear bold, and text in <PLAIN> tags will appear plain. Note that these two tags override each other, because these text attributes are "either-or"—you can't mix them.

Let's put this example together now. Because this is a graphical application, we start by creating a window, placing the textbrowser applet in that window, and adding the Browse button we'll use:

```
import java.awt.*;
import java.applet.Applet;

public class textbrowser extends Applet{

    static String filename;
    Button button1;

    public static void main(String args[])
    {
        textbrowserFrame frame = new textbrowserFrame("The
            textbrowser
            application");

        frame.show();
        frame.hide();
        frame.resize(320, 320);

        textbrowser applet = new textbrowser();

        frame.add("Center", applet);
        applet.init();
        applet.start();
        frame.show();
    }

    public void init(){
        button1 = new Button("Browse");
        add(button1);
    }
```

When the user clicks the Browse button, we can read in the textbrowser XML document, **textbrowser.xml**:

```
import com.ms.xml.ParseException;
import com.ms.xml.Document;
import com.ms.xml.Element;

import java.awt.*;
import java.net.*;
import java.applet.Applet;

public class textbrowser extends Applet{

    static String filename;
```

```
        Button button1;
            .
            .
            .
    public boolean action (Event e, Object o){
        URL url = null;
        filename = "file:////c://xml//textbrowser//
            textbrowser.xml";

        try {
            url = new URL(filename);
        } catch (MalformedURLException e1) {
            System.out.println("Cannot create URL for: " +
                filename);
            System.exit(0);
        }

        Document d = new Document();

        try {
            d.load(url);
        }
        catch (ParseException e3) {
            d.reportError(e3, System.out);
        }
            .
            .
            .
    }
```

Now that the document is read in, the program should interpret the <BOLD> and <PLAIN> tags and display that document accordingly.

As with the other browsers we've developed, we'll work through the tree structure of the XML document recursively, so we set up a new method named **doTree()**. We pass the document's **root** element to **doTree()** to get that method started, and we also pass an integer flag, **doBold**, which indicates whether or not this element's text should appear bold or plain. We will set **doBold** to **0** for plain text and to **1** for bold text. When we call **doTree()** with the root element, we'll set **doBold** to **0**, but the setting of that flag doesn't actually matter here because we don't display the root element in any case. Note that we also call **repaint()** to make sure the document is displayed when **doTree()** is done processing:

```
import com.ms.xml.ParseException;
import com.ms.xml.Document;
import com.ms.xml.Element;

import java.util.Enumeration;
import java.awt.*;
import java.net.*;
```

```
import java.applet.Applet;

public class textbrowser extends Applet{

    static String filename;
    Button button1;
        .
        .
        .
    public boolean action (Event e, Object o){

        URL url = null;
        filename = "file:////c://xml//textbrowser//
            textbrowser.xml";

        try {
            url = new URL(filename);
        } catch (MalformedURLException e1) {
            System.out.println("Cannot create URL for: " +
                filename);
            System.exit(0);
        }

        Document d = new Document();

        try {
            d.load(url);
        }
        catch (ParseException e3) {
            d.reportError(e3, System.out);
        }

        if (d != null) {
            doTree(d.getRoot(), 0);
            repaint();
        }
        return true;
    }
```

Now we'll write the **doTree()** method to store the document in a form that we can display it in, and the **paint()** method to actually display the document. We start with **doTree()**:

```
void doTree(Element elem, int doBold)
{

}
```

The **doTree()** method has two tasks: if the item we pass to **doTree()** is text, we should store that text in a way that's easy to display after interpreting if it should be displayed as bold or plain text. If the item we're passed is an element—either <BOLD> or <PLAIN>—we should use **doBold** to match the new font weight and call **doTree()** again to process the children of the element, which includes any text in the element.

To store the text in a way that's easy to display, we'll set up two new arrays, **displayStrings[]** and **displayAttributes[]**. The **displayStrings[]** array will hold the text strings we're supposed to display, line after line, and the **displayAttributes[]** array will hold the **doBold** settings for each line (0 = plain text, 1 = bold text). Here's how the **textbrowser.xml**'s data will be stored when **doTree()** is done:

displayStrings []	displayAttributes []
Britta	1
Adam	1
Phoebe	0
Fred	0
Edward	1
Sammy	1
	0

We'll make use of these two arrays in the **paint()** method when it's time to display the document. We add those new arrays to the program now, along with an index into them, **numberDisplayLines**:

```
public class textbrowser extends Applet{

    static String filename;
    Button button1;
    static String displayStrings[] = new String[100];
    static int displayAttributes[] = new int[100];
    static int numberDisplayLines = 0;
        .
        .
        .
```

In **doTree()**, then, we loop over the children of the element passed to us and check to see whether each child is of type **Element.ELEMENT**; if not, we'll treat this item as text:

```
void doTree(Element elem, int doBold)
{
    Enumeration enum = elem.getChildren();

    while (enum.hasMoreElements()) {
        Element elem2 = (Element)enum.nextElement();
```

```
        if(elem2.getType() != com.ms.xml.Element.ELEMENT){
            .
            .
            .
        }
    }
}
```

If this item is text, we store the text in the **displayStrings[]** array and the current setting of **doBold,** which was passed to us in **doTree()**) in the **displayAttributes[]** array. Finally, we increment the index of those two arrays, **numberDisplayLines:**

```
void doTree(Element elem, int doBold)
{
    Enumeration enum = elem.getChildren();

    while (enum.hasMoreElements()) {
        Element elem2 = (Element)enum.nextElement();
        if(elem2.getType() != com.ms.xml.Element.ELEMENT){
            displayStrings[numberDisplayLines] =
                elem2.getText();
            displayAttributes[numberDisplayLines++] =
                doBold;
        }
        .
        .
        .
    }
}
```

That handles the text-storing process. Next we'll handle the two elements, <BOLD> and <PLAIN>. Because these two tags override each other, we first save the current **doBold** setting:

```
void doTree(Element elem, int doBold)
{
    Enumeration enum = elem.getChildren();

    while (enum.hasMoreElements()) {
        Element elem2 = (Element)enum.nextElement();
        if(elem2.getType() != com.ms.xml.Element.ELEMENT){
            displayStrings[numberDisplayLines] =
                elem2.getText();
            displayAttributes[numberDisplayLines++] =
                doBold;
        }
        else{
            int doBoldOld = doBold;
            .
            .
```

```
            }
        }
    }
```

Next, we handle the <BOLD> tag by setting doBold to 1:

```
void doTree(Element elem, int doBold)
{
    Enumeration enum = elem.getChildren();

    while (enum.hasMoreElements()) {
        Element elem2 = (Element)enum.nextElement();
        if(elem2.getType() != com.ms.xml.Element.ELEMENT){
            displayStrings[numberDisplayLines] =
                elem2.getText();
            displayAttributes[numberDisplayLines++] =
                doBold;
        }
        else{
            int doBoldOld = doBold;
            if(elem2.getTagName().equals("BOLD")){
                doBold = 1;
            }
                .
                .
                .

        }
    }
}
```

Then we handle the <PLAIN> tag by setting the doBold flag to 0:

```
void doTree(Element elem, int doBold)
{
    Enumeration enum = elem.getChildren();

    while (enum.hasMoreElements()) {
        Element elem2 = (Element)enum.nextElement();
        if(elem2.getType() != com.ms.xml.Element.ELEMENT){
            displayStrings[numberDisplayLines] =
                elem2.getText();
            displayAttributes[numberDisplayLines++] =
                doBold;
        }
        else{
            int doBoldOld = doBold;
            if(elem2.getTagName().equals("BOLD")){
                doBold = 1;
            }
            if(elem2.getTagName().equals("PLAIN")){
                doBold = 0;
            }
```

.
.
.

```
        }
    }
}
```

Now that we've interpreted the <BOLD> or <PLAIN> tag, we call
doTree() again, this time passing the new **doBold** setting. After return-
ing from the **doTree()** call, we restore the old **doBold** setting:

```
void doTree(Element elem, int doBold)
{
    Enumeration enum = elem.getChildren();

    while (enum.hasMoreElements()) {
        Element elem2 = (Element)enum.nextElement();
        if(elem2.getType() != com.ms.xml.Element.ELEMENT){
            displayStrings[numberDisplayLines] =
elem2.getText();
            displayAttributes[numberDisplayLines++] =
doBold;
        }
        else{
            int doBoldOld = doBold;
            if(elem2.getTagName().equals("BOLD")){
                doBold = 1;
            }
            if(elem2.getTagName().equals("PLAIN")){
                doBold = 0;
            }
            doTree(elem2, doBold);
            doBold = doBoldOld;
        }
    }
}
```

That completes the **doTree()** method; next, we'll write the **paint()**
method, seeing how to display text as bold or plain.

Displaying Bold Text

In the **paint()** method, we will display the XML document's data as interpreted by the **doTree()** method. The **doTree()** method has filled the
displayStrings[] and **displayAttributes[]** arrays with the data we're
supposed to display: **displayStrings[]** holds the text to display, and **displayAttributes[]** tells us how to display that text (**0** = plain, **1** = bold):

```
displayStrings []              displayAttributes []
```

displayStrings []	displayAttributes []
Britta	1
Adam	1
Phoebe	0
Fred	0
Edward	1
Sammy	1
	0

We begin the **paint()** method with a loop over all the lines we're supposed to display:

```
public void paint(Graphics g)
{
    for(int index = 0; index < numberDisplayLines;
        index++){
        .
        .
        .
    }
}
```

To display the current line in bold or plain text, we will create a new Java Font object. The Font object specifies three aspects of the text font—its name (such as Roman, Courier, and so on), its style (set with the constants **Font.PLAIN**, **Font.BOLD**, **Font.ITALIC**) and the font size. In this case, we declare our new Font object, named **font**, and set an integer named style to **Font.PLAIN**:

```
public void paint(Graphics g)
{
    for(int index = 0; index < numberDisplayLines;
        index++){
        Font font;
        int style = Font.PLAIN;
        .
        .
        .
    }
}
```

On the other hand, if the **doBold** flag for this line (now stored in the **displayAttributes[]** array) is **1**, we should make this line bold, which we do by setting the style integer to **Font.BOLD**:

```
public void paint(Graphics g)
{
    for(int index = 0; index < numberDisplayLines;
        index++){
        Font font;
        int style = Font.PLAIN;
        if(displayAttributes[index] == 1){
            style = Font.BOLD;
        }
            .
            .
            .
    }
}
}
```

Next, we create the font object using Roman typeface, the style integer, and make the font 12 points (a point is 1/72 of an inch) high:

```
public void paint(Graphics g)
{
    for(int index = 0; index < numberDisplayLines;
        index++){
        Font font;
        int style = Font.PLAIN;
        if(displayAttributes[index] == 1){
            style = Font.BOLD;
        }
        font = new Font("Roman", style, 12);
            .
            .
            .
    }
}
}
```

After we've created our font object, we can install that object into the Graphics object, **g**, passed to us in **paint()**; to install the new font, we use the **setFont()** method:

```
public void paint(Graphics g)
{
    for(int index = 0; index < numberDisplayLines;
        index++){
        Font font;
        int style = Font.PLAIN;
        if(displayAttributes[index] == 1){
            style = Font.BOLD;
        }
        font = new Font("Roman", style, 12);
        g.setFont(font);
            .
```

```
            .
            .
        }
    }
}
```

As we display each line in the application's window, we have to keep skipping down by the height of each line. We determine the height of each line as displayed in the window by getting a **FontMetrics** object for the current font this way:

```
public void paint(Graphics g)
{
    for(int index = 0; index < numberDisplayLines;
        index++){
        Font font;
        int style = Font.PLAIN;
        if(displayAttributes[index] == 1){
            style = Font.BOLD;
        }
        font = new Font("Roman", style, 12);
        g.setFont(font);

        FontMetrics fontmetrics =
            getFontMetrics(getFont());
            .
            .
            .
    }
}
```

Now we increment the y-screen location of the current line by the display-line height and draw that line of text, as stored in **displayStrings[]**, in the window:

```
public void paint(Graphics g)
{
    int y = 0;

    for(int index = 0; index < numberDisplayLines;
        index++){
        Font font;
        int style = Font.PLAIN;
        if(displayAttributes[index] == 1){
            style = Font.BOLD;
        }
        font = new Font("Roman", style, 12);
        g.setFont(font);
        FontMetrics fontmetrics =
            getFontMetrics(getFont());
```

```
                    y += fontmetrics.getHeight();

                    g.drawString(displayStrings[index], 0, y);
                }
            }
        }
```

That's it—run the application now, as shown in Figure 7-1.

When the user clicks the Browse button, the program reads in the **textbrowser.xml** document and displays the text in that document in the application's window, formatted according to the <BOLD> and <PLAIN> tags, as shown in Figure 7-2.

Our textbrowser application is a success. Now we're using different font weights in an XML browser. The code for this application, **textbrowser.java**, appears in Listing 7-1, and the XML document it reads in, **textbrowser.xml**, appears in Listing 7-2.

Figure 7-1.
The textbrowser application.

Figure 7-2.
Displaying text with different font weights.

Listing 7-1.
textbrowser.java

```java
import com.ms.xml.ParseException;
import com.ms.xml.Document;
import com.ms.xml.Element;

import java.util.Enumeration;
import java.awt.*;
import java.net.*;
import java.applet.Applet;


public class textbrowser extends Applet{

    static String filename;
    Button button1;
    static String displayStrings[] = new String[100];
    static int displayAttributes[] = new int[100];
    static int numberDisplayLines = 0;

    public static void main(String args[])
    {
        textbrowserFrame frame = new textbrowserFrame("The
            textbrowser application");

        frame.show();
        frame.hide();
        frame.resize(320, 320);

        textbrowser applet = new textbrowser();

        frame.add("Center", applet);
        applet.init();
        applet.start();
        frame.show();
    }

    public void init(){
        button1 = new Button("Browse");
        add(button1);
    }

    public boolean action (Event e, Object o){

        URL url = null;
        filename = "file:////c://xml//textbrowser//
            textbrowser.xml";

        try {
            url = new URL(filename);
        } catch (MalformedURLException e1) {
```

Continues

Listing 7-1.
Continued.

```
            System.out.println("Cannot create URL for: "
                + filename);
            System.exit(0);
        }

        Document d = new Document();

        try {
            d.load(url);
        }
        catch (ParseException e3) {
            d.reportError(e3, System.out);
        }

        if (d != null) {
            doTree(d.getRoot(), 0);
            repaint();
        }
        return true;
    }


    void doTree(Element elem, int doBold)
    {
        Enumeration enum = elem.getChildren();

        while (enum.hasMoreElements()) {
            Element elem2 = (Element)enum.nextElement();
            if(elem2.getType() !=
                com.ms.xml.Element.ELEMENT){
                displayStrings[numberDisplayLines] =
                    elem2.getText();
                displayAttributes[numberDisplayLines++] =
                    doBold;
            }
            else{
                int doBoldOld = doBold;
                if(elem2.getTagName().equals("BOLD")){
                    doBold = 1;
                }
                if(elem2.getTagName().equals("PLAIN")){
                    doBold = 0;
                }
                doTree(elem2, doBold);
                doBold = doBoldOld;
            }
        }
    }

    public void paint(Graphics g)
    {
        int y = 0;
```

```
        for(int index = 0; index < numberDisplayLines;
            index++){
            Font font;
            int style = Font.PLAIN;
            if(displayAttributes[index] == 1){
                style = Font.BOLD;
            }
            font = new Font("Roman", style, 12);
            g.setFont(font);
            FontMetrics fontmetrics =
                    getFontMetrics(getFont());
            y += fontmetrics.getHeight();

            g.drawString(displayStrings[index], 0, y);
        }
    }
}
class textbrowserFrame extends Frame
{
    public textbrowserFrame(String str)
    {
        super (str);
    }

    public boolean handleEvent(Event evt)
    {
        switch (evt.id)
        {
            case Event.WINDOW_DESTROY:
                dispose();
                System.exit(0);
                return true;

            default:
                return super.handleEvent(evt);
        }
    }

}
```

```
<?XML version = "1.0" ?>
<!DOCTYPE DOCUMENT [
<!ELEMENT DOCUMENT (BOLD|PLAIN)*>
<!ELEMENT BOLD (#PCDATA|BOLD|PLAIN)*>
<!ELEMENT PLAIN (#PCDATA|BOLD|PLAIN)*>
]>
<DOCUMENT>
```

Continues

Listing 7-2.
Continued.

```
<BOLD>Britta</BOLD>
<BOLD>
<BOLD>
Adam
</BOLD>
<PLAIN>
Phoebe
<BOLD>
<PLAIN>Tom</PLAIN>
<BOLD>Fred</BOLD>
Edward
</BOLD>
</PLAIN>
</BOLD>
<PLAIN>
Sammy
</PLAIN>
</DOCUMENT>
```

We've gotten some experience with handling text in XML browsers now. Let's make a quick modification to the textbrowser example to enable it to display text in different size fonts.

The `fontsize` Example

In this next example, we'll modify our textbrowser example into a new example, fontsize, that will let us interpret XML documents that specify fontsize. These new documents will use two new tags: <BIGFONT> and <SMALLFONT>. Here's how a document, **fontsize.xml**, that uses these new tags looks:

```
<?XML version = "1.0" ?>
<!DOCTYPE DOCUMENT [
<!ELEMENT DOCUMENT (BIGFONT|SMALLFONT)*>
<!ELEMENT BIGFONT (#PCDATA|BIGFONT|SMALLFONT)*>
<!ELEMENT SMALLFONT (#PCDATA|BIGFONT|SMALLFONT)*>
]>
<DOCUMENT>
<BIGFONT>Britta</BIGFONT>
<BIGFONT>
<BIGFONT>
```

```
Adam
</BIGFONT>
<SMALLFONT>
Phoebe
<BIGFONT>
<SMALLFONT>Tom</SMALLFONT>
<BIGFONT>Fred</BIGFONT>
Edward
</BIGFONT>
</SMALLFONT>
</BIGFONT>
<SMALLFONT>
Sammy
</SMALLFONT>
</DOCUMENT>
```

When the user starts the fontsize application, the program displays a window with a button in it labeled Browse:

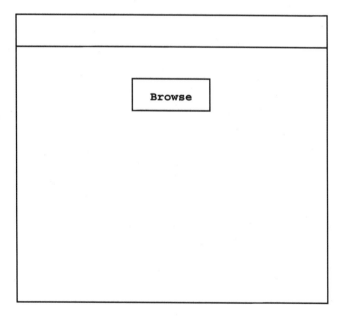

When the user clicks the Browse button, we read in the **fontsize.xml** document and display the text in that document:

```
┌─────────────────────────────────────────┐
│                                         │
├─────────────────────────────────────────┤
│  Britta                                 │
│  Adam                                    │
│  Phoebe        ┌──────────────┐          │
│                │   Browse     │          │
│  Tom           └──────────────┘          │
│  Fred                                    │
│  Edward                                  │
│  Sammy                                   │
│                                         │
│                                         │
│                                         │
│                                         │
│                                         │
└─────────────────────────────────────────┘
```

In this case, the text between the <BIGFONT> tags is in large font, and the text between the <SMALLFONT> tags is in small font.

We'll start this program as we did with the textbrowser example, creating a window and adding a Browse button:

```
import com.ms.xml.ParseException;
import com.ms.xml.Document;
import com.ms.xml.Element;

import java.util.Enumeration;
import java.awt.*;
import java.net.*;
import java.applet.Applet;

public class fontsize extends Applet{

    Button button1;
    String filename;
    static String displayStrings[] = new String[100];
    static int displayAttributes[] = new int[100];
    static int numberDisplayLines = 0;

    public static void main(String args[])
    {
        fontsizeFrame frame = new fontsizeFrame("The
            fontsize application");

        frame.show();
```

```
                        frame.hide();
                        frame.resize(320, 240);

                        fontsize applet = new fontsize();

                        frame.add("Center", applet);
                        applet.init();
                        applet.start();
                        frame.show();
                    }

                public void init(){
                        button1 = new Button("Browse");
                        add(button1);
                    }
```

When the user clicks the Browse button, we read in the new document, fontsize.xml, and call doTree():

```
            public boolean action (Event e, Object o){

                    URL url = null;
                    filename = "file:////c://xml//fontsize//fontsize.xml";

                    try {
                        url = new URL(filename);
                    } catch (MalformedURLException e1) {
                        System.out.println("Cannot create URL for: " +
                                filename);
                        System.exit(0);
                    }

                    Document d = new Document();

                    try {
                        d.load(url);
                    }
                    catch (ParseException e2) {
                            d.reportError(e2, System.out);
                    }

                    if (d != null) {
                        doTree(d.getRoot(), 0);
                        repaint();
                    }
                    return true;
                }
```

Here, we pass doTree() two arguments—the root element and a font size. We'll support two font sizes in this example—12 point (for the <SMALLFONT> tag) and 24 point (for the <BIGFONT> tag). Besides these changes, doTree() is essentially the same as in the last example;

we store the lines of text in the array `displayStrings[]` and the display attributes (i.e., the font size) in the `displayAttributes[]` array:

displayStrings []	displayAttributes []
Britta	24
Adam	24
Phoebe	12
Tom	12
Fred	24
Edward	24
Sammy	12

Here's the new version of `doTree()`:

```
void doTree(Element elem, int currentfontsize)
{
    Enumeration enum = elem.getChildren();

    while (enum.hasMoreElements()) {

        Element elem2 = (Element)enum.nextElement();
        if(elem2.getType() != com.ms.xml.Element.ELEMENT){

            displayStrings[numberDisplayLines] =
                elem2.getText();
            displayAttributes[numberDisplayLines++] =
                currentfontsize;

        }
        else{

            int oldfontsize = currentfontsize;
            if(elem2.getTagName().equals("BIGFONT")){
                currentfontsize = 24;
            }
            if(elem2.getTagName().equals("SMALLFONT")){
                currentfontsize = 12;
            }
            doTree(elem2, currentfontsize);
            currentfontsize = oldfontsize;

        }
    }
}
```

In the `paint()` method, we create a new font object as we did in the previous example, but this time, we set the font's size, not its style. In fact, we can set the font's size directly from the **displayAttributes[]** array, because we've stored the font size for each line, 12 or 24 points, in that array:

```
public void paint(Graphics g)
{
    int y = 0;

    for(int index = 0; index < numberDisplayLines;
        index++){

        Font font;
        int type = Font.PLAIN;
        font = new Font("Roman", Font.PLAIN,
            displayAttributes[index]);
        g.setFont(font);
        FontMetrics fontmetrics =
            getFontMetrics(font);
        y += fontmetrics.getHeight();

        g.drawString(displayStrings[index], 0, y);

    }
}
}
```

That's all we need—now run the program as shown in Figure 7-3.

When the user clicks the Browse button, we read in the **fontsize.xml** document and display it, as shown in Figure 7-4. As you can see in that figure, we interpret the <BIGFONT> and<SMALLFONT> tags and display the text accordingly.

The fontsize application is a success. Now we can control the size of the font that we use to display XML documents. The code for this application appears in Listing 7-3, and the XML document it reads in, **fontsize.xml**, appears in Listing 7-4.

Figure 7-3.
The fontsize application.

Figure 7-4.
Displaying text with
different font sizes.

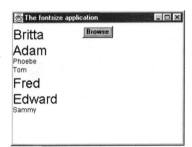

Figure 7-4.
Displaying text with
different font sizes.

Listing 7-3.
`fontsize.java`.

```java
import com.ms.xml.ParseException;
import com.ms.xml.Document;
import com.ms.xml.Element;

import java.util.Enumeration;
import java.awt.*;
import java.net.*;
import java.applet.Applet;

public class fontsize extends Applet{

    Button button1;
    String filename;
    static String displayStrings[] = new String[100];
    static int displayAttributes[] = new int[100];
    static int numberDisplayLines = 0;

    public static void main(String args[])
    {
        fontsizeFrame frame = new fontsizeFrame("The
            fontsize application");

        frame.show();
        frame.hide();
        frame.resize(320, 240);

        fontsize applet = new fontsize();

        frame.add("Center", applet);
        applet.init();
        applet.start();
        frame.show();
    }

    public void init(){
        button1 = new Button("Browse");
        add(button1);
    }
```

Listing 7-3.
Continued.

```
public boolean action (Event e, Object o){

    URL url = null;
    filename = "file:////c://xml//fontsize//
        fontsize.xml";

    try {
        url = new URL(filename);
    } catch (MalformedURLException e1) {
        System.out.println("Cannot create URL for: "
            + filename);
        System.exit(0);
    }

    Document d = new Document();

    try {
        d.load(url);
    }
    catch (ParseException e2) {
            d.reportError(e2, System.out);
    }

    if (d != null) {
        doTree(d.getRoot(), 0);
        repaint();
    }
    return true;
}


void doTree(Element elem, int currentfontsize)
{
    Enumeration enum = elem.getChildren();

    while (enum.hasMoreElements()) {

        Element elem2 = (Element)enum.nextElement();
        if(elem2.getType() !=
            com.ms.xml.Element.ELEMENT){

                displayStrings[numberDisplayLines] =
                    elem2.getText();
                displayAttributes[numberDisplayLines++] =
                    currentfontsize;

        }
        else{

            int oldfontsize = currentfontsize;
            if(elem2.getTagName().equals("BIGFONT")){
```

Continues

Listing 7-3.
Continued.

```
                                    currentfontsize = 24;
                }
                if(elem2.getTagName().equals
                    ("SMALLFONT")){
                    currentfontsize = 12;
                }
                doTree(elem2, currentfontsize);
                currentfontsize = oldfontsize;


            }
        }
    }

    public void paint(Graphics g)
    {
        int y = 0;

        for(int index = 0; index < numberDisplayLines;
            index++){

            Font font;
            int type = Font.PLAIN;
            font = new Font("Roman", Font.PLAIN,
                displayAttributes[index]);
            g.setFont(font);
            FontMetrics fontmetrics =
                getFontMetrics(font);
            y += fontmetrics.getHeight();

            g.drawString(displayStrings[index], 0, y);


        }
    }
}

class fontsizeFrame extends Frame
{
    public fontsizeFrame(String str)
    {
        super (str);
    }

    public boolean handleEvent(Event evt)
    {
        switch (evt.id)
        {
            case Event.WINDOW_DESTROY:
                dispose();
                System.exit(0);
                return true;

            default:
                return super.handleEvent(evt);
```

```
            }
        }
    }
```

```
<?XML version = "1.0" ?>
<!DOCTYPE DOCUMENT [
<!ELEMENT DOCUMENT (BIGFONT|SMALLFONT)*>
<!ELEMENT BIGFONT (#PCDATA|BIGFONT|SMALLFONT)*>
<!ELEMENT SMALLFONT (#PCDATA|BIGFONT|SMALLFONT)*>
]>
<DOCUMENT>
<BIGFONT>Britta</BIGFONT>
<BIGFONT>
<BIGFONT>
Adam
</BIGFONT>
<SMALLFONT>
Phoebe
<BIGFONT>
<SMALLFONT>Tom</SMALLFONT>
<BIGFONT>Fred</BIGFONT>
Edward
</BIGFONT>
</SMALLFONT>
</BIGFONT>
<SMALLFONT>
Sammy
</SMALLFONT>
</DOCUMENT>
```

The first two examples in this chapter were text-oriented, but that doesn't mean XML browsers have to be text-oriented. And in fact we should steer away from that idea, because many people have a bias already built-in about how browsers should work after using the World Wide Web. Our next example will display XML documents entirely as nontext graphics; there's no reason XML documents shouldn't work in such a way, and we'll take a look at that now.

The circles Examples

In this next example, we'll display an XML document in a nontext graphical manner. For example, we might create an XML document that is represented in a browser as a series of circles and ellipses. To do this, we'll create two new empty tags, <CIRCLE> and <ELLIPSE>, in a new XML document named `circles.xml`:

```
<?XML version = "1.0" ?>
<!DOCTYPE DOCUMENT [
<!ELEMENT DOCUMENT (CIRCLE|ELLIPSE)*>
<!ELEMENT CIRCLE EMPTY>
<!ELEMENT ELLIPSE EMPTY>
        .
        .
        .
```

Since these elements are empty, they have no text content, but we can store the data we need to specify each ellipse or circle—location, radius, and so on—in the attributes of the <CIRCLE> and <ELLIPSE> tags. We'll need an (x, y) location to specify a circle and a radius:

```
<?XML version = "1.0" ?>
<!DOCTYPE DOCUMENT [
<!ELEMENT DOCUMENT (CIRCLE|ELLIPSE)*>
<!ELEMENT CIRCLE EMPTY>
<!ELEMENT ELLIPSE EMPTY>
<!ATTLIST CIRCLE
    X CDATA #IMPLIED
    Y CDATA #IMPLIED
    RADIUS CDATA #IMPLIED>
        .
        .
        .
```

To specify an ellipse, we'll need an (x, y) location as well as the width and height of the box in which to place the ellipse:

```
<?XML version = "1.0" ?>
<!DOCTYPE DOCUMENT [
<!ELEMENT DOCUMENT (CIRCLE|ELLIPSE)*>
<!ELEMENT CIRCLE EMPTY>
<!ELEMENT ELLIPSE EMPTY>
<!ATTLIST CIRCLE
    X CDATA #IMPLIED
    Y CDATA #IMPLIED
    RADIUS CDATA #IMPLIED>
<!ATTLIST ELLIPSE
    X CDATA #IMPLIED
    Y CDATA #IMPLIED
    WIDTH CDATA #IMPLIED
    HEIGHT CDATA #IMPLIED>
]>
        .
        .
        .
```

Having set up the tags we need, we can specify as many circles and ellipses as we want, like this in `circles.xml`:

```
<?XML version = "1.0" ?>
<!DOCTYPE DOCUMENT [
<!ELEMENT DOCUMENT (CIRCLE|ELLIPSE)*>
<!ELEMENT CIRCLE EMPTY>
<!ELEMENT ELLIPSE EMPTY>
<!ATTLIST CIRCLE
    X CDATA #IMPLIED
    Y CDATA #IMPLIED
    RADIUS CDATA #IMPLIED>
<!ATTLIST ELLIPSE
    X CDATA #IMPLIED
    Y CDATA #IMPLIED
    WIDTH CDATA #IMPLIED
    HEIGHT CDATA #IMPLIED>
]>
<DOCUMENT>
<CIRCLE X="100" Y="100" RADIUS="25">
<CIRCLE X="200" Y="160" RADIUS="50">
<CIRCLE X="170" Y="100" RADIUS="15">
<ELLIPSE X="150" Y="100" WIDTH="100" HEIGHT="50">
<ELLIPSE X="220" Y="130" WIDTH="100" HEIGHT="50">
<ELLIPSE X="60" Y="240" WIDTH="80" HEIGHT="100">
</DOCUMENT>
```

When we start the circles browser, we simply display a Browse button:

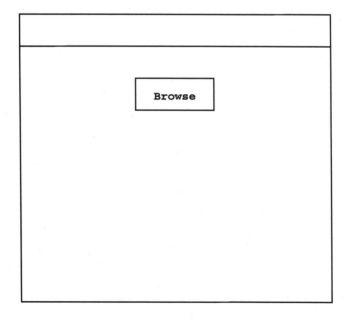

When the user clicks the Browse button, we read in the `circles.xml` document and display the circles and ellipses indicated in the document:

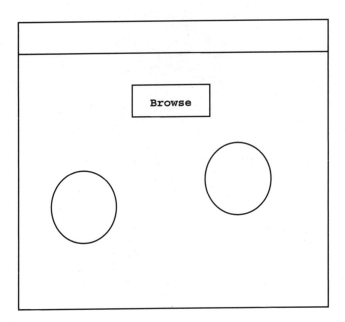

Let's put this example to work. We start with the `main()` method in which we set the application and its window up; we also install the Browse button in the `init()` method:

```
import com.ms.xml.ParseException;
import com.ms.xml.Document;
import com.ms.xml.Element;

import java.util.Enumeration;
import java.awt.*;
import java.net.*;
import java.applet.Applet;

public class circles extends Applet{

    Button button1;
    String filename = null;

    public static void main(String args[])
    {
        circlesFrame frame = new circlesFrame("The circles
            application");

        frame.show();
```

```
        frame.hide();
        frame.resize(400, 400);

        circles applet_app = new circles();

        frame.add("Center", applet_app);
        applet_app.init();
        applet_app.start();
        frame.show();
    }

    public void init(){
        button1 = new Button("Browse");
        add(button1);
    }
```

When the user clicks the Browse button, we read in the **circles.xml** document and call the **doTree()** method with that document's **root**:

```
public boolean action (Event e, Object o){

    URL url = null;
    String filename;

    filename = "file:////c://xml//circles//circles.xml";

    try {
        url = new URL(filename);
    } catch (MalformedURLException e1) {
        System.out.println("Cannot create URL for: "
                + filename);
        System.exit(0);
    }

    Document d = new Document();

    try {
        d.load(url);
    }
    catch (ParseException e3) {
        d.reportError(e3, System.out);
    }

    if (d != null) {
        doTree(d.getRoot());
        repaint();
    }
    return true;
}
```

Now that we've read in the **circles.xml** document, we will need some way to store the data in that document for each circle and ellipse specified there. We can store the total number of figures to draw in an integer named **numberFigures**:

```
public class circles extends Applet{

    Button button1;
    String filename = null;
    int numberFigures = 0;
        .
        .
        .
```

In addition, we store the (x, y) location for each figure in two new arrays, **x[]** and **y[]**; We will set aside enough storage for 100 figures. We also store the width and height of our figures in two additional arrays, **width[]** and **height[]**; we'll simply store a value of two times the radius value for the width and height of circles:

```
public class circles extends Applet{

    Button button1;
    String filename = null;
    int numberFigures = 0;
    int x[] = new int[100];
    int y[] = new int[100];
    int width[] = new int[100];
    int height[] = new int[100];
        .
        .
        .
```

Now that we've set up storage for the data we'll need, we will write the **doTree()** method to decode that XML document. First in **doTree()**, we loop over the current element's children:

```
void doTree(Element elem)
{
    Enumeration enum = elem.getChildren();

    while (enum.hasMoreElements()) {
        Element elem2 = (Element)enum.nextElement();
            .
            .
            .

    }
}
```

Then we check to see whether the current child element is of type **Element.ELEMENT**:

```
void doTree(Element elem)
{
    Enumeration enum = elem.getChildren();

    while (enum.hasMoreElements()) {
        Element elem2 = (Element)enum.nextElement();

        if(elem2.getType() == com.ms.xml.Element.ELEMENT){
                    .
                    .
                    .

        }
    }
}
```

If so, then this element must be of type <CIRCLE> or type <ELLIPSE>. We'll handle the circles first:

```
void doTree(Element elem)
{
    Enumeration enum = elem.getChildren();

    while (enum.hasMoreElements()) {
        Element elem2 = (Element)enum.nextElement();

        if(elem2.getType() == com.ms.xml.Element.ELEMENT){
            if(elem2.getTagName().equals("CIRCLE")){
                    .
                    .
                    .

            }
        }
    }
}
```

To handle a circle element, we simply store the location of the circle in the **x[]** and **y[]** arrays and place twice the radius value in the **width[]** and **height[]** arrays, and we get all this data from the <CIRCLE> tag's attributes. Note that we also increment **numberFigures**, the number of figures to draw:

```
void doTree(Element elem)
{
    Enumeration enum = elem.getChildren();

    while (enum.hasMoreElements()) {
        Element elem2 = (Element)enum.nextElement();

        if(elem2.getType() == com.ms.xml.Element.ELEMENT){
            if(elem2.getTagName().equals("CIRCLE")){
                x[numberFigures] =
```

```
                    Integer.parseInt(elem2.getAttribute
                        ("X"));
                y[numberFigures] =
                    Integer.parseInt(elem2.getAttribute
                        ("Y"));
                width[numberFigures] =
                    2 * Integer.parseInt
                        (elem2.getAttribute("RADIUS"));
                height[numberFigures] =
                    2 * Integer.parseInt
                        (elem2.getAttribute("RADIUS"));
                numberFigures++;
                repaint();
            }
        }
    }
}
```

If the element is an <ELLIPSE> element, we store the data we need from the tag's attributes in the **x[]**, **y[]**, **width[]** and **height[]** arrays:

```
void doTree(Element elem)
{
    Enumeration enum = elem.getChildren();

    while (enum.hasMoreElements()) {
        Element elem2 = (Element)enum.nextElement();

        if(elem2.getType() == com.ms.xml.Element.ELEMENT){
            if(elem2.getTagName().equals("CIRCLE")){
                x[numberFigures] =
                    Integer.parseInt
                        (elem2.getAttribute("X"));
                y[numberFigures] =
                    Integer.parseInt
                        (elem2.getAttribute("Y"));
                width[numberFigures] =
                    2 * Integer.parseInt
                        (elem2.getAttribute("RADIUS"));
                height[numberFigures] =
                    2 * Integer.parseInt
                        (elem2.getAttribute("RADIUS"));
                numberFigures++;
                repaint();
            }
            if(elem2.getTagName().equals("ELLIPSE")){
                x[numberFigures] =
                    Integer.parseInt
                        (elem2.getAttribute("X"));
                y[numberFigures] =
                    Integer.parseInt
                        (elem2.getAttribute("Y"));
                width[numberFigures] =
```

```
                            Integer.parseInt
                                (elem2.getAttribute("WIDTH"));
                        height[numberFigures] =
                            Integer.parseInt
                                (elem2.getAttribute("HEIGHT"));
                        numberFigures++;
                        repaint();
                    }
                }
            }
        }
```

Finally, to process any children of this element, we call **doTree()** again:

```
void doTree(Element elem)
{
    Enumeration enum = elem.getChildren();

    while (enum.hasMoreElements()) {
        Element elem2 = (Element)enum.nextElement();

        if(elem2.getType() == com.ms.xml.Element.ELEMENT){
            if(elem2.getTagName().equals("CIRCLE")){
                x[numberFigures] =
                    Integer.parseInt
                        (elem2.getAttribute("X"));
                y[numberFigures] =
                    Integer.parseInt
                        (elem2.getAttribute("Y"));
                width[numberFigures] =
                    2 * Integer.parseInt
                        (elem2.getAttribute("RADIUS"));
                height[numberFigures] =
                    2 * Integer.parseInt
                        (elem2.getAttribute("RADIUS"));
                numberFigures++;
                repaint();
            }
            if(elem2.getTagName().equals("ELLIPSE")){
                x[numberFigures] =
                    Integer.parseInt
                        (elem2.getAttribute("X"));
                y[numberFigures] =
                    Integer.parseInt
                        (elem2.getAttribute("Y"));
                width[numberFigures] =
                    Integer.parseInt
                        (elem2.getAttribute("WIDTH"));
                height[numberFigures] =
                    Integer.parseInt
                        (elem2.getAttribute("HEIGHT"));
                numberFigures++;
                repaint();
```

```
            }
            doTree(elem2);
        }
    }
}
```

And that's it. All that's left is to draw the required figures in the
paint() method:

```
    public void paint(Graphics g)
    {

    }
}
_H
```

All we have to do in the **paint()** method is use the data we've stored with
the Java Graphics class' **drawOval()** method. We start by looping over all
the figures we want to draw; that total number is stored in **numberFigures**:

```
    public void paint(Graphics g)
    {
        for(int index = 0; index < numberFigures;
            index++){
            .
            .
            .
        }
    }
}
```

We use the Java Graphics class' **drawOval()** to draw both ellipses and
circles. We simply pass the x and y location of the figure we want to draw
and its width and height this way:

```
    public void paint(Graphics g)
    {
        for(int index = 0; index < numberFigures;
            index++){
            g.drawOval(x[index], y[index], width[index],
                height[index]);
        }
    }
}
```

Run the application now, as shown in Figure 7-5.

When the user clicks the Browse button, the program reads in the
circles.xml document and interprets the XML there, displaying the re-
sulting figures in the application's window, as shown in Figure 7-6.

Our circles application is a success; now we're depicting the contents of XML documents graphically. The code for this example, **circles.java**, appears in Listing 7-5, and the XML document it reads in, **circles.xml**, appears in Listing 7-6.

Figure 7-5.
The circles application.

Figure 7-6.
Displaying the contents of an XML document graphically.

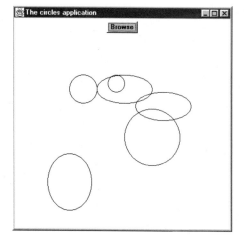

Listing 7-5.
circles.java.

```
import com.ms.xml.ParseException;
import com.ms.xml.Document;
import com.ms.xml.Element;

import java.util.Enumeration;
```

Continues

Listing 7-5.
Continued.

```java
import java.awt.*;
import java.net.*;
import java.applet.Applet;

public class circles extends Applet{

    Button button1;
    String filename = null;
    int numberFigures = 0;
    int x[] = new int[100];
    int y[] = new int[100];
    int width[] = new int[100];
    int height[] = new int[100];

    public static void main(String args[])
    {
        circlesFrame frame = new circlesFrame("The circles
            application");

        frame.show();
        frame.hide();
        frame.resize(400, 400);

        circles applet_app = new circles();

        frame.add("Center", applet_app);
        applet_app.init();
        applet_app.start();
        frame.show();
    }

    public void init(){
        button1 = new Button("Browse");
        add(button1);
    }

    public boolean action (Event e, Object o){

        URL url = null;
        String filename;

        filename = "file:////c://xml//circles//
            circles.xml";

        try {
            url = new URL(filename);
        } catch (MalformedURLException e1) {
            System.out.println("Cannot create URL for: "
                + filename);
            System.exit(0);
        }
```

```
                    Document d = new Document();

                    try {
                        d.load(url);
                    }
                    catch (ParseException e3) {
                        d.reportError(e3, System.out);
                    }

                    if (d != null) {
                        doTree(d.getRoot());
                        repaint();
                    }
                    return true;
                }


            void doTree(Element elem)
            {
                Enumeration enum = elem.getChildren();

                while (enum.hasMoreElements()) {
                    Element elem2 = (Element)enum.nextElement();

                    if(elem2.getType() ==
                        com.ms.xml.Element.ELEMENT){
                        if(elem2.getTagName().equals("CIRCLE")){
                            x[numberFigures] =
                                Integer.parseInt
                                    (elem2.getAttribute("X"));
                            y[numberFigures] =
                                Integer.parseInt
                                    (elem2.getAttribute("Y"));
                            width[numberFigures] =
                                2 * Integer.parseInt(elem2
                                    .getAttribute("RADIUS"));
                            height[numberFigures] =
                                2 * Integer.parseInt(elem2
                                    .getAttribute("RADIUS"));
                            numberFigures++;
                            repaint();
                        }
                        if(elem2.getTagName().equals("ELLIPSE")){
                            x[numberFigures] =
                                Integer.parseInt(elem2
                                    .getAttribute("X"));
                            y[numberFigures] =
                                Integer.parseInt(elem2
                                    .getAttribute("Y"));
                            width[numberFigures] =
                                Integer.parseInt(elem2
```

Continues

Listing 7-5.
Continued.

```
                                      .getAttribute("WIDTH"));
                    height[numberFigures] =
                        Integer.parseInt(elem2
                            .getAttribute("HEIGHT"));
                    numberFigures++;
                    repaint();
                }
                doTree(elem2);
            }
        }
    }

    public void paint(Graphics g)
    {
        for(int index = 0; index < numberFigures;
            index++){
            g.drawOval(x[index], y[index], width[index],
                height[index]);
        }
    }
}

class circlesFrame extends Frame
{
    public circlesFrame(String str)
    {
        super (str);
    }

    public boolean handleEvent(Event evt)
    {
        switch (evt.id)
        {
            case Event.WINDOW_DESTROY:
                dispose();
                System.exit(0);
                return true;

            default:
                return super.handleEvent(evt);
        }
    }
}
```

Listing 7-6.
textbrowser.xml.

```
<?XML version = "1.0" ?>
<!DOCTYPE DOCUMENT [
<!ELEMENT DOCUMENT (CIRCLE|ELLIPSE)*>
<!ELEMENT CIRCLE EMPTY>
<!ELEMENT ELLIPSE EMPTY>
```

Listing 7-6.
Continued.

```
<!ATTLIST CIRCLE
    X CDATA #IMPLIED
    Y CDATA #IMPLIED
    RADIUS CDATA #IMPLIED>
<!ATTLIST ELLIPSE
    X CDATA #IMPLIED
    Y CDATA #IMPLIED
    WIDTH CDATA #IMPLIED
    HEIGHT CDATA #IMPLIED>
]>
<DOCUMENT>
<CIRCLE X="100" Y="100" RADIUS="25">
<CIRCLE X="200" Y="160" RADIUS="50">
<CIRCLE X="170" Y="100" RADIUS="15">
<ELLIPSE X="150" Y="100" WIDTH="100" HEIGHT="50">
<ELLIPSE X="220" Y="130" WIDTH="100" HEIGHT="50">
<ELLIPSE X="60" Y="240" WIDTH="80" HEIGHT="100">
</DOCUMENT>
```

We've seen one graphically oriented example; now we'll turn to another to see how to create other types of graphical figures: lines and rectangles.

The `lines` Example

In the next example, we'll expand our graphics capability by seeing how to draw lines and rectangles. Here, we will read in a new XML document named **lines.xml**; in this document, we store the data we'll need to draw lines and rectangles. In Java, both those figures are drawn using two points—a start point, (x1, y1), and an end point (x2, y2):

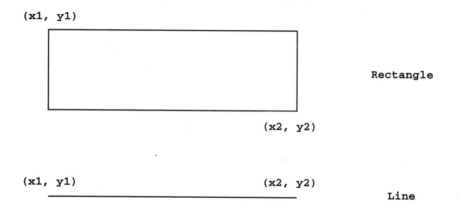

We'll specify lines with a new <LINE> tag and rectangles with the <RECTANGLE> tag like this in the `lines.xml` document. Note that we store the X1, Y1, X2, and Y2 data we need as attributes of these tags:

```
<?XML version = "1.0" ?>
<!DOCTYPE DOCUMENT [
<!ELEMENT DOCUMENT (LINE|RECTANGLE)*>
<!ELEMENT LINE EMPTY>
<!ELEMENT RECTANGLE EMPTY>
<!ATTLIST LINE
    X1 CDATA #IMPLIED
    Y1 CDATA #IMPLIED
    X2 CDATA #IMPLIED
    Y2 CDATA #IMPLIED>
<!ATTLIST RECTANGLE
    X1 CDATA #IMPLIED
    Y1 CDATA #IMPLIED
    X2 CDATA #IMPLIED
    Y2 CDATA #IMPLIED>
]>
<DOCUMENT>
    <LINE X1="100" Y1="100" X2="50" Y2="70">
    <LINE X1="200" Y1="160" X2="100" Y2="30">
    <LINE X1="170" Y1="100" X2="30" Y2="300">
    <RECTANGLE X1="150" Y1="100" X2="100" Y2="50">
    <RECTANGLE X1="220" Y1="130" X2="100" Y2="50">
    <RECTANGLE X1="60" Y1="240" X2="80" Y2="100">
</DOCUMENT>
```

When the user starts this program, we'll present the user with a Browse button as shown at the top of the following page.

When the user clicks the Browse button, we read in the `lines.xml` document and display the lines and rectangles in the application's window as shown at the bottom of the following page.

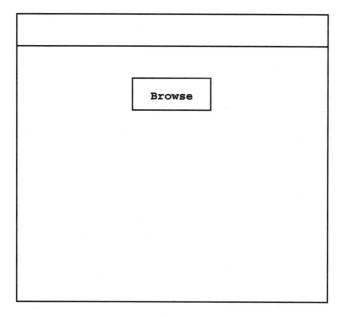

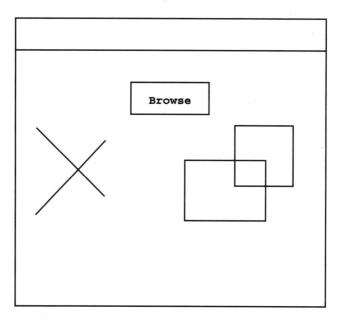

We start the `lines.java` application by creating a window, the applet we'll need, and the button we'll use:

```java
import java.awt.*;
import java.applet.Applet;

public class lines extends Applet{

    Button button1;

    public static void main(String args[])
    {
        linesFrame frame = new linesFrame("The lines
            application");

        frame.show();
        frame.hide();
        frame.resize(400, 400);

        lines applet = new lines();

        frame.add("Center", applet);
        applet.init();
        applet.start();
        frame.show();
    }

    public void init(){
        button1 = new Button("Browse");
        add(button1);
    }
```

When the user clicks the button, we read in the `lines.xml` file and call the recursive method `doTree()`:

```java
public boolean action (Event e, Object o){

    URL url = null;
    filename = "file:////c://xml//lines//lines.xml";

    try {
        url = new URL(filename);
    } catch (MalformedURLException e1) {
        System.out.println("Cannot create URL for: " +
            filename);
        System.exit(0);
    }

    Document d = new Document();

    try {
```

```
            d.load(url);
        }
        catch (ParseException e3) {
            d.reportError(e3, System.out);
        }

        if (d != null) {
            doTree(d.getRoot());
            repaint();
        }
        return true;
    }
```

We will write the **doTree()** method now. In that method, we will store the data we need to draw lines in a two-dimensional array named **lines[][]** and the data we need to draw rectangles in a two-dimensional array named **rectangles[][]**. We also store the total number of lines in the new integer **numberLines** and the total number of rectangles in the new integer **numberRectangles**:

```
public class lines extends Applet{

    Button button1;
    String filename;
    int numberLines = 0, numberRectangles = 0;
    int lines[][] = new int[100][4];
    int rectangles[][] = new int[100][4];
        .
        .
        .
```

Now in **doTree()**, we can loop over the children of the element passed to us, first checking to make sure the current child is of type **Element.ELEMENT**:

```
void doTree(Element elem)
{
    Enumeration enum = elem.getChildren();

    while (enum.hasMoreElements()) {
        Element elem2 = (Element)enum.nextElement();
        if(elem2.getType() == com.ms.xml.Element.ELEMENT){
            .
            .
            .
        }
    }
}
```

With the **getTagName()** method, we can check to see whether the current element is a <LINE> element:

```
void doTree(Element elem)
{
    Enumeration enum = elem.getChildren();

    while (enum.hasMoreElements()) {
        Element elem2 = (Element)enum.nextElement();
        if(elem2.getType() == com.ms.xml.Element.ELEMENT){
            if(elem2.getTagName().equals("LINE")){
                    .
                    .
                    .

            }
        }
    }
}
```

If this is a <LINE> element, we store the (x1, y1) and (x2, y2) data from the <LINE> element's attributes in the `lines[][]` array. Note that we also increment the total number of lines to draw, `numberLines`:

```
void doTree(Element elem)
{
    Enumeration enum = elem.getChildren();

    while (enum.hasMoreElements()) {
        Element elem2 = (Element)enum.nextElement();
        if(elem2.getType() == com.ms.xml.Element.ELEMENT){
            if(elem2.getTagName().equals("LINE")){
                lines[numberLines][0] =
                    Integer.parseInt(elem2.getAttribute
                        ("X1"));
                lines[numberLines][1] =
                    Integer.parseInt(elem2.getAttribute
                        ("Y1"));
                lines[numberLines][2] =
                    Integer.parseInt(elem2.getAttribute
                        ("X2"));
                lines[numberLines][3] =
                    Integer.parseInt(elem2.getAttribute
                        ("Y2"));
                numberLines++;
                repaint();
            }
        }
    }
}
```

If the current element is not a <LINE> element, we check to see whether it's a <RECTANGLE> element:

```
void doTree(Element elem)
{
```

```
              Enumeration enum = elem.getChildren();

          while (enum.hasMoreElements()) {
              Element elem2 = (Element)enum.nextElement();
              if(elem2.getType() == com.ms.xml.Element.ELEMENT){
                  if(elem2.getTagName().equals("LINE")){
                      lines[numberLines][0] =
                          Integer.parseInt(elem2.getAttribute
                          ("X1"));
                      lines[numberLines][1] =
                          Integer.parseInt(elem2.getAttribute
                          ("Y1"));
                      lines[numberLines][2] =
                          Integer.parseInt(elem2.getAttribute
                          ("X2"));
                      lines[numberLines][3] =
                          Integer.parseInt(elem2.getAttribute
                          ("Y2"));
                      numberLines++;
                      repaint();
                  }
                  if(elem2.getTagName().equals("RECTANGLE")){
                               .
                               .
                               .
                  }
              }
          }
      }
```

We will store the data we need to draw the rectangle in the **rectangles[][]** array and increment the total number of rectangles to draw, **numberRectangles**, this way:

```
  void doTree(Element elem)
  {
      Enumeration enum = elem.getChildren();

      while (enum.hasMoreElements()) {
          Element elem2 = (Element)enum.nextElement();
          if(elem2.getType() == com.ms.xml.Element.ELEMENT){
              if(elem2.getTagName().equals("LINE")){
                  lines[numberLines][0] =
                      Integer.parseInt(elem2.getAttribute
                          ("X1"));
                  lines[numberLines][1] =
                      Integer.parseInt(elem2.getAttribute
                          ("Y1"));
                  lines[numberLines][2] =
                      Integer.parseInt(elem2.getAttribute
                          ("X2"));
                  lines[numberLines][3] =
```

```
                                Integer.parseInt(elem2.getAttribute
                                    ("Y2"));
                        numberLines++;
                        repaint();
                    }
                    if(elem2.getTagName().equals("RECTANGLE")){
                        rectangles[numberRectangles][0] =
                            Integer.parseInt(elem2.getAttribute
                                ("X1"));
                        rectangles[numberRectangles][1] =
                            Integer.parseInt(elem2.getAttribute
                                ("Y1"));
                        rectangles[numberRectangles][2] =
                            Integer.parseInt(elem2.getAttribute
                                ("X2"));
                        rectangles[numberRectangles][3] =
                            Integer.parseInt(elem2.getAttribute
                                ("Y2"));
                        numberRectangles++;
                        repaint();
                    }
                }
            }
        }
    }
```

Finally, we call **doTree()** again to handle any child elements like this:

```
void doTree(Element elem)
{
    Enumeration enum = elem.getChildren();

    while (enum.hasMoreElements()) {
        Element elem2 = (Element)enum.nextElement();
        if(elem2.getType() == com.ms.xml.Element.ELEMENT){
            if(elem2.getTagName().equals("LINE")){
                lines[numberLines][0] =
                    Integer.parseInt(elem2.getAttribute
                        ("X1"));
                lines[numberLines][1] =
                    Integer.parseInt(elem2.getAttribute
                        ("Y1"));
                lines[numberLines][2] =
                    Integer.parseInt(elem2.getAttribute
                        ("X2"));
                lines[numberLines][3] =
                    Integer.parseInt(elem2.getAttribute
                        ("Y2"));
                numberLines++;
                repaint();
            }
            if(elem2.getTagName()
                .equals("RECTANGLE")){
```

```
                        rectangles[numberRectangles][0] =
                            Integer.parseInt(elem2
                                .getAttribute("X1"));
                        rectangles[numberRectangles][1] =
                            Integer.parseInt(elem2.getAttribute
                                ("Y1"));
                        rectangles[numberRectangles][2] =
                            Integer.parseInt(elem2.getAttribute
                                ("X2"));
                        rectangles[numberRectangles][3] =
                            Integer.parseInt(elem2.getAttribute
                                ("Y2"));
                        numberRectangles++;
                        repaint();
                    }
                    doTree(elem2);
                }
            }
        }
```

All that remains is to write the **paint()** method to draw the lines and rectangles as directed in the **lines.xml** document. We start by looping over all the lines we are to draw:

```
        public void paint(Graphics g)
        {
            for(int index = 0; index < numberLines; index++){
                .
                .
                .
            }
        }
```

We use the Java Graphics class' **drawLine()** method to actually draw the line. We pass that method the four coordinates which we've stored to display the current line this way:

```
        public void paint(Graphics g)
        {
            for(int index = 0; index < numberLines; index++){
                g.drawLine(lines[index][0], lines[index][1],
                    lines[index][2],
                    lines[index][3]);
            }
            .
            .
            .
        }
```

To draw the rectangles, we loop over all the rectangles we are to draw and call the Graphics class' `drawRect()` method:

```
public void paint(Graphics g)
{
    for(int index = 0; index < numberLines; index++){
        g.drawLine(lines[index][0], lines[index][1],
            lines[index][2],
            lines[index][3]);
    }
    for(int index = 0; index < numberRectangles;
        index++){
        g.drawRect(rectangles[index][0],
            rectangles[index][1],
            rectangles[index][2],
            rectangles[index][3]);
    }
}
```

That's it—run the application now, as shown in Figure 7-7.

When the user clicks the Browse button, the program reads in the `lines.xml` document and displays the lines and rectangles described in that document, as shown in Figure 7-8.

The lines application works as planned. The code for this application, `lines.java`, appears in Listing 7-7, and the XML document it reads in, `lines.xml`, appears in Listing 7-8.

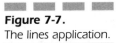

Figure 7-7.
The lines application.

Figure 7-8.
Drawing lines and
rectangles as indi-
cated in an XML
document.

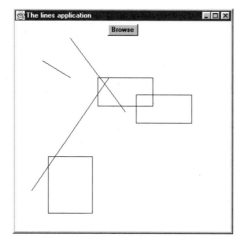

Listing 7-7.
lines.java.

```
import com.ms.xml.ParseException;
import com.ms.xml.Document;
import com.ms.xml.Element;

import java.util.Enumeration;
import java.awt.*;
import java.net.*;
import java.applet.Applet;

public class lines extends Applet{

    Button button1;
    String filename;
    int numberLines = 0, numberRectangles = 0;
    int lines[][] = new int[100][4];
    int rectangles[][] = new int[100][4];

    public static void main(String args[])
    {
        linesFrame frame = new linesFrame("The lines
            application");

        frame.show();
        frame.hide();
        frame.resize(400, 400);

        lines applet = new lines();

        frame.add("Center", applet);
        applet.init();
```

Continues

Listing 7-7.
Continued.

```
        applet.start();
        frame.show();
}

public void init(){
    button1 = new Button("Browse");
    add(button1);
}

public boolean action (Event e, Object o){

    URL url = null;
    filename = "file:////c://xml//lines//lines.xml";

    try {
        url = new URL(filename);
    } catch (MalformedURLException e1) {
        System.out.println("Cannot create URL for: "
                + filename);
        System.exit(0);
    }

    Document d = new Document();

    try {
        d.load(url);
    }
    catch (ParseException e3) {
        d.reportError(e3, System.out);
    }

    if (d != null) {
        doTree(d.getRoot());
        repaint();
    }
    return true;
}


void doTree(Element elem)
{
    Enumeration enum = elem.getChildren();

    while (enum.hasMoreElements()) {
        Element elem2 = (Element)enum.nextElement();
        if(elem2.getType() ==
            com.ms.xml.Element.ELEMENT){
            if(elem2.getTagName().equals("LINE")){
                lines[numberLines][0] =
                    Integer.parseInt
                        (elem2.getAttribute("X1"));
                lines[numberLines][1] =
```

Listing 7-7.
Continued.

```
                                    Integer.parseInt(elem2
                                        .getAttribute("Y1"));
                            lines[numberLines][2] =
                                Integer.parseInt
                                    (elem2.getAttribute("X2"));
                            lines[numberLines][3] =
                                Integer.parseInt(elem2
                                    .getAttribute("Y2"));
                            numberLines++;
                            repaint();
                        }
                        if(elem2.getTagName().equals
                            ("RECTANGLE")){

                            rectangles[numberRectangles][0] =
                                Integer.parseInt
                                    (elem2.getAttribute("X1"));
                            rectangles[numberRectangles][1] =
                                Integer.parseInt
                                    (elem2.getAttribute("Y1"));
                            rectangles[numberRectangles][2] =
                                Integer.parseInt(elem2
                                    .getAttribute("X2"));
                            rectangles[numberRectangles][3] =
                                Integer.parseInt
                                    (elem2.getAttribute("Y2"));
                            numberRectangles++;
                            repaint();
                        }
                        doTree(elem2);
                    }
                }
            }

    public void paint(Graphics g)
    {
        for(int index = 0; index < numberLines; index++){
            g.drawLine(lines[index][0], lines[index][1],
                lines[index][2],
                lines[index][3]);
        }
        for(int index = 0; index < numberRectangles;
            index++){
            g.drawRect(rectangles[index][0],
                rectangles[index][1],
                rectangles[index][2],
                    rectangles[index][3]);
        }
    }
}
```

Continues

Listing 7-7.
Continued.

```java
class linesFrame extends Frame
{
    public linesFrame(String str)
    {
        super (str);
    }

    public boolean handleEvent(Event evt)
    {
        switch (evt.id)
        {
            case Event.WINDOW_DESTROY:
                dispose();
                System.exit(0);
                return true;

            default:
                return super.handleEvent(evt);
        }
    }

}
```

Listing 7-8.
lines.xml.

```xml
<?XML version = "1.0" ?>
<!DOCTYPE DOCUMENT [
<!ELEMENT DOCUMENT (LINE|RECTANGLE)*>
<!ELEMENT LINE EMPTY>
<!ELEMENT RECTANGLE EMPTY>
<!ATTLIST LINE
    X1 CDATA #IMPLIED
    Y1 CDATA #IMPLIED
    X2 CDATA #IMPLIED
    Y2 CDATA #IMPLIED>
<!ATTLIST RECTANGLE
    X1 CDATA #IMPLIED
    Y1 CDATA #IMPLIED
    X2 CDATA #IMPLIED
    Y2 CDATA #IMPLIED>
]>
<DOCUMENT>
    <LINE X1="100" Y1="100" X2="50" Y2="70">
    <LINE X1="200" Y1="160" X2="100" Y2="30">
    <LINE X1="170" Y1="100" X2="30" Y2="300">
    <RECTANGLE X1="150" Y1="100" X2="100" Y2="50">
    <RECTANGLE X1="220" Y1="130" X2="100" Y2="50">
    <RECTANGLE X1="60" Y1="240" X2="80" Y2="100">
</DOCUMENT>
```

SUMMARY

That's it for this chapter. Here, we've expanded our abilities in writing XML browsers considerably. We've seen how to handle text of different font weights and sizes, and we've seen how to create graphical XML browsers that create figures such as circles, ellipses, lines, and rectangles.

In the next chapter, we'll increase our XML skills further as we work with XML image handling.

CHAPTER **8**

XML
Image Handling

In this chapter, we'll see how to use XML with image handling. We'll see how to load in and make use of images in this chapter, including how to create and use image browsers and image maps. Because image maps require the use of the mouse, we'll also see how to use the mouse in this chapter.

To use the MSXML parser, we've enclosed our applets in Java windows instead of opening them in Web browsers (because the MSXML classes won't work in Web browsers currently). However, this is a problem when we want to load in images, because Java applets usually pass this task off to Web browsers. In this chapter we'll see how to load in images in applets without needing support from a Web browser. In fact, let's start with that process immediately—how to load images into our programs.

The `images` Example

In the first example of this chapter, we'll load an image into our applet. We present the user with a window in which there is a button labeled Click Me:

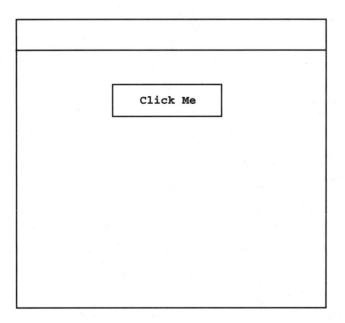

When the user clicks that button, we will load an image into the window as shown on the following page.

The image we'll use, **figure.jpg**, appears in Figure 8-1.

We start this new application, **images.java**, by declaring the **images** class as an applet:

```
import java.awt.*;
import java.applet.Applet;

public class images extends Applet{
        .
        .
        .
}
```

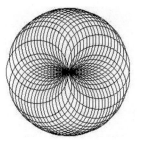

Figure 8-1.
The **figure.jpg**
image.

Next, we create the window class we'll use, **imagesFrame**:

```
class imagesFrame extends Frame
{
    public imagesFrame(String str)
    {
        super (str);
    }

    public boolean handleEvent(Event evt)
    {
        switch (evt.id)
        {
            case Event.WINDOW_DESTROY:
                dispose();
                System.exit(0);
                return true;
```

```
                    default:
                        return super.handleEvent(evt);
                }
            }
        }
```

This is the window that will take the place of a Web browser for us when it comes time to load in images. Next we add a **main()** method to the applet:

```
import java.awt.*;
import java.applet.Applet;

public class images extends Applet{

    public static void main(String args[])
    {
        .
        .
        .

    }
}
```

Then we create a new object of the **imagesFrame** class in the **main()** method, a new applet object of the **images** class, place the applet into the window, call the applet's **init()** method, and show the window:

```
import java.awt.*;
import java.applet.Applet;

public class images extends Applet{

    public static void main(String args[])
    {
        imagesFrame frame = new imagesFrame("The images
            application");

        frame.resize(400, 400);

        images applet = new images();

        frame.add("Center", applet);
        applet.init();
        applet.start();
        frame.show();
    }
```

In the **init()** method, we add the button we'll use, labeling that button Click Me:

```
import java.awt.*;
import java.applet.Applet;

public class images extends Applet{

    Button button1;
        .
        .
        .
    public void init(){
        button1 = new Button("Click Me");
        add(button1);
    }
```

Then, in the **action()** method, we'll check to see whether the user has clicked the Click Me button:

```
public boolean action(Event e, Object o)
{
    if(e.target.equals(button1)){
        .
        .
        .
    }
}
```

If the user has clicked the button, we should load in and display the image file **figure.jpg**. Usually, you load in image files in applets with a call to the applet's **context** object—that is, the Web browser—using the Applet class' **getImage()** method. However, we don't have a Web browser here, so that call would generate an error. This raises the question: how do we load images in our applications?

Loading Images without Web Browsers

The part of the Java framework that handles the applet context is called the toolkit; to host Java, Web browsers implement the methods of the toolkit. However, we don't want to have to implement the entire (very large) toolkit here. Instead (and this is something many Java programmers don't know about), we can use the Java Toolkit class' **getDefaultToolkit()** method to get a *default toolkit*. With that default toolkit, we can load in the image using the **getImage()** method. This method takes either an URL of an image or just the filename as a string (in Java this is called *overloading* a method; an overloaded method can take arguments of different types and know what to do based on the argument's type). Here, we'll just store the **figure.jpg** in the same directory as the images application (i.e., the **c:\xml\images** directory), and then we pass that filename to **getImage()**:

```
public class images extends Applet{

    Image image;
    Button button1;

    public boolean action(Event e, Object o)
    {
        if(e.target.equals(button1)){
            image = Toolkit.getDefaultToolkit()
                .getImage("figure.jpg");
                    .
                    .
                    .

        }
            return true;
    }
```

Loading in an image creates an object of the Java Image class, and we'll call our new object image. This is the image we'll display in our application's window using code in the **paint()** method. Note, however, that we don't want the **paint()** method to try to display the image until the user clicks the button and loads it in, so we set up a flag, **DisplayOK**, which we set to true when the user loads in the image:

```
public class images extends Applet{

    Image image;
    boolean DisplayOK = false;
    Button button1;
            .
            .
            .

    public boolean action(Event e, Object o)
    {
        if(e.target.equals(button1)){
            image = Toolkit.getDefaultToolkit()
                    .getImage("figure.jpg");
            DisplayOK = true;
                    .
                    .
                    .

        }
    }
```

Finally, we make sure the **paint()** method is called to display the image by calling **repaint()**:

```
public class images extends Applet{

    Image image;
    boolean DisplayOK = false;
    Button button1;
        .
        .
        .
    public boolean action(Event e, Object o)
    {
        if(e.target.equals(button1)){
            image = Toolkit.getDefaultToolkit()
                .getImage("figure.jpg");
            DisplayOK = true;
            repaint();
        }

        return true;
    }
```

All that remains is to write the **paint()** method. In this method, we want to display the image we've loaded in, if that image is ready to be displayed. We check to see whether the image is ready by checking the **DisplayOK** flag in **paint()**:

```
public void paint (Graphics g) {

    if(DisplayOK){
            .
            .
            .

    }
  }
}
```

If the image has been loaded in, we can display it. We'll need the width and height of the image to use the **Graphics** class' **drawImage()** method, and we store those in integers named **drawWidth** and **drawHeight**:

```
public void paint (Graphics g) {
    int drawWidth, drawHeight;
    if(DisplayOK){
        drawWidth = 243;
        drawHeight = 242;
            .
            .
            .

    }
  }
}
```

We can also display a border around our image by drawing a rectangle around it like this:

```
public void paint (Graphics g) {
    int drawWidth, drawHeight;
    if(DisplayOK){
        drawWidth = 243;
        drawHeight = 242;
        g.drawRect(60, 40, drawWidth + 1, drawHeight
            + 1);
            .
            .
            .
    }
}
}
```

Finally, we draw the image with the Java **Graphics** class' **drawImage()** method. We pass the image to draw, the (x, y) location of its upper-left corner, its height and width, and a Java **ImageObserver** object to **drawImage()**. The **ImageObserver** class lets you watch the progress of images as they are read in (this is useful over slow Web connections). Here, we'll just use the applet's default **ImageObserver** by passing a reference to the applet with the keyword named **this**:

```
public void paint (Graphics g) {
    int drawWidth, drawHeight;
    if(DisplayOK){
        drawWidth = 243;
        drawHeight = 242;
        g.drawRect(60, 40, drawWidth + 1, drawHeight
            + 1);
        g.drawImage(image, 61, 41, drawWidth,
            drawHeight, this);
    }
}
}
_H
```

And that completes the images application. Run the application now, as shown in Figure 8-2.

When the user clicks the Click Me button in the application, the application reads in the **figure.jpg** file and displays it, as shown in Figure 8-3. The images application works as we designed it.

The code for this program, **images.java**, appears in Listing 8-1.

Now that we've seen how to read in images, let's create XML documents that make use of images.

Figure 8-2.
The images
application.

Figure 8-3.
Loading an image
into an application.

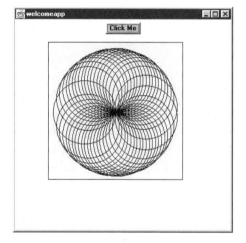

Listing 8-1.
images.java.

```
import java.awt.*;
import java.applet.Applet;

public class images extends Applet{

    Image image;
    boolean DisplayOK = false;
    Button button1;

    public static void main(String args[])
    {
            imagesFrame frame = new imagesFrame("The images
                                                       Continues
```

Listing 8-1.
Continued.

```
            application");
            frame.resize(400, 400);

            images applet = new images();

            frame.add("Center", applet);
            applet.init();
            applet.start();
            frame.show();
        }

        public void init(){
            button1 = new Button("Click Me");
            add(button1);
        }

        public boolean action(Event e, Object o)
        {
            if(e.target.equals(button1)){
                image = Toolkit.getDefaultToolkit()
                    .getImage("figure.jpg");
                DisplayOK = true;
                repaint();
            }
            return true;
        }

        public void paint (Graphics g) {
            int drawWidth, drawHeight;
            if(DisplayOK){
                drawWidth = 243;
                drawHeight = 242;
                g.drawRect(60, 40, drawWidth + 1, drawHeight
                    + 1);
                g.drawImage(image, 61, 41, drawWidth,
                    drawHeight, this);
            }
        }
    }

class imagesFrame extends Frame
{
    public imagesFrame(String str)
    {
        super (str);
    }

    public boolean handleEvent(Event evt)
    {
        switch (evt.id)
        {
            case Event.WINDOW_DESTROY:
```

Listing 8-1.
Continued.

```
                              dispose();
                              System.exit(0);
                              return true;

                      default:
                              return super.handleEvent(evt);
              }
      }
}
```

The `imagebrowser.java` Example

In our next example, we'll create an XML image browser. This XML browser will be able to read in any image you like, depending on which image you refer to in your XML documents. To load in images in XML documents, we'll create a new <IMG> tag, based on the HTML <IMG> tag. Using attributes in the <IMG> tag, we'll specify the (x, y) location of the upper left of the image as it should be displayed in the application's window, its width and height, and the name of the file to load (note that we make all these attributes required) like this in XML:

```
<!ELEMENT IMG EMPTY>
<!ATTLIST IMG
    X        CDATA #REQUIRED
    Y        CDATA #REQUIRED
    WIDTH    CDATA #REQUIRED
    HEIGHT   CDATA #REQUIRED
    SRC      CDATA #REQUIRED>
]>
```

Let's use this new tag in an XML document now. Here's how we might create such a document, **imagebrowser.xml**, which reads in the **figure.jpg** file we used in the last example:

```
<?XML version = "1.0"?>
<!DOCTYPE DOCUMENT [
<!ELEMENT DOCUMENT (#PCDATA|IMG)*>
<!ELEMENT IMG EMPTY>
<!ATTLIST IMG
    X        CDATA #REQUIRED
    Y        CDATA #REQUIRED
    WIDTH    CDATA #REQUIRED
    HEIGHT   CDATA #REQUIRED
    SRC      CDATA #REQUIRED>
]>
<DOCUMENT>
```

```
<IMG X="30" Y="30" WIDTH="243" HEIGHT="242"
     SRC="figure.jpg" >
</DOCUMENT>
```

When we run the image browser, we display a Browse button:

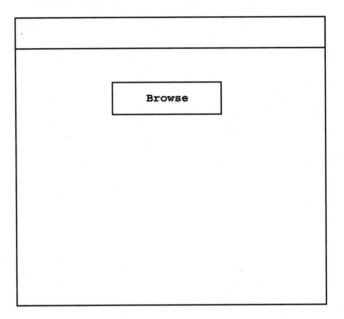

When the user clicks the browse button, we load in the **imagebrowser.xml** document and process the <IMG> tag in that document, displaying the image as shown on the following page.

We start by creating a window for the applet, inserting the applet into the window and adding the Browse button:

```java
import com.ms.xml.ParseException;
import com.ms.xml.Document;
import com.ms.xml.Element;

import java.util.Enumeration;
import java.awt.*;
import java.net.*;
import java.applet.Applet;

public class imagebrowser extends Applet{

    static String filename;
    Button button1;
    boolean imageReady = false;
    Image image = null;
```

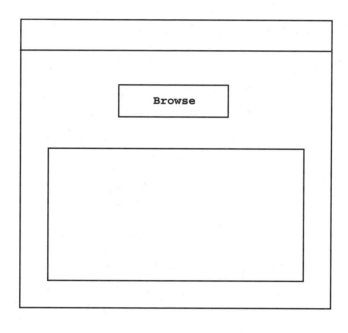

```
Element imageElement = null;

public static void main(String args[])
{
    imagebrowserFrame frame = new
        imagebrowserFrame("The
        imagebrowser application");

    frame.resize(320, 320);

    imagebrowser applet = new imagebrowser();

    frame.add("Center", applet);
    applet.init();
    applet.start();
    frame.show();
}

public void init(){
    button1 = new Button("Browse");
    add(button1);
}
```

We also set up the window class, **imagebrowserFrame,** we'll need this way:

```
class imagebrowserFrame extends Frame
{
    public imagebrowserFrame(String str)
    {
```

```
        super (str);
    }

    public boolean handleEvent(Event evt)
    {
        switch (evt.id)
        {
            case Event.WINDOW_DESTROY:
                dispose();
                System.exit(0);
                return true;

            default:
                return super.handleEvent(evt);
        }
    }
}
```

When the user clicks the Browse button, we will load in the
imagebrowser.xml document in the **action()** method:

```
public boolean action (Event e, Object o)
{
    filename = "file:////c://xml//imagebrowser//
        imagebrowser.xml";
    URL url = null;

    try {
        url = new URL(filename);
    } catch (MalformedURLException e1) {
        System.out.println("Cannot create URL for: "
            + filename);
        System.exit(0);
    }

    Document d = new Document();

    try {
        d.load(url);
    }
    catch (ParseException e3) {
        d.reportError(e3, System.out);
    }
        .
        .
        .
```

If the document was loaded without problem, we will start searching
for the <IMG> tag in order to load in the image and display it. We start
by looping over all the **child** elements of the **root** element this way:

```
public boolean action (Event e, Object o)
{
    filename = "file:////c://xml//imagebrowser//
        imagebrowser.xml";
    URL url = null;
        .
        .
        .
    if (d != null) {
        Element elem = d.getRoot();
        Enumeration enum = elem.getChildren();

        while (enum.hasMoreElements()) {
            Element elem2 = (Element)enum.nextElement();
                .
                .
                .
        }
    }
}
```

To search for the <IMG> tag, we check to see whether the current
child element is of type Element.ELEMENT:

```
public boolean action (Event e, Object o)
{
    filename = "file:////c://xml//imagebrowser//
        imagebrowser.xml";
    URL url = null;
        .
        .
        .
    if (d != null) {
        Element elem = d.getRoot();
        Enumeration enum = elem.getChildren();

        while (enum.hasMoreElements()) {
            Element elem2 = (Element)enum.nextElement();
            if(elem2.getType() ==
                com.ms.xml.Element.ELEMENT){
                    .
                    .
                    .
            }
        }
    }
}
```

If the current child element is of the type Element.ELEMENT, we check
to see whether the element's tag name is "IMG":

```
public boolean action (Event e, Object o)
{
    filename = "file:////c://xml//imagebrowser//
        imagebrowser.xml";
    URL url = null;
    .
    .
    .
    if (d != null) {
        Element elem = d.getRoot();
        Enumeration enum = elem.getChildren();

        while (enum.hasMoreElements()) {
            Element elem2 = (Element)enum.nextElement();
            if(elem2.getType() ==
                com.ms.xml.Element.ELEMENT){
                if(elem2.getTagName().equals("IMG")){
                    .
                    .
                    .

                }
            }
        }
    }
}
```

If this element is indeed the <IMG> element, we load in the image by getting the attribute SRC from this element:

```
public boolean action (Event e, Object o)
{
    filename = "file:////c://xml//imagebrowser//
        imagebrowser.xml";
    URL url = null;
    .
    .
    .
    if (d != null) {
        Element elem = d.getRoot();
        Enumeration enum = elem.getChildren();

        while (enum.hasMoreElements()) {
            Element elem2 = (Element)enum.nextElement();
            if(elem2.getType() ==
                com.ms.xml.Element.ELEMENT){
                if(elem2.getTagName().equals("IMG")){

                    image = Toolkit.getDefaultToolkit()
                        .getImage(elem2.getAttribute
                        ("SRC"));

                    .
                    .

                }
```

```
                           }
                     }
                 }
           }
```

Because we may be loading in this image over the Web, we will wait until it's all loaded before trying to display it, and we can do that with a Java **MediaTracker** object:

```
public boolean action (Event e, Object o)
{
      filename = "file:////c://xml//imagebrowser//
            imagebrowser.xml";
      URL url = null;
           .
           .
           .
      if (d != null) {
          Element elem = d.getRoot();
          Enumeration enum = elem.getChildren();

          while (enum.hasMoreElements()) {
              Element elem2 = (Element)enum.nextElement();
              if(elem2.getType() ==
                    com.ms.xml.Element.ELEMENT){
                  if(elem2.getTagName().equals("IMG")){

                      image = Toolkit.getDefaultToolkit()
                          .getImage(elem2.getAttribute
                          ("SRC"));
                      MediaTracker tracker = new
                          MediaTracker(this);
                              .
                              .
                              .
                  }
              }
          }
      }
}
```

First, we add the current image to the media tracker with **addImage()**:

```
public boolean action (Event e, Object o)
{
      filename = "file:////c://xml//imagebrowser//
            imagebrowser.xml";
      URL url = null;
           .
           .
           .
      if (d != null) {
```

```
Element elem = d.getRoot();
Enumeration enum = elem.getChildren();

while (enum.hasMoreElements()) {
    Element elem2 = (Element)enum.nextElement();
    if(elem2.getType() ==
        com.ms.xml.Element.ELEMENT){
        if(elem2.getTagName().equals("IMG")){

            image =
Toolkit.getDefaultToolkit().getImage(elem2.getAttribute
    ("SRC"));
            MediaTracker tracker = new
            MediaTracker(this);
            tracker.addImage(image, 0);
                        .
                        .
                        .


        }
    }
}
}
}
```

Next, we wait for the image to be loaded in with the `waitForAll()`
method, which returns after the image is fully loaded:

```
public boolean action (Event e, Object o)
{
    filename = "file:////c://xml//imagebrowser//
        imagebrowser.xml";
    URL url = null;
    .
    .
    .

    if (d != null) {
        Element elem = d.getRoot();
        Enumeration enum = elem.getChildren();

        while (enum.hasMoreElements()) {
            Element elem2 = (Element)enum.nextElement();
            if(elem2.getType() ==
                com.ms.xml.Element.ELEMENT){
                if(elem2.getTagName().equals("IMG")){

                    image = Toolkit.getDefaultToolkit()
                        .getImage(elem2.getAttribute
                        ("SRC"));
MediaTracker tracker = new MediaTracker(this);
                    tracker.addImage(image, 0);
                    try{
                        tracker.waitForAll();
                    }
```

```
                            catch(InterruptedException e0){
                            }
                                .
                                .
                                .
                        }
                    }
                }
            }
        }
```

When the image is loaded in, we store the <IMG> element in a global element named **imageElement** (we make this element global so we can read its attributes when we need them in the **paint()** method), set a flag named **imageReady** to indicate that we can draw the image in the **paint()** method, and call **repaint()**:

```
    public class imagebrowser extends Applet{

        static String filename;
        Button button1;
        boolean imageReady = false;
        Image image = null;
        Element imageElement = null;
            .
            .
            .

        public boolean action (Event e, Object o)
        {
            filename = "file:////c://xml//imagebrowser//
                imagebrowser.xml";
            URL url = null;
                .
                .
                .

            if (d != null) {
                Element elem = d.getRoot();
                Enumeration enum = elem.getChildren();

                while (enum.hasMoreElements()) {
                    Element elem2 =
                        (Element)enum.nextElement();
                    if(elem2.getType() ==
                        com.ms.xml.Element.ELEMENT){
                        if(elem2.getTagName().equals("IMG")){

                            image = Toolkit
                                .getDefaultToolkit()
                                .getImage(elem2.getAttribute
                                ("SRC"));
    MediaTracker tracker = new MediaTracker(this);
                            tracker.addImage(image, 0);
```

```
                              try{
                                  tracker.waitForAll();
                              }
                              catch(InterruptedException e0){
                              }
                              imageElement = elem2;
                              imageReady = true;
                          }
                      }
                  }
                  repaint();
              }
              return true;
          }
```

Finally, we write the **paint()** method; in this method, we first check to
see whether the image is ready to display:

```
public void paint(Graphics g)
{
    if(imageReady){
                .
                .
                .
    }
}
```

If the image is ready, we display it with the **drawImage()** method, getting the (x, y), width, and height data we need from the attributes of the
<IMG> element this way:

```
public void paint(Graphics g)
{
    if(imageReady){
        g.drawImage(image,
        Integer.parseInt
            (imageElement.getAttribute("X")),
        Integer.parseInt
            (imageElement.getAttribute("Y")),
        Integer.parseInt
            (imageElement.getAttribute("WIDTH")),
        Integer.parseInt
            (imageElement.getAttribute("HEIGHT")),
        this);
    }
}
```

That's it—run the application now, as shown in Figure 8-4.

When the user clicks the Browse button, the image browser application reads in the **imagebrowser.xml** document and decodes the <IMG> element in that document, displaying the **figure.jpg** image, as shown in Figure 8-5.

The **imagebrowser.java** application is a success, and now we've created an XML image browser. The code for this application, **imagebrowser.java**, appears in Listing 8-2. The document this application reads in, **imagebrowser.xml**, appears in Listing 8-3.

Now we'll turn to something new—handling image maps. An image map is a graphical image with "clickable" *hotspots* in it; when the user clicks one of those hotspots, the program does something, typically reading in a new document. In order to work with image maps, we'll have to understand how to use the mouse, so we'll take a look at a Java mouse example, mouser, first.

Figure 8-4.
The imagebrowser application.

Figure 8-5.
Loading an image into an application.

Listing 8-2.
imagebrowser
.java

```java
import com.ms.xml.ParseException;
import com.ms.xml.Document;
import com.ms.xml.Element;

import java.util.Enumeration;
import java.awt.*;
import java.net.*;
import java.applet.Applet;

public class imagebrowser extends Applet{

    static String filename;
    Button button1;
    boolean imageReady = false;
    Image image = null;
    Element imageElement = null;

    public static void main(String args[])
    {
        imagebrowserFrame frame = new
            imagebrowserFrame("The imagebrowser
            application");

        frame.resize(320, 320);

        imagebrowser applet = new imagebrowser();

        frame.add("Center", applet);
        applet.init();
        applet.start();
        frame.show();
    }

    public void init(){
        button1 = new Button("Browse");
        add(button1);
    }

    public boolean action (Event e, Object o)
    {
        filename = "file:////c://xml//imagebrowser//
            imagebrowser.xml";
        URL url = null;

        try {
            url = new URL(filename);
        } catch (MalformedURLException e1) {
            System.out.println("Cannot create URL for: "
                + filename);
            System.exit(0);
        }
        Document d = new Document();
```

Listing 8-2.
Continued.

```
    try {
        d.load(url);
    }
    catch (ParseException e3) {
        d.reportError(e3, System.out);
    }

    if (d != null) {
        Element elem = d.getRoot();
        Enumeration enum = elem.getChildren();

        while (enum.hasMoreElements()) {
            Element elem2 =
                (Element)enum.nextElement();
            if(elem2.getType() ==
                com.ms.xml.Element.ELEMENT){
                if(elem2.getTagName().equals("IMG")){

                    image = Toolkit
                        .getDefaultToolkit()
                        .getImage(elem2
                        .getAttribute("SRC"));
MediaTracker tracker = new MediaTracker(this);
                    tracker.addImage(image, 0);
                    try{
                        tracker.waitForAll();
                    }
                    catch(InterruptedException e0){

                    }
                    imageElement = elem2;
                    imageReady = true;
                }
            }
        }
        repaint();
    }
    return true;
}

public void paint(Graphics g)
{
    if(imageReady){
        g.drawImage(image,
        Integer.parseInt
            (imageElement.getAttribute("X")),
        Integer.parseInt
            (imageElement.getAttribute("Y")),
        Integer.parseInt
            (imageElement.getAttribute("WIDTH")),
```

Continues

Listing 8-2.
Continued.

```
                          Integer.parseInt
                               (imageElement.getAttribute("HEIGHT")),

                     this);
              }
         }
}

class imagebrowserFrame extends Frame
{
     public imagebrowserFrame(String str)
     {
          super (str);
     }

     public boolean handleEvent(Event evt)
     {
          switch (evt.id)
          {
               case Event.WINDOW_DESTROY:
                    dispose();
                    System.exit(0);
                    return true;

               default:
                    return super.handleEvent(evt);
          }
     }
}
```

Listing 8-3.
`imagebrowser.xml`

```
<?XML version = "1.0"?>
<!DOCTYPE DOCUMENT [
<!ELEMENT DOCUMENT (#PCDATA|IMG)*>
<!ELEMENT IMG EMPTY>
<!ATTLIST IMG
    X       CDATA #REQUIRED
    Y       CDATA #REQUIRED
    WIDTH   CDATA #REQUIRED
    HEIGHT  CDATA #REQUIRED
    SRC     CDATA #REQUIRED>
]>
<DOCUMENT>
    <IMG X="30" Y="30" WIDTH="243" HEIGHT="242"
         SRC="figure.jpg" >
</DOCUMENT>
```

The mouser Example

To prepare the way for our image map work—and to provide a valuable resource in itself—we'll take a look at how to handle the mouse in XML browsers now. We will call this new example mouser; in this application, we'll prompt the user with the text `Click or move the mouse` as shown:

```
Click or move the mouse.
```

When the user does move the mouse, we'll indicate the new mouse position's (pixel) coordinates in a text field as shown at the top of the following page.

When the user presses the left or right mouse button, we can indicate that as well at the bottom of the following page.

```
┌─────────────────────────────────────────────┐
│                                             │
├─────────────────────────────────────────────┤
│                                             │
│   ┌─────────────────────────────────────┐   │
│   │ Mouse position: (222, 15)           │   │
│   └─────────────────────────────────────┘   │
│                                             │
│                                             │
│                                             │
│             Click or move the mouse.        │
│                                             │
│                                             │
│                                             │
│                                             │
│                                             │
└─────────────────────────────────────────────┘
```

```
┌─────────────────────────────────────────────┐
│                                        .    │
├─────────────────────────────────────────────┤
│                                             │
│                                             │
│   ┌─────────────────────────────────────┐   │
│   │ Left mouse button is down           │   │
│   └─────────────────────────────────────┘   │
│                                             │
│                                             │
│                                             │
│             Click or move the mouse.        │
│                                             │
│                                             │
│                                             │
│                                             │
└─────────────────────────────────────────────┘
```

If the user moves the mouse without dragging it (i.e., moves the mouse without holding any buttons down), we can report that as shown:

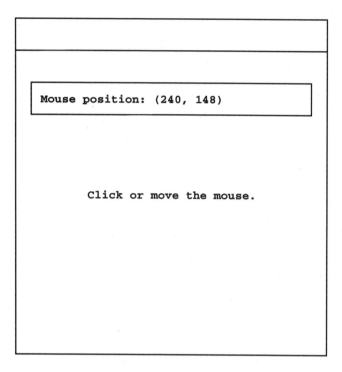

Mouse position: (240, 148)

Click or move the mouse.

If the user drags the mouse, we will report that action as **Mouse being dragged** as shown at the top of the following page.

Finally, when the user moves the mouse cursor out of the applet's display area, we display the message shown at the bottom of the following page.

We start this new example, **mouser.java**, by creating the applet and installing it in a window and then adding the text field we'll use:

```
import java.awt.*;

public class mouser extends java.applet.Applet{

    TextField text1;

    public static void main(String args[])
    {
        mouserFrame frame = new mouserFrame("The mouser
            application");
```

```
┌─────────────────────────────────────────────┐
│                                             │
├─────────────────────────────────────────────┤
│                                             │
│   ┌───────────────────────────────────┐     │
│   │ Mouse being dragged               │     │
│   └───────────────────────────────────┘     │
│                                             │
│                                             │
│         Click or move the mouse.            │
│                                             │
│                                             │
│                                             │
│                                             │
└─────────────────────────────────────────────┘
```

```
┌─────────────────────────────────────────────┐
│                                             │
├─────────────────────────────────────────────┤
│                                             │
│   ┌───────────────────────────────────┐     │
│   │ Mouse is out of applet            │     │
│   └───────────────────────────────────┘     │
│                                             │
│                                             │
│         Click or move the mouse.            │
│                                             │
│                                             │
│                                             │
│                                             │
└─────────────────────────────────────────────┘
```

```
        frame.resize(400, 300);

        mouser applet = new mouser();

        frame.add("Center", applet);
        applet.init();
        applet.start();
        frame.show();
    }

    public void init(){
        text1 = new TextField(40);
        add(text1);
    }
```

Now we're ready to start handling the mouse. We do that by setting up methods like **mouseDown()** to handle the case when the user presses the mouse button (this is called a **mouseDown** *event*), or **mouseUp()** to handle the case when the user releases the mouse button. We'll start with **mouseDown()**.

The **mouseDown** Event

The event-handling method **mouseDown()** looks like this:

```
public boolean mouseDown(Event e, int x, int y)
{
    .
    .
    .
}
```

Here, we are passed three parameters—a Java **Event** object, **e**, and the (x, y) location of the mouse (in pixels, as usual). The **Event** object holds information about the mouse event—for example, if the member data **e.modifiers** is equal to **0**, the user pressed the left mouse button, and we indicate that with a message in the text field:

```
public boolean mouseDown(Event e, int x, int y)
{
    if(e.modifiers == 0){
        text1.setText("Left mouse button is down");
    }
    .
    .
    .
}
```

The `e.modifiers` value is **2** if the middle mouse button went down and **4** if the right mouse button went down; since it's a rare mouse that has a middle mouse button these days, we'll just cover the right mouse button event this way:

```
public boolean mouseDown(Event e, int x, int y)
    {
        if(e.modifiers == 0){
            text1.setText("Left mouse button is down");
        }
        if(e.modifiers == 4){
            text1.setText("Right mouse button is down");
        }
    }
```

TIP *If the user is holding more than one mouse button down, the* `e.modifiers` *value reflects that and is set to some sum of its single-button values (*0, 2, *and* 4*).*

At the end of `mouseDown()`, we return a value of **true** to indicate that we have handled the event:

```
public boolean mouseDown(Event e, int x, int y)
{
    if(e.modifiers == 0){
        text1.setText("Left mouse button is down");
    }
    if(e.modifiers == 4){
        text1.setText("Right mouse button is down");
    }
    return true;
}
```

That's how to handle the `mouseDown` event; let's look at the `mouseUp` event next.

The `mouseUp` Event

You handle the `mouseUp` event just as you handle the `mouseDown` event; the only difference is that the user has released a mouse button instead of pressing one. Here's how we add the `mouseUp()` event handler to our mouser example:

```
public boolean mouseUp(Event e, int x, int y){
    .
    .
    .
}
```

We can use the same code that we've developed for the **mouseDown** event, adding that code like this:

```
public boolean mouseUp(Event e, int x, int y){
    if(e.modifiers == 0){
        text1.setText("Left mouse button is up");
    }
    if(e.modifiers == 4){
        text1.setText("Right mouse button is up");
    }
    return true;
}
```

That takes care of **mouseDown()** and **mouseUp()**. We will take a look at the **mouseDrag()** event handler next.

The mouseDrag Event

When the user drags the mouse, that action generates **mouseDrag** events. We handle those events in a **mouseDrag()** method:

```
public boolean mouseDrag(Event e, int x, int y){
    .
    .
    .
}
```

Here, x and y give us the current location of the mouse; in this case, we'll simply indicate that the user is dragging the mouse:

```
public boolean mouseDrag(Event e, int x, int y){
    text1.setText("Mouse is being dragged");
    return true;
}
```

When the user simply moves the mouse (as opposed to holding a button down and dragging the mouse), that action generates a **mouseMove** event, and we'll look at that now.

The mouseMove Event

You handle mouse movements with the **mouseMove()** event-handling method:

```
public boolean mouseMove(Event e, int x, int y){

}
```

Let's report the new position of the mouse using the x and y parameters we are passed in this method:

```
public boolean mouseMove(Event e, int x, int y){
    text1.setText("Mouse position: (" + x + ", " + y + a
        ")");
    return true;
}
```

Now we've handled **mouseDown** events, **mouseUp** events, **mouseDrag** events, and **mouseMove** events. There are two more events we'll cover: **mouseEnter**, which occurs when the user moves the mouse into the applet's area on the screen; and **mouseExit**, which occurs when the user moves the mouse out of the applet.

The mouseEnter Event

The **mouseEnter()** method is set up like any other mouse event handler:

```
public boolean mouseEnter(Event e, int x, int y){
    .
    .
    .
}
```

In this method, we can indicate to the user that the mouse has entered the applet's area on the screen with a message like this:

```
public boolean mouseEnter(Event e, int x, int y){
    text1.setText("Mouse is in applet");
    return true;
}
```

And that's it. There's just one more mouse event to handle in mouser: the **mouseExit** event.

The mouseExit Event

When the user moves the mouse out of the applet's space on the screen, we generate a mouseExit event, which we handle in the mouseExit() event handler:

```
public boolean mouseExit(Event e, int x, int y){
    .
    .
    .
}
```

In this case, we will indicate to the user that the mouse has left the applet:

```
public boolean mouseExit(Event e, int x, int y){
    text1.setText("Mouse is out of applet");
    return true;
}
```

That completes the mouse events; all that's left in mouser is to display the **Click or move the mouse.** prompt to the user, and we do that in the **paint()** method:

```
public void paint( Graphics g )
{
    g.drawString( "Click or move the mouse.", 110, 100 );
}
```

The mouser application is complete—run it now, as shown in Figure 8-6.

When the user moves the mouse, the program reports the new mouse position, as shown in Figure 8-7.

Figure 8-6.
The mouser application.

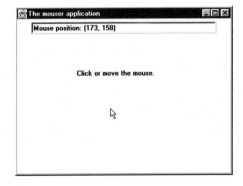

Figure 8-7.
Moving the mouse
in the mouser
application.

When the user drags the mouse, we report that as well, as shown in Figure 8-8.

When the mouse leaves the applet, the program indicates that fact, as shown in Figure 8-9.

Our mouser application is a success. Now we're able to use the mouse in our XML browsers. The code for this application appears in Listing 8-4.

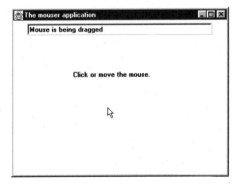

Figure 8-8.
Dragging the
mouse in mouser.

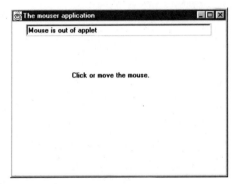

Figure 8-9.
The mouse has left
the mouser applet.

Listing 8-4.
mouser.java.

```
import java.awt.*;

public class mouser extends java.applet.Applet{

    TextField text1;

    public static void main(String args[])
    {
        mouserFrame frame = new mouserFrame("The mouser
            application");

        frame.resize(400, 300);

        mouser applet = new mouser();

        frame.add("Center", applet);
        applet.init();
        applet.start();
        frame.show();
    }

    public void init(){
        text1 = new TextField(40);
        add(text1);
    }

    public boolean mouseDown(Event e, int x, int y)
    {
        if(e.modifiers == 0){
            text1.setText("Left mouse button is down");
        }
        if(e.modifiers == 4){
            text1.setText("Right mouse button is down");
        }
        return true;
    }

    public boolean mouseDrag(Event e, int x, int y){
        text1.setText("Mouse is being dragged");
        return true;
    }

    public boolean mouseUp(Event e, int x, int y){
        if(e.modifiers == 0){
            text1.setText("Left mouse button is up");
        }
        if(e.modifiers == 4){
            text1.setText("Right mouse button is up");
        }
        return true;
    }
```

Continues

Listing 8-4.
Continued.

```java
    public boolean mouseMove(Event e, int x, int y){
        text1.setText("Mouse position: (" + x + ", " + y
            + ")");
        return true;
    }

    public boolean mouseEnter(Event e, int x, int y){
        text1.setText("Mouse is in applet");
        return true;
    }

    public boolean mouseExit(Event e, int x, int y){
        text1.setText("Mouse is out of applet");
        return true;
    }

    public void paint( Graphics g )
    {
        g.drawString( "Click or move the mouse.", 110,
            100 );
    }
}

class mouserFrame extends Frame
{
    public mouserFrame(String str)
    {
        super (str);
    }

    public boolean handleEvent(Event evt)
    {
        switch (evt.id)
        {
            case Event.WINDOW_DESTROY:
                dispose();
                System.exit(0);
                return true;

            default:
                return super.handleEvent(evt);
        }
    }
}
```

Now that we've seen how to use the mouse, we're ready to put the mouse to use in an XML browser. We'll turn to that now when we develop an image map application.

The imagemap Example

In this next example, imagemap, we'll display an image with two labeled areas **Target 1** and **Target 2**:

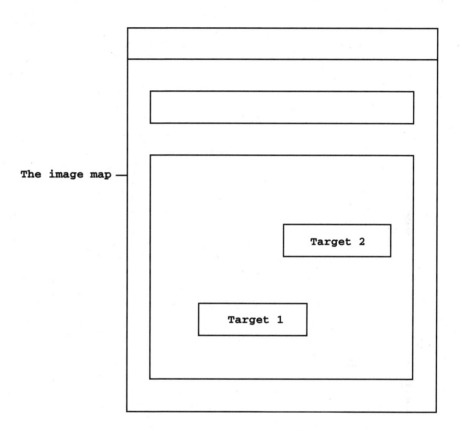

The image map

Target 2

Target 1

This image is an *image map*, which the user can click; the two labeled parts of this image map are *hotspots*, and when the user clicks one of these hotspots, we'll load in a new document and display its text in the text field at the top of the application. For example, when the user clicks the **Target 1** hotspot, we can load in this document, **target1.xml**:

```
<?XML VERSION = "1.0" ?>
<DOCUMENT>

Here is Target 1.

</DOCUMENT>
```

We'll display this document's text in the imagemap application's text field:

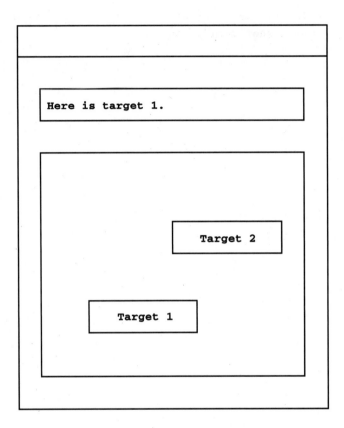

If the user clicks the **Target 2** hotspot, we load in the document **target2.xml**:

```
<?XML VERSION = "1.0" ?>
<DOCUMENT>
```

Here is **Target 2**.

```
</DOCUMENT>
```

After loading **target2.xml** in, we display its text in the text field:

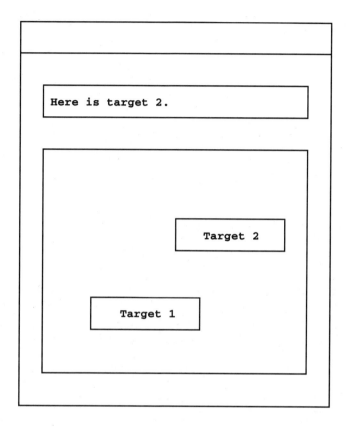

Let's write this application now. We start by creating this application's window and applet:

```
import java.awt.*;
import java.net.*;
import java.applet.Applet;

public class imagemap extends Applet{

    public static void main(String args[])
    {
        imagemapFrame frame = new imagemapFrame("The
            imagemap application");

        frame.resize(320, 320);

        imagemap applet = new imagemap();

        frame.add("Center", applet);
        applet.init();
        applet.start();
```

```
                    frame.show();
            }
```

Next, in the **init()** method, we add the text field we'll use:

```
public class imagemap extends Applet{

    TextField text1;
            .
            .
            .
    public void init(){
        text1 = new TextField(30);
        add(text1);
            .
            .
            .

    }
```

In addition, we load the image map we'll use into an **Image** object. The image file we'll use, **imagemap.gif**, appears in Figure 8-10.

We load the image in, as we did in the images example at the beginning of this chapter, by getting the default toolkit:

```
public class imagemap extends Applet{

    TextField text1;
    Image image = null;
            .
            .
            .
    public void init(){
        text1 = new TextField(30);
        add(text1);
        image = Toolkit.getDefaultToolkit()
                .getImage("Imagemap.gif");
            .
            .
            .
```

We'll also use a **MediaTracker** object to make sure this image map is read in before we use it:

Figure 8-10.
The **imagemap.gif**
file.

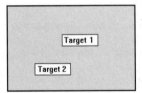

```
public class imagemap extends Applet{

    TextField text1;
    Image image = null;
        .
        .
        .

    public void init(){
        text1 = new TextField(30);
        add(text1);
        image = Toolkit.getDefaultToolkit()
            .getImage("Imagemap.gif");
        MediaTracker tracker = new MediaTracker(this);
        .
        .
        .

    }
```

Next, we wait until we are sure the image has been read in:

```
public class imagemap extends Applet{

    TextField text1;
    boolean imageReady = false;
    Image image = null;
        .
        .
        .

    public void init(){
        text1 = new TextField(30);
        add(text1);
        image = Toolkit.getDefaultToolkit()
            .getImage("Imagemap.gif");
        MediaTracker tracker = new MediaTracker(this);
        tracker.addImage(image, 0);
        try{
            tracker.waitForAll();
        }
        catch(InterruptedException e0){
        }
            .
            .
            .

    }
```

When the image is ready, we set a boolean flag named **imageReady** to
true and call **repaint()** to make sure the image is drawn in the applet:

```
public class imagemap extends Applet{

    TextField text1;
    boolean imageReady = false;
```

```
Image image = null;
    .
    .
    .

public void init(){
    text1 = new TextField(30);
    add(text1);
    image = Toolkit.getDefaultToolkit()
            .getImage("Imagemap.gif");
    MediaTracker tracker = new MediaTracker(this);
    tracker.addImage(image, 0);
    try{
        tracker.waitForAll();
    }
    catch(InterruptedException e0){
    }
    imageReady = true;
    repaint();
}
```

In the **paint()** method, we draw the image like this if the image is ready:

```
public void paint(Graphics g)
{
    if(imageReady){
        g.drawImage(image, 10, 40, 240, 155, this);
    }
}
}
```

Now the image appears in the window, and we're ready to work with the mouse.

Handling Mouse Clicks in the `imagemap` Example

When the user clicks a hotspot (such as Target 1 or Target 2 in Figure 8-10), we are supposed to handle that mouse click by reading in an XML document. We'll handle the mouse click in the **mouseDown()** event handler:

```
public class imagemap extends Applet{

    public boolean mouseDown(Event e, int x, int y)
    {
        .
        .
        .
    }
```

First, we'll check to see whether the user has clicked the first hotspot, **Target** 1. We do that by taking a look at the x and y coordinates of the mouse location and matching that to the **Target** 1 hotspot:

```
public class imagemap extends Applet{

    public boolean mouseDown(Event e, int x, int y)
    {
        if( x > 104 + 10 && x < 171 + 10 && y > 53 + 40
            && y < 75 + 40){
            .
            .
            .
        }
    }
}
```

If the user did indeed click the first hotspot, we can load in the XML document **target1.xml**:

```
public class imagemap extends Applet{

    URL url;
        .
        .
        .
    public boolean mouseDown(Event e, int x, int y)
    {
        URL newURL = null;

        if( x > 104 + 10 && x < 171 + 10 && y > 53 + 40
            && y < 75 + 40){
            try {
                url = new URL("file:////c://xml//
                    imagemap//target1.xml");
            }
            catch (MalformedURLException e1){
            }

            Document d = new Document();

            try {
                d.load(url);
            }
            catch (ParseException e3) {
                d.reportError(e3, System.out);
            }
            .
            .
            .
        }
    }
```

Finally, we can display the `target1.xml` document's text in the application's text field:

```
public class imagemap extends Applet{

    public boolean mouseDown(Event e, int x, int y)
    {
        URL newURL = null;

        if( x > 104 + 10 && x < 171 + 10 && y > 53 +
            40 && y < 75 + 40){
            try {
                url = new URL("file:////c://xml//
                    imagemap//target1.xml");
            }
            catch (MalformedURLException e1){
            }

            Document d = new Document();

            try {
                d.load(url);
            }
            catch (ParseException e3) {
                d.reportError(e3, System.out);
            }

            if (d != null) {
                text1.setText(d.getText());
            }
        }
    }
```

That handles the first hotspot. Next, we check to see whether the user has clicked the second hotspot:

```
public class imagemap extends Applet{

    public boolean mouseDown(Event e, int x, int y)
    {
        URL newURL = null;

        if( x > 104 + 10 && x < 171 + 10 && y > 53 + 40
            && y < 75 + 40){
                .
                .
                .

        }

        if( x > 54 + 10 && x < 118 + 10 && y > 105 + 40
            && y < 125 + 40){
                .
```

```
        }
    }
```

If the user has indeed clicked the second hotspot, we read in the
`target2.xml` document:

```java
public class imagemap extends Applet{

    public boolean mouseDown(Event e, int x, int y)
    {
        URL newURL = null;

        if( x > 104 + 10 && x < 171 + 10 && y > 53 +
            40 && y < 75 + 40){
                    .
                    .
                    .

        }

        if( x > 54 + 10 && x < 118 + 10 && y > 105 + 40
            && y < 125 + 40){
            try {
                url = new URL("file:////c://xml//
                    imagemap//target2.xml");
            }
            catch (MalformedURLException e1) {
            }

            Document d = new Document();

            try {
                d.load(url);
            }
            catch (ParseException e3) {
                d.reportError(e3, System.out);
            }
                .
                .
                .

        }
    }
```

Then we display `target2.xml`'s text in the text field:

```java
public boolean mouseDown(Event e, int x, int y)
{
    URL newURL = null;

    if( x > 104 + 10 && x < 171 + 10 && y > 53 + 40 && y
        < 75 + 40){
```

```
                        .
                        .
                        .
            }

            if( x > 54 + 10 && x < 118 + 10 && y > 105 + 40 && y
                < 125 + 40){
                try {
                    url = new URL("file:////c://xml//imagemap//
                        target2.xml");
                }
                catch (MalformedURLException e1) {
                }

                Document d = new Document();

                try {
                    d.load(url);
                }
                catch (ParseException e3) {
                    d.reportError(e3, System.out);
                }

                if (d != null) {
                    text1.setText(d.getText());
                }
            }
        }
```

At the end of `mouseDown()`, we return a value of **true** to indicate that we've handled the event:

```
public boolean mouseDown(Event e, int x, int y)
{
    URL newURL = null;

    if( x > 104 + 10 && x < 171 + 10 && y > 53 + 40 &&
        y < 75 + 40){
                    .
                    .
                    .
    }

    if( x > 54 + 10 && x < 118 + 10 && y > 105 + 40 && y
        < 125 + 40){
        try {
            url = new URL("file:////c://xml//imagemap//
                target2.xml");
        }
        catch (MalformedURLException e1) {
        }

        Document d = new Document();
```

```
        try {
            d.load(url);
        }
        catch (ParseException e3) {
            d.reportError(e3, System.out);
        }

        if (d != null) {
            text1.setText(d.getText());
        }
    }
    return true;
}
```

And that's it—run the imagemap application now, as shown in Figure 8-11.

When you click a hotspot in the imagemap application, that application reads in the required XML document and displays its text in the text field, as shown in Figure 8-12.

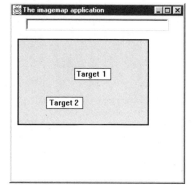

Figure 8-11.
The imagemap application.

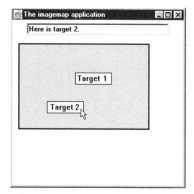

Figure 8-12.
Clicking a hotspot in the imagemap application.

The imagemap application is a success. Now we're supporting image maps applications that use XML documents. The code for this program, `imagemap.java`, appears in Listing 8-5.

Listing 8-5.
imagemap.java.

```java
import com.ms.xml.ParseException;
import com.ms.xml.Document;
import com.ms.xml.Element;

import java.util.Enumeration;
import java.awt.*;
import java.net.*;
import java.applet.Applet;

public class imagemap extends Applet{

    static String filename;
    TextField text1;
    boolean imageReady = false;
    Image image = null;
    URL url;

    public static void main(String args[])
    {
        imagemapFrame frame = new imagemapFrame("The
            imagemap application");

        frame.resize(320, 320);

        imagemap applet = new imagemap();

        frame.add("Center", applet);
        applet.init();
        applet.start();
        frame.show();
    }

    public void init(){
        text1 = new TextField(30);
        add(text1);
        image = Toolkit.getDefaultToolkit()
        .getImage("Imagemap.gif");
        MediaTracker tracker = new MediaTracker(this);
        tracker.addImage(image, 0);
        try{
            tracker.waitForAll();
        }
        catch(InterruptedException e0){
        }
        imageReady = true;
    }
```

Listing 8-5.
Continued.

```
public boolean mouseDown(Event e, int x, int y)
{
    URL newURL = null;

    if( x > 104 + 10 && x < 171 + 10 && y > 53 + 40
        && y < 75 + 40){
        try {
            url = new URL("file:////c://xml//
                imagemap//target1.xml");
        }
        catch (MalformedURLException e1){
        }

        Document d = new Document();

        try {
            d.load(url);
        }
        catch (ParseException e3) {
            d.reportError(e3, System.out);
        }

        if (d != null) {
            text1.setText(d.getText());
        }
    }

    if( x > 54 + 10 && x < 118 + 10 && y > 105 + 40
        && y < 125 + 40){
        try {
            url = new URL("file:////c://xml//
                imagemap//target2.xml");
        }
        catch (MalformedURLException e1) {
        }

        Document d = new Document();

        try {
            d.load(url);
        }
        catch (ParseException e3) {
            d.reportError(e3, System.out);
        }

        if (d != null) {
            text1.setText(d.getText());
        }
    }
    return true;
}
```

Continues

Listing 8-5.
Continued.

```
        public void paint(Graphics g)
        {
            if(imageReady){
                g.drawImage(image, 10, 40, 240, 155, this);
            }
        }
    }

class imagemapFrame extends Frame
{
    public imagemapFrame(String str)
    {
        super (str);
    }

    public boolean handleEvent(Event evt)
    {
        switch (evt.id)
        {
            case Event.WINDOW_DESTROY:
                dispose();
                System.exit(0);
                return true;

            default:
                return super.handleEvent(evt);
        }
    }
}
```

SUMMARY

That's it for our image-handling chapter. In this chapter, we've seen how to load images into our Java applications, how to create an XML image browser that uses a special XML <IMG> tag, how to use the mouse, and how to create and support image maps. We've come a long way.

In the next chapter, we'll explore Part III of the XML specification—XML stylesheets.

XML Stylesheets

In this chapter, we're going to look at Part III of the XML specification: XML stylesheets. This part of the specification is far from formalized yet, and in fact, there is not even a W3C working draft of this specification at this writing. There is a preliminary document, which you can find at: **http://sunsite.unc.edu/pub/sun-info/ standards/dsssl/xs/xs970522.ps.zip** and which unzips to a postscript document discussing Part III. There is also an RTF (Rich Text Format) version of this document at: **http://sunsite.unc.edu/pub/sun-info/standards/ dsssl/xs/xs970522.rtf.zip**. This document describes the subset of *Document Style Semantics and Specification Language* (DSSSL) used in XML.

DSSSL is a standardized stylesheet language as specified in "ISO/IEC 10179:1996," and you use it to format your documents in a way that's platform and application independent. We'll find out what that means in this chapter. Briefly, it means you can take standard text-oriented documents like XML documents and specify how they are to appear in XML browsers, formatting text in italics, different fonts, colors, and so on. You use DSSSL to specify how documents marked up in SGML (and XML is a subset of SGML) should be presented visually.

We'll spend this chapter getting acquainted with DSSSL stylesheets of the kind that are to be supported in XML browsers. You can find information about the DSSSL standard at **http://sunsite.unc.edu/pub/ sun-info/standards/dsssl**.

There is no XML-specific software yet that handles XML stylesheets, so we'll work with SGML documents in this chapter (the SGML documents in this chapter differ in only one way from XML documents, and we'll see what that way is in a moment) and point out what subset of DSSSL XML is intended to support. In particular, we'll be using the Jade DSSSL processor, written by James Clark, which you can find on the CD-ROM that accompanies this book or at **http://www.jclark.com/jade**.

Unzipping the Jade zip file creates several new directories, including a documentation directory, **doc**, with Jade documentation in HTML format. We'll use **jade.exe** in this chapter, along with several of the DTD files that come with Jade.

Using Jade, we'll be able to process DSSSL stylesheets (Jade expects these documents to have the extension **.dsl**) and use them with our SGML documents to produce formatted output documents. To be able to see the results of our formatting, we'll create output documents in RTF format, which we can view directly.

All this may sound very new and theoretical, so let's get to work on an example at once to make it concrete; in this example, we'll see where the DSSSL stylesheets fit into the whole process and what they look like.

Our First Stylesheet Example

We'll see our first DSSSL example now. Our first example will display some text in a large font and will be called **bigfont.sgml**. Note that here the only difference between this document and an XML document of the type we're familiar with is the **o o** and **- o** strings in the element declarations:

```
<!DOCTYPE DOCUMENT [
<!ELEMENT DOCUMENT O O (p*, BIGP*)>
<!ELEMENT p - O (#pcdata)>
<!ELEMENT BIGP - O (#pcdata)>
]>
<DOCUMENT>
<p>
Welcome to...
<BIGP>
XML Style!
</DOCUMENT>
```

This document is pretty straightforward: we're just setting up three new tags, <DOCUMENT>, <p>, and <BIGP>. The <DOCUMENT> tag is for the root element, the <p> tag is a paragraph tag, and the <BIGP> tag is for a paragraph of large-font (24 point) text.

SGML Versus XML

The "O O" and "- O" strings represent the only way in which the SGML documents in this chapter will differ from the XML documents in the other chapters. In SGML, you specify if the tag you're declaring may be omitted as either a start tag or an end tag. For example, this declaration says that the <p> start tag is required to start a paragraph, but the end tag is optional—that is, the </p> tag is optional:

```
<!ELEMENT p - O (#pcdata)>
```

This declaration says that both <p> and </p> are required:

```
<!ELEMENT p - - (#pcdata)>
```

An "O O" string means both start and end tags are optional.

NOTE   We use SGML declarations in this chapter because the Jade DSSSL tool requires them. However, these declarations, with o o type strings, are the only differences between the SGML documents in this chapter and XML documents.]

The Whole Point of Using Stylesheets in XML

Up until now, interpreting the <p> and <BIGP> tags were up to the XML browser we ourselves wrote. The point of XML stylesheets, however, is that you can use the XML subset of DSSSL to direct prewritten XML browsers (the larger commercial browsers intend to support this aspect of XML at some point) exactly how to display your document. How do we do that? We do that with a DSSSL stylesheet like this one, **bigfont.dsl**, (we'll see how to construct stylesheets like this one in this chapter):

```
<!doctype style-sheet PUBLIC "-//James Clark//DTD DSSSL
        Style Sheet//EN">

(root (make simple-page-sequence))

(element p (make paragraph))

(element BIGP (make paragraph
          font-size: 24pt
          space-before: 12pt))
```

Here we direct the Jade DSSSL processor to make the <p> tag a standard paragraph tag, but to use an extra large font, 24 point, for the <BIGP> paragraph tag. In this way, we are able to use the standard, prewritten items available to us in DSSSL to format our documents in a browser-independent and platform-independent way.

When we run the preceding SGML document through the Jade DSSSL processor using the preceding DSSSL stylesheet, we can produce an output document in rich text format, **bigfont.rtf**. Microsoft Word can read RTF documents, so we take a look at that document now in Figure 9-1, using Word.

As you can see in Figure 9-1, we've been able to specify the formatting of our document using DSSSL. You can think of DSSSL as a language with which to speak to an XML browser. It tells that browser exactly how it should handle each formatting tag you place in your XML documents in order to create the visual effects (such as italics or bold type) and visual organization you want. It doesn't matter which browser you use ei-

Figure 9-1.
Our first DSSSL-
formatted document.

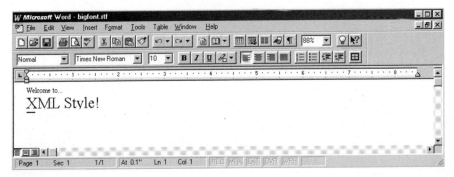

ther (when they become available!)—if it supports XML stylesheets, you're all set. We'll see that there is a terrific number of formatting aspects that you can set yourself in DSSSL.

XML does not support all of DSSSL, however; in fact, it only supports a subset. We'll take a look at that subset now.

XML DSSSL: XML-Style

For reference, we'll discuss the XML subset of DSSSL now. If you're not familiar with DSSSL, this list will make little sense right now, but we'll examine some of these elements throughout this chapter as we get an introduction to DSSSL. (If you want to understand DSSSL more thoroughly, there are whole books on the subject.) If you are familiar with DSSSL, or for reference purposes otherwise, let's take a look at what the XML DSSSL specification includes.

Here are the XML-Style (XS) features that must be supported by an XS application:

- Table
- Table-auto-width
- Online
- Simple-page
- Keyword
- Sideline
- Aligned-column

The following DSSSL language components must be supported in any application conforming to the XS specification:

- DSSSL core query language
- core expression language
- lambda
- #!key
- letrec
- let*
- let (including named let).

An XS application must also support these *flow object classes* (we'll see what flow object classes are soon):

- Sequence
- Display-group
- Simple-page-sequence
- Paragraph
- Paragraph-break
- Line-field
- Sideline
- Character
- Leader
- Rule
- External-graphic
- Score
- Box
- Alignment-point
- Aligned-column
- Table
- Table-part
- Table-column
- Table-row
- Table-cell
- Table-border
- Scroll
- Multi-mode
- Link
- Marginalia

Here are the optional components of DSSSL that an XS application need not support:

- Page
- Multicolumn
- Nested-column-set
- Combine-char
- General-indirect
- Font-info
- Included-container

- actual-characteristic
- expression
- multiprocess
- regexp
- word
- hytime
- side-by-side
- cross-reference
- bidi
- vertical
- inline-note
- glyph-annotation
- emphasizing-mark
- math
- query

Finally, here are the optional flow classes that an XS application need not support:

- Page-sequence
- Column-set-sequence
- Anchor
- Embedded-text
- Included-container-area
- Side-by-side
- Side-by-side-item
- Glyph-annotation
- Multiline-inline-note
- Emphasizing-mark
- Math-sequence
- Unmath
- Subscript
- Superscript
- Script
- Mark
- Fence

- Fraction
- Radical
- Math-operator
- Grid
- Grid-cell

If you aren't familiar with DSSSL, the preceding terms probably don't mean much. Let's make all this clearer by continuing our DSSSL exploration now, starting with the two parts that make up DSSSL.

The Two Parts of DSSSL

There are two parts to DSSSL: a style language and a transformation language. We've already seen an example of the style language in our first DSSSL example. You use the style language to specify the way you want to format your documents. The transformation language specifies how to transform SGML documents that use one DTD into documents that use another.

Currently, XML-Style only uses the style language. You use this language as we've seen: you create an XML document with a DTD, as well as a XS stylesheet, and use an XS application to read in that document. The application formats the document according to the stylesheet and displays it.

In the style language, DSSSL treats the documents it formats as a set of *nodes* organized into *groves*. That is, we've seen how XML documents can be treated as trees, and "groves" are trees of trees, and each connection where a new branch is connected to the tree is a node. Even the DTD is considered a tree attached to the main document. We won't get into the concept of groves too deeply here, but if you're interested, you will find a great deal on this topic in the DSSSL documentation.

Let's put DSSSL to work now as we see how to create and work with DSSSL stylesheets.

Creating Stylesheets

A stylesheet is made up of a collection of *construction rules*. A construction rule tells the XS application how to construct and format a particular element. For example, we've seen construction rules for elements like <p> and <BIGP> in the **bigfont.dsl** example:

```
<!doctype style-sheet PUBLIC "-//James Clark//DTD DSSSL
     Style Sheet//EN">

(root (make simple-page-sequence))

(element p (make paragraph))

(element BIGP (make paragraph
        font-size: 24pt
        space-before: 12pt))
```

Using construction rules, you can specify the color, size, location, and other presentation aspects of the elements you define.

In the preceding example, we're telling the XS application that when it finds a <p> element, it is to make a **paragraph** *flow* object:

```
<!doctype style-sheet PUBLIC "-//James Clark//DTD DSSSL
     Style Sheet//EN">

(root (make simple-page-sequence))

(element p (make paragraph))

(element BIGP (make paragraph
        font-size: 24pt
        space-before: 12pt))
```

That brings up our next question: what's a flow object?

Flow Objects

Just like objects and classes in Java, the XS application uses **flow object** classes to make **flow** objects. There are certain standard **flow object** classes defined in XS, and we've seen their names. For example, one of these classes is the **paragraph** class. Using this class, you can create a new **paragraph flow** object, and by placing text into such a **flow** object, you format it; that is, the **flow** object *flows* to fit the object's formatting area in the document. In the case of the <p> element, then, we indicate to the XS application that the text inside <p> tags should be formatted using a standard **paragraph flow** object:

```
<!doctype style-sheet PUBLIC "-//James Clark//DTD DSSSL
     Style Sheet//EN">

(root (make simple-page-sequence))

(element p (make paragraph))
```

```
(element BIGP (make paragraph
        font-size: 24pt
        space-before: 12pt))
```

You can customize **flow** objects by making use of their *characteristics*.

Flow Object Characteristics

Flow objects like the **paragraph flow** object take values in variables called *characteristics*. These characteristics are predefined for each flow object and specify various aspects of the **flow** object. For example, we specify the font size and the vertical space before the <BIGP> paragraphs using the **paragraph flow** object's font-size and space-before characteristics this way:

```
<!doctype style-sheet PUBLIC "-//James Clark//DTD DSSSL
  Style Sheet//EN">

(root (make simple-page-sequence))

(element p (make paragraph))

(element BIGP (make paragraph
        font-size: 24pt
        space-before: 12pt))
```

We've gotten the terminology down now, so it's time for our first example that we'll create from beginning to end.

The **style** Example

We'll create this next, simple example from scratch. In this example, we'll see how to create and how to use a stylesheet using the Jade processor. We'll start with the SGML document, **style.sgml**. Create that document now and add this DTD:

```
<!DOCTYPE DOCUMENT [
   .
   .
   .
]>
```

Next, we declare the **root** element, <DOCUMENT>, this way (note that we use the SGML type of declaration that jade requires, with an **o o** string:

```
<!DOCTYPE DOCUMENT [
<!ELEMENT DOCUMENT o o (p*)>
       .
       .
       .
]>
```

Here we indicate that the document contains elements of the <p> type, which we'll use to create paragraphs. We declare that element this way in the DTD:

```
<!DOCTYPE DOCUMENT [
<!ELEMENT DOCUMENT o o (p*)>
<!ELEMENT p - o (#pcdata)>
]>
```

Now let's add the body of the document; we start with a <p> tag:

```
<!DOCTYPE DOCUMENT [
<!ELEMENT DOCUMENT o o (p*)>
<!ELEMENT p - o (#pcdata)>
]>
<DOCUMENT>
<p>
   .
   .
   .
```

Then we place some text in the document (this text will go into the **paragraph flow** object and be formatted by that object):

```
<!DOCTYPE DOCUMENT [
<!ELEMENT DOCUMENT o o (p*)>
<!ELEMENT p - o (#pcdata)>
]>
<DOCUMENT>
<p>
Welcome to...
   .
   .
   .
```

We've made the </p> tag optional, so we'll omit that tag at the end of the paragraph (as is the common usage in HTML). We'll just add one more paragraph now and finish the document this way:

```
<!DOCTYPE DOCUMENT [
<!ELEMENT DOCUMENT o o (p*)>
<!ELEMENT p - o (#pcdata)>
]>
```

```
<DOCUMENT>
<p>
Welcome to...
<p>
XML style!
</DOCUMENT>
```

Now let's create the stylesheet for this example, telling the DSSSL processor how to handle the <p> tag. We do that with Jade by creating and using a document with the extension **.dsl**; if we pass the **style.sgml** document to Jade, it will expect to find a corresponding stylesheet as well, named **style.dsl** (i.e., with the same name as the SGML document, but the extension **.dsl**).

Creating a DSSSL Stylesheet

We start the DSSSL stylesheet **style.dsl** with a DTD:

```
<!doctype style-sheet PUBLIC "-//James Clark//DTD DSSSL
    Style Sheet//EN">
    .
    .
    .
```

Here, we use the public key **-//James Clark//DTD DSSSL Style Sheet//EN** to associate the actual DTDs we need to use Jade with this document. We'll need two DTDs to process our SGML files using Jade, and these DTDs come with Jade: **dsssl.dtd** and **style-sheet.dtd**. To use these DTDs with Jade, you place a file named **catalog** (with no filename extension) connecting the public keys to DTD files. The contents of the catalog file look like this (notice that we connect the public keys to the **dsssl.dtd** and **style-sheet.dtd** files):

```
PUBLIC "ISO/IEC 10179:1996//DTD DSSSL Architecture//EN"
    "dsssl.dtd"
PUBLIC "-//James Clark//DTD DSSSL Style Sheet//EN"
    "style-sheet.dtd"
```

Next in the stylesheet **style.dsl**, we define the root of the document as a simple-page-**sequence flow** object. This is a standard **flow** object to construct documents with (we use this flow object in particular because it's one supported in XS):

```
<!doctype style-sheet PUBLIC "-//James Clark//DTD DSSSL
    Style Sheet//EN">
```

```
(root (make simple-page-sequence))
        .
        .
        .
```

Note the syntax here: we specify the element in the construction rule, followed by directions for making that element. In this case, we construct the document's root with the directive **make simple-page-sequence**. This creates a new simple-page-sequence for the **root**.

To create the <p> element, we make a new **paragraph flow** object (the **paragraph flow** object is also supported by XS):

```
<!doctype style-sheet PUBLIC "-//James Clark//DTD DSSSL
Style Sheet//EN">

(root (make simple-page-sequence))

(element p (make paragraph))
```

That completes this example's code. To combine **style.sgml** and **style.dsl** and create **style.rtf** (which we can read in Microsoft Word), we use Jade with the **-trtf** switch, which indicates we want the output in RTF format:

```
C:\jade>jade -trtf style.sgml
```

NOTE *The Jade version on the CD-ROM and the Jade Web site runs under Windows 95 or Windows NT; if you use another operating system, you'll have to rebuild Jade as described at the Jade Web site. The Win32 version of Jade needs access to several DLL files as well as the catalog file and the two DTD files mentioned previously. These DLL files also come with Jade. Also, make sure you place the two DTD files,* **dsssl.dtd** *and* **style-sheet.dtd**, *in the same directory as the* **.dsl** *file.*

TIP *Jade also includes a switch for converting SGML documents into XML ones:* **-txml**

The preceding code line creates **style.rtf**, and we can take a look at that file in Microsoft Word, as shown in Figure 9-2.

As you can see in Figure 9-2, each new paragraph that we've created starts on a new line, just as it should. In this way, we've created our first stylesheet example from beginning to end. The code for this example, **style.sgml**, appears in Listing 9-1, and **style.dsl** appears in Listing 9-2.

Figure 9-2.
The style example.

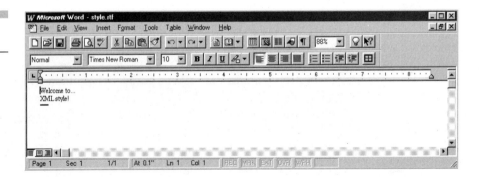

Listing 9-1.
`style.sgml`.

```
<!DOCTYPE DOCUMENT [
<!ELEMENT DOCUMENT o o (p*)>
<!ELEMENT p - o (#pcdata)>
]>
<DOCUMENT>
<p>
Welcome to...
<p>
XML style!
</DOCUMENT>
```

Listing 9-2.
`style.dsl`.

```
<!doctype style-sheet PUBLIC "-//James Clark//DTD DSSSL
     Style Sheet//EN">

(root (make simple-page-sequence))

(element p (make paragraph))
```

We've seen how to work one example now in detail, but that example is very simple. Let's elaborate the style example into one we've gotten a little exposure to already: the bigfont example.

Stylesheet Characteristics: the `bigfont` Example

The bigfont example will give us some exposure to the idea of **flow** object characteristics, which we've seen are special data items associated with **flow** objects that you can use to customize what that **flow** object does.

In the bigfont example, then, we'll use some of the **paragraph flow** object's characteristics to create a <BIGP> element that formats its enclosed text in a large font.

We start the bigfont example with **bigfont.sgml**. This is the document that contains the text to be formatted, and we start that document by defining the elements we'll use in a DTD:

```
<!DOCTYPE DOCUMENT [
    .
    .
    .
]>
```

First we declare the root, indicating that this root can include <p> elements and <BIGP> elements:

```
<!DOCTYPE DOCUMENT [
<!ELEMENT DOCUMENT o o (p*, BIGP*)>
    .
    .
    .
]>
```

The <p> element is defined as we defined it in the last example:

```
<!DOCTYPE DOCUMENT [
<!ELEMENT DOCUMENT o o (p*, BIGP*)>
<!ELEMENT p - o (#pcdata)>
    .
    .
    .
]>
```

And we declare the <BIGP> tag the same way:

```
<!DOCTYPE DOCUMENT [
<!ELEMENT DOCUMENT o o (p*, BIGP*)>
<!ELEMENT p - o (#pcdata)>
<!ELEMENT BIGP - o (#pcdata)>
]>
    .
    .
    .
```

Now the DTD is done. We add a <p> element to the document this way, giving it some text:

```
<!DOCTYPE DOCUMENT [
<!ELEMENT DOCUMENT o o (p*, BIGP*)>
<!ELEMENT p - o (#pcdata)>
```

```
<!ELEMENT BIGP - o (#pcdata)>
]>
<DOCUMENT>
<p>
Welcome to...
        .
        .
        .
```

We also add a <BIGP> element with some text this way:

```
<!DOCTYPE DOCUMENT [
<!ELEMENT DOCUMENT o o (p*, BIGP*)>
<!ELEMENT p - o (#pcdata)>
<!ELEMENT BIGP - o (#pcdata)>
]>
<DOCUMENT>
<p>
Welcome to...
<BIGP>
XML Style!
</DOCUMENT>
```

Now let's write the `bigfont.dsl` stylesheet. We start that stylesheet with a DTD that loads in the actual DTDs we need:

```
<!doctype style-sheet PUBLIC "-//James Clark//DTD DSSSL
    Style Sheet//EN">
        .
        .
        .
```

Then we set up the document itself as before, with a simple-page-**sequence flow** object:

```
<!doctype style-sheet PUBLIC "-//James Clark//DTD DSSSL
    Style Sheet//EN">

(root (make simple-page-sequence))
        .
        .
        .
```

Next, we set up the <p> element with the following construction rule:

```
<!doctype style-sheet PUBLIC "-//James Clark//DTD DSSSL
    Style Sheet//EN">

(root (make simple-page-sequence))

(element p (make paragraph))
```

.
.
.

Finally, we set up the <BIGP> element:

```
<!doctype style-sheet PUBLIC "-//James Clark//DTD DSSSL
    Style Sheet//EN">

(root (make simple-page-sequence))

(element p (make paragraph))

(element BIGP (make paragraph
```
.
.
.

Here, we'll use two **paragraph flow** object characteristics to specify the formatting for our <BIGP> paragraphs. We start by specifying the font-size characteristic, making the font size for the paragraph 24 points:

```
<!doctype style-sheet PUBLIC "-//James Clark//DTD DSSSL
    Style Sheet//EN">

(root (make simple-page-sequence))

(element p (make paragraph))

(element BIGP (make paragraph
        font-size: 24pt
```
.
.
.

To avoid overwriting the previous paragraph's text, now that we're using large font, we should add extra space before the current paragraph, and we do that with the space-before characteristic:

```
<!doctype style-sheet PUBLIC "-//James Clark//DTD DSSSL
    Style Sheet//EN">

(root (make simple-page-sequence))

(element p (make paragraph))

(element BIGP (make paragraph
        font-size: 24pt
        space-before: 12pt))
```

That's it—now the example is complete. We run the Jade processor this way on the **bigfont.sgml** document:

```
C:\jade>jade -trtf bigfont.sgml
```

This creates **bigfont.rtf**, which we've already seen in Figure 9-1. Using **flow** object characteristics like this, we can specify the properties of **flow** objects.

Some common **flow** objects include font-family-name, which specifies the font type to use (e.g., **Roman**); font-size, which gives the font size (usually specified in points—**24pt** or **12pt** and so on); space-before, the space before the formatting area; start-after, which gives the space after the area and before the next area; quadding, which means the justification of the formatting area. You can use values like **'start**, **'end**, and **'center** here (note the **'** before these terms, which indicate that these terms are predefined symbols); and start-indent, gives the indentation of an area.

You can find complete lists of characteristics for DSSSL flow objects in DSSSL documentation. The "xs970522.rtf" document lists all the flow objects and characteristics in XML-Style, along with their standard and default values. For example, all the XS **paragraph flow** object's characteristics appear in Table 9-1. In that table, the Inherited column indicates if this characteristic is inherited for nested objects (also, note that the symbol **#f** stands for false in DSSSL and **#t** for true; both symbols are used in Table 9-1).

NOTE   *The term* **sosofo** *in Table 9-1 stands for specification of a sequence of flow objects. A* **sosofo** *is what you make up construction rules from, like this* **sosofo**: *(make paragraph). Each* **sosofo** *can itself contain child sequences.]*

Table 9-1.

The **paragraph flow** Object's Characteristics.

Characteristic	Inherited	Standard Values	Init/Default
alignment-point-offset	Y	**#f**, number between 0 and 100	50
asis-truncate-char	Y	**#f**, char object	**#f**
asis-wrap-char	Y	**#f**, char object	**#f**
asis-wrap-indent	Y	**#f**, length-spec	**#f**
break-after	N	**#f**, page, page-region*, column*, column-set*	**#f**

Table 9-1.

Continued.

Characteristic	Inherited	Standard Values	Init/Default
break-before	N	**#f**, page, page-region*, column*, column-set*	**#f**
country	Y	**#f**, ISO 3166 country code	**#f**
end-indent	Y	length-spec	0pt
expand-tabs?	Y	**#f**, integer greater than zero	8
first-line-align	Y	**#f**, **#t**, char object	**#f**
first-line-start-indent	Y	length-spec	0pt
font-family-name	Y	**#f**, string	iso-serif
font-name	Y	**#f**, public identifier	**#f**
font-posture	Y	**#f**, not-applicable*, upright, oblique, back-slanted-oblique*, italic, back-slanted-italic*	upright
font-proportionate-width	Y	**#f**, not-applicable*, ultra-condensed*, extra-condensed*, condensed, semi-condensed*, medium, semi-expanded*, expanded, extra-expanded*, ultra-expanded*	medium
font-size	Y	length	10pt
font-structure	Y	**#f**, not-applicable, solid, outline	solid
font-weight	Y	**#f**, not-applicable*, ultra-light*, extra-light*, light, semi-light*, medium, semi-bold*, bold, extra-bold*, ultra-bold*	medium
glyph-alignment-mode	Y	base, center, top, bottom, font	font
hanging-punct?	Y	**#f**, **#t**	**#f**
hyphenation-char	Y	character	**#\-)**
hyphenation-exceptions	Y	list of strings	empty list

Continues

Characteristic	Inherited	Standard Values	Init/Default
hyphenation-keep	Y	**#f**, spread, page, column	**#f**
hyphenation-ladder-count	Y	**#f**, integer greater than zero	**#f**
hyphenation-push-char-count	Y	positive integer	2
hyphenation-remain-char-count	Y	positive integer	2
ignore-record-end?	Y	**#f**, **#t**	**#f**
implicit-bidi-method	Y	**#f**, public identifier	**#f**
justify-glyph-space-max-add	Y	length-spec	0pt
justify-glyph-space-max-remove	Y	length-spec	0pt
keep-with-next?	N	**#f**, **#t**	**#f**
keep-with-previous?	N	**#f**, **#t**	**#f**
keep	N	**#f**, page, column-set*, column*, **#t***	**#f**
language	Y	**#f**, ISO 639 language code	**#f**
last-line-end-indent	Y	length-spec	0pt
last-line-justify-limit	Y	length-spec	0
last-line-quadding	Y	relative, start, end, spread-inside, spread-outside, page-inside, page-outside, center, justify	relative
line-breaking-method	Y	**#f**, public identifier	**#f**
line-composition-method	Y	**#f**, public identifier	**#f**
line-number-sep	Y	length-spec	none
line-number-side	Y	start, end, spread-inside, spread-outside, page-inside, page-outside	none
line-number	Y	**#f**, unlabeled **sosofo**	**#f**
line-spacing-priority	Y	force, integer	0
line-spacing	Y	length-spec	12pt

Table 9-1.

Continued.

Characteristic	Inherited	Standard Values	Init/Default
lines	Y	wrap, asis, asis-wrap*, asis-truncate*, none	wrap
may-violate-keep-after?	N	#f, #t	#f
may-violate-keep-before?	N	#f, #t	#f
min-leading	Y	#f, length-spec	#f
min-post-line-spacing	Y	#f, length-spec	#f
min-pre-line-spacing	Y	#f, length-spec	#f
numbered-lines?	Y	#f, #t	#t
orphan-count	Y	positive integer	2
position-preference	N	#f, top, bottom	#f
quadding	Y	start, end, spread-inside*, spread-outside*, page-inside*, page-outside*, center, justify*	start
space-after	N	display space	no space after
space-before	N	display space	no space before
span-weak?	Y	#f, #t	#f
span	Y	integer greater than zero	1
start-indent	Y	length-spec	0pt
widow-count	Y	positive integer	2
writing-mode	Y	left-to-right, right-to-left, top-to-bottom	left-to-right

The bigfont example is a success. This document, **bigfont.sgml**, appears in Listing 9-3, and its associated stylesheet appears in Listing 9-4.

As we can see, using **flow** object characteristics can tailor various display elements as we want them; for example, here's how you might simulate the <H1> to <H6> HTML header tags in a SGML document (this is a traditional example when discussing DSSSL):

```
<!doctype style-sheet PUBLIC "-//James Clark//DTD DSSSL
    Style Sheet//EN">
```

Listing 9-3.
bigfont.sgml

```
<!DOCTYPE DOCUMENT [
<!ELEMENT DOCUMENT o o (p*, BIGP*)>
<!ELEMENT p - o (#pcdata)>
<!ELEMENT BIGP - o (#pcdata)>
]>
<DOCUMENT>
<p>
Welcome to...
<BIGP>
XML Style!
</DOCUMENT>
```

Listing 9-4.
bigfont.dsl

```
<!doctype style-sheet PUBLIC "-//James Clark//DTD DSSSL
     Style Sheet//EN">

(root (make simple-page-sequence))

(element p (make paragraph))

(element BIGP (make paragraph
        font-size: 24pt
        space-before: 12pt))
```

```
(element HTML (make simple-page-sequence))

(element H1
    (make paragraph
        font-weight: 'bold
        font-size: 24pt
        line-spacing: 24pt
        space-before: 10pt
        space-after: 10pt))

(element H2
    (make paragraph
        font-weight: 'bold
        font-size: 18pt
        line-spacing: 18pt
        space-before: 8pt
        space-after: 8pt))

(element H3
    (make paragraph
        font-weight: 'bold
        font-size: 12pt
        line-spacing: 12pt
        space-before: 6pt
```

```
                        space-after: 6pt))

      (element H4
          (make paragraph
              font-weight: 'bold
              font-size: 10pt
              line-spacing: 10pt
              space-before: 6pt
              space-after: 6pt))

      (element H5
          (make paragraph
              font-weight: 'bold
              font-size: 9pt
              line-spacing: 9pt
              space-before: 6pt
              space-after: 6pt))

      (element H6
          (make paragraph
              font-weight: 'bold
              font-size: 8pt
              line-spacing: 8pt
              space-before: 6pt
              space-after: 6pt))
```

We can do more with DSSSL. For example, we can define our own terms. Let's look into that next.

The defines Example

In this next example, we'll see how to define new terms in a DSSSL stylesheet. In particular, we'll define three new terms: **standardfontsize**, **bigfontsize**, and **bigfontweight**, and use these terms in a DSSSL stylesheet.

In this example, we'll create a new document that, when formatted, will support a <HEADER> tag that produces large-font headers. We will start this example by creating a new stylesheet, **defines.dsl**. We begin that stylesheet with a DTD:

```
<!doctype style-sheet PUBLIC "-//James Clark//DTD DSSSL
      Style Sheet//EN">
          .
          .
          .
```

Next, we define our **root** element:

```
<!doctype style-sheet PUBLIC "-//James Clark//DTD DSSSL
    Style Sheet//EN">

(root (make simple-page-sequence))
              .
              .
              .
```

Now we can create the <HEADER> element. We do that like this:

```
<!doctype style-sheet PUBLIC "-//James Clark//DTD DSSSL
    Style Sheet//EN">

(root (make simple-page-sequence))

(element HEADER (make paragraph
    .
    .
    .
```

We'll use a value of 'bold for the font-weight characteristic here to make the header appear in bold letters. In this case, we'll see how we can define a new term in the stylesheet and then use that term in the construction rule for the <HEADER> element.

We first define a new term, **bigfontweight**, like this, setting it equal to the DSSSL symbol **'bold**:

```
<!doctype style-sheet PUBLIC "-//James Clark//DTD DSSSL
    Style Sheet//EN">

(root (make simple-page-sequence))

        (define bigfontweight 'bold)

(element HEADER (make paragraph
    .
    .
    .
```

Now we can make use of that term in the <HEADER> construction rule:

```
<!doctype style-sheet PUBLIC "-//James Clark//DTD DSSSL
    Style Sheet//EN">

(root (make simple-page-sequence))

        (define bigfontweight 'bold)

(element HEADER (make paragraph
                    font-weight: bigfontweight
```

.
.
.

In a similar way, we define another new term, **bigfontsize**:

```
<!doctype style-sheet PUBLIC "-//James Clark//DTD DSSSL
    Style Sheet//EN">

(root (make simple-page-sequence))

        (define bigfontsize 24pt)
        (define bigfontweight 'bold)

(element HEADER (make paragraph
            font-weight: bigfontweight
                .
                .
                .
```

We make use of the new **bigfontsize** term in the <HEADER> construction rule this way:

```
<!doctype style-sheet PUBLIC "-//James Clark//DTD DSSSL
    Style Sheet//EN">

(root (make simple-page-sequence))

        (define bigfontsize 24pt)
        (define bigfontweight 'bold)

(element HEADER (make paragraph
            font-weight: bigfontweight
            font-size: bigfontsize
                .
                .
                .
```

In this way, you can define your own terms for use in your stylesheet. We finish the <HEADER> construction rule by specifying values for the space-before and space-after characteristics:

```
<!doctype style-sheet PUBLIC "-//James Clark//DTD DSSSL
    Style Sheet//EN">

(root (make simple-page-sequence))

        (define bigfontsize 24pt)
        (define bigfontweight 'bold)

(element HEADER (make paragraph
            font-weight: bigfontweight
```

```
                    font-size: bigfontsize
                    space-before: 10pt
                    space-after: 10pt))
```

Finally, we can define a standard font size, **standardfontsize**, and use it in a normal <p> tag:

```
<!doctype style-sheet PUBLIC "-//James Clark//DTD DSSSL
      Style Sheet//EN">

(root (make simple-page-sequence))

        (define standardfontsize 12pt)
        (define bigfontsize 24pt)
        (define bigfontweight 'bold)

(element HEADER (make paragraph
                  font-weight: bigfontweight
                  font-size: bigfontsize
                  space-before: 10pt
                  space-after: 10pt))

(element p (make paragraph font-size: standardfontsize))
```

That completes the stylesheet; let's put this stylesheet to work in a new SGML document, **defines.sgml**. We start that document with a DTD:

```
<!DOCTYPE DOCUMENT [
   .
   .
   .
]>
```

Next, we declare our **root** element, which can hold both <HEADER> and <p> elements:

```
<!DOCTYPE DOCUMENT [
<!ELEMENT DOCUMENT o o (HEADER*,p*)>
      .
      .
      .
]>
```

Finally, we declare our <HEADER> and <p> elements:

```
<!DOCTYPE DOCUMENT [
<!ELEMENT DOCUMENT o o (HEADER*,p*)>
<!ELEMENT HEADER - o (#pcdata)>
<!ELEMENT p - o (#pcdata)>
]>
```

That completes the DTD. We add a <HEADER> element to our document's body now like this, where we set up a header with the text **Header 1**:

```
<!DOCTYPE DOCUMENT [
<!ELEMENT DOCUMENT o o (HEADER*,p*)>
<!ELEMENT HEADER - o (#pcdata)>
<!ELEMENT p - o (#pcdata)>
]>
<DOCUMENT>
<HEADER>
Header 1
</HEADER>
</DOCUMENT>
```

We can also place a standard paragraph in the document like this:

```
<!DOCTYPE DOCUMENT [
<!ELEMENT DOCUMENT o o (HEADER*,p*)>
<!ELEMENT HEADER - o (#pcdata)>
<!ELEMENT p - o (#pcdata)>
]>
<DOCUMENT>
<HEADER>
Header 1
</HEADER>
<p>
```

Here is a header showing how to use the define keyword:

```
</p>
</DOCUMENT>
```

That's it—run this document through Jade now, producing **defines.rtf**, as shown in Figure 9-3.

Figure 9-3.
The result of formatting **defines.sgml**.

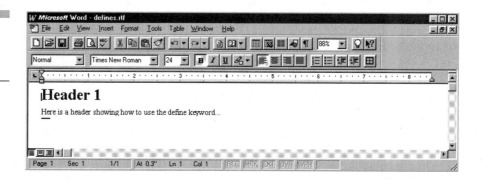

As you can see in Figure 9-3, we've created a header with large, bold letters. Now we're able to define new terms in DSSSL. The SGML document for this example, **defines.sgml**, appears in Listing 9-5, and the stylesheet for this example, **defines.dsl**, appears in Listing 9-6.

Here is a header showing how to use the **define** keyword:

```
</p>
</DOCUMENT>
```

So far, all the elements we've formatted in DSSSL have started with a new paragraph, but what if we don't want to start a new paragraph for the element or elements we're formatting? What if we want everything to fit on the same line? We'll take a look at that now.

**Listing 9-5.
defines.sgml**.

```
<!DOCTYPE DOCUMENT [
<!ELEMENT DOCUMENT o o (HEADER*,p*)>
<!ELEMENT HEADER - o (#pcdata)>
<!ELEMENT p - o (#pcdata)>
]>
<DOCUMENT>
<HEADER>
Header 1
</HEADER>
<p>
```

**Listing 9-6.
defines.dsl**.

```
<!doctype style-sheet PUBLIC "-//James Clark//DTD DSSSL
      Style Sheet//EN">

(root (make simple-page-sequence))

        (define fontsize 12pt)
        (define bigfontsize 24pt)
        (define bigfontweight 'bold)

(element HEADER (make paragraph
                font-weight: bigfontweight
                font-size: bigfontsize
                space-before: 10pt
                space-after: 10pt))

(element p (make paragraph font-size: fontsize) )
```

Sequences: the ands Example

In this next example, we'll see how to base our elements not on the **paragraph flow** object, but on the *sequence flow* object. In particular, we'll create a new tag—the <and> tag—that we can use wherever we need the word **and** to connect two other words in a document:

Here are items connected with ands:

```
Item 1 and Item 2 and Item 3.
```

Here's how we declare the <and> tag in a new document, **ands.sgml**. Note that we declare this element as EMPTY so that we won't need a closing tag:

```
<!DOCTYPE DOCUMENT [
<!ELEMENT DOCUMENT o o (p*, and*)>
<!ELEMENT p - - (#pcdata|and)*>
<!ELEMENT and - o EMPTY>
]>
     .
     .
     .
```

TIP *Although we can indicate that the </and> tag is optional in SGML, that won't allow us to use lines like this: "Item 1 <and> Item 2 <and> Item 3" because that turns the text strings "Item 2" and so on into the content of the <and> tag. To use a line like "Item 1 <and> Item 2 <and> Item 3", we have to make the <and> tag empty.*

Next, we add the body of the document to **ands.sgml**:

```
<!DOCTYPE DOCUMENT [
<!ELEMENT DOCUMENT o o (p*, and*)>
<!ELEMENT p - - (#pcdata|and)*>
<!ELEMENT and - o EMPTY>
]>
<DOCUMENT>
<p>
```

Here are items connected with ands:

```
</p>
<p>
Item 1
<and>
Item 2
```

```
<and>
Item 3.
</p>
</DOCUMENT>
```

Now it's up to us to set up the <and> tag in the stylesheet so that it simply inserts the word **and**, but no new paragraph. We start **ands.dsl** with a DTD and format the root:

```
<!doctype style-sheet PUBLIC "-//James Clark//DTD DSSSL
    Style Sheet//EN">

(root (make simple-page-sequence))
              .
              .
              .
```

Then we add the simple paragraph element, <p>, this way:

```
<!doctype style-sheet PUBLIC "-//James Clark//DTD DSSSL
    Style Sheet//EN">

(root (make simple-page-sequence))

(element p (make paragraph))
           .
           .
           .
```

Now we can set up the <and> tag. We do that by using the **sequence flow** object this way:

```
<!doctype style-sheet PUBLIC "-//James Clark//DTD DSSSL
    Style Sheet//EN">

(root (make simple-page-sequence))

(element p (make paragraph))

(element and (make sequence
                 .
                 .
                 .
```

The **sequence flow** object is a flow object that does not start a new paragraph, and you can use it to format lines of text. In this case, we'll just insert the string **and** as a *literal* into the sequence:

```
<!doctype style-sheet PUBLIC "-//James Clark//DTD DSSSL
    Style Sheet//EN">

(root (make simple-page-sequence))
```

```
(element p (make paragraph))

(element and (make sequence
                    (literal "and ")))
```

That's it—now process this file with Jade to create **ands.rtf**:

```
C:\jade>jade -rtf ands.sgml
```

When we open the **ands.rtf** document in MS Word, we see that the
<and> tag has done just what it should: placed **and** in the correct places,
as shown in Figure 9-4. The **ands.sgml** example is a success.

This document, **ands.sgml**, appears in Listing 9-7, and **ands.dsl** appears in Listing 9-8.

Here are items connected with ands:

```
</p>
<p>
Item 1
<and>
Item 2
<and>
Item 3.
</p>
</DOCUMENT>
```

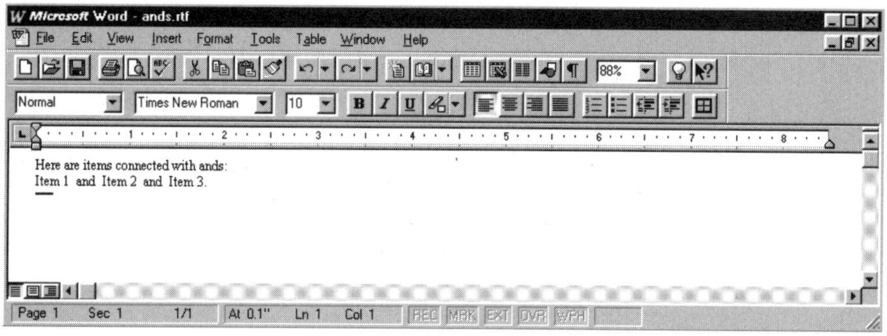

Figure 9-4.
Placing elements on
the same line.

Listing 9-7.
ands.sgml.

```
<!DOCTYPE DOCUMENT [
<!ELEMENT DOCUMENT o o (p*, and*)>
<!ELEMENT p - - (#pcdata|and)*>
<!ELEMENT and - o EMPTY>
]>
<DOCUMENT>
<p>
```

Listing 9-8.
ands.dsl.

```
<!doctype style-sheet PUBLIC "-//James Clark//DTD DSSSL
     Style Sheet//EN">

(root (make simple-page-sequence))

(element p (make paragraph))

(element and (make sequence
                    (literal "and ")))
```

We can nest **flow** objects in DSSSL. For example, now that we've seen how to create both **paragraph** and **sequence flow** objects, let's combine the two with a sequence in a paragraph.

The **indents** Example

In this next example, we'll combine paragraphs and sequences. In particular, we'll create a new tag, <INDENTS>, which will preface text with . . . and place that same string after the text. For example, this SGML,

```
<p>
Here are items indented with dots:
<INDENTS>
Item 1
<INDENTS>
Item 2
<INDENTS>
Item 3
```

will be formatted this way:

```
Here are items indented with dots:
          ...Item 1...
          ...Item 2...
          ...Item 3...
```

Each <INDENTS> element creates a new paragraph and then a sequence with . . . followed by the element's content, followed by . . . again.

Let's put this example to work now. We start placing a DTD in an SGML document, **indents.sgml**, as well as declaring a <p> and <INDENTS> tag:

```
<!DOCTYPE DOCUMENT [
<!ELEMENT DOCUMENT o o (p*, INDENTS*)>
<!ELEMENT p - o (#pcdata)>
```

```
<!ELEMENT INDENTS - o (#pcdata)>
]>
```

Now we add the body of the document:

```
<!DOCTYPE DOCUMENT [
<!ELEMENT DOCUMENT o o (p*, INDENTS*)>
<!ELEMENT p - o (#pcdata)>
<!ELEMENT INDENTS - o (#pcdata)>
]>
<DOCUMENT>
<p>
Here are items indented with dots:
<INDENTS>
Item 1
<INDENTS>
Item 2
<INDENTS>
Item 3
</DOCUMENT>
```

All that's left now is to create the stylesheet, **indents.dsl**. We start that process by declaring the document's **root** and a <p> tag:

```
<!doctype style-sheet PUBLIC "-//James Clark//DTD DSSSL
    Style Sheet//EN">

(root (make simple-page-sequence))

(element p (make paragraph))
                    .
                    .
                    .
```

Now we set up the <INDENTS> element. Each new <INDENTS> element places its text on a new line, so we start the specification of this tag by making a new paragraph:

```
<!doctype style-sheet PUBLIC "-//James Clark//DTD DSSSL
    Style Sheet//EN">

(root (make simple-page-sequence))

(element p (make paragraph))

(element INDENTS (make paragraph
                    .
                    .
                    .
```

Now we have to construct the contents of the new line, which has several parts. To place those parts on the same line, we start a new sequence:

```
<!doctype style-sheet PUBLIC "-//James Clark//DTD DSSSL
    Style Sheet//EN">

(root (make simple-page-sequence))

(element p (make paragraph))

(element INDENTS (make paragraph
        (make sequence
                      .
                      .
                      .
```

Then we place the literal string **. . .** first on the new line:

```
<!doctype style-sheet PUBLIC "-//James Clark//DTD DSSSL
    Style Sheet//EN">

(root (make simple-page-sequence))

(element p (make paragraph))

(element INDENTS (make paragraph
        (make sequence
                  (literal "...")
                      .
                      .
                      .
```

We also want to place the content of the <INDENTS> tag on the line, but how do we do that? We format the content (which may contain other elements) and add it to our sequence with the DSSSL functions **process-children** or **process-children-trim** (the second version trims off white-spaces):

```
<!doctype style-sheet PUBLIC "-//James Clark//DTD DSSSL
    Style Sheet//EN">

(root (make simple-page-sequence))

(element p (make paragraph))

(element INDENTS (make paragraph
        (make sequence
                  (literal "...")
                  (process-children-trim)
                      .
                      .
                      .
```

Finally, we display the trailing **. . .** literal string this way:

```
<!doctype style-sheet PUBLIC "-//James Clark//DTD DSSSL
      Style Sheet//EN">

(root (make simple-page-sequence))

(element p (make paragraph))

(element INDENTS (make paragraph
        (make sequence
              (literal "...")
              (process-children-trim)
              (literal "...")))))
```

And that's it—process **indents.sgml** with Jade now to create **indents.rtf**, which we can open in MS Word, as shown in Figure 9-5.

As you can see in Figure 9-5, we've formatted our SGML document as intended. The indents example is a success. The **indents.sgml** document appears in Listing 9-9, and the stylesheet **indents.dsl** is in Listing 9-10.

Figure 9-5.
Combining
paragraphs and
sequences.

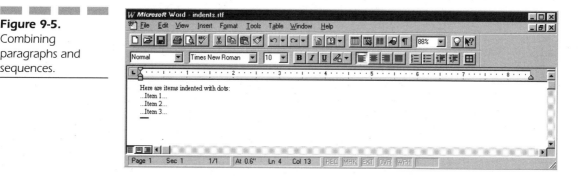

Listing 9-9.
indents.sgml.

```
<!DOCTYPE DOCUMENT [
<!ELEMENT DOCUMENT o o (p*, INDENTS*)>
<!ELEMENT p - o (#pcdata)>
<!ELEMENT INDENTS - o (#pcdata)>
]>
<DOCUMENT>
<p>
Here are items indented with dots:
<INDENTS>
Item 1
<INDENTS>
Item 2
<INDENTS>
Item 3
</DOCUMENT>
```

Listing 9-10.
indents.dsl.

```
<!doctype style-sheet PUBLIC "-//James Clark//DTD DSSSL
     Style Sheet//EN">

(root (make simple-page-sequence))

(element p (make paragraph))

(element INDENTS (make paragraph
        (make sequence
                (literal "...")
                (process-children-trim)
                (literal "...")))))
```

In fact, we can gain even more control over the parts of an individual line; we can even specify their width, as we'll see next.

The tabs Example

In this next example, we'll see how to specify the actual width of various parts of a line. For example, we might create an sample that simulates the use of tabs so that we can tab text in a document, moving it towards the right, like this:

```
                        This text has been tabbed...
```

Let's see how this works now. We start by creating a new <tab> element in the SGML document **tabs.sgml**:

```
<!doctype document [
<!element document o o (#pcdata|tab)*>
<!element tab - o EMPTY>
]>
```

Now we use that element to add a tag to the beginning of a line like this:

```
<!doctype document [
<!element document o o (#pcdata|tab)*>
<!element tab - o EMPTY>
]>
<document>
<tab>
This text has been tabbed...
</document>
```

That completes the SGML document here, and in fact, the stylesheet
for this example is quite simple. We start with the DTD and describe the
root in **tabs.dsl**:

```
<!doctype style-sheet PUBLIC "-//James Clark//DTD DSSSL
    Style Sheet//EN">

(root (make simple-page-sequence))
    .
    .
    .
```

Then we set up the <tab> element this way:

```
<!doctype style-sheet PUBLIC "-//James Clark//DTD DSSSL
    Style Sheet//EN">

(root (make simple-page-sequence))

(element tab
    .
    .
    .
```

Now, to specify a length of the line with a certain definite width, we
make a *line-field* flow object this way:

```
<!doctype style-sheet PUBLIC "-//James Clark//DTD DSSSL
    Style Sheet//EN">

(root (make simple-page-sequence))

(element tab
        (make line-field
            .
            .
            .
```

One of the characteristics of **line-field flow** objects is the field-
width characteristic, and we use that to specify an exact width for our
tab:

```
<!doctype style-sheet PUBLIC "-//James Clark//DTD DSSSL
    Style Sheet//EN">

(root (make simple-page-sequence))

(element tab
        (make line-field
              field-width: 120pt))
```

> **TIP**   *If you want to include text in the* **line-field***, use the* **process-children** *function when you set up the tab element in* **tabs.dsl***.*

That's it. Use Jade now to create **tabs.rtf**, which we can open in MS Word, as shown in Figure 9-6.

As you can see in Figure 9-6, our fixed-width **line-field** object acts like a tab for us, moving the rest of the text on the line over to the right. The tabs example is a success. The SGML document in this example, **tabs.sgml**, appears in Listing 9-11, and the stylesheet, **tbs.dsl**, appears in Listing 9-12.

As you might imagine, there is a lot more we can do in DSSSL. For example, we can get and display the current page number, as we'll see next.

Figure 9-6.
Using the field-width characteristic to create tabs.

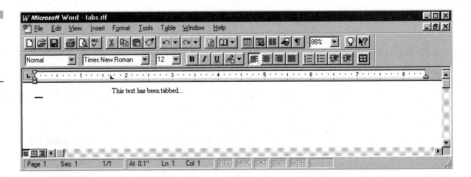

Listing 9-11.
tabs.sgml.

```
<!doctype document [
<!element document o o (#pcdata|tab)*>
<!element tab - o EMPTY>
]>
<document>
<tab>
This text has been tabbed...
</document>
```

Listing 9-12.
tabs.dsl.

```
<!doctype style-sheet PUBLIC "-//James Clark//DTD DSSSL
     Style Sheet//EN">

(root (make simple-page-sequence))

(element tab
     (make line-field
          field-width: 120pt))
```

The pagenumber Example

You can print the current page number using DSSSL. To do that, we will use a new empty element, <PAGENUMBER>:

```
<!DOCTYPE DOCUMENT [
<!ELEMENT DOCUMENT o o (p|#pcdata|PAGENUMBER)*>
<!ELEMENT p - - (#pcdata|PAGENUMBER)*>
<!ELEMENT PAGENUMBER - o EMPTY>
]>
```

Here's a document, **pagenumber.sgml**, that uses the <PAGENUMBER> tag to display the page number:

```
<!DOCTYPE DOCUMENT [
<!ELEMENT DOCUMENT o o (p|#pcdata|PAGENUMBER)*>
<!ELEMENT p - - (#pcdata|PAGENUMBER)*>
<!ELEMENT PAGENUMBER - o EMPTY>
]>
<p>This is page <PAGENUMBER>.</p>
```

We will design the stylesheet for this document, **pagenumber.dsl**, now. We start with the DTD and **root** this way:

```
<!doctype style-sheet PUBLIC "-//James Clark//DTD DSSSL
     Style Sheet//EN">

(root (make simple-page-sequence))
          .
          .
          .
```

Next, we add the <PAGENUMBER> element:

```
<!doctype style-sheet PUBLIC "-//James Clark//DTD DSSSL
     Style Sheet//EN">

(root (make simple-page-sequence))
```

```
(element p (make paragraph font-size: 12pt))

(element PAGENUMBER
                .
                .
                .
```

We start this new element by making a new sequence:

```
<!doctype style-sheet PUBLIC "-//James Clark//DTD DSSSL
     Style Sheet//EN">

(root (make simple-page-sequence))

(element p (make paragraph font-size: 12pt))

(element PAGENUMBER
          (make sequence
```

The <PAGENUMBER> element will use the DSSSL function **page-number-sosofo**, which returns a **page number sosofo**. As mentioned earlier in this chapter, **sosofo** stands for specification of a sequence of flow objects; we build construction rules using these **sosofos**. The **page-number-sosofo** function returns the page number in a form we can display immediately:

```
<!doctype style-sheet PUBLIC "-//James Clark//DTD DSSSL
     Style Sheet//EN">

(root (make simple-page-sequence))

(element p (make paragraph font-size: 12pt))

(element PAGENUMBER
          (make sequence
              (page-number-sosofo)))
```

And that's it. Now the <PAGENUMBER> element will be replaced by the current page number in the document. When we use Jade to create **pagenumber.rtf** and open that document in MS Word, for example, we see that the first page is indeed page 1, as shown in Figure 9-7.

Our pagenumber example is a success. Now we're able to access page numbers in DSSSL documents. The SGML document for this example, **pagenumber.sgml**, appears in Listing 9-13, and the associated stylesheet, **pagenumber.dsl**, appears in Listing 9-14.

Another powerful feature of DSSSL is that we can retrieve attributes from SGML tags directly when processing a document. We'll take a look at how that works now.

Figure 9-7.
Finding the page
number using DSSSL.

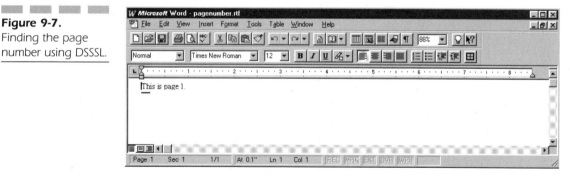

Listing 9-13.
pagenumber.sgml.

```
<!DOCTYPE DOCUMENT [
<!ELEMENT DOCUMENT o o (p|#pcdata|PAGENUMBER)*>
<!ELEMENT p - - (#pcdata|PAGENUMBER)*>
<!ELEMENT PAGENUMBER - o EMPTY>
]>
<p>This is page <PAGENUMBER>.</p>
```

Listing 9-14.
pagenumber.dsl.

```
<!doctype style-sheet PUBLIC "-//James Clark//DTD DSSSL
    Style Sheet//EN">

(root (make simple-page-sequence))

(element p (make paragraph font-size: 12pt))

(element PAGENUMBER
        (make sequence
                (page-number-sosofo)))
```

The font Example

In this next example, we'll set up a <FONT> tag. We can store the name of the font we want to use for the content of the <FONT> tag in an attribute of that tag. Here's how we declare the <FONT> tag in a new document, **font.sgml**; note that we give the <FONT> tag an attribute with the name FONTNAME:

```
<!DOCTYPE DOCUMENT [
<!ELEMENT DOCUMENT o o (FONT|p|FONTNAME|#PCDATA)*>
<!ELEMENT p - - (#pcdata|FONT|FONTNAME)*>
<!ELEMENT FONT - - (#pcdata)>
```

```
<!ATTLIST FONT
         FONTNAME      CDATA #implied>
]>
```

Here's how we can use the <FONT> tag in the **font.sgml** document, where we indicate that we want to use the Courier font by setting the FONTNAME attribute to **"Courier"**:

```
<!DOCTYPE DOCUMENT [
<!ELEMENT DOCUMENT o o (FONT|p|FONTNAME|#PCDATA)*>
<!ELEMENT p - - (#pcdata|FONT|FONTNAME)*>
<!ELEMENT FONT - - (#pcdata)>
<!ATTLIST FONT
         FONTNAME      CDATA #implied>
]>
<p>Here is some...<FONT FONTNAME = "Courier">text in
     Courier font!</FONT></p>
```

Now let's put together the stylesheet for this example, **font.dsl**, starting with the DTD and root:

```
<!doctype style-sheet PUBLIC "-//James Clark//DTD DSSSL
     Style Sheet//EN">

(root (make simple-page-sequence))
            .
            .
            .
```

Next, we add a simple paragraph element, <p>:

```
<!doctype style-sheet PUBLIC "-//James Clark//DTD DSSSL
     Style Sheet//EN">

(root (make simple-page-sequence))

(element p (make paragraph font-size: 12pt))
            .
            .
            .
```

We are ready to declare the <FONT> element, which we do this way, by making a new sequence:

```
<!doctype style-sheet PUBLIC "-//James Clark//DTD DSSSL
     Style Sheet//EN">

(root (make simple-page-sequence))

(element p (make paragraph font-size: 12pt))
```

```
(element FONT (make sequence
                .
                .
                .
```

We use the attribute-string function here to get the font name we should use, because we've stored the font name in the <FONT> tag's FONTNAME attribute. We get the name of the font and make it the new font in this sequence this way:

```
<!doctype style-sheet PUBLIC "-//James Clark//DTD DSSSL
    Style Sheet//EN">

(root (make simple-page-sequence))

(element p (make paragraph font-size: 12pt))

(element FONT (make sequence
            font-family-name: (attribute-string
                "FONTNAME")
            .
            .
            .
```

Using this new font, then, we can process the children of this <FONT> element:

```
<!doctype style-sheet PUBLIC "-//James Clark//DTD DSSSL
    Style Sheet//EN">

(root (make simple-page-sequence))

(element p (make paragraph font-size: 12pt))

(element FONT (make sequence
            font-family-name: (attribute-string
                "FONTNAME")
            (process-children)))
```

That completes the font example—using Jade, create `font.rtf` now. We can open this new file in MS Word, as shown in Figure 9-8.

As you can see in Figure 9-8, we've been able to retrieve the font name from a tag's attribute and install that new font in our document, formatting text in that font. The font example is a success—now we're using tag attributes in DSSSL.

For the final example in this chapter, we'll make use of the skill we've just learned—reading an attribute directly from a tag—to support *cross references* in SGML documents.

Figure 9-8.
Using tag attributes
to specify a font.

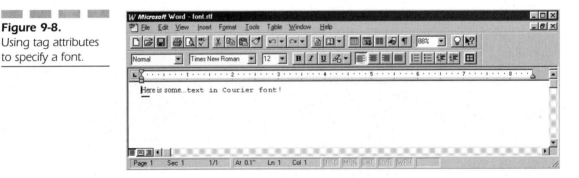

Listing 9-15.
`font.sgml`.

```
<!DOCTYPE DOCUMENT [
<!ELEMENT DOCUMENT o o o (FONT|p|FONTNAME|#PCDATA)*>
<!ELEMENT p - - (#pcdata|FONT|FONTNAME)*>
<!ELEMENT FONT - - (#pcdata)>
<!ATTLIST FONT
          FONTNAME    CDATA #implied>
]>
<p>Here is some...<FONT FONTNAME = "Courier">text in
    Courier font!</FONT></p>
```

Listing 9-16.
`font.dsl`.

```
<!doctype style-sheet PUBLIC "-//James Clark//DTD DSSSL
    Style Sheet//EN">

(root (make simple-page-sequence))

(element p (make paragraph font-size: 12pt))

(element FONT (make sequence
          font-family-name: (attribute-string
                "FONTNAME")
          (process-children)))
```

The xref Example

In this next example, we'll see how to create cross references in SGML documents as we format them. For example, we might place three notes in a document like this:

```
Note 1 Flowers are nice.
Note 2 Ponds can be nice.
Note 3 Thunderstorms are fun.
```

.
.
.

Then we might add some intervening text:

```
Note 1 Flowers are nice.
        Note 2 Ponds can be nice.
        Note 3 Thunderstorms are fun.
        text...text...text...
```

.
.
.

Then we could introduce a cross reference to one of the notes into our text like this:

```
Note 1 Flowers are nice.
Note 2 Ponds can be nice.
Note 3 Thunderstorms are fun.
text...text...text...
As we said (see Note 1), flowers are nice.
```

Using DSSSL, we can insert such cross references automatically. Let's see how this works now. We start by defining a new element, <NOTE>, and we'll display the content of this tag (e.g., **Note 1**, **Note 2** and so on) in bold:

```
<!DOCTYPE DOCUMENT [
<!ELEMENT DOCUMENT o o (NOTE|p|#PCDATA)*>
<!ELEMENT p - - (#pcdata|NOTE)*>
<!ELEMENT NOTE - o (#pcdata)>
]>
<p><NOTE>Note 1</NOTE> Flowers are nice.</p>
<p><NOTE>Note 2</NOTE> Ponds can be nice.</p>
<p><NOTE>Note 3</NOTE> Thunderstorms are fun.</p>
```

.
.
.

Now we insert a line of text to simulate the text that intervenes between the notes and a cross reference to them:

```
<!DOCTYPE DOCUMENT [
<!ELEMENT DOCUMENT o o (NOTE|p|#PCDATA)*>
<!ELEMENT p - - (#pcdata|NOTE)*>
<!ELEMENT NOTE - o (#pcdata)>
]>
<p><NOTE>Note 1</NOTE> Flowers are nice.</p>
<p><NOTE>Note 2</NOTE> Ponds can be nice.</p>
```

```
<p><NOTE>Note 3</NOTE> Thunderstorms are fun.</p>
text...text...text...
        .
        .
        .
```

To be able to cross reference the various notes, we'll give the <NOTE> tag an ID attribute like this:

```
<!DOCTYPE DOCUMENT [
<!ELEMENT DOCUMENT o o (NOTE|p|#PCDATA)*>
<!ELEMENT p - - (#pcdata|NOTE)*>
<!ELEMENT NOTE - o (#pcdata)>
<!ATTLIST NOTE
         ID        ID    #implied>
]>
<p><NOTE ID="Note1">Note 1</NOTE> Flowers are nice.</p>
<p><NOTE ID="Note2">Note 2</NOTE> Ponds can be nice.</p>
<p><NOTE ID="Note3">Note 3</NOTE> Thunderstorms are
fun.</p>
text...text...text...
        .
        .
        .
```

Now we add a cross reference to the note first. We will create a new <NOTEREFERENCE> tag for this purpose. To indicate which note this <NOTEREFERENCE> element is a cross reference to, we give the <NOTEREFERENCE> tag a new attribute, REFERENCE, and give that attribute the ID value of the note we are referencing, Note1:

```
<!DOCTYPE DOCUMENT [
<!ELEMENT DOCUMENT o o (NOTE|p|NOTEREFERENCE|#PCDATA)*>
<!ELEMENT p - - (#pcdata|NOTE|NOTEREFERENCE)*>
<!ELEMENT NOTE - o (#pcdata)>
<!ATTLIST NOTE
         ID        ID    #implied>
<!ELEMENT NOTEREFERENCE - o EMPTY>
<!ATTLIST NOTEREFERENCE
         REFERENCE CDATA #implied>
]>
<p><NOTE ID="Note1">Note 1</NOTE> Flowers are nice.</p>
<p><NOTE ID="Note2">Note 2</NOTE> Ponds can be nice.</p>
<p><NOTE ID="Note3">Note 3</NOTE> Thunderstorms are
      fun.</p>
text...text...text...
<p>As we said <NOTEREFERENCE REFERENCE = "Note1">, flowers
      are nice.</p>
```

This is a common way of handling cross references in DSSSL-formatted SGML documents—to give the tags you'll cross reference ID values and then to refer to those ID values in the cross references. When we format the preceding document, the <NOTEREFERENCE> element will be replaced with a cross reference to note 1, and we'll be able to display the content of that note, **Note 1**, in the cross reference itself.

Let's create the **xref.dsl** stylesheet document now to complete the xref example. We start with the DTD and the **root**:

```
<!doctype style-sheet PUBLIC "-//James Clark//DTD DSSSL
        Style Sheet//EN">

(root (make simple-page-sequence))
        .
        .
        .
```

We add the <NOTE> element next; we make the text of this element appear in bold, this way:

```
<!doctype style-sheet PUBLIC "-//James Clark//DTD DSSSL
        Style Sheet//EN">

(root (make simple-page-sequence))

(element p (make paragraph font-size: 12pt))

(element NOTE (make sequence
                font-weight: 'bold
                font-size: 12pt
                (process-children)))
        .
        .
        .
```

Now we'll create the <NOTEREFERENCE> tag. We use that tag like this:

```
<p><NOTE ID="Note1">Note 1</NOTE> Flowers are nice.</p>
<p><NOTE ID="Note2">Note 2</NOTE> Ponds can be nice.</p>
<p><NOTE ID="Note3">Note 3</NOTE> Thunderstorms are
        fun.</p>
text...text...text...
<p>As we said <NOTEREFERENCE REFERENCE = "Note1">, flowers
        are nice.</p>
```

We will read the REFERENCE attribute of the <NOTEREFERENCE> tag; that attribute holds the string **"Note1"**. We then want to find the element with the ID **"Note1"**; that element is the first note:

```
<p><NOTE ID="Note1">Note 1</NOTE> Flowers are nice.</p>
<p><NOTE ID="Note2">Note 2</NOTE> Ponds can be nice.</p>
<p><NOTE ID="Note3">Note 3</NOTE> Thunderstorms are
fun.</p>
```

```
text...text...text...
<p>As we said <NOTEREFERENCE REFERENCE = "Note1">, flowers
are nice.</p>
```

We can display the cross reference by putting together a sequence like this: "(see xxxxx)"; where we'll replace xxxxx with the content of the cross-referenced note, which gives us this cross reference: "(see Note 1)".

Here's how we start formatting the <NOTEREFERENCE> tag, by creating a sequence:

```
<!doctype style-sheet PUBLIC "-//James Clark//DTD DSSSL
    Style Sheet//EN">

(root (make simple-page-sequence))

(element p (make paragraph font-size: 12pt))

(element NOTE (make sequence
            font-weight: 'bold
            font-size: 12pt
            (process-children)))

(element NOTEREFERENCE (make sequence
                  .
                  .
                  .
```

Next, we add the string "(see ":

```
<!doctype style-sheet PUBLIC "-//James Clark//DTD DSSSL
    Style Sheet//EN">

(root (make simple-page-sequence))

(element p (make paragraph font-size: 12pt))

(element NOTE (make sequence
            font-weight: 'bold
            font-size: 12pt
            (process-children)))

(element NOTEREFERENCE (make sequence
          (literal "(see ")
                  .
                  .
                  .
```

Then we need the cross reference itself; we need the ID of the tag to cross reference, and we get that from the REFERENCE attribute of the <NOTEREFERENCE> tag with the attribute-string **function**.

But how do we get the content of the element we're supposed to cross reference? It turns out that cross-referencing is a common enough task in DSSSL, so DSSSL supports a function named **process-element-with-id**. We pass the ID of the element to cross reference to this function, and the function formats the first note's content for our cross reference:

```
<!doctype style-sheet PUBLIC "-//James Clark//DTD DSSSL
    Style Sheet//EN">

(root (make simple-page-sequence))

(element p (make paragraph font-size: 12pt))

(element NOTE (make sequence
            font-weight: 'bold
            font-size: 12pt
            (process-children)))

(element NOTEREFERENCE (make sequence
        (literal "(see ")
        (process-element-with-id (attribute-string
    "REFERENCE"))
                .
                .
                .
```

TIP *Because cross referencing is so common, XML even defines a special attribute type (like the ID or CDATA attribute types) that you use to refer to elements with a particular ID value—IDREF. You typically get the IDREF attribute's value from the cross reference element and then search for the element with the matching ID.*

Finally, we place the closing parenthesis into the sequence this way:

```
<!doctype style-sheet PUBLIC "-//James Clark//DTD DSSSL
Style Sheet//EN">

(root (make simple-page-sequence))

(element p (make paragraph font-size: 12pt))

(element NOTE (make sequence
            font-weight: 'bold
            font-size: 12pt
            (process-children)))

(element NOTEREFERENCE (make sequence
        (literal "(see ")
```

```
(process-element-with-id (attribute-string
        "REFERENCE"))
(literal ")")))
```

That's it—the xref example is complete. In this example, we've used cross-referencing techniques standard in DSSSL. Use Jade to create **xref.rtf** now. We can open the RTF document in MS Word now, as shown in Figure 9-9.

As you can see in Figure 9-9, our cross reference works just as we want it to; now we're using cross references in DSSSL!

The SGML document for this example appears in Listing 9-17, **xref.sgml**, and the stylesheet **xref.dsl** appears in Listing 9-18.

Figure 9-9.
Supporting DSSSL
cross references.

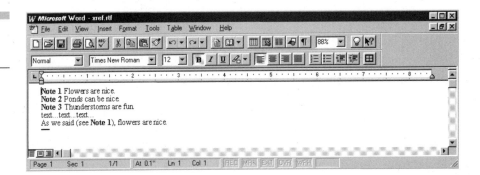

Listing 9-17.
xref.sgml.

```
<!DOCTYPE DOCUMENT [
<!ELEMENT DOCUMENT o o (NOTE|p|NOTEREFERENCE|#PCDATA)*>
<!ELEMENT p - - (#pcdata|NOTE|NOTEREFERENCE)*>
<!ELEMENT NOTE - o (#pcdata)>
<!ATTLIST NOTE
        ID        ID    #implied>
<!ELEMENT NOTEREFERENCE - o EMPTY>
<!ATTLIST NOTEREFERENCE
        REFERENCE CDATA #implied>
]>
<p><NOTE ID="Note1">Note 1</NOTE> Flowers are nice.</p>
<p><NOTE ID="Note2">Note 2</NOTE> Ponds can be nice.</p>
<p><NOTE ID="Note3">Note 3</NOTE> Thunderstorms are
    fun.</p>
text...text...text...
<p>As we said <NOTEREFERENCE REFERENCE = "Note1">, flowers
    are nice.</p>
```

```
<!doctype style-sheet PUBLIC "-//James Clark//DTD DSSSL
    Style Sheet//EN">

(root (make simple-page-sequence))

(element p (make paragraph font-size: 12pt))

(element NOTE (make sequence
          font-weight: 'bold
          font-size: 12pt
          (process-children)))

(element NOTEREFERENCE (make sequence
          (literal "(see ")
          (process-element-with-id (attribute-string
              "REFERENCE"))
          (literal ")")))
```

SUMMARY

That completes our look at DSSSL and XML-Style. Although XML-Style is not yet finalized as a specification, XS is a subset of the DSSSL standard, and we've gotten an introduction to that standard in this chapter. As we've seen, DSSSL presents us with a powerful set of tools for formatting our documents using stylesheets.

INDEX

F

I

J

Y

ABOUT THE AUTHOR

Steven Holzner is one of the most prolific programming authors in the industry. With more than 35 books to his credit, he has taught more than a million people how to program more effectively. Among his most popular titles is *Java 1.1: No Experience Required*. Holzner lives in Cambridge, Massachusetts.